History of African Civilization

E. Jefferson Murphy

Foreword by Hollis R. Lynch
Director, Institute of African Studies
Columbia University

Thomas Y. Crowell Company
New York, Established 1834

HISTORY OF

AFRICAN

CIVILIZATION

916
M97h

ACKNOWLEDGMENTS

Acknowledgment is gratefully made to the following authors and publishers for permission to use quotations from their works.

Richard A. Pankhurst and Oxford University Press, London, for material from *The Ethiopian Royal Chronicles,* quoted on pages 50-51 and 55.

D. T. Niane and Longman Group, London, and Humanities Press, Inc., New York, for material from *Sundiata: An Epic of Old Mali,* quoted on pages 114-115.

Basil Davidson and Atlantic, Little, Brown and Company, Boston, for material from *The African Past,* quoted on pages 120, 190-191, 193, and 346-347.

Thomas Hodgkin and Oxford University Press, London, for material from *Nigerian Perspectives,* quoted on pages 135 and 172.

Routledge & Kegan Paul, Ltd., London, and Praeger Publishers, New York, for material from Sir Richard Burton, *A Mission to Gelele,* quoted on pages 165 and 167.

G. S. P. Freeman-Granville and Clarendon Press, Oxford, for material from *The East African Coast,* quoted on pages 226, 231, and 232.

Robin Hallett and Routledge & Kegan Paul, Ltd., London, and Praeger Publishers, New York, for material from *The Penetration of Africa,* quoted on pages 265, 296, 297, 300-301, and 306-307.

Hollis Lynch and Oxford University Press, London, for material from *Edward Wilmot Blyden: Pan-Negro Patriot,* quoted on pages 377, 378, 379, and 380-381.

Acknowledgment is also gratefully made to Louise E. Jefferson, Graphic Design, New York, for her generous advice and assistance, and for the many photographs from her files which appear in this volume (pages 50, 61, 160, 180, 209, and 397).

In addition, grateful acknowledgment is made to the following for permission to use photographs: Alinari-Art Reference Bureau, page 194; British Museum, page 173; Frank Cass & Company Ltd., London, pages 158, 159; *Congopresse,* page 197; Cooper Square Publishers, New York, page 166; Durban Local History Museum, page 214; Johnson Reprint Corporation, New York, for reprint from Olfert Dapper, *Beschreibung von Afrika,* 1958, page 195; New York Public Library Picture Collection, pages 227, 237, 269, 281, and 318; Oriental Institute, University of Chicago, page 42; Zambia National Monuments Commission and Thames and Hudson, Ltd., London, page 202.

Designed by Abigail Moseley

Manufactured in the United States of America

L.C. Card 72-78274
ISBN 0-690-38194-8

1 2 3 4 5 6 7 8 9 10

For HKH

By the Author

Understanding Africa
History of African Civilization

Foreword

The emergence of independent African countries from the 1950's stimulated a considerable and widespread scholarly interest in Africa. As a result, in academic circles the prevalent European view that Africa had no history worth recording or studying was largely laid to rest. In the last decade or so, universities on all five continents have introduced courses and programs in African Studies. Even so, ignorance about Africa is still the rule, not least among the vast majority of Americans, including those who are college-trained. And this makes all the more lamentable the fact that currently there is a major and critical decline in support of African Studies at universities on the part of the federal government and the foundations. For, as yet, too many Americans still cling to the old derogatory stereotypes about Africa, which are still sometimes projected in the media, much to the annoyance of the growing numbers among the 23,000,000 Afro-Americans who are taking an intelligent interest in Africa. There thus remains a major job to be done to inform Americans generally about the history and culture of a continent with which their own history and culture have been vitally and inextricably linked.

One obvious first step is to make available up-to-date, readable, general studies on Africa, suitable for both the student and the layman. But compared with the proliferation of monographic and other specialized historical studies, there have been very few works attempting to cover the full history of the African continent. Despite its brevity and the fact that some of its interpretations have been seriously questioned, *A Short History of Africa* (Harmondsworth, 1962) by the English scholars R. A. Oliver and J. D. Fage has been the best general source.

Since then, there have been about seven major general histories of Africa.* But while each possesses considerable merit, none is satisfying as a balanced synthesis. Their limitations—very often deliberately imposed by the authors—consist of undue emphasis on modern and political history or, contrariwise, omitting the colonial and independence eras altogether and giving virtually exclusive attention to Africa south of the Sahara. But, happily, the need which until now has existed for a balanced history of all Africa is very admirably met in this felicitiously written volume, which takes account of the latest scholarly research, gives the precolonial period the careful and extended treatment it deserves, and is as much concerned with cultural as with political history.

The author, E. Jefferson Murphy, has had the advantages of a background in anthropology as well as in history, and of having lived and worked in all the major regions of Africa during more than a decade. His dual disciplinary training is a major asset in piecing together the relatively sparse information available for the reconstruction of African history, which depends, particularly in the precolonial period, on a wide variety of disciplines. His knowledge of anthropology is essential to the first chapter, "Early Man in Africa"—now a topic which has relevance beyond the continent because of the now generally accepted view that man first evolved in Africa. And throughout the book Mr. Murphy gives us a firm sense of the culture history of typical or significant peoples in various parts of Africa—their religion, their art, their social customs, as well as their economic and political institutions. There is, in short, much more ethnographic material in this book than is to be found in other histories of Africa, and thus there is a proper focus on the ordinary African. But leaders and other men of exploits are not neglected: and here the author's portraits are as sharp and clear as current evidence would allow.

There are other merits, too, in Mr. Murphy's book. It is intelligently organized around major African civilizations—from ancient Egypt to the Bantu states of southern Africa—with unity achieved by attention to the interconnections between them, as well as to the impact of European and Islamic cultures and the African reaction to them. He clearly has a preference for the broad canvas, and seeks to convey a sense of the epic qualities evident in the rise and fall of great states and empires; in the Bantu migrations which the author describes as "one of the truly

---

* 1. Donald Wiedner, *A History of Africa South of the Sahara* (New York, 1962); 2. Robert Rotberg, *A Political History of Tropical Africa* (New York, 1965); 3. Basil Davidson, *Africa: History of a Continent* (New York, 1966); 4. Robin Hallet, *Africa to 1875* (Ann Arbor, 1970); 5. Robert July, *A History of the African People* (New York, 1970); 6. *The Horizon History of Africa* (New York, 1971); 7. Lewis Gann and Peter Duignan, *Africa and the World: History of Sub-Saharan Africa . . . to 1840* (San Francisco, 1971).

great population movements of human history"; in the far-reaching consequences of the disastrous slave trade; and in the clashes of major cultures and interests in Africa.

He has been diligent and painstaking in incorporating the latest scholarly research. Two examples will suffice. From this volume we learn that the finds in 1969 of Patrick Munson, a young American archaeologist, show the new and important fact that there existed in central Mauritania a flourishing agricultural society of black Africans more than a thousand years before the rise of ancient Ghana in the early centuries of the Christian era; and in the author's discussion of the slave trade, he judiciously uses Professor Curtin's findings in *The Atlantic Slave Trade: A Census* (Madison, 1969), which among other contributions, revises downward to about ten million the number of Africans bought as slaves in the Americas.

In addition, Mr. Murphy has systematically and effectively interspersed his book with apt selections drawn from primary African, Arabic, and European sources. What more telling way, for instance, to reflect African resistance to the imposition of European rule than to quote from the letter of an East African chief, Macemba, to a German colonial official which says, *inter alia* "I . . . find no reason why I should obey you—I would rather die first."

Finally, the author's description of ruins and other physical sites, as well, perhaps, as his general sensibility, betrays the fact that he has had a close acquaintance with Africa.

With new research almost constantly changing the contours and content of African history, no general book is up to date for long, but this volume is bound to prove highly serviceable for several years to come.

Hollis R. Lynch
Professor of History and Director,
Institute of African Studies,
Columbia University, New York City,
May 1972

Author's Note

This book has a bias. It is based on the premise that the history of the Africans is a moving story, a story of the largely successful efforts of the Black African to create his own distinctive civilization in response to the African environment.

A careful and honest study of the efforts to reconstruct Africa's history, especially the accelerating research since the achievement of independence by most Africans, corroborates and ramifies this view. Yet only a few years ago it required an act of faith to assert that the Black African had a proud past. A few scholars and believers did, and were ignored or ridiculed. Today ample hard evidence is available to bear out this positive interpretation of African history, vindicating those whose assertions in favor of the African achievement met such skeptical response from the learned and scholarly men of Europe and America.

My own original attachment to this bias came from William Leo Hansberry, one of the most ardent of this small band of historians, whom I was honored to know for many years as a friend. The late Leo Hansberry was Professor of History at Howard University, where he inspired many students to appreciate Africa's past. He devoted himself tenaciously and with unswerving loyalty, throughout his life, to studying the African past. Normally a mild and deeply modest man, Leo Hansberry defended and argued the African case with passion and perseverance. Nor was his partisanship limited to the Africa of antiquity; he labored vigorously to assist African students in America, to arouse American interest in Africa, and to urge American support for the liberation and regeneration of modern Africa.

When he died, in 1965, Leo Hansberry left drafts of several major works on African history. When these works are published, his deep, empathetic understanding of African history, based on both knowledge and faith, will become much more widely known. They will expand the recognition that Hansberry's long advocacy of the African cause had begun to receive toward the end of his nearly fifty years of scholarship and teaching.

This book is not the appropriate medium to convey Hansberry's sensitive comprehension of the great panorama of Africa's past. Yet his love for Africa, and his passion to see Africa, and its heritage, treated justly, had a deep and lasting influence on me, as they did on all who knew him well.

William Leo Hansberry was, in a very personal sense, one of the greatest men I have known. I hope this book will serve as a small tribute to his life, to the love he bore for Africa, and to the great achievements of the African past which he recognized and bespoke many years before it was fashionable to do so.

Contents

Maps

Introduction

Africa—all of Africa—has a history. Ironically, it is still not generally recognized that this is true. In popular and often educated thinking, most of Africa simply has no history prior to the arrival of white slavers and explorers. Africa's ancient and sophisticated civilizations are little known. Man has walked on the moon, but he has not yet come to understand himself in all his diversity.

The study of history is a relatively recent endeavor, and it has been peculiarly concentrated on the literate civilizations of Europe and the Mediterranean world. In the past century or so history was extended to include the study of Egypt and the Near East, and gradually, rather peripherally, India and China were brought in. As archaeology has been refined and expanded, history has finally come to include ancient civilizations, such as those of the Aztec and the Maya, that were nonliterate or that have left writing that has not been deciphered.

But despite the gradual broadening of the study of history, the past of much of the human race is still unknown—or worse still, is often assumed to be unworthy of study. Of all the great communities of mankind that have remained outside the mainstream of historical inquiry, Africa is the most notable.

This does not apply, of course, to the civilization of Egypt, which is prominently included in standard histories of the world. The Mediterranean coast of northern Africa, which has been in touch with the peoples of Europe and the Near East since ancient times, is well enough known to claim a place at least on the edge of "world" history. But the peoples of virtually all the rest of Africa, especially south of the vast

Sahara Desert, are perceived, if they are thought of at all, as a blurred mass, of no particular consequence.

It has been only in the past few decades that the bits and pieces of historical evidence known to the few specialists on Africa have been pieced together into a coherent outline of history for the rest of Africa. Although this outline still remains obscure to most people—including most historians—it is now slowly demanding recognition.

The reconstruction of Africa's history, still very incomplete, has been a difficult task. Two serious problems have hindered it: the paucity of both written and archaeological evidence, and the deeply rooted myth, long prevalent in America and Europe, that the despised Black men of Africa had languished in savagery for thousands of years. Before we can look clearly at an African history we must examine these two problems, taking the second, and more serious one, first.

Before the fifteenth century, Europeans, who have been largely responsible for most of the modern world's knowledge of history, had no direct contact with or knowledge of most of Africa. For centuries Europeans traded with Africans along that continent's coasts, but these traders came for profit, not understanding. As the traffic in slaves swelled, eventually dominating the entire European system of trade with Africa, there developed a positive disinterest in such matters as the African past. It was difficult enough for a Christian civilization to justify to itself the odious and inhuman practice of enslaving "savages"; recognition of the African as a respectable member of the human race, with a long history of accomplishment behind him, might have complicated the situation intolerably.

There grew, during the centuries of the slave trade, a deeply rooted and widely held European view of the African as a savage without culture and without a past, wallowing in a natural state of barbarism. This pejorative view, we now must recognize, was flatly contradictory to fact. We must also recognize that the Europeans who helped to establish this myth could not even plead ignorance: at least a few European visitors to Africa in the fifteenth, sixteenth, and seventeenth centuries wrote reasonable and objective accounts of their favorable impressions of the majesty of African kings and the affluence and order they encountered in several African cities. A Dutch geographer, Olfert Dapper, writing in 1668, for example, compared Benin quite favorably with his own Amsterdam, on the basis of its broad and long streets, the quality of its buildings, and even on its cleanliness, a quality important to the tidy Dutch.

But these favorable records of Africa were either ignored or gradually forgotten, filed away in musty archives and libraries. Evidences of

African civilization were inconsistent with the myths that were developing to save the European conscience during the slavery period.

By the beginning of the colonial conquest, at the end of the nineteenth century, the dismal European stereotype of the African was almost universally accepted. When the European powers divided Africa into spheres of influence in 1885, and almost immediately began forcible occupation of the continent, the stereotype was elevated to the status of an official truth. It served to exalt the frantic conquest of Africa from the sordid imposition of imperialism that it really was to a righteous campaign to bring the benefits of civilization to the supposedly wretched Negro savages of the continent. In Europe and America little attention was paid to the dogged and valiant resistance many African states offered their colonial deliverers: these struggles, now becoming recognized as legitimate wars against alien invaders, were generally portrayed at the time as illegitimate responses to Europe's "benign pacification." The unfavorable stereotype of the African was reinforced by the view that this pacification brought to the constantly squabbling Africans the only peace they had ever known.

This Western judgment on the African persisted tenaciously up to the very end of the colonial period, as late as 1960, even among some specialists in African affairs. For decades before the end of the colonial era research was producing convincing evidence that the popular, officially ramified stereotype was false, but only a handful of scholars and specialists in Africa, Europe, and America were convinced.

It was only with the mushrooming emergence of independent African states between 1957 and 1961 that the opinion of the outside world began seriously to change. Almost overnight Africans were featured in the mass media as diplomats, leaders of liberation movements, and men of intellect. At the same time outsiders, from Europe and America, sought increasingly to read about or even visit Africa. Schools and universities rapidly expanded their curricula to include African studies. Americans and Europeans, sensing that Africa had suddenly emerged from obscurity and was gaining a place in world affairs, hastened to update their centuries-old view of the African. Especially in the United States, this process was spurred by the explosive demand of Black Americans (many of whom aptly refer to themselves as "Africans of the diaspora") to establish their own identity and history.

In this precipitate surge to revise perceptions of the African, to see him in the same terms as men from more familiar parts of the world, there appeared a long-belated recognition that he was also a man with a past. Before this, the meager study of African history that had developed had been the history of European contact with and exploration of

Africa; it was not *African* history, but the history of Europeans in Africa.

Even before the colonial conquest the African continent itself was becoming better known as adventurous European explorers—Mungo Park, James Bruce, Rene Caillié, Hugh Clapperton, John Hanning Speke, David Livingstone, Henry Morton Stanley, and dozens of others—ventured into the interior and returned to write about it for the European audience. During their period, and the colonial era that followed, the continent was mapped and delineated so that every schoolboy could learn in his geography lessons the basic facts about its size, land features, products, and rivers, and in the history lessons could trace the adventures of the explorers, conquerers, and famous colonial figures.

But in this whole period, especially before the 1950's, the African himself remained ignominiously obscure. Well-known and respected Europeans, such as Lord Milverton, a former governor of Kenya, could assert as late as 1952 that the African had stagnated in primitive savagery during the thousands of years that men in the rest of the world were creating their civilizations. The myth of the African's supposed lack of progress was so complete that whole generations of African schoolchildren themselves were taught that they had no past.

This myth is steadily disintegrating. Research to illuminate African history has burgeoned. Many gaps remain and may never be filled in, but each year brings fresh facts to light that increase the historian's understanding of what happened in African history and why.

The disintegration of the myth of African inferiority is helping with the second of the two problems that have hindered the reconstruction of African history. The problem of the paucity of written and archaeological records is not yet fully solved, but much has been done to lessen it. The scholar of African history is using what written and archaeological evidence he has with great effectiveness and is supplementing it with a variety of other forms of evidence.[1]

Written records, long assumed to be virtually nonexistent where African history is concerned, have been much more helpful in recording a history of Africa than used to be thought possible. Diligent searches in recent years have brought to light a number of informative and accurate accounts of visits to Africa and descriptions of Africa, based on eye-witness accounts, by Arab travelers and scholars. These have been invaluable for the period before the sixteenth century, and it is to be hoped that others will be found that will add further useful evidence.

[1] The reader who wishes to explore the development of the methodology by which African history is being reconstructed will find one volume of special interest: *Africa in Time Perspective: A Discussion of Historical Reconstruction from Unwritten Sources*, by Daniel F. McCall, New York, Oxford University Press, 1969.

Between the eighth and the fifteenth centuries at least two dozen Arabic writers are known to have written about Africa in books of history, geography, or travel. Not all these have been studied carefully; indeed, not all are translated into European languages as yet. But from several of these works has come vital information about the western Sudanic belt and the east coast of Africa. Seven authors may be singled out for identification here because of their great importance to modern reconstructions of African history.

The earliest of these writers is al-Mas'udi, a native of Baghdad who wrote during the first half of the tenth century of the Christian era. He traveled widely in the Muslim world and is believed to have visited East Africa and Madagascar. His best-known surviving work is *Meadows of Gold and Mines of Gems,* which includes a description of the "land of the Zanj," or coastal Africa, and the ivory trade. Al-Mas'udi's writings influenced many later Arabic scholars.

Ibn Haukal was also a native of Baghdad and roughly contemporary with al-Mas'udi. He visited the interior of West Africa, and left bits of information about Awdoghast and Kumbi, two important cities in the empire of Ghana. He saw the Niger, flowing eastward, but erroneously believed it to be the Nile. Regrettably Haukal was also one of the first racially prejudiced foreign visitors to black Africa, asserting that the African Blacks "and other peoples of the torrid zones" were not worth dignifying by writing about their countries. Fortunately later Muslim scholars were able to see Africa more objectively!

One of the best of the Muslim writers was al-Bakri, a Moor from Cordoba who lived during the eleventh century. Among several illustrious works he produced a geography that described both North Africa and the Sudan; his treatment of the Sudan is the earliest known attempt at a general survey, and it is especially useful in its account of the empire of Ghana.

In the twelfth century al-Idrisi, a native of Morocco who lived in Sicily in the service of the Norman king Roger, produced a comprehensive and widely read geography of most of the known world, called *The Book of Roger.* It contains several sections on Africa, especially the East Coast.

The best of all the early Arabic accounts of Africa were produced during the fourteenth century. Al-Omari, a native of Damascus who spent several years in the service of the sultan of Egypt, left a valuable record of the famous visit to Cairo of Mansa Musa, the emperor of Mali.

Ibn Battuta, much less well known to Western readers than Marco Polo, traveled more widely than Polo. He covered approximately 75,000 miles, including China, India, and the Maldive Islands, and wrote brilliantly clear accounts of his travels. He was a Berber from Tangier, well educated and widely acclaimed in the Muslim world as a scholar and jurist. His last great adventure was a visit to West Africa, which he described in considerable detail.

Ibn Khaldun was one of the last of the great Arabic writers whose works have survived; he was born in Tunis in 1332 and died in Cairo in 1406. He did not travel nearly so extensively as Ibn Battuta, spending most of his life in Tunisia and Egypt except for short trips into Asia Minor. But he collected a variety of records of the travels of others and produced a monumental history. When he died he was widely recognized as one of the greatest scholars of his time.

In addition to these, and a number of less important writers, Black Africans themselves produced several important and useful works in the Arabic language which still survive. Islam was adopted by some Sudanic Africans as early as the tenth century, and through it a tradition of literacy was established in the thriving trading cities of the Sudan. Very few written records from these cities survive from times prior to the sixteenth century, but during the sixteenth and seventeenth centuries several works were produced that are now translated, at least in part. Three scholars are of special significance.

Ahmad Baba was a scholar of Timbuktu, born in 1556, whose name is still remembered in West African Islamic circles. He refused to serve the Moroccan invaders of Songhai and was sent as a prisoner to Morocco to prevent his fomenting resistance to the conquest. He is known to have produced over fifty works, mostly on Islamic law, but not all survive.

Mahmad Kati, another scholar of Timbuktu, was a Soninke (a member of the nation that founded the early empire of Ghana) in the service of Askia Muhammed, the great ruler of the Songhai Empire. Born in 1468, Kati is reputed to have lived to the age of one hundred and twenty-five. He wrote, with the help of a grandson, the *Tarikh al-Fettash,* which described Songhai in detail, including some of its early history gleaned from both oral and written accounts.

Still another scholar of Timbuktu, Abderrahman as-Sadi, wrote the *Tarikh al-Sudan* in the seventeenth century, carrying forward the contemporary history of Songhai begun by Kati. As-Sadi lived through the successful Moroccan conquest of Songhai, and witnessed the collapse of the proud Songhai civilization.

The histories of Kati and as-Sadi were continued by the unknown writer of the *Tedzkiret en-Nisian,* which outlined up to 1750 the names of rulers and principal events of the reign of the pashas who ruled the remnants of Songhai after the conquest.

West Africa, especially Songhai, was described in substantial detail by one other prolific writer in the sixteenth century, a North African who lived in Italy and served Pope Leo X. Leo Africanus, whose Arabic name was Hassan ibn Mohammed el Wazzan el Zayyati, had traveled throughout North Africa and the Sudan before his capture by Christian pirates, and was well educated and cultured. He was handed over by his captors to Leo X, who freed him and converted him to Christianity. He wrote a history and description of Africa that combined many valuable first-hand accounts with some faulty deductions, such as his assertion that the Niger flowed westward.

From the sixteenth century onward written records of Africa's history increased in number and detail. There are many accounts by Africans themselves, written in Arabic, Swahili, and later in European languages. Accounts of travel, letters, ship's logs, and other documents by Europeans become increasingly frequent after the sixteenth century.

Although historians are naturally enough frustrated that there are not more and fuller documents available, these writings are sufficient to give some sense of African history from the tenth century onward. Through them some light has been shed on the impressive states and empires of the Sudan—Ghana, Mali, Songhai, and Kanem-Bornu—and on the East African coastal cities of Mogadishu, Malindi, Zanzibar, Mafia, Kilwa, and Sofala. Largely from letters and documents in Portuguese we have information about the great kingdoms of Kongo and Mwene Mutapa in the sixteenth and seventeenth centuries. And from a variety of written European accounts sketches of history are possible for the several West African coastal and forest states that grew to great heights of power and accomplishment in the past five hundred years: Ashanti, Dahomey, Oyo, Ife, and Benin.

But the known written sources, important though they are, give only tantalizing glimpses of the larger mosaic of African development, and mainly for the last ten centuries. Other ways of reconstructing African history have been essential.

Archaeology has proved especially useful. The great buildings and monuments of Egypt have been the subject of intensive archaeological research for many years. Less intensive, but nevertheless revealing, research has been carried out in the ruins of the ancient land of Nubia, in modern Sudan, especially its cities of Napata and Meroe. Other good archaeological work has been done on Axum, in modern Ethiopia, and on the cities left by the Phoenicians, Greeks, Romans, and Arabs in North Africa. A great contribution is the relatively recent, and not very well publicized, investigations of scattered finds, covering both stone age and iron age settlements, in Mauritania, Mali, Nigeria, Kenya, Tanzania, Zambia, Rhodesia, and South Africa.

The archaeology of these areas is still in its infancy, but it has nonetheless illuminated a pattern of African development that no written records covered. Added to the written records noted above, archaeological research is helping to complete a picture of early migrations and increasing cultural development in almost the entire continent south of the Sahara.

For a time research south of the Sahara concentrated on very ancient stone age cultures, and the paleontological study of man's early evolution. The work of Raymond Dart and Robert Broom in South Africa, and of Louis S. B. Leakey in East Africa, has greatly clarified the evolution of man from his anthropoid ancestors. But in more recent years archaeologists have paid increasing attention to neolithic and iron age investigations, especially in central and southern Africa, pursuing the story of the development of African farmers and iron workers who have dominated most of the continent for the past two thousand years.

Studying the distribution of stone tools, iron tools and ornaments, pottery fragments, human and animal bones, and other articles, archaeologists have discovered a pattern of diffusion from north to south of a culture that may have the same roots as those of the Sudanic states in West Africa. The evidence, although scanty, suggests an underlying cultural unity among almost all the Negroid Africans of the sub-Saharan region.

Both ethnology and linguistics have been used with good result to reconstruct African history, and their conclusions tend to confirm those of archaeology. Linguists have been able to demonstrate that most African languages south of the Sahara belong to one large language family, the Congo-Kordofanian, called by some the Niger-Congo family, while ethnologists have found highly significant similarities among widely spread economic, political, and religious systems. Linguistic and ethnological study of the Bantu languages and peoples have helped to clarify their rapid and far-reaching spread over most of central, southern, and eastern Africa in the past two thousand years.

The combined findings of archaeology, ethnology, and linguistics have begun to suggest a history for central and southern Africa that written records do not cover at all. Evidence is growing that the ancestors of the modern Bantu peoples originated somewhere to the south and west of Lake Chad, moved over the first few centuries before Christ to an area of secondary concentration south of the Congo rain forests, then exploded southward, eastward, and northeastward to populate, within a few centuries, most of the continent south of the equator. Their population explosion was made possible by a great leap forward in technology: the mastery of iron working and the discovery of how to cultivate a number of new crops that came to Africa from southeast Asia.

The history of Africa that archaeology, ethnology, and linguistics are constructing is far from being clear and specific. All three of these sciences have barely scratched the surface in sub-Saharan Africa. Far more research, especially in archaeology, is essential.

Another specific discipline has yielded good results: ethno-botany, or historical botany. Botanists have studied preserved seeds found in excavations, and impressions or drawings of plants on pottery, to help trace the migration of plants and crops. They have been able to trace the place of origin of many plants, which in turn helps the historian trace the movement and cultural contacts of peoples who use these plants. Many basic food-producing plants used in Africa are not indigenous. The yam, coco-yam, banana, maize, coconut, sweet potato, manioc, and cassava are all staples that have come to Africa from the Americas or Malaysia. They were brought to Africa by men traveling by ship, which gives the historian definite clues about when they were introduced and how they probably spread.

The study of oral tradition is also proving to be very useful. Until the past few decades oral history was dismissed contemptuously as fancy and fabrication, but it has been found that the widespread African practice of recounting history from one generation to the next can provide valuable data unavailable from any other source. Where it is possible to compare the events and chronologies of oral histories with written accounts, the former have been shown to be sometimes quite reliable when recorded by a trained and careful historian.

In most of Africa oral histories are reliable only for two or three centuries or less, although in some cases, such as the histories recounted by the "griots" (a caste of bards and history tellers) of some Sudanic peoples, they may be reliable for much longer periods. Where it is possible to validate portions of an oral history by written accounts, the reliability of the oral history can be extended for longer periods into the past: in Rhodesia, for example, the ethno-historian D. P. Abraham has been able to reconstruct a history that is fairly complete for over five hundred years by skillfully combining oral histories and Portuguese documents.

The study of African art is another fruitful source of information. There are vast numbers of rock paintings in the Sahara and in southern and central Africa, and a few in western Africa. Careful study of the Saharan rock paintings, especially by Henri Lbote in the Tassili mountains, has shown that the Sahara was settled by Africans long before it became a desert. For thousands of years, in the Tassili, unknown artists recorded scenes of the life of their times on sheltered rock faces, sometimes with deep sensitivity and skill. In Nigeria William Fagg, the discoverer of the Nok artifacts, has been able to suggest a possible historical connection between the art styles of the Nok people, before the time of Christ, and the much later artists of Ife, who worked in clay and bronze in the fourteenth and fifteenth centuries.

Among other approaches, studies of human remains and the distribution of physical traits in existing populations cast useful light on history. Geology helps provide both time perspective and information about the natural environment in ancient times. Physics and chemistry, especially through the carbon-14 method of analyzing ancient organic materials, help to determine the age of bones, wood, charcoal, and other materials. Geography and geology help to establish the climatic and soil conditions in ancient times, dendrochronology determines the age of trees, and paleontology helps provide information on human types at various periods.

As the information gleaned from all these techniques is ordered and combined, there emerges a view of African history that utterly confounds the surviving proponents of the unflattering myths about Africa.

This book is an effort to summarize African history in very broad outline, synthesizing the findings of an ever growing number of studies. There is risk in attempting even this broad an outline, for new evidence is regularly being discovered that alters the unfolding picture of African history; like all other history, it will never be totally known or finished. Yet the risk must be taken. Now, despite the vast areas in which too little research has been done, enough is known to give a confident sense of the vital development of African societies over thousands of years.

1 | Early Man in Africa

Knowledge of Africa's most ancient past is essential to understanding man's origins and development over a period of at least three million years, for it is now widely accepted that Africa is the birthplace of man. Until recently many scholars argued that man originated elsewhere, possibly in Asia. Then, in July 1959, Dr. and Mrs. Louis S. B. Leakey announced the discovery (in Tanzania's Olduvai Gorge) of a fossil skull of a hominid (a creature either human or ancestral to humans) dating to nearly 2,000,000 B.C. With the skull were found simple stone tools and fragments of the bones of animals that had apparently been eaten at the site. Although this was by no means the first hominid fossil found in Africa, its association with tools suggested strongly the very ancient existence of proto-human creatures who possessed a rudimentary technology. The vigorous search for additional evidence that this dramatic find precipitated has produced many new fossils and tools, and a reexamination of the whole question of human evolution.

The Leakeys named their discovery *Zinjanthropus boisei* (it has since been renamed *Australopithecus boisei,* because of its fundamental similarity to australopithecine finds in southern Africa); it has also been called Nutcracker man because of its huge molar teeth, which may have been used for cracking and crunching tough vegetable foods and bones. This man-ape, as reconstructed through a study of the skull, shows nearly as much similarity to the large anthropoid apes as to man, but the high probability that he fashioned tools from stone and depended upon them for killing and butchering game, plus the skull and teeth characteristics that are clearly evolved in man's direction, gives him a very special claim to human kinship.

Thirty-five years before the Leakeys uncovered *Australopithecus boisei,* Professor Raymond Dart unearthed (at Taungs, in modern Botswana) part of the skull and teeth of a very young creature, which he named *Australopithecus africanus,* or the Southern Ape of Africa. Professor Dart was very much aware that he had discovered something of rare significance: an animal that combined many apelike characteristics with features definitely suggestive of man. The brain size and shape were primarily apelike, whereas the teeth resembled man's. The contour of the skull was, however, the most unusual feature: it indicated, in terms quite clear to the anatomist, that the skull had been balanced fairly directly on top of the spinal column, which meant that *Australopithecus* habitually walked more or less upright.

Professor Dart, after a careful study of the skull of young *Australopithecus,* inferred that it represented a clear departure from the ape, in the definite direction of man. Though he found no tools associated with the skull, he speculated that *Australopithecus* was capable of using tools. But many scholars expressed reservations about drawing such conclusions, preferring to classify *Australopithecus* as an evolved ape who had adapted to living on the ground and walking upright.

In the years following, other discoveries of fossil remains in southern Africa were made, all of them tending to amplify and clarify the picture of *Australopithecus* originally based on Dart's find. Dr. Robert Broom, excavating at Kromdraai and Sterkfontein in northern South Africa, discovered a number of skulls, teeth, and portions of the skeleton of creatures similar to the one from Taungs. Though Dr. Broom gave these separate names, he and later specialists have agreed that his discoveries belong to the same family, the australopithecines.

Since Leakey's find in Tanzania a number of other australopithecine fossils have been discovered in other parts of southern Africa, in East Africa (Leakey, his son, and various colleagues have found more at Olduvai Gorge, as well as at Olorgesailie, Kenya, and near Lake Omo in southern Ethiopia), near Lake Chad in central Africa, in North Africa, and in Java. These finds make it clear that there were at least two species or groups of the genus *Australopithecus.* One group, and very probably the first to appear, is represented by Dart's find at Taungs, known by the name Dart originally coined: *Australopithecus africanus.* Small in height (less than five feet) and build, with relatively slender bones, *A. africanus* lived on the dry and grassy plains of southern and eastern Africa, probably near shallow lakes, and collected a variety of vegetables as well as meat.

The second group, called *Australopithecus robustus,* apparently developed somewhat later than *A. africanus* and tended to be heavier, with an exaggerated jaw, brow ridge, and facial features; his teeth, like those of Leakey's Nutcracker man (who may well have been *A. robustus*), were often enormous. *A. robustus* lived on the dry plains, like his relative *A. africanus,* but may also have lived in forested regions as well.

Although Dr. Leakey long felt that *Zinjanthropus* represented a third type of australopithecine, most authorities now tend to class it with the more robust of the two groups.

The australopithecines appeared at least by 3,500,000 B.C., and they may well have originated even earlier. They used stone tools, although it is not clear that they possessed much skill in making them. Of the two types, *A. africanus* seems to have been the more capable, and if stone tools were manufactured, rather than used in naturally occurring forms, he is the more likely to have produced them.

The australopithecine ancestors of modern man were small brained (cranial capacities of about 400 to 600 cc., compared to the average human size of about 1,300 cc.); but their brains were larger relative to their body size than those of any known apes. They lived on dry, grassy plains, never wandering far from ponds, lakes, or streams since they had no way of transporting water. They foraged in small groups for edible roots, fruits, nuts, and leafy plants, and they ate the meat of a variety of animals, both small and large. Their meat came both from dead animals, killed by predators or accidentally, and from animals they killed, by throwing stones and heavy sticks or perhaps by running them down in hunting groups and capturing them. Their behavior must have been more like that of modern chimpanzees than modern *Homo sapiens,* yet they were more intelligent than apes, probably had a better ability to communicate with each other and a more varied ability to use tools.

Some two million years ago a new, more highly evolved manlike creature appeared in Africa. He was similar in many respects to *A. africanus,* but with a larger brain and the ability to walk and probably stride in a vaguely human fashion (rather than to shuffle, often with knuckles on the ground) and to make stone tools in an intelligent fashion; this creature has been named *Homo habilis* (man who could manipulate tools). There are indications that *H. habilis* evolved from *A. africanus,* possibly because the tool-using abilities of the latter helped, over a period of a million or more years, to create superior adaptation conditions for its line. *A. robustus* seems to have died out by about 1,000,000 B.C., leaving the arena of competition for foods and territory to even more adaptable relatives.

H. habilis (and possibly later forms of *A. africanus*) was definitely an accomplished toolmaker; his remains have been found in several places associated with tools of the Olduwan industry, the most ancient stone-tool technology yet discovered. Olduwan tools have often been described as "pebble tools," from a common misconception that they were shaped entirely from naturally available pebbles; but as more finds have been made it has become clear that many Olduwan stone tools were chipped from angular lumps and flakes of quartz and lava. Pebbles were used where they abounded and were suitable for shaping, but clearly the Olduwan toolmakers were capable of fashioning hand tools from other materials. In Olduwan sites (at Olduvai Gorge, in several lake beds in East Africa, and in Morocco and Tunisia) a considerable variety of tools has been found: choppers, worked on one or both faces to form a sharp edge; discoids, the use of which is uncertain; flake knives of several types; scrapers, used for scraping the tough outer surface from edible roots and plants and the skin off animals; and spheroids, probably used for bashing, crushing, throwing, and pounding. All the Olduwan tools are small, generally no more than three or four inches in length or width, and clearly were not made nor used by giant ape-men or phenomenally strong "missing links." They were made by *H. habilis* and perhaps later forms of *A. africanus,* both smallish creatures under five feet in height and probably little better muscled than modern men.

The living habits of *H. habilis* were generally similar to those of both australopithecines. He lived in small groups, probably varying from ten or twelve up to fifty or sixty. From the brain size (which ran about 600 cc.) and the fact that the skill of manufacturing tools required teaching, it is assumed that he had a rudimentary culture. Probably the young had to be protected by adults for some years, food and defense were shared, and the range of communication sounds was increasing, even if speech, as we know it, had not yet developed. None of the early hominids were primarily vicious, predatory carnivores, a notion that has been romantically popular for some years. They depended more on vegetable foods than meat, they probably often abandoned camp sites rather than defend them continuously against other hominid or carnivorous enemies, and they hunted cautiously and selectively those animals that were needed for food and were relatively easy prey. There is no certain evidence to indicate whether the early hominids hunted large and dangerous game at all; they definitely ate early forms of elephants, giant baboons, and large antelopes, but they may have scavenged these.

The introduction of new methods of dating these ancient fossils has pushed back their time of existence much further than was once thought likely. The use of the potassium-argon method of dating gave Leakey's *Zinjanthropus* an age of about 1,750,000 years. The Dart-Broom finds in southern Africa date back to the same general period as *Zinjanthropus,* and finds at Lake Omo in Ethiopia have proved that australopithecines were present as long ago as 3,500,000 B.C. Thus the process of evolution leading to modern man is a very long one indeed.

At some time before about 1,000,000 B.C. a more highly evolved, more definitely human type appeared (possibly in a direct evolutionary step from *H. habilis*): *Homo erectus*. The first known find of *H. erectus* (man who stood erect) was in Java, when a Dutch anthropologist, Eugene Dubois, found the skull cap, part of the lower jaw and teeth, and thighbone of a creature he named *Pithecanthropus erectus*, in the late nineteenth century. Subsequently there have been numerous discoveries of related creatures in Java, China, England, Germany, North Africa, East Africa, and southern Africa, and all of these have been classed together into one populous genus of *H. erectus*.

H. erectus bones have been found in many sites associated with the widely distributed Acheulian Stone Industry, named after St. Acheul, in France, where such stone tools were first found. Judging by the number of African sites at which Acheulian tools have been found, and the number of tools at the sites, St. Acheul was virtually an outpost of the people who made these tools, and East Africa was their center of greatest concentration. In East Africa literally tens of thousands of Acheulian tools have been found in deep strata as well as on the surface of areas where winds and rains have washed away sediments deposited over many hundreds of thousands of years.

H. erectus was a man, rather than an ape or even a man-ape; his brain capacity, ranging from 775 to 1,225 cc., in its larger sizes is well within the human range (which runs from about 1,000 to more than 1,600 cc.), he stood and walked erect (albeit with slightly more stoop and shuffle of gait than *Homo sapiens*), and he had the ability both to manufacture tools and to communicate to others the best ways of doing it. His face, though still massive with a heavy jaw and brow ridge, was more recognizably human than that of either *Australopithecus* or *H. habilis*.

The Acheulian tools made by *H. erectus* are larger than those of the Olduwan industry, better fashioned, and of much greater variety. Especially characteristic are stout hand axes and cleavers, up to eight inches long, formed from large flakes of quartz or other suitable stone and sharpened into quite effective tools. At one bed at Olduvai the tools consisted of 47 percent hand axes, cleavers, and scrapers; 10.5 percent of choppers; 11.5 percent of spheroids; and the remainder of miscellaneous heavy stones of various shapes, the uses of which are difficult to determine. Almost all the tools in this bed were made from large flakes of lava that were chipped off outcroppings and large boulders. The cutting faces show multiple facets, indicating that the toolmakers intelligently used a piece of hard stone to strike small flakes from another stone to produce the tool they were making; the tools also show a certain uniformity of style, indicating a pattern that in turn reflects a definite method of manufacture passed on from individual to individual and generation to generation.

The Acheulian industry was a very long-lived one: beginning as early as 1,000,000 B.C., it persisted in several parts of Africa until as late as about 40,000 B.C. Although it evolved to a certain extent, the change was a very slow one. Perhaps the greatest single instance of progress was the discovery that "soft hammers" of bone, antler, or hardwood would produce thinner, more delicate flakes from the core being worked than the "hard hammers" of stone that had been used in the Olduwan and earlier Acheulian industries. This refinement of technique allowed the stone artisan to take a suitable core, such as quartz or lava (flint was rarely found in Africa but was used in Europe), and gradually shape it, by repeatedly striking off small flakes, into a quite delicately shaped ax, cleaver, or scraper; this in turn opened the way for the introduction of aesthetic expression in toolmaking, and later Acheulian implements often show much more flaking, to produce just the right shape, than would have been necessary if the stone worker had been concerned solely with utility.

H. erectus also seems to have been conscious of beauty in personal appearance; in one of the beds at Olduvai pieces of hematite, still used in places for red color to adorn the skin, were found alongside stone tools, and since the nearest source of hematite was some fifty miles away, *H. erectus* and his mates presumably had brought some to the camp site.

The distribution of *H. erectus* over so many parts of Africa, Asia, and Europe indicates that he was an adaptable creature, able to use his tools and intelligence to find food and shelter, to protect himself from the elements, and to defend himself against natural enemies in a variety of environments ranging from cold to warm. In Africa he apparently did not inhabit the forest regions, but he was spread widely over the grassy plains of northern, eastern, and southern Africa. In France there is evidence that he constructed a type of shelter with poles supporting a roof; in Africa, several sites, such as the large one at Olorgesailie in Kenya, contain piles of stones that may have formed the base of windbreaks or other shelters. Both in Europe and in China, where Acheulian tools and some *H. erectus* bones have been found in cold climates, there are remains of ancient hearths, so it seems that *H. erectus* had also mastered the use of fire, at least for warmth if not for cooking.

H. erectus is believed to have lived on the same omnivorous diet as *Australopithecus* and *H. habilis,* but there is evidence that he hunted large game as well as small. At Isimila in Tanzania and at Olorgesailie there are finds where disarticulated hippopotamus skeletons have been found alongside rare heavy-duty tools, presumably made specifically for butchering these large and tough animals; similar tools have been found at several sites in Spain with the skeletons of elephants. Throughout Africa and Europe Acheulian tools, the hallmark of *H. erectus,* are found associated with the bones of large animals, and it is now believed possible that *H. erectus* employed a variety of techniques for finding, capturing, and killing large animals. At several European sites wooden spears with sharpened points have been found, and the African *H. erectus* must have used spears also. He may have been able to control fire sufficiently well to have set brush fires for the purpose of driving game toward a point where other hunters waited with spears, clubs, and heavy throwing stones.

Although we know a fair amount about *H. erectus,* we do not know for certain how well he could communicate. Some communication is definitely implied by the group hunting and semipermanent living arrangements he employed, and especially by the great standardization of manufacture in his tools. The same basic techniques were employed worldwide, and, since these techniques were relatively sophisticated (more so than probably could have been learned by observation alone), it is almost certain that *H. erectus* had sufficient language ability to communicate such skills.

Yet for all his superiority over previous hominid forms, *H. erectus* was inferior in intelligence and creativity to his descendant *Homo sapiens.* For more than half a million years *H. erectus* continued to live basically the same kind of life, manufacture the same kind of tools, with a very slow rate of development. Like his predecessor hominids, he then became extinct, ultimately giving way before modern man, *Homo sapiens.*

The disappearance of *H. erectus* and the appearance of the first *H. sapiens* forms coincides roughly with a major climatic change that affected all of Africa as it did most other parts of the world. This was the last major glaciation period of the ice age, beginning about seventy thousand years ago. Temperatures lowered all over the globe and the ice caps around both the North and South Poles increased greatly in size. Much of northern and eastern Africa became moister as a result of these ice age changes, resulting in the spread of forests into what had been, and are now again, grasslands. Along the western part of Africa, on the other hand, drying winds caused desert conditions in places that had been grassy, and forced the tropical rainforests to retreat and contract in size. These great changes affected both flora and fauna; it was during this period that many of the large herbivores and ungulates of Africa became extinct, leaving modern species in possession of the continent.

The nature of the difficulties and challenges that the ice age must have created for *H. erectus* and his successor, *Homo sapiens,* is not fully understood, but both tool types and fossil remains show considerable change during the period between about 70,000 and 35,000 B.C. *H. erectus* disappeared, while numerous fossil remains of *Homo sapiens neanderthalensis,* or Neanderthal man, appeared. In Europe, adjacent Asia, and northern Africa a relatively homogeneous Neanderthal population lived, while in sub-Saharan Africa a related type, called Rhodesian man from the site where his remains were first discovered, held sway.

The physique of Neanderthal man is virtually indistinguishable from that of modern man, except in being slightly heavier. His head and face, however, were different: he had the massive jaws and teeth of *H. erectus* and earlier hominids, with heavy brow ridges and a thick cranial-bone structure to support the powerful muscles of the jaw. Rhodesian man *(Homo sapiens rhodesiensis)* differs little from the classic Neanderthals of Europe and North Africa, although the skulls and skull fragments (found in central Africa) all have especially heavy brow ridges and unusually thick cranial bones. Where parts of the body were found, however, as they were at Broken Hill, they were indistinguishable from those of modern man: the Rhodesian man of Broken Hill was about five feet ten inches tall, standing fully erect. The differences between Rhodesian and Neanderthal man are so slight, in fact, that several finds have been classed by some authorities in one group and by others in the other group.

The size and shape of the brain of Neanderthal and Rhodesian men were close to those of modern men, ranging in cranial capacity from about 1,200 cc. upward. From this evidence, as well as from the tool-making techniques associated with the type, Neanderthal-Rhodesian man seems undoubtedly to have been an early and primitive form of modern man, little different in intelligence or ability.

With the disappearance of *H. erectus* and the appearance of the Neanderthaloids over much of the world in a wide variety of climatic and ecological zones, tool industry underwent an almost revolutionary process of change, at least compared to the half million years during which the Acheulian industry changed so little. One of the last Acheulian sites found anywhere in the world was at Kalambo Falls, in southern Tanzania, and radiocarbon dating gives it a date of 60,000-50,000 B.C. Between that time and about 35,000 B.C. there appeared in many places in Africa a variety of new techniques in working stone, many new kinds of tools, and tools made of bone, ivory, and other materials. By about 35,000 B.C., man was producing tools in a number of identifiably different styles and traditions, each apparently adapted to the needs of the regions in which it was characteristic.

During this period there emerged in Africa three main regional cultural-technological traditions. In North Africa, all the way from the Atlantic coast of Morocco to the Nile valley, the stone tools form part of the great Mousterian industry of the middle stone age, which was practiced in much of Europe at the same general period.

The major innovation characterizing the Mousterian was the use of hard punches (similar to leather punches) of wood or bone to strike flakes from specially prepared cores of flint, quartz, quartzite, obsidian, or other crystalline stone. These flakes were then used as blanks from which highly refined tools were fashioned. Using this basic method, the Mousterian craftsmen of Europe, Asia, and North Africa made dozens of types of tools: knives, scrapers, awls, spear points, ax blades, chisels, etc. Both the needs of differing environments and economies and the creative adaptations of the craftsmen produced regional and local traditions of stone working. In North Africa three major Mousterian traditions appeared during this period, before about 30,000 B.C.: the Maghribian, in Morocco and adjacent areas; the Cyrenaican, in Libya (and Palestine); and the Nubian, in the Nile valley. All of the traditions seem to have been created for an economy based on a combination of hunting and gathering.

In southern Africa and eastern Africa, where the predominant environment was grasslands stretching from the Cape to Ethiopia, a tradition usually called the Fauresmith (from the site at Fauresmith in South Africa) evolved directly from the Acheulian, with a continuation of the hand axes and cleavers that had typified the Acheulian tradition. But the *Homo sapiens* (probably Rhodesioids) who developed the Fauresmith tradition introduced refinements into the manufacture of these tools, shaping them into sharper and more exact forms, reducing their size still further, and standardizing their manufacture so that craftsmen could turn out tool after tool nearly identical in size and shape.

Fauresmith craftsmen also used the prepared-core technique in much the same way as the Mousterians, producing thin, broad flakes and long blade forms. From these flakes were produced a variety of cutting and scraping tools, retouched carefully for sharpness and precision of shape. Since there was little change in the environment of southern, central, and eastern Africa from the time of *H. erectus* through the early *H. sapiens* period, it is presumed that the latter evolved tool forms from the earlier tradition because their needs were similar. The same types of roots were dug, the same types of animals were hunted, the same fruits, nuts, and vegetables were gathered, and the basic way of life remained similar. Yet the greater intelligence of *H. sapiens* produced tools that were in every respect more refined, more skillfully prepared, and presumably more effective in the many digging, killing, skinning, butchering, and leather-working activities that were the basis of middle stone age life.

To the west of the Fauresmith peoples, from modern Angola north to the Great Lakes region, climatic conditions favored the growth of savannah woodlands, forests, and mosaics of forest and grassland. The Sangoan peoples lived in this region, and developed a tool tradition that differed considerably from the earlier Acheulian. The same basic method of producing flakes from prepared cores continued, but the results were in two quite different styles. One type consisted ʻof small scraping and cutting tools, smaller and more refined than those of the Acheulian industry. The other was a group of large, rather crude heavy-duty tools designed for scraping, chopping, and cutting. These latter tools were made to cut trees and work them, in order to produce wooden tools—clubs, spears, ax handles—and conceivably even materials for shelters. Sangoan craftsmen, in other words, concentrated on woodwork, which has perished, and the stone tools they needed for this purpose appear crude but were most effective.

The Sangoan and Fauresmith peoples depended upon both hunting and gathering wild foods; the Sangoan, because of their more densely vegetated habitat, may have depended proportionally less on hunting and more on a vegetable diet. (Of the few surviving human groups that depend on hunting and gathering, the intake of food is invariably more vegetable than animal: usually the animal portion of the diet, on an annual basis, comprises only 30 to 40 percent of the total.)

In Europe there are several camp sites of *H. sapiens neanderthalensis* that indicate he believed in an afterlife, and took special precautions with burials; in several sites skeletons have been found carefully buried in graves, with food and weapons buried with them. Although no similar finds have been made in Africa, it is probable that the African Neanderthaloids and Rhodesioids would have practiced the same rituals. In both Africa and Europe hematite and several other ores that produce stains and cosmetic coloring are found alongside skeletal remains and tool kits.

There are many other indications that the Neanderthaloid *H. sapiens* represented a major step forward compared to earlier hominids. In many of the sites that have been studied, the number of animal bones is quite large, both absolutely and in ratio to the number of tools at the same site, indicating that the practice of hunting had become more efficient. The larger number of sites found also indicates a larger population. In Africa *H. sapiens* had become skilled enough in the techniques of survival that he was able to multiply and spread over most regions of the continent. He also was able to kill a wide variety of animals; in a few sites as many as thirty-eight different species are represented in the bones scattered about the campsite. At the same time, however, he was sufficiently knowledgeable and skilled to specialize, hunting certain animals at certain periods when they presumably were most abundant, or in places where they abounded; some sites contain the bones of only two or three species, indicating that the early men had come to that area to hunt that kind of game.

The hunting methods can only be guessed at, but the find of a number of sites below cliffs suggests that the hunters organized drives to force their quarry over the cliffs, then butchered them and feasted at the base of the cliffs. It is believed that fire was used to drive game, and that some species may have been driven into water, where it was easier to overtake and kill them. Weapons had certainly improved. In addition to the bolo stones previously mentioned, these early men used throwing sticks (one fossilized arced stick has been found at Florisbad, South Africa), throwing clubs with stone heads and heavy wooden knob heads, throwing axes, and spears. There is much evidence that stone blades and points were hafted onto wood or bone handles, to form spears, knives, and axes, and wood alone was used for spears, with carefully sharpened points.

Shelter was used wherever possible. Numerous sites have been found in caves and rock shelters, and several finds of semicircles of stones indicate the building of windbreaks. In two sites there are interesting finds of shallow depressions about six feet long, filled with the remains of grass stems and leafy plants, suggesting the possibility of beds. Fire was widely used, for warmth, probably for cooking food, and for working wood; early *H. sapiens* had discovered that it is much easier to sharpen a wooden spear by charring its end, then shaving off the soft charred area, than to cut the raw wood into a point.

Men had learned to fight each other, if they had not long done so. In several sites skulls with holes that might have been made by spears have been found, and other skulls have crushed portions at the front or back, such as would have been produced by a club.

From the evidence, early *H. sapiens* must have lived in well-defined social groups, with a carefully specified system of kinship relationships and obligations; he would have shared food with other members of the group, participated in mutual defense, and assisted in the common pursuit of game. Presumably he had developed rituals and beliefs, with taboos against antisocial behavior and perhaps rites to be performed before and after the hunt. His technology could not have been trans-

mitted in its standardized, precise forms unless he also possessed rudimentary language ability, especially the ability to assign names to
objects.

The exact time and place of modern man's appearance in any part
of the world is a mystery; it is not known whether he originated in one
particular area as a result of mutation or highly selective breeding, then
spread all over the world, or originated in several different places
independently. But it is in Africa that we find the most of his ancient
fossilized remains. Many years ago at Kanjera, near the Kavirondo Gulf
of Lake Victoria in western Kenya, Dr. Leakey discovered a number of
cranial fragments that were completely modern in appearance. Estimated
to be 55,000-60,000 years old, they are the oldest known remains of
modern *Homo sapiens,* or *Homo sapiens sapiens.*

Other finds also indicate that Africa was at least one of the earliest
homes of modern man, whether he originated there or not. The Florisbad skull and limb bones from South Africa have been dated to between
35,000 and 40,000 years ago; recent skeletal finds in the Omo basin of
southwestern Ethiopia are also essentially modern in appearance and
believed to be roughly contemporary with the Kanjera skull.

Modern skeletal fragments dating to between 40,000 and 30,000 B.C.
have been found in both Europe and Asia, but finds earlier than this
generally resemble the Neanderthal or other earlier types, and cannot
be regarded as being as definitely modern as the African fossils.

At any event, modern *H. sapiens* had spread himself over most
of the world, and had completely supplanted his Neanderthaloid-
Rhodesioid kin, by 40,000-30,000 B.C.; whether he warred against and
exterminated his earlier relatives, or whether he blended in with them
so that the genetic traits that made them different were gradually lost
in an evolutionary process, is not known. Until recent years it had been
romantically fancied, even by scholars, that modern man invaded
Europe and other regions of the "primitive" Neanderthal, and by his
superior intellect and skills drove the latter out. However, the differences between the two types of men were not nearly so great as this
theory implies. Given the close similarity between the two kinds of men
a process of genetic blending seems the more likely explanation.

The process by which modern races were formed is more subject
to controversy and uncertainty than any other aspect of the study of
human evolution. Until recently scientists tended to accept skeletal mea-
surements as accurate indices of race, and have eagerly studied new
finds to determine their racial type. Modern anthropologists, however,
increasingly question the validity of skeletal evidence for determining
race: there are too many other genetic factors involved (hair, skin,
blood type) for one to describe an individual's race by his skeletal

characteristics after several thousand years have passed. Race is, after all, basically a statistical abstraction, derived by measuring dozens of traits of a population, then using averages, medians, norms, and other statistical (and arbitrary) points to formulate a description; the individual rarely possesses all the traits of his race.

In Africa the only safe conclusions, therefore, are highly general ones. In northern Africa a population sharing many skeletal similarities with the peoples of southern Europe appeared at least fifteen or twenty thousand years ago. In southern Africa a short-statured people with slight Rhodesioid affinities but resembling modern Bushmen had begun to appear at least ten thousand years ago; in the same general area, and well up into eastern Africa, a people resembling modern Hottentots began to appear even earlier. In the upper Nile region, and in parts of central and western Africa, remains of individuals who seem to resemble modern Negroes date from as early as ten to twelve thousand years ago. In West Africa, the area in which Negroid peoples have historically been concentrated, the soil is unfortunately unkind to skeletal remains; acids eat away organic materials within centuries. The earliest human skeleton from West Africa has been found at Iwo Eleru, near Benin, Nigeria. Generally Negroid in appearance, it dates to about 9000 B.C.

Whatever the racial types of Africa's early humans, however, their stone tools (and eventually their pottery and other artifacts) have been found in great quantities in every part of the continent from about 35,000 B.C. Specializations evolving out of the three main technological traditions (Mousterian, Fauresmith, Sangoan) of earlier man began to multiply as modern *H. sapiens* spread over the continent. Between 35,000 B.C. and 1000 B.C. these tool traditions diversified steadily, much as human cultures and languages must have done during the same period.

In the drier inland areas of southern and eastern Africa where the Fauresmith technology had flourished, modern types of men continued to live much the same kind of life as their predecessors, and their tool traditions were based on similar needs. In a fairly direct line of descent three major industrial traditions followed one another: the Proto-Stillbay and Stillbay (32,000-10,000 B.C.), the Magosian (10,000-2500 B.C.), and the Wilton (2500 B.C. to recent times). All three are believed to have been practiced by Khoisan peoples, and most Bushmen and Hottentot sites of the past millennium have yielded Wilton-type tools and potsherds. Beginning with the many points, blades, scrapers, cleavers, axes, and other tools of the Fauresmith tradition, the originators of the Stillbay industry developed more refined stone-working techniques which allowed them to produce tools of increasingly greater sharpness and utility. Flakes became smaller, and techniques were developed to work them on both faces, yielding much greater symmetry than in earlier tools. Hafting techniques improved, so that more and more stone tools were affixed to handles of wood or bone to form knives, axes, adzes, spears, and (by at least 8000-7000 B.C.) arrows for use with bows.

Throughout this period the basic economy seems to have changed little; hunting, for much the same kinds of game, and gathering, for much the same kinds of fruits, nuts, roots, and leaves, continued to provide sustenance. But as the modern men who followed this ancient economic pattern became better and better at making tools, their ability to kill game improved and their butchering techniques became more refined.

The process was much the same in the more densely vegetated areas of central, western, and interior eastern Africa, where the Sangoan tradition had been developed. The Sangoan was followed by the Lupemban (40,000-11,000 B.C.) and the Tshitolian (11,000 B.C.-present). In the later period of the Lupemban industry and during the Tshitolian which succeeded it, the wood-working tools of the Sangoan culture became highly refined and included numerous types of axes, gouges, adzes, planers-scrapers, borers. By the later period of the Tshitolian (which is still practiced by the Pygmies, and was until recent times widely used by forest peoples in the Congo), the stone technology was in the service of the wood-working industry, stone tools being used to work wood into bowls, weapons, canoes, eating utensils, stools, and dozens of other utilitarian objects.

In North Africa a number of local stone-working traditions developed, but the most widespread and influential was the Aterian, which succeeded the Mousterian-Levalloisian, and in many places continued, with refinements, up to the neolithic period when agriculture began and the use of metals was introduced. The hallmark of the Aterian tradition was the invention and invariable use of a tang (a difficult thing to make on a stone tool until the technique is known) for affixing the stone implement onto wooden handles.

In all these stone traditions developed by modern man the emphasis was on innovation, over a period of time, to produce the most refined and most efficient tools for a wide variety of uses, in hunting, butchering, working animals skins, wood working, digging roots, warfare, and, eventually, harvesting grains and other vegetable foods, both wild and cultivated. As the middle stone age gave way to the later stone age (in general about 8000 to 5000 B.C.) the tools in all the African traditions tended to become smaller—finally, in most parts of the continent, becoming microlithic in type. The Tshitolian, Magosian, and Wilton traditions were later stone age industries, and all included stone tools of tiny size, beautifully worked for maximum sharpness, hardness, and beauty; some points and scrapers were only half an inch in diameter, yet were finely symmetrical with razor-sharp edges.

The rate of this developmental process seems slow by modern standards; but when judged by what had preceded it, it was rapid indeed. More advances were made in ten or fifteen thousand years than in the million years that had gone before. All this development was made possible by the ability of modern *H. sapiens* to speak: to create words to describe not only objects but attitudes and concepts, and to use these words in a complex system of language. Men could not only think creatively and therefore experiment, but they could communicate both their ideas and the results of their experiments to others in terms that were both concrete and abstract. *H. sapiens* early developed a fully fledged culture, of which his languages were a part, which served to elaborate the societies of his predecessors into infinitely more complex units, and his language enabled him to perpetuate this culture and complex social system from generation to generation.

The technological ability which *H. sapiens* expressed by rapidly developing better and more varied stone tools was applied to other materials as well. Sangoan men (Rhodesioids as well as modern men) had long used wood, and we have already noted the increasing use to which their cultural successors, the Lupembans and Tshitolians, put the wood that was so abundantly available to them. All the modern *H. sapiens,* regardless of location and tradition of stone working, also developed great skill in working bones and tusks into tools and utilitarian articles such as combs, toothpicks, spoons, needles, fishhooks, and pins. Increasingly they decorated their bone implements with carved symbols and designs; presumably they did the same with their wooden artifacts, but these have not survived from early times. In the late part of the middle stone age and the early part of the later stone age the bow and arrow came into general use; where it was invented, or whether it was invented in several places, is unknown, but the earliest bow to have been preserved was found in Germany, dating to about 8000 B.C. Judging by the many small points that were being made in Africa at about the same time, the bow and arrow may well have been in use just as early there.

During this same general period of accelerating development, man first learned to domesticate wild animals; the first to ally itself with man was the dog, which was domesticated and probably trained to assist in the hunt by the very first modern *H. sapiens,* forty to fifty thousand years ago. But during the later stone age (and the new stone age, which came into being with the discovery of agriculture) many other animals were added. Where the dog was first domesticated is not known; there were wild species in Africa, Asia, and Europe, any of which could have been used for the purpose. However, most other domestic animals were first domesticated in Africa or Asia.

During the later stone age the conceptual and aesthetic abilities of modern man led him to paint and draw pictures of his exploits and daily life on convenient surfaces, usually on smooth rock walls in caves or on the sides of rock overhangs. Rock paintings abound in Africa, in every part of the continent except the forest regions. The Bushmen, whose ancestors are certainly responsible for the extraordinary paintings found in many parts of eastern and southern Africa, kept this art vital until this century. In the Sahara there are hundreds of drawings and paintings, some of exquisite artistic quality.

In many parts of the world toolmaking traditions passed through the old stone age (paleolithic), the middle stone age (the mesolithic), and the new stone age (neolithic). In this broad sequence of development, the new stone age is traditionally associated with the development of agriculture: stone tools became increasingly refined and diversified, then began to give way to metal tools as the use of copper, tin, bronze, and eventually iron was discovered and became widespread. Where these metals are available in reasonable quantity, and men know how to work them, their superiority for toolmaking spells the death of toolmaking from stone (although there is always a long period when both types of tools are used, stone tools being less expensive and more widely available until society can mine or buy enough metal to make metal tools available to all who need them).

Several parts of Africa passed through this "typical" sequence of technological development, but many areas moved from the middle stone age into a later stone age, when highly sophisticated stone tools were manufactured, then directly into the iron age, usually entering this latter stage between about 500 B.C. and A.D. 500. A few peoples, such as the hunting-gathering peoples of southern Africa (the Bushmen) and eastern Africa (Ndorobo and others), continued to make stone tools until the past few centuries, even though they lived in close proximity to iron-using agriculturalists and pastoralists. The reason for Africa's deviation from the sequence followed in so many parts of the world is simply the unsuitability of much of the continent for the early development of agriculture.

There are only four regions of Africa where the conditions of fertile soil, adequate rainfall or water supplies, and potentially domesticable wild grains or tubers encouraged the development of agriculture by early man: the middle and lower Nile valley; the highland plateau of northern Ethiopia; the grasslands of the far western Sudan (north of the headwaters of the Niger and Senegal rivers); and the highland plateaus in the central Sahara, which was much moister seven or eight thousand years ago than it is today. In these areas men, from around 6000 to 3000 B.C., would have been in position to use agricultural knowledge brought to them from elsewhere even if they did not independently discover how to cultivate the wild plants they were already using as a source of food. Egypt began to practice agriculture in the Nile valley by at least 5000 B.C., but it is likely the ancient Egyptians acquired the knowledge from men farther east in Mesopotamia.

Ethiopians began to practice agriculture at some time before about 1500 B.C., perhaps as early as 3000 B.C.; the men of the western Sudan are known to have practiced grain agriculture at least as early as 1000 B.C., and it is possible that they began it much earlier, before 3500 B.C. There are hints that men in the Sahara may have planted wheat and millet between 6000 and 5000 B.C. (perhaps even earlier than the Egyptians) but by that time the Sahara was entering a period of gradual desiccation, which, over the next few thousand years, would have eliminated the pursuit of agriculture.

In Egypt and Ethiopia the middle stone age evolved into the new stone age, in common with much of Europe and Asia; there are local regions farther south in East Africa where the fashioning of tiny stone tools for agricultural and domestic uses, in the manner of the new stone age, occurred before the iron age began. But in most of the continent, men continued to make tools of stone for their ancient practices of hunting and gathering. Africa's failure to pass through the neolithic period in no way reflects a lack of ability on the part of the Africans: their stone tools became increasingly refined and efficient, and represent some of the finest stonework made in any part of the world. They were the right tools for the hunting-gathering economy to which the environment lent itself. When agriculture was developed in more favorable environments, Africans quickly spread it into every suitable part of their continent, leaping in their technology over the neolithic phase and the bronze age directly into the iron age.

The history of the many societies and cultures formed by Africans begins, to a large extent, with the discovery of agriculture and its spread to the various parts of the continent. The earliest mastery of agriculture was in ancient Egypt, often called the cradle of civilization.

2 Ancient Egypt

At a time when men in most of Africa, as well as in much of the rest of the world, were primitive stone age hunters, the ancient Egyptians had built a resplendent civilization in the Nile valley. Their culture, which is rightly famous for its awe-inspiring accomplishments, had its roots deeply buried in the soils of prehistoric Africa.

Until recent years it was frequently claimed that the Egyptian civilization was not truly "African," on the ground that both its peoples and their cultural affinities were more related to those of the Near East. While it is true that the Egyptians were a racially mixed people, with fewer Negroid genes than their Nubian neighbors to the south, they were fundamentally an African people. The history of Africa is the history of the migrations and intermingling of peoples; the further back one traces the history of Egypt, the more evident is the deep commonality of cultural roots over all of northern Africa, regardless of the facial composition of the peoples in various regions. Indeed, these deep cultural ties include the Mediterranean area in general. We are slowly learning that in prehistoric times there was far more communication among peoples and exchange among cultures than was formerly imagined.

The foundations of the Egyptian civilization were laid between 6000 B.C. and 5000 B.C. During this period the cultivation of wheat and barley significantly altered the pattern of life of a people who had previously been limited to hunting, fishing, and gathering wild seeds, roots, and fruits. It is not certain whether the early Egyptians discovered agriculture independently, or whether they acquired it from

Asia, where people had been cultivating crops for over a thousand years in the Tigris-Euphrates area and on the Anatolian plateau. But whatever its origin, agriculture quickly became the main means of livelihood in the Nile valley.

The early Egyptian farmers lived on the plains to the east and west of the Nile, rather than directly in the river's narrow valley. At that time the Nile valley and its great delta in the north were largely swamps, densely vegetated by thickets of reeds. The first crops were very probably sown in the wadis, ancient riverbeds that lead down from the plateau flanking the Nile into the lower area of the river valley. Nowadays the wadis are bone dry, carrying water only on the rare occasions when it rains over the desert. But in 5000 B.C. they were more regularly moist and carried water for at least a few months of each year. Flat areas in the wadis would have been fertile and relatively clear of the swamp growth of the Nile valley.

The area of the Nile valley probably became a population center as a result of the desiccation of the grassy savannahs of the Sahara in about 6000 B.C. Both the great game herds that had populated the Sahara and the hunters who had preyed on them gradually retreated to the north, south, and east. On the east lay the Nile River, forming a long narrow environmental ribbon that affords a sharp contrast to the now parched desert through which it runs. The Saharan hunters who moved toward the Nile found a region almost unmatched for its fertility and potential productivity.

These early settlers were apparently a heterogeneous group. Judging from the rock paintings in the central and eastern Sahara, and from skeletal remains, they included physical types that were ancestral to modern Berbers in the northern zone and to modern Negroes in the southern zone, with a great deal of mixture in between. At various times, the physical characteristics seem to vary, implying frequent movements and migrations of peoples. The Nile valley, despite being bordered by hostile deserts, was a land where peoples and ideas met—where periodic infusions of new peoples and new ideas contributed to the creative development of its unique environment.

The basis of the Egyptian civilization was the tremendous agricultural potential of the Nile valley. Each July, with rarely failing regularity, the Nile swells and overflows its banks from the rains that fall in the Ethiopian highlands. As the rain waters flow from Ethiopia in the Blue Nile, they carry tons of rich soils. In November the Nile subsides, leaving a new layer of loamy silt on the flats adjacent to its banks, thus constantly refertilizing them. By 4000 B.C. the early Egyptian farmers were clearing the natural vegetation, creating flats where the grains they sowed grew and yielded abundantly. Soon they learned to expand the cultivable areas by draining swamps and building irrigation systems, utilizing the potential of the valley with dramatic results.

The population of the Nile valley probably numbered no more than a few tens of thousands of people when agriculture was first introduced. By the end of the Old Kingdom, in the late third millennium B.C., the population had increased to about six million. The abundant production of food had made possible an explosion of population. It also enabled a major diversification of society, since the labor of the farming peasantry could support a large and complex structure of administrators, priests, craftsmen, soldiers, artists, and others who themselves produced no food.

The earliest history of the peoples who developed the basic African culture pattern from which the Egyptian civilization emerged is now known in part. Techniques of using grain appeared extremely early in the Nubian region of the Nile valley. The favored grains were very probably millet and wheat. Archaeologists have found numerous worn grinding stones, almost certainly used for making meal, and small tools fashioned from stone flakes that closely resemble the blades used on sickles for harvesting grain in later agricultural societies. These date from 15,000 to 12,000 B.C. Since no calcified seeds have been found to indicate whether wild or cultivated grain was used, it cannot be asserted that the ancient inhabitants of the valley had learned agriculture so early, millennia before any other people in the world, but they certainly used grain for food.

The evidence for the use of grain comes entirely from Nubia rather than Lower Egypt, arguing that this profoundly important economic innovation originated among the ancient Nubians, who then later passed it on to their Egyptian relatives. Nubia and Upper Egypt were, by 10,000 B.C., the most progressive areas in the world, judging by the highly refined developments in stonework now being found in that region.

At about 5000 B.C., the people of Lower Egypt began to overtake their neighbors to the south. A different neolithic culture began to emerge, clearly associated with the stone tools, grinding stones, and pots of a sedentary, agricultural people, who still hunted and fished, but were beginning to depend upon cultivation of grains and vegetables.

Excavations at Merimda, in the delta of the Nile, and at Fayum, the fertile site of an ancient lake to the west of the Nile, show this pattern of settled life. At the same period the peoples of Upper Egypt, from just below the first cataract (at modern Aswan) south through Nubia into the modern Sudan, had begun to practice cultivation, but seem to have been less permanently settled and somewhat more reliant on animal husbandry and hunting. However, these people, named the Tasians from the first excavated site of their culture, worked stone and pottery with a skill equal to that of the craftsmen of Fayum and Merimda.

In about 4000 B.C. the Tasians were succeeded by a more vigorous group who have been named Badarians. The Badarians, whose skeletal remains show numerous Negroid characteristics, quickly spread up and down the Nile, except for the area immediately south of the delta, which was still populated by the descendants of the Merimda and Fayum peoples. The Badarian art and stonework was more developed than the earlier Tasian, the agricultural techniques were apparently more effective, and the population more numerous.

The regional specialization of prehistoric Egyptians foreshadowed the later division of the country into Upper Egypt in the south and Lower Egypt in the north. It is generally felt that the prehistoric peoples of Lower Egypt were more powerful than those of Upper Egypt between about 5000 and 4000 B.C. Egyptian religious legends hold that the gods of Lower Egypt successfully invaded Upper Egypt at least a millennium before the founding of the First Dynasty, perhaps around 4500 to 4200 B.C. And there is some evidence to support the legend; stone vases and rectangular house foundations characteristic of Lower Egypt appeared in many parts of Upper Egypt about 4200 B.C.

Tantalizingly little is known of Egypt's history during this predynastic period between about 4500 and 3200 B.C. The delta, in which so much of the progressive development that underlay Egyptian civilization was taking place, has so silted up from the mud of the Nile that material remains are deeply buried and largely unexcavated. Fragments of pottery and stone tools, bits of ivory and bone, scattered writings from the dynastic period which mention earlier events, occasional carvings and paintings on stone all give hints, but too few to put together a comprehensive historical picture. But the Egyptian calendar, dating definitely from 4241 B.C., was devised during this hazy period, and hieroglyphic writing must have been invented, though no writing of the period has survived.

The Egyptians of this time were racially mixed, with the balance of Caucasoid and Negroid traits varying from time to time and region to region. The Caucasoid traits tended to be stronger in the delta area, the Negroid in Upper Egypt. In the delta close contact between the Libyans and the Egyptians blurred the differences between the two, while in the far south the Upper Egyptians shared many similarities with the neighboring Nubians. Material culture was rich. The people wore kilts and cloaks of skins and woven materials, probably linen, and sometimes sandals. They made highly refined pottery to decorate their homes, carved increasingly well in stone, wood, and ivory, made jewelry and hair ornaments of stone, ivory, and bone, ate with ivory spoons, and used boats along the Nile and its waterways. Their houses were made of dried mud and wattle, but sun-dried bricks had appeared by 4000 B.C.

A number of petty kingdoms must have dotted the Nile valley during the predynastic period. By 3400 B.C. two kingdoms had matured, one in Lower Egypt and one in Upper; these seem clearly to have incorporated smaller preexisting kingdoms. Classes of nobles and serfs almost certainly existed by 4000 B.C., as they are known to have done after about 3400 B.C. The art of irrigation had developed to a high point and, under the organization imposed by strong kings, had resulted in the claiming and regular irrigation of most of the cultivable land in the Nile valley. This in turn produced expanding wealth and a growing population. Cities appeared early in the predynastic age, though little is known of them other than their names: Nekheb, Buto, Thinis, El Kab. Probably settled during this early period were other cities that were important centers during the early historic period, such as Hierakonpolis, Abydos, Sais, and Heracleopolis.

Archaeologists often refer to the culture that was established during this period as the Gerzean, after El-Gerza, where excavation first revealed it. The Gerzean culture, borrowing from several of the earlier cultures such as the Badarian and Tasian, seems to have emerged first in Lower Egypt; the site at El-Gerza dates to about 3600 B.C. Its hallmarks were refined pottery, delicate stonework, copper utensils and ornaments, rectangular houses and tombs of sun-dried brick, and well-sculpted statuary and figurines of stone and ivory. By fusing earlier regional and foreign traditions into one cohesive culture which soon spread throughout Egypt, the Gerzean culture represented perhaps the first national tradition of the country, encompassing both north and south.

In about 3400 B.C. hostilities intensified between the kingdoms of Upper and Lower Egypt, culminating in the total conquest of Lower Egypt by the king of Upper Egypt some time between 3400 and 3200 B.C. This major conquest united the peoples of all Egypt into one kingdom, cementing the linguistic and cultural unity that had been developing for centuries. The man responsible for the conquest that launched Egypt on its course of five thousand years of known history was King Narmer, who is believed to be the same as the legendary Menes, as the Greeks referred to him, who founded the First Dynasty. Narmer is the first Egyptian king (or pharaoh, to use the later term) about whom definite information has survived. The sources are a brick tomb close to his place of birth and burial near Abydos, and several plaques and tablets found in tombs of his successors. Born and probably buried in the town of Thinis, near the city of Abydos of later times, Narmer must have been a brilliant soldier, administrator, and statesman. He marshaled the forces to unite Egypt and forge a political system that survived, at least in broad outline, for millennia.

According to an account recorded by Herodotus, Narmer transferred his capital to a new, more centrally located area between Upper and Lower Egypt. Here he built a great dam to divert the Nile's course and a town called the White Wall, later to become the royal center of Memphis. He identified himself with the great god Horus, represented by a hawk in early inscriptions. He also customarily had inscribed in the hieroglyphs of his title the bee, symbol of Lower Egypt, and the lily plant, symbol of his own Upper Egypt. Where his portrait appeared, he (like his successors) is shown wearing alternately the White Crown of Upper Egypt, an elongated conical hat representing the lily plant, and the Red Crown of Lower Egypt, a shorter, flared hat. Similarly demonstrating the unity of Egypt, Narmer and his successor kings often included religious symbols from both north and south in representations of their titles: Nekhbet, the vulture-goddess of the south's city of El Kab, and Buto, the serpent-goddess of the north's capital of Buto. Scenes on tableaus from this early period show Narmer appearing in state on ceremonious occasions, flanked by retainers, wearing a simple garment suspended by a strap over one shoulder, to which a lion's tail is attached. In a tradition that is by now well established, he is shown celebrating great victories, opening canals, or inaugurating other public works.

At the time of Narmer's conquest of Lower Egypt there was a broad "personality" for each Egypt which tended to endure throughout the dynastic period. Lower Egypt was generally richer and more refined in the arts and sciences, while Upper Egypt was more militarily and politically skilled. The culture and language of the two Egypts were the same, but the broad differences of national character served to set them slightly apart from each other.

Narmer's conquest marked the beginning of a historic dynastic era which lasted for some three thousand years, during which thirty dynasties of approximately three hundred and thirty monarchs, whose reigns lasted from a few days to as long as ninety years, rose and fell, until final conquest by foreign powers ushered in a new period of history under alien rule. During the three millennia following Narmer's unification virtually all the monarchs were native Egyptians, despite relatively brief periods of rule by families whose origins lay in Asia, Libya, or Nubia. During each of the thirty dynasties there reigned a line of kings who traced their legitimacy, usually by blood, to the founder of the dynasty, and new dynasties came to power when an able king or alliance of nobles was able to wrest power from the line that had previously ruled. The First Dynasty, for example, founded by

Narmer, included six other kings drawn from his family, all coming from the city of Thinis, all being buried in tombs in the neighboring city of Abydos, despite their use of the new center of the White Wall as capital. The Second Dynasty, made up of eleven kings, also came from Thinis, though of a different family. Together the two dynasties, sometimes referred to as Thinites, ruled Egypt for roughly four hundred twenty years, before being succeeded by a new line of kings native to Memphis (but possibly related by marriage to the Thinites).

Throughout Egyptian history the founding of new dynasties followed no set pattern. In some cases the transition between an old dynasty and a new was smooth and peaceful, sometimes resulting simply from assumption of power by an able new king of different family with little opposition. At other times the transition was violent and radical, resulting from foreign invasion or from civil war, with a new king seizing power with every intention of eradicating all influence and claims from the old dynasty. During several periods of internal weakness two or more kings ruled parts of Egypt, each claiming legitimacy over the whole, so that there are years of overlap between dynasties until one clearly emerged as the undisputed authority over the country.

Yet despite the occasional periods of weakness and political confusion, the mighty Egyptian civilization that rose to such heights of achievement in the millennia following Narmer predated every other civilization in the world in many of its achievements, and had enjoyed over two millennia of glory before a European civilization began to flower during the ancient Greek and Roman periods. Because of the immense longevity of the Egyptian civilization and the paucity of records for some periods, its history has to be looked at as through a telescope, from a far distance, picking out broad periods and signal events. There is in existence no exact list of all the kings of ancient Egypt, nor a record of the dates and lengths of their reigns. The ancient and very accurate Egyptian calendar was never applied to a cumulative chronology. Dates, where known, normally referred only to the reign of each king; a new chronology began with each new king, with no reference to the years of the kings he had succeeded.

Egyptian history is customarily divided into several broad periods: the Predynastic Period, the Archaic Period, the Old Kingdom, the Middle Kingdom, the New Kingdom, and the Late Period. Known dynasties, beginning with the Archaic Period in about 3400 B.C., cover roughly three thousand years, ending with the conquest of Egypt by Alexander the Great and the installation of foreign kings.

During the Archaic Period, which began when Narmer united the two Egypts, a foundation was laid down for almost every area of the civilization that developed over the next three thousand years. Politically, the key advance was the pharaonic system, which provided Egypt with a permanent concept of national unity. After Narmer's reign all Egyptians accepted the standard of a single legitimate king; even during later periods of anarchy, when petty nobles struggled to gain power over each other, they sought the ultimate goal of becoming king of the entire country.

Under the pharaonic system the power of all lesser kings and princes was swept away, and their titles abolished. Egypt was to have but one ruler, and administration of the country was provided by governors and deputies whom he appointed. Taxes were levied on local towns and former kingdoms, and the country was divided into a series of "nomes," or provinces, that accorded approximately with older kingdoms.

In the arts the Archaic Period laid a foundation for later development or institutionalized developments that had originated long before in the predynastic ages. Hieroglyphic writing, developed much earlier, was perfected and regularized, as the kings and their courts encouraged scribes to record and glorify their deeds. On the sun-dried bricks commonly used in buildings, on smooth stone slabs that were designed as monuments, the scribes carved and painted descriptions of the hunt, of military victories, and of ceremonies. Pens and ink came into use for writing on papyrus sheets and tablets of slate. A form of cursive writing, much more rapid than hieroglyphic, was developed, although it was used only for notes and computations, never for permanent or royal records and inscriptions.

Around the king's court grew a class of learned men who aided the king in government and devoted a portion of their time to medicine, religion, writing, architecture, engineering, or art. There is no evidence that guilds of specialists developed during the Archaic Period, but learning was common among the nobles and senior administrators. Narmer is believed to have been the first king to cause the Nile to be dammed and diverted in order to regulate the flow of water into the fields along its banks. Large-scale irrigation projects thus added new cultivable land and allowed greater production on lands already cultivated. Throughout later history the wealth of Egypt depended upon the basic system of irrigation developed during the Archaic Period; when a strong king held the throne so that irrigation works covering hundreds of miles up and down the Nile could be coordinated, prosperity followed. When weak kings failed to provide the requisite coordination, crops suffered in many areas and productivity declined.

The importance of maintaining the complex irrigation system developed during the Archaic Period cannot be overemphasized. The technique of simple irrigation, drawing up water from the Nile by bucket, had been known long before the Archaic Period. But utilization of all the potential valley and delta lands for regular crop production year round was possible only when diversion dams were built. By means of these dams, flood waters were retained in canals and pools and kept clear of silt. The water was released in measured amounts during the dry periods. In the delta organized effort was needed to keep the undergrowth away, to build dykes in order to keep cleared areas dry, and to keep drainage and irrigation canals open for providing water when and where it was needed.

In architecture, the chief building material for tombs, palaces, and public buildings was sun-dried brick, but gradually stone slabs came into use for foundations and the lower reaches of walls, presaging the use of massive stone blocks in later times for building immense pyramids and temples. Large brick tombs built for kings of the Archaic Period were the prototypes of the great stone pyramids that the kings of the succeeding Old Kingdom built to house their remains and provide permanent shrines.

Stone was commonly used during the Archaic Period for tools, jewelry, bowls, pots, and points for spears and arrows, but copper working began to replace it for many uses before the period ended. Cold copper was hammered into spear and arrow points and utensils, and the art of melting and casting copper was highly developed well before the end of the Archaic Period.

In foreign affairs, little is known from direct records, but there is considerable indirect evidence of contact between Egypt and its neighbors in Libya and Nubia, as well as with the other great contemporary civilization of Mesopotamia in the Near East valleys of the Tigris and Euphrates rivers. Egyptian boat designs, writing forms, art, and pottery styles show Mesopotamian influence, although there is less evidence of Egyptian influence in Mesopotamia.

Both trade and occasional conflict characterized ancient Egypt's relations with its African neighbors, the Libyans to the west and the Nubians to the south. In Egyptian history and even prehistory, relationships with the Libyans and Nubians were always inextricably linked with the affairs of Egypt itself. No natural boundaries exist between Egypt and either Libya or Nubia, and the peoples of the three areas have mingled and exchanged goods and ideas for thousands of years. The Libyans and Egyptians are related in language and basic culture, both speaking languages belonging to the Afro-Asiatic language stock. Libyans and Egyptians of the delta area were in such close contact that many families had representatives living in both countries. Their differences were primarily those of politics and way of life, with the Egyptians committed to the pharaonic kingdom and a settled, urban life, and the Libyans committed to a more pastoral and seminomadic life, acknowledging allegiance only to their own clans and village councils.

Although greater racial and cultural differences existed between the Egyptians and the Nubians, who spoke a language of the Sudanic stock, their proximity in the Nile valley facilitated close contact and trade, as well as the exchange of ideas and culture traits. From the days of the Middle Kingdom on, the Egyptians deliberately extended their influence and culture as far into Nubia as their military strength permitted, so that northern Nubians adopted many traits of Egyptian religion and culture and often were forced to acknowledge Egyptian suzerainty. Intermarriage seems to have been common between southern Egyptians and northern Nubians, helping to blur differences even more. Nevertheless, these differences never completely ceased to exist.

Egyptian records from the earliest days on imply a consciousness of the importance of its relationship to both Libya and Nubia. Toward Nubia, especially, Egypt felt a special regard, since it was the source of a never failing supply of goods that Egyptians prized: gold, skins, feathers, ebony, gum, spices, slaves, and, on occasion, men for military service.

Egypt, however, felt very differently toward Asia, despite the fact that the ancient Arabs, Hebrews, Syrians, and Palestinians spoke languages related to Egyptian and shared many common elements of race and culture. Asians were regarded as foreigners. Trade was constant across the Sinai, but the Asiatics on its eastern side were never regarded in quite the same light as the neighboring Libyans on the west and Nubians on the south. In a deep sense, the Egyptians regarded themselves as an African people.

The transition between the Archaic and Old Kingdom periods came in about 2980 B.C. when Zoser, the young leader of a noble family of Memphis, succeeded to the throne and established the Third Dynasty. By this time, the White Wall built by Narmer had become a glittering complex of palaces, public buildings, temples, and gardens, though it was not a large center of population. More and more noble families of the court developed permanent homes there and ceased to identify with their cities of origin. The great family that Zoser headed was one of these and may have been related to the Thinites, since there is no evidence of conflict or upheaval when he assumed the throne.

The Old Kingdom, in some respects the golden age of Egyptian civilization, stretched from Zoser's reign to the end of the Sixth Dynasty, in about 2475 B.C. Egypt was then a land of plenty, vastly increasing its population, reclaiming much of the delta for cultivation, enjoying a satisfactory standard of living for the peasantry and a plentiful income for the pharaoh. Mechanics and engineering reached heights of development never surpassed in later Egyptian history, and inscriptions of the period emphasize bountiful harvests and the good life. Immense buildings and monuments, the greatest of which were the pyramids, still survive to symbolize the glories of the Old Kingdom and its kings.

During the Archaic Period the kings had begun to identify themselves with favored gods, so that by the time of Zoser's reign there was a strong belief in the king's divinity; he was a god in human form. Pharaonic tombs grew ever larger and more ornate, with altars and small temples surrounding them in which rites could be performed to worship the king after death. The logical culmination of the tomb development was the creation of tombs that were so large, so impressive, and so permanent as to seem eternal monuments to the divine kings whose remains they held.

The first of the great pyramids was built for King Zoser, by his vizier, or prime minister, Imhotep, whose fame persisted in later Egyptian tradition as strongly as Zoser's. Imhotep must have been an intellectual giant, numbering among his talents architecture, governmental administration, medicine, and the priesthood. For three thousand years after his death his name was revered as the semidivine patron of scribes and as the father of medicine.

Throughout the Third and Fourth dynasties kings continued to build great pyramids, culminating in the several huge pyramids at Gizeh, just outside modern Cairo, which have symbolized the awesome grandeur of ancient Egypt for millions of visitors over the centuries, and which now attract tourists as one of the wonders of the world.

The centering of wealth, power, and talent around the pharaoh and his court during the Old Kingdom brought advances in art comparable to those in architecture. Large statues of granite, marble, alabaster, and soapstone representing the pharaohs and chief nobles were carved by brilliant sculptors. Stone vases and bowls, jewelry of copper and silver studded with semiprecious stones, and other personal ornaments of great beauty were fashioned for the royal and noble families. Artists and craftsmen adhered to traditional styles, which were formal, and tended toward the abstract and static; yet individual expression and freedom of form were allowed to some extent in the creation of artifacts and jewelry, setting a standard that Egyptian artists of many later eras envied and strove to emulate.

The Old Kingdom fell into ruin about 2475 B.C., and a long period of unrest and disunity followed; its duration is not known for certain, but it may have lasted as long as three centuries. The cause of its collapse was the gradual growth of dozens of petty principalities in the nomes. As originally organized by Narmer, each of these administrative areas was run by an appointed governor having no hereditary right to the office. But as the centuries wore on, these governors, often called nomarchs, acquired titles and local tracts of land which traditionally remained in their families. They came to regard themselves as hereditary nobility, almost as princes or kings of their own domains. They remained loyal to the strong pharaohs, and the government seemingly functioned effectively as a monarchy throughout the Archaic and Old Kingdom periods. But a change in the balance of power signaled the end of the Old Kingdom and the old system of government.

During the period of anarchy that followed, the jealous nomarchs struggled incessantly against each other and against weak pharaohs. In the struggles there was resentment against the former divine authority of the Old Kingdom pharaohs, and armed bands frequently ravaged and destroyed tombs and statuary commemorating them. Royal bodies were taken from the tombs and burned, and the precious jewels and possessions buried with them pillaged. Only the sheer immenseness and durability of some of the monuments saved them to give modern man some conception of the greatness achieved by Old Kingdom Egypt.

The Middle Kingdom took shape in 2160 B.C. when Mentuhotep II, a Theban king, completed a process of conquest of Lower Egypt which his family had begun as early as 2250 B.C. Just as Narmer had swept out of Upper Egypt over a thousand years before to unite all Egypt, the kings of Thebes, in the same region, were the only nomarchs strong enough to reestablish unity and restore pharaonic rule over the whole country. But their task was made difficult by the power accumulated by other nomarchs, and in the end pharaonic rule was restored only by accepting the hereditary rights of the nomarchs and allowing them to retain a measure of power. Thus the chief characteristic of government and politics under the Middle Kingdom was a type of feudalism, under which pharaohs were prevented from acquiring absolute power and were forced to govern by consent of the powerful nomarchs.

During the feudal era of the Middle Kingdom Egypt again prospered; irrigation systems which had fallen into disuse were repaired and expanded, trade inside the country and with other countries again flourished, and peace was restored. But the wealth of the pharaoh's court was limited. Each nomarch maintained his own court, complete with scribes, architects, nobles, retainers, and administrators, and these courts of the nomes replicated the royal court on a smaller scale.

The wider distribution of wealth under this system stimulated a general flourishing of arts and letters. Palaces, tombs, statues, public buildings, and works of art characterized the courts of the nomarchs as well as that of the pharaoh. Literature was widely appreciated, and included excellent poetry, discourses on religion, philosophy, and ethics, and real or artificial folk tales recorded for entertainment. Schools were popular and literacy was commonplace among both the nobility and a middle class of artists, craftsmen, merchants, and petty officials.

Perhaps the greatest economic achievement of the Middle Kingdom was the creation of a vast agricultural complex in the Fayum depression, through the construction of dams and walled reservoirs. At least twenty-seven thousand acres of highly productive new land in the Fayum alone were brought under cultivation, and the Fayum delta region became a center of great wealth. Eventually, in fact, the pharaoh built a new center of government there, based on a vast administrative building, over a thousand feet long and eight hundred wide, that came to be known as the Labyrinth; it was compared by later Greeks, who saw it before it fell into ruin, with the famous Cretan labyrinth of Greek tradition.

The enormous wealth of Egypt that the Middle Kingdom produced was best exemplified by the new middle class that it supported; never before, during the Archaic or Old Kingdom periods, had a middle class emerged. As it grew in size and prosperity it developed a distinct pride in its achieved position. Individuals of the middle class were sometimes wealthy enough to erect tombs. Here the inscriptions refer to the buried person simply as "goldsmith," "coppersmith," "sandalmaker," or "citizen." In one cemetery of the period at Abydos one fourth of the eight hundred burials show no inscriptions of titles of rank or office, and the majority of the titles themselves refer to minor, non-noble office-holders, such as "assistant treasurer."

Art was greatly encouraged during the Middle Kingdom, especially sculpture and jewelry making. Statues of kings, nomarchs, and nobles of the period have been found in many places, and they tend to be massive in size, often exceeding twenty feet in height. Rigid in form and mechanical in execution, they show little freedom of expression, but they are skillfully executed by artists who were obviously masters of their technique. The jewelry of the Middle Kingdom, in contrast, included numerous pieces of exquisite beauty and supreme technical skill. Often delicate, with gold, silver, and various alloys soldered so smoothly as to be difficult to detect, the best Middle Kingdom jewelry is the equal of any ever produced in the world.

The Middle Kingdom came to an end with the Twelfth Dynasty about 1788 B.C. The pharaohs again became unable to govern effectively over the still powerful, often ambitious nomarchs. There followed a time of darkness of which we known little. The ruins from this time are few and modest. The country must have been economically depressed, with the irrigation systems in disuse and internal commerce sporadic and perilous, as petty nomarchs battled each other for power or for booty.

During this period the first conquest of Egypt by foreigners took place, when the Hyksos kings from Asia invaded the delta and set up a dynasty over Lower Egypt. The century of their rule has been almost completely obscured. Their stronghold was the delta, in which ruins gradually disappear under the silt deposited by the Nile, and even their capital city there, Avaris, has disappeared without a trace. We do not even know definitely their origins. Later Egyptian tradition refers to them as Asiatics, as well as barbarians; they were despised by Egyptians of later times because they never accepted Egyptian gods and presumably remained aliens in language and culture during their reign. When they were expelled in about 1580 B.C. they are known to have retreated into Syria, then eastward as pursuing Egyptian armies routed them. A few stelae referring to them have been found in, Syrian excavations, but not enough to clarify their ethnic character.

The New Kingdom began in 1580 B.C., when Theban forces, who had never been conquered by the Hyksos, drove the Hyksos out of Egypt and defeated a number of nomarchs in middle and Lower Egypt who had supported them. The cumulative successes of several Theban leaders resulted in the restoration of virtually absolute power to the throne and the crushing of all nomarchies that had offered resistance. Within a few decades Egypt was at peace, and prosperity began to return under the firm guidance of a throne whose power rested upon military strength, led by pharaohs who had proven their superiority in war, as heads of the largest and most professional army Egypt had ever produced.

With the power of most nomarchs totally eliminated by the pharaoh's army, Egypt became a military state, ruled by the pharaoh through the thousands of loyal officers who had helped him restore the throne's legitimacy. Feudal nomarchs were replaced by efficient military governors, responsible only to the pharaoh's and fully committed to the new destiny for Egypt which he symbolized. Even though the original military government gradually grew into a civilian government during the course of the New Kingdom, the clear lines of authority from nome administrator to the crown remained the salient feature of the political system, and for centuries the nomes were little more than administrative units in a highly centralized state.

The professional army developed by Thebes during the restoration had acquired the use of the horse and chariot, introduced to Egypt by the Hyksos, and it developed strategies, tactics, and forms of organization that made it a formidable force—for centuries clearly the most formidable army in the world. The lust of conquest and the enthusiasm for plunder that developed during the restoration remained as a motivating force for army and throne alike, so that foreign campaigns and imperial expansion followed soon after peace returned internally. The New Kingdom became Egypt's imperial age, as victorious Egyptian troops marched into Libya, Nubia, and Asia, crushing all who offered resistance and erecting monuments to the glory of Egypt and the pharaoh. Within a few decades Egypt's empire extended to the Euphrates River in Asia, into the Libyan desert on the west, and up the Nile to the fourth cataract, deep into Nubian territory.

As in previous times of national unity, the productivity of Egypt's farms expanded with the rebuilding of ruined irrigation systems and the enforcement of coordinated water use and labor organization. By 1500 B.C. Egypt's prosperity was equal to that achieved under the Old and Middle kingdoms, but under the New Kingdom booty and tribute from foreign conquests and dominions swelled the pharaoh's coffers even further. Inscriptions in tombs and palaces of the period have as a regular theme divine pharaohs receiving great stores of gold, silver, slaves, spices, ivory, gems, and other riches from conquered chiefs and foreign vassals. Much of the wealth undoubtedly was needed to support the vast bureaucracy of professional soldiers and administrators through whom the pharaoh ruled Egypt and its empire, but there was also enough to support costly public works and palaces, temples, statues, and works of art.

Another hallmark of the New Kingdom was the formulation and implementation of a comprehensive code of laws, drawn both from age-old common law and from the pharaoh's edicts, and of a uniform system of justice, binding even the pharaoh to lawful behavior. The office of vizier, used by pharaohs throughout Egyptian history, was expanded to include supervision of justice, so that in later history good viziers of the New Kingdom were remembered as those who administered the law fairly and wisely to all, both high born and low.

The more professional government of the New Kingdom encouraged the further growth of the middle class, far beyond that of the Middle Kingdom, and emphasis was placed on individual achievement. Numerous tomb inscriptions and records emphasize the ease with which humble men could rise in prominence and position by virtue of superior performance in administration, military service, or crafts. For the first time in Egyptian history a large corps of professional priests appeared, devoted to keeping the many temples built by the pharaohs and helping worshipers attain a good destiny in the afterlife by correct behavior and pious conduct.

About 1150 B.C. the New Kingdom collapsed, following the rule of a number of weak pharaohs and repeated struggles with Asian powers on one side and the Libyans on the other. Power passed from the throne to the nomarchies, this time in the hands of men who had been professional soldiers or foreign mercenaries, rewarded by the crown with title to vast estates in appreciation for their military service. Among the mercenaries who had acquired power in this way were many Libyans, who controlled large parts of the delta and Lower Egypt, and upon whom the crown had increasingly come to depend. In about 950 B.C. Libyan families based in the delta seized the throne, and installed a new dynasty of Egyptianized Libyan kings who ruled, sometimes with sufficient success to unite most of Egypt for brief periods, for over a century.

The period following the end of the New Kingdom, until the conquest of Egypt by Persia, then Greece, is the Late Period, or the Decadence. Numerous kings and dynasties ruled during this long period, some of them of Libyan or Nubian origin. In about 722 B.C. Nubia conquered Egypt and reunified the country under a series of strong Nubian kings for nearly a century, until Assyrian invasions forced them to retreat back into Nubia. For much of the Late Period Egypt was able to maintain a semblance of unity and peaceful internal prosperity, but no line of kings was sufficiently powerful to provide the country with the leadership needed to reach heights of greatness. The New Kingdom was the last period in which Egypt was able to harness its remarkable natural and human resources to produce the outstanding feats of civilization that characterized the Old, Middle, and New kingdoms. More often than not the achievements of the more productive kings and dynasties of the Late Period, creditable though they sometimes were, imitated the glories of the Old Kingdom rather than branching out into new areas; this was especially true in art, dress, ornamentation, and literature. The deeply rooted talents of Egyptian artists, craftsmen, architects, and administrators often found means of expression and strong encouragement from the throne, but the great innovations and glittering pinnacles of accomplishment of the past failed to appear.

The Late Period was broken in the sixth century B.C., by Persian conquest and rule, followed by another period of rule by native pharaohs, then by a second Persian conquest at the end of the fifth century. It ended with the Greek conquest in 332 B.C., resulting in three centuries of Greek rule under Ptolemy I and his successors, who reigned until Roman conquest in 30 B.C. Following the gradual breakup of the Roman Empire in the fourth and fifth centuries of the Christian era, Egyptian Christian kings reigned, until the Arab invasions of the seventh century and the eventual Islamization of the country.

During the more than three thousand years of ancient Egypt's sovereignty a truly great civilization was created that endured persistently despite times of internal chaos and misery, changing its form as new periods took shape, yet never losing its distinctively Egyptian character. Its social structure and culture evolved from prehistoric African patterns that appear in various forms in other African nations.

Egyptian civilization rested throughout its illustrious career on the labors of the Egyptian peasant, the ordinary serf whose constant hard work produced such abundant grains, vegetables, and fruits. His existence was simple and poor.

The land tilled by the serfs was often owned collectively by their villages, but the taxes of the pharaoh and nomarch left only enough food for subsistence. The serfs had minimal rights, but their lot in life was toil, that they might produce the surpluses upon which the nobility and government depended. The serfs, or "fellahin" as they have come to be known, were essentially sturdy individuals whose primary concerns were their work and family, unchanging certainties throughout the millennia of change. Monogamy was the rule, and relations between husband and wife were based on an intimate sharing of experiences: tilling the land, rearing the children, suffering common woes, together enjoying the few pleasures afforded by village social life. The wife's position was a strong one, since inheritance was through the female line, and the wife's labor in the home and the field was as important as the husband's in maintaining life.

Their material possessions were few: simple cots on which to sleep, several tools, usually of stone, pots for cooking and food preparation, a bit of linen for simple garb—often discarded entirely when working in the field—and bits of treasured jewelry in the form of beads, stone or bone amulets, and small objects of copper.

The village was the widest social or political unit that normally concerned the fellahin. Although the growth of cities created a new and different environment for some, the majority always lived in the villages and tilled the soil. In a society where land was precious, villages were crowded onto the smallest possible area, with mud houses jammed together and separated only by narrow lanes, widening in places for a few shops where shoemakers, carpenters, and other artisans plied their trades. Social life consisted of occasional religious ceremonials, dancing, gossip among groups of men and women separated by sex, occasional swimming and fishing in the Nile, and occasional social gatherings in which beer of barley or honey was consumed.

The fellahin traditionally resisted change and eschewed the affairs of the nobles and the coming and going of new rulers; even toward the priests and required religious observances the fellahin tended to be dutiful rather than devout. Accepting the eternal obligation of hard work on the land, and the giving over of a portion of his labor and harvest to the landlord and the tax collector, the fellah concentrated his attention on his family and his village, there finding his pleasure and satisfaction in life.

As previously noted, a middle class grew up during the Middle Kingdom, and expanded greatly under the New Kingdom. Very largely urban, the middle class consisted of a variety of artisans, soldiers, petty administrators, scribes, priests, and court functionaries in the nomes and the capital. During periods of great stability and productivity the middle class flourished, and from it came much of the arts and crafts, engineering works, building, and government service that Egypt produced so abundantly. In some cases there was no sharp distinction between the more humble members of the middle class and the fellahin, since village artisans counted themselves part of the middle class, but the more gifted and recognized members of the middle class were often intimate participants in the life of the court. During the New Kingdom, for example, when an efficient professional government encouraged and rewarded individual achievement, one proud artisan recorded his deep satisfaction at the position he had achieved:

". . . I was one whose family was poor and whose town was small, but the Lord of the Two Lands [the pharaoh] recognized me; I was accounted great in his heart, the king in his role as sun-god in the splendor of his palace saw me. He exalted me more than the royal companions, introducing me among the princes of the palace. . . . He appointed me to conduct works while I was a youth, he found me, I was made account of in his heart, I was introduced into the gold-house to fashion the figures and images of all the gods."

In art and science Egypt achieved great heights early in the Old Kingdom, rarely in later periods surpassing the achievements of that time. Egyptian science was practically oriented rather than theoretical: mathematics, developed even before the Archaic Period, was built around the needs of commerce, taxation, architecture, and surveying, for example, and never grew into a comprehensive system of theoretical solutions to problems. Astronomers early catalogued the stars and recognized the consistency of solar and lunar movements, but their knowledge was used to determine exact directions, to calculate the times of the rise and fall of the Nile, and to keep the calendar accurate; no effort was made to use astronomical knowledge to formulate scientific theories of the universe and the movements of stellar and planetary bodies.

Medicine at its best was remarkably sophisticated, including a sufficient understanding of the bones of the body for setting fractures and minor surgery, a knowledge of simple brain surgery, and some comprehension of the function of blood vessels. But folk remedies and magical incantations remained part of the Egyptian medical system, apparently deemed by most practitioners to be as efficacious as healing based on practical experience and a knowledge of physiology.

Egyptian architecture represents perhaps the most majestic achievement of its civilization, and still staggers the imagination even though most of its architectural heritage was destroyed by deliberate and wanton ravaging by conquerers, by the gradual action of rain and wind, or by slowly sinking beneath the vast acres of silt in Lower Egypt and the delta. Yet the numerous ruined buildings, tombs, and monuments that remain, some four and five thousand years old, point to a great civilization which devoted enormous wealth, labor, and creative talent to architecture and engineering.

In the most impressive structures, such as the great pyramids of Gizeh, the limestone and granite slabs weigh as much as five tons. The huge pyramid of Khufu at Gizeh required some two million three hundred thousand stone blocks, weighing an average of two and a half tons each. Incredible work was necessary to quarry these blocks from stone formations many miles away, float them during the flood periods to the site of the pyramid, move them upon wooden rollers to the structure itself, then lift them to their positions.

In addition to the tremendous wealth and labor involved, mathematical skills of great complexity were required. The Great Pyramid is laid out with fine precision: its sides align almost exactly with the four cardinal points of the compass, its slabs fit together so tightly that the cracks are almost invisible, and the relationship of its height to the circumference of the base is the same as that of the radius of a circle to its circumference. Until the last century few, if any, engineers have possessed the vast knowledge and skill that the Egyptians employed to erect such consummate edifices.

To achieve the soaring heights attained during its three millennia of supreme achievement, ancient Egypt invented and devised many ideas and techniques, while it borrowed others from the even more ancient civilization of Sumeria in Mesopotamia. Whether by independent innovation or borrowing, however, Egypt accumulated and utilized a wide range of complex and sophisticated skills to create a system of awesome monuments that are unique in the history of man. At a time when the ancestors of most modern peoples were living in a state of primitivism, the Egyptians attained, and maintained for an unprecedented span of time, a civilization of such grandeur and luster that it still inspires the awe and respect of all men.

3 Nubia and Kush

Nubia is the traditional name of the vast lands that lie around the upper Nile, in the modern nation of the Sudan, between Egypt and Ethiopia. Its earliest civilization of note was that of the Kushites, who lived above the third cataract of the Nile, just south of the modern Egypt-Sudan border.

The kingdom of Kush, as the Egyptians named it, was the principal power of Nubia from very early times and was referred to in Egyptian records at least as early as 2000 B.C. It grew powerful enough to conquer Egypt during the eighth century B.C., and might have flourished as an empire had it not been for a series of invasions by the powerful Assyrians, who were armed with weapons of iron. (At that time iron was little used in either Egypt or Nubia.) As it was, however, Kush continued to develop in its own homeland for centuries after this brief experience as a major world power and, in fact, reached the zenith of its civilization more than three hundred years later.

Most regrettably, the history of Kush, especially in the centuries following the rise of Meroe, is much less well known than that of Egypt. This is due partly to a lack of archaeological study; most of Meroe is still unexcavated. But partly it is due to the fact that Meroitic writing has never been adequately translated.

At first Kush used standard Egyptian hieroglyphic writing for its records, but in the third century B.C. it invented its own cursive script and soon abandoned hieroglyphics. Meroitic script has been deciphered, by comparing it to hieroglyphic records describing the same event, but the language of Meroe in which the script was written has never been translated. Scholars working on the problem of the Meroitic language are searching for an extant language that may be sufficiently close to the ancient Kushite language to allow translation. Although ancient Kushitic bears a slight resemblance to modern Nubian, it clearly is a separate language, related only distantly to the modern languages of the area. Scholars believe it was a language of the eastern group of the Sudanic language family, many of which have not been studied sufficiently to be sure of their relationship to ancient Kushitic. To the historian of Africa the task of finding a language that would permit ancient Kushitic to be translated is an exciting priority.

The relationship between Egypt and Kush was generally characterized by the dominance of the highly organized Egyptians, who raided, policed, traded with, and sometimes invaded and annexed their weaker and less developed neighbors. Kush borrowed much from Egyptian culture: styles in art and architecture (including pyramids), hieroglyphic writing, and religious beliefs, to name only a few. This has led many scholars, especially Egyptologists, to dismiss the Kushites as a backward and barbaric people who could, at best, only imitate their more creative Egyptian neighbors.

Such invidious comparisons between Kush and Egypt are exaggerated, but to the extent they are based on fact they do gross injustice to the Kushites and by inference to other Black Africans. They fail to take into account the tremendous achievements made in the face of physical environments far more isolated and far less hospitable than the lush lower Nile valley and delta. For, as one ascends the Nile ever farther to the south, into Nubia and beyond, the amount of arable land and its fertility generally decrease. The environment simply does not support as dense a population as in the north, nor does it permit the farmer to be as productive.

Until about 5000 B.C. the peoples of Egypt and Nubia were not far apart in cultural development—in fact, the Nubians were apparently somewhat more advanced. But as the Egyptians began to farm the rich lower Nile and the delta, their economic base and growing population enabled a rapid advance; and being in relatively frequent contact with other developing peoples at the eastern end of the Mediterranean, they were in a position to borrow new ideas. The Nubians, poorer, sparsely scattered, and more isolated from the outside world, also progressed steadily, but fell increasingly behind their more fortunate neighbors to the north. By 2000 B.C., the Nubians were a sturdy lot of pastoral and agricultural tribesmen, prosperous by comparison to many other peoples, but weak and bucolic compared to the civilized Egyptians.

Shortly after 2000 B.C. the pharaoh Sesostris I, of the Twelfth

Dynasty, led his troops into Nubia as far as the third cataract, annexing a number of the northern tribes, building forts, and securing the rights to unrestricted trade for Nubia's gold, ivory, ebony, and other prized goods. He passed through the land of Kush, according to records of his expedition, but was unable to secure control so far from his base of operations. From this time onward, until the period of Hyksos rule in Egypt, the northern portions of Nubia were dominated by Egypt, and the Nubians farther south, including the Kushites, were in close contact with Egyptian culture. Just outside the sphere of Egyptian control, near the third cataract, a Nubian state came into being near Kerma in about 1800 B.C. that may have been the ancestor of the later kingdom of Kush.

In about 1500 B.C., during the New Kingdom, Egypt extended her control further, and Egyptian troops often penetrated as far south as the fourth cataract; they may even have reached the sixth cataract area, near modern Khartoum. The Kushite homeland, and the city of Napata (near the fourth cataract), which was to become its capital, fell under close Egyptian supervision, and became increasingly Egyptianized in culture. The Theban god Amon-re attracted many Kushite devotees, Egyptian art and pottery styles were adopted, Egyptian buildings and temples appeared in large numbers, and Egyptian hieroglyphic writing became common. Although the culture of the common people probably remained Nubian, the high culture of the court and the nobility inexorably became Egyptian.

Toward the close of the second millennium B.C., as the power of Egypt's New Kingdom waned, Kushite strength and resentment of Egyptian control grew steadily. Under the rulership of Egyptianized Kushite kings, Napata, strategically situated to control the rich trade between Nubia and Egypt, became a center of wealth and power. During the eighth century Kushite forces under King Kashta, the first Kushitic king whose name survives, invaded southern Egypt; Kashta's successor, Piankhi, completed the task of conquest by occupying Memphis and the delta and establishing a dynasty of Kushite rulers of Egypt.

Little information is available to describe the customs and manners of the conquering Kushites. Piankhi is known to have made brilliant use of naval facilities in his sweep down the Nile, and his successful assault on the great city of Memphis rested on a massive assemblage of amphibious troops. Carved murals on temples of the period tended to emphasize the bow and arrow as a weapon, so apparently the Kushites relied upon bowmen.

The Kushite kings united Egypt and ruled for a hundred years, but they had so deeply absorbed Egyptian culture that they left no clear

Kushitic legacy. A distinctive Kushite culture did not emerge until several centuries later, when a new center of power grew up in the city of Meroe.

Kushite control of Egypt was ended by Assyrian invasions less than a century after Piankhi's conquest. The Assyrians, based in the Fertile Crescent, in what is now Syria, Lebanon, Israel, and Jordan, had long regarded Egypt as a threatening rival. During the period of internal weakness that followed the end of the New Kingdom, relations between Egypt and Assyria had been relatively peaceful, but Assyrian fears apparently were revived as the Kushite dynasty restored unity and power to Egypt. Soon Assyrian and Egyptian forces began to clash in the Sinai desert region, and Assyria launched an invasion. The Assyrian troops, well armed with iron spears and swords and bronze shields, and well equipped with cavalry, soon proved superior to the Egyptian-Kushite troops, who had no iron weapons, fewer cavalry forces, and more troops shielded by leather rather than bronze. Gradually they were forced back into Egypt, then, as Lower Egypt fell, up the Nile as far as Thebes.

Although the Assyrians withdrew from Egypt after their military success, the power of the Kushite nobility was mortally weakened, and they abandoned their imperial role in Egypt to return to their homeland in Napata.

Less than a century later Napata itself was invaded, either by Egyptian or Persian forces, and was despoiled. Perhaps as a result the Kushite royal family moved farther up the Nile to the city of Meroe near the modern Sudanese capital of Khartoum. For many generations the kings ruled from Meroe, but traveled to Napata for investiture, and their bodies were returned after death to the Napata area for burial. As time wore on, however, Napata fell into ruins and Meroe supplanted it as the political, religious, and economic capital of Kush.

Meroe had three major advantages over Napata: it was in a region with sufficient rainfall to permit grass and trees to grow, it had large iron deposits, and it was far enough from the center of Egyptian power to be relatively invulnerable to attack or unwanted influence. Located in a small triangle between the Nile and the Atbara rivers, through which run several wadis that permit intensive cultivation, the city of Meroe was able to sustain a far denser population than most of northeastern Africa. Caravans could cover the distance between Meroe and the Red Sea easily in a few weeks, so that it lay astride a growing trade between interior Africa and the Red Sea-Indian Ocean traders of Arabia, India, Persia, Rome, and Greece.

Meroe was heavily engaged in commerce and iron working, and the presence of numerous members of the nobility and religious and military leaders made it a great capital city.

Established about the beginning of the sixth century B.C., Meroe had become a major center by the fourth century, and continued as a cultural, political, and commercial metropolis until the third century A.D., when it was destroyed either by encroaching peoples from the west (usually thought to be the Noba) or by troops from the Ethiopian kingdom of Axum. Today it is uninhabited, marked only by long rows of crumbling pyramids, great mounds of earth that cover ruined temples, palaces, and dwellings, and huge heaps of slag from the iron works that sustained Meroe's power for many centuries. Only a few of the temples and pyramids have been explored with any thoroughness, so that the exact size and plan of the city are still not fully known, but its population must have numbered at least in the tens of thousands, judging by its apparent extent. For some miles to the east, in the relatively fertile area between the Nile and the Atbara, are the ruins of a number of other towns filled with crumbled buildings and stone figures in Meroitic style.

The builders of Meroe worked in stone and especially brick. Some buildings were constructed entirely of sun-dried bricks made of mud and straw, others were built of sun-dried brick but were faced with harder, fired brick, and some were built of brick on stone foundations. Most of the dwellings in the city itself were of brick, but murals indicate that the ordinary people of the countryside around Meroe and its tributary cities lived in beehive-shaped huts of straw and reed, similar to those built today by many rural Sudanese.

There is little evidence of industry except for iron tools and weapons and pottery, although there may have been cotton weaving. Agriculture was carried on outside the city, in the rich area along the Nile's banks and in the plains between the Nile and the Atbara, with cattle herding and the growing of millet being the chief occupations; what vegetables and fruits may have been produced are unknown.

From Meroe the Kushites carried on a lively trade with Egypt, Arabia, and India, through Red Sea ports and through the kingdom of Axum in Ethiopia. It is not known how the trade was organized, although the ruins of a large stone quay on the banks of the Nile at Meroe indicate barge and boat traffic. Numerous glass bottles, pieces of jewelry, pots, and other objects of foreign origin, from Greece, Rome, Egypt, Arabia, and India, have been found in Kushite ruins, and Kush was a major exporter of elephants, ivory, ostrich feathers, and hides. The trade brought wealth and ideas into Meroe. Many luxury goods were imported from the Mediterranean area and from as far afield as India, which at that time engaged in a lively trade with eastern Africa. Out of Meroe, across the Sudan to Adulis and other Red Sea ports, flowed the goods of Africa—gold, ivory, ebony, spices, gums,

skins and hides, and iron—and into Meroe poured glass bottles, exotic jewelry, bowls and lamps of bronze and silver, and other goods.

The temples, palaces, stelae, and carved stone figures found in Meroe and other Kushite towns show the influence of Egyptian, Greek, and Roman architectural styles and construction, yet they are distinctively Meroitic in certain respects. Bold and vividly contrasting colors were used with a freshness that differs sharply from Egyptian art. Carved and painted engravings and murals cover most of the stone walls and columns, portraying Kushitic kings, queens, and gods; the artists who created these scenes had obviously been schooled in the Egyptian style—for example, figures are done only in profile—yet their work was uniquely Kushite. Female figures are plump and lushly rounded; features are often clearly Negroid and were sometimes painted black. Elephants and lions are ubiquitously present in scenes of battle and conquest, and the lion god Apedemak, a Kushitic deity, was a favorite subject. In later Meroitic art Apedemak is often portrayed with multiple heads and arms, with the face full rather than in profile, showing possible Indian and Persian influence.

As the Meroitic civilization developed its own quality and style, blending ideas from many sources into its traditions, Egyptian cultural influence gradually waned. The peak period of Meroe's greatness seems to have been between about 250 B.C. and A.D. 150, when its power and culture spread over an area stretching nearly a thousand miles up and down the Nile. At this time it was secure in its distinctive identity yet not totally isolated from the rest of the world.

During this period the artists and craftsmen of Meroe showed high productivity and skill. Pottery, which is to be found in great abundance in all the ruins, was of especially high standard; the more refined pots, evidently made to adorn the homes of the wealthy, were beautifully finished and decorated with drawings done in ochre paints. Meroitic pottery, at its best, was artistically and technically the equal of any in the ancient world. Lovely ornaments in gold, silver, and copper, often studded with semiprecious stones, show the artistry of Meroe's metal craftsmen and jewelers.

Trade was vital to the prosperity of Meroe because of the relatively limited productivity of the land, which was too small in area and insufficiently fertile to have supported a centralized, wealthy state for long. As long as Meroe straddled the main routes by which goods from the interior of Africa reached the seacoast, the power of the kingdom was secure. Therefore when Meroe began to decline, in the second century A.D, it was very probably because its trading preeminence was deteriorating. A rival state in the Ethiopian highlands, Axum, was growing rapidly in strength about this time and was in a more favorable

Pyramid in Meroe: monument to King Ntekemani.

trading position, being located nearer the seaports and just as near sources of African goods. Moreover, Sudanic western Africa, a rich source of goods, was beginning to trade across the Sahara to North Africa. And the Romans, who ruled much of the world at the time, dominated African commerce, trading all along the northern edge of the continent.

Whatever the cause, the ruins of Meroe show a significant deterioration in quality of craftsmanship from about A.D. 100 onward. In about A.D. 325 King Ezana of Axum initiated a war of reprisal against the Kushites and their neighbors the Noba. The Noba, as Ezana called them, were another Nubian people who had moved into Kushite territory from the still dessicating region just south of the Sahara to the west of Kush. In this war Ezana destroyed Meroe and a number of other towns of the kingdom, and thereafter the Meroitic civilization disappeared; for two centuries the area languished in obscurity.

The fall of Meroe, however, did not lead to a permanent decline in Nubia, for a number of independent kingdoms continued in existence, the largest of which were Nobadia in the north, Makuria in the center, and Alwa in the south. These were to become the nucleus of Christianized Nubia, a wealthy and educated society that endured for more than five hundred years.

Unfortunately, once again we know little of Nubian history of this period. From the fourth to the sixth centuries there are virtually no records available, but in A.D. 540 the missionary Julian (who also visited Axum) was sent to Nubia by the Emperor Justinian and his wife Theodora. Julian energetically preached Christianity and succeeded in converting much of Nobadia. He was succeeded by Longinius, who spent many years in Nubia and was equally successful in his evangelization; by 563 the kings of Nobadia and Makuria (which was becoming increasingly powerful) had accepted Christianity. In 580, following a sojourn in Constantinople, Longinius returned to Nubia, this time concentrating on the south and the kingdom of Alwa, where he also succeeded in his mission.

By the beginning of the seventh century most of Nubia was Christianized, and a great program of building churches and monasteries had been started. The northern part of the area was united under the kingdom of Makuria, with its capital at Dongola, while the south was united under Alwa, with its capital at Soba. The Greek, Coptic, and Nubian languages were all used in the liturgies of the Nubian church, and parts of the Bible were soon translated into Nubian. Learning was encouraged, especially among the priesthood, and close communication was developed with the Patriarch of Alexandria and with the Ethiopian church.

It is difficult now to reconstruct the Nubian civilization under the Kushite Christian kingdoms. Virtually all the churches, of which hundreds were built, lie in crumbled ruins, their brick walls having gradually deteriorated. The present-day mosque at Old Dongola, converted from the Christian cathedral in that capital, reveals that some of the ancient churches were large and impressive structures reflecting Byzantine influence, but provides no detail of their art and finish. Religious and other books, in both Greek and Nubian, that are known to have abounded have disappeared. An unknown Arab historian, writing in the thirteenth century, leaves a hint of what Makuria must have been like in its prime:

"Here lies the abode of the king. The town is large and lies on the blessed Nile. There are many Churches and brick houses in it and its streets are wide. The king's house is decorated with a number of domes, built of red bricks and it resembles houses in Iraq."

Of Alwa, the same historian noted:

"Soba, the capital of Alwa, lies to the east of the big island which stretches between the two Niles, the Green [i.e., Blue] and the White. In it, there are beautiful buildings and large monasteries, full of gold. The town is beautified by splendid gardens. The ruler of Alwa is wealthier than that of Makuria because his country is bigger and more fertile and yields better returns. Well bred horses abound in Soba. The books are in Greek."

Crumbled ruins and an occasional mention in Arabic writings or in Coptic records in Alexandria, together with countless sherds of beautiful and finely crafted pottery, are all that survive. After Egypt became predominantly Islamic, the close connection between the Christian churches of Nubia and Alexandria deteriorated, and by the thirteenth and fourteenth centuries Islam was spreading into the isolated lands of Nubia. In 1317 the king of Makuria accepted Islam, and Christianity soon disappeared. Alwa continued as a Christian kingdom until the invasions by the Muslim Funj peoples, from the north and west, early in the sixteenth century. Soba was destroyed in 1504, and the kingdom ceased to exist. The Funj, ruled by a sultan based at the town of Sennar, gradually intermarried with the indigenous Nubians, and Christianity faded out of existence. From the sixteenth century on, the history of Nubia became the history of the Sudan, dominated by Islam and Arabic influences.

The relationship between ancient Kush and the rest of Africa, to its south and west, remains a major unsolved question, generating much speculation among historians. Many have held that Kush was in long, close contact with western Africa across the Sudanic belt south of the Sahara, and that it was the transmitter of a range of ideas and developments to the people of West Africa. Iron working, for example, was thought to have been transmitted by the Kushites across the Sudan to northern Nigeria and the Lake Chad area. The belief in divine kingship, according to this view, diffused from Egypt to Kush to western and central Africa, as did many basic religious and cosmological ideas. Some have maintained that the rulers of Kush fled, after the fall of Meroe, westward to the Chad area, there to provide leadership to Africans in building such western states as Ghana, Kanem-Bornu, and Yoruba.

The legends of several West African peoples would seem to support the theory of Kushite influence. The Yoruba and Akan peoples, of modern Nigeria and Ghana respectively, have traditions that their ancestors came from the east, and are popularly believed to have been of Kushitic or Egyptian origin. Several modern. Yoruba and Akan scholars support this interpretation.

Critics of the theory of Kushite diffusion point to the lack of solid evidence of Kushite artifacts or cultural influences in western Africa, and to the lack of mention in Egyptian or Kushite records of any contact with western Africa. They point to the indisputable evidence of long trade contacts north and south across the Sahara, which could have provided as ready a source of new ideas as the still unproved east-west pattern.

Perhaps more important still is recent evidence that West Africans, at least in northern Nigeria, were mining and smelting iron about as early as the Kushites, in about 400 B.C., and that agricultural states had begun to appear in the far west, in the modern state of Mauritania, around 1000 B.C., although no such states appeared in the territory between Mauritania and Kush until centuries later. These facts would argue that West Africans either discovered iron working and agriculture independently or acquired them across the western Sahara from North Africa.

Further research will undoubtedly clear up the two great Kushitic mysteries: its influence, if any, on the rest of Africa, and the detailed account of its history and affairs that may be revealed when its script is translated. In the meantime, research on the ruins of Meroe and neighboring cities continues to dramatize the impressive achievements of the Nubian peoples.

4 Ethiopia

The nation of Ethiopia has an ancient and unbroken history stretching back well over 2,000 years. Many another African civilization flourished and then crumbled. Others were supplanted by quite different later civilizations. But the present empire of Ethiopia traces its roots into biblical times, to the mythical union of Solomon and the Queen of Sheba.

The Ethiopians claim that the land of Sheba, near the foot of the Red Sea, was part of their ancient kingdom of Axum. According to the Bible, the Queen of Sheba visited King Solomon in Israel to discover whether his wisdom was as great as reputed. Both the oral and written legends of Ethiopia tell that Sheba agreed to sleep with Solomon if, during her visit to his palace, she took anything that belonged to him. The legends note that Solomon fed Sheba a dinner of highly spiced delicacies and then feigned sleep but maintained a watch over her. During the night she arose to drink water, and Solomon claimed his rights on the ground that she had taken water belonging to him. The legend holds that Solomon and Sheba slept together and that upon her return to Ethiopia Sheba bore Solomon's son, Ebna Hakim. As a young man the son returned to Israel to receive Solomon's royal blessing and became ruler of Axum, taking the title Menelik I. With the exception of one dynasty of the twelfth and thirteenth centuries, all Ethiopian rulers, including the present emperor, Haile Selassie I, have claimed to trace their ancestry back to Menelik I, founder of the nation's Solomonic dynasty.

This legend, carefully nurtured and jealously defended for centuries by church and state, together with Ethiopia's long-lived Christian church, has provided the country with a sense of history few nations can rival. Although there is no proof that the biblical story is authentic, or that Sheba came from Ethiopia, if she did indeed exist, the legend is tenaciously cherished in Ethiopian history.

Ethiopia's geography has helped to ensure its continuous development relatively free of outside encroachment. Most of the country lies on a high and uneven mountain plateau, which along most of its northeastern rim plunges abruptly to the Red Sea, dropping as much as 7,000 feet to the dry and hot coastal plains. On its western rim it drops in a series of jagged escarpments down to the equally arid plains and deserts of the upper Nile. On the southeast, dry plains descend more gradually to the Red Sea. In all, the plateau stretches, with irregular borders, well over 500 miles east and west, and nearly 1,000 miles from north to south. In general, Ethiopia has a cool, bracing climate with plentiful rainfall and rich soils. The jagged topography creates problems in internal communication and has tended to make the country difficult to unify. But the entire mountainous mass has rendered the Ethiopians in the northern regions quite secure from attack, especially as their population and military potential have expanded over the past two and a half millennia.

In old stone age times, the population of Ethiopia seems to have included groups of Bushmanoid peoples who lived in the southern, eastern, and western portions of the country. But in very ancient times, perhaps before 5000 B.C., Cushites (not related to the Kushites of Nubia, but rather to the Berbers of northern Africa and the Arabs and Jews of Arabia) spread into Ethiopia, eventually erasing every trace of the ancient Bushmen. A mixed Negroid-Caucasoid people, with tan to brown skin, thin noses and lips, and dark wavy or frizzled hair, the ancient Cushites became the basic population group from which most modern Ethiopian peoples have descended.

The very ancient Ethiopians were subject to numerous invasions from outside groups. As a result there is considerable modern heterogeneity in race, language, culture, and religion. Negroes from the west and the south pressed into the area; Somalis and Galla came from the southeast and east; Semites came from Yemen. The influence of Yemeni Semites was so pervasive during the first millennium B.C. that most Ethiopians of the northern and central regions are more closely related in language and basic culture to Arabians than to most other Africans.

Yemeni influence began with the conquest of what are now Eritrea and the Tigre province of northern Ethiopia in about 700 B.C. These northern areas are high and moist, with an equable climate and good soils. The indigenous inhabitants, the Agau, a people of the Cushitic-speaking group, were prosperous, progressive, and creative. They had already mastered the cultivation of millet, sorghum, coffee, castor, safflower, and several other plants, and possibly had domesticated the donkey. From the new mixed population of Agau and Arab, the first major civilization of Ethiopia emerged in the region of Axum.

Semitic languages, especially Tigrinya (the language spoken in Shoa province), soon became established in most of northern and central Ethiopia. Agau farmers were generally governed by a ruling Arab aristocracy, and Semitic customs, social structure, and religious beliefs gradually became dominant. Within a few centuries, much of northern Ethiopia had become Semitized.

The blending of the Semitic with the Agau nurtured a virile new civilization, taking its name from the town of Axum in the north. By the first century A.D., the kingdom of Axum was a powerful agricultural and commercial state, engaged in trade and close contact with Meroe on its west and Yemen across the Red Sea on its east.

Today Axum is a sleepy, dusty town. Its once splendid temples, dwellings, and monuments are covered by debris or broken into stone slabs, having suffered the ravages of 1,000 years of war, neglect, and weather. A few awesome stelae still stand. The largest ever made, over 110 feet in length, lies broken into pieces. One of the most exquisite stelae, sixty-five feet long, was transported to Italy by Mussolini during the Italian occupation of Ethiopia in the 1930's. Other towns, smaller than Axum but obviously part of the once great Axumite Empire, dot the area with ruins that are largely unexcavated and unstudied. But the massive stones that were used in buildings and monuments and the numerous eroded coins still found by children playing in the ruins suggest that the region was once prosperous and highly developed.

First written knowledge of Axum comes from the *Periplus of the Erythraean Sea,* a guide to trade and navigation in the Red Sea and Indian Ocean. Written by an unknown Greek mariner in about A.D. 60, the *Periplus* describes the port of Adulis on the Red Sea coast of Eritrea as Axum's chief seaport. The king of Axum is identified as Zoscales, probably King Za Hakele, whose name is inscribed on coins of the period. He is described as wealthy and powerful, and "a covetous and grasping man, but otherwise noble and imbued with Greek education." The *Periplus* also notes that Adulis is a busy port, importing substantial quantities of soft copper, small axes, Italian wine, gold and silver plate, military cloaks, Indian iron, steel, and cotton cloth. Adulis was destroyed, either by earthquake or warfare, in the ninth century, but massive stone ruins from its piers and bulwarks have been found on the Eritrean coast. The local people still refer to the area as "Azuli."

Another record of ancient Axum, dating probably to the third

century, was written by an unidentified king of Axum and later transcribed by one Cosma of Alexandria. This account of war and conquest indicates that Axum was penetrating southward into the central Ethiopian highlands and westward into Nubia and the lands of Meroe. It indicates that Axum defeated forces across the Red Sea in part of Yemen, allowing her to claim suzerainty over a small part of Arabia as well as over northern Ethiopia and eastern Nubia. The extent of Axum's territory during its period of greatness, however, is unknown.

Perhaps the zenith of Axum's development came during the fourth century, when King Ella Amida and his son, Ezana, reigned. Ella Amida came to the throne at about the end of the third century. He waged major campaigns in Nubia and effectively destroyed whatever remnants of Meroe's power may have survived previous Axumite attacks and commercial superiority. Little is known of him, although many of his coins and several stelae with inscriptions commemorating his campaigns have survived. His son Ezana, who came to the throne between about 320 and 330, claims a special place in African history. He is the general who finally destroyed Meroe and adopted Christianity as the state religion of Ethiopia.

The remarkably well-preserved stelae inscriptions attributed to Ezana were writen in several languages—Greek, Sabean (the ancient language of Yemen), Ge'ez (the classical language of Axum)—and at least one inscription reproduces the same narrative in all three tongues.

In one very famous inscription, on a black basalt stela, Ezana describes a vigorous punitive campaign against the "Kasu" (the Kushites of Meroe) and the "Noba" (a people of the Nuba mountain region, who migrated from the west into Meroe, eventually engulfing the indigenous population and laying the basis for the later Christian states of Alwa and Makuria):

> By the might of the Lord of All I made war upon Noba, for the peoples of Noba had rebelled and made a boast of it. The peoples of Noba had said: "they [the Axumites] will not cross the Takazze". . . . And two or three times they had broken their solemn oaths and had killed their neighbors mercilessly, and they had stripped bare and stolen the properties of our envoys and messengers which I had sent to them to enqurie into their thefts, and had stolen from them their weapons of defense.
>
> And as I have sent warnings to them, and they would not listen to me and refused to stop their [evil] deeds and heaped insults upon me and then took a flight, I made war upon them. And I rose up in the might of the Lord of the Land, and I fought them on the Takazze, at the ford of Kemalke. Thereupon they took to flight and would not make a stand. And I followed the fugitives for 23 days, killing and making prisoners and

Axumite Stelae.

capturing booty wherever I stopped. My people who marched into the country brought back prisoners and booty.

Meanwhile I burnt their towns, [both] those built of brick and those built of reeds, and my soldiers carried off their food, as well as copper, iron, and brass; they destroyed the statues in their temples, as well as their storehouses for food, and their cotton trees, casting them in the river Sida [the Nile]. And there were many men who died in the water, their number being unknown to me. The soldiers sank their ships crowded with people, men and women, in the river. And I captured two chieftains, who had come as spies riding on female camels. . . . And I captured an Angabenawi nobleman. . . . The chieftains who died were five in number. . . .

And I came to Kasu and I fought a battle and made prisoners of its people at the junction of the rivers Sida and Takazze. And the day after I arrived I sent out the army . . . to raid the country upstream of Sida, and the cities built of brick and those of reeds. The names of the cities built of brick were Alwa and Daro. And they killed and captured prisoners and cast people into the water, and they arrived safe and sound having terrified their enemies and conquered them by the might of the Lord of the Land. And after that I sent the army . . . down the Sida against the towns of Noba which are made of reeds . . . . The towns of brick which the Noba had taken were Tabito and Fertoti. And my people arrived at the frontier of the red Noba and they returned safe and sound, having captured prisoners and slain the Noba and taken booty from them by the might of the Lord of Heaven. And I set up a throne in that country at the place where the rivers Sida and Takazze join, opposite the town with brick houses. . . .

The things which the Lord of Heaven has given me are: men captives, 214, women captives, 415, total captives, 629. Men slain, 602, women and children slain, 156, total slain, 758. Total of prisoners and slain, 1,387. Booty, 10,560 cattle and 51,050 sheep. . . .

Considerable evidence substantiates the Ethiopian legend that Christianity was introduced into the country during Ezana's reign. Legend holds that two Syrian youths, well educated and of good family, were brought to Axum as slaves after being either shipwrecked or captured by pirates in the Red Sea. These youths, Frumentius and Aedisius, were attached to the court of Ella Amida, where Frumentius' learning made him a scribe. Frumentius attained considerable favor and standing, and apparently formed a friendship with young Ezana, then heir apparent.

A Christian, Frumentius preached the new faith and was eventually allowed to visit Alexandria, where St. Athanasius, the bishop, consecrated him as the first archbishop of Axum. Upon returning to Axum, Frumentius preached tirelessly, soon converting Ezana, who had by then succeeded to the throne. Coins in the latter part of Ezana's reign bear the cross, providing one point of corroboration of the legend.

Frumentius is mentioned in several letters found in Coptic archives in Alexandria. One letter from the Emperor Constantine in Rome was sent on to Axum. Constantine asked that the Ethiopians depose Frumentius in order that a man loyal to the imperial court could be appointed. This letter dates Frumentius' consecration in 356, whereas Ethiopian legend sets it soon after 330. Despite this discrepancy, the letter clearly serves to substantiate the Frumentius story in general.

Frumentius, with the patronage of Ezana, sank deep roots for the church in Ethiopia. During his tenure, dozens of churches were built and a lasting bond was forged between church and state. Christianity and learning had become important to the life of Axum.

By the end of the fourth century Ge'ez was beginning to supplant Greek as the language of church ritual. In the fifth century a group of priests who had migrated from Syria translated the scriptures into Ge'ez. These priests have become part of the holy legends of the Ethiopian church and are revered as "the Nine Saints."

During the fifth and sixth centuries Axum's trade fostered continuous contact with Rome, Greece, Persia, and the Mediterranean world. Roman literature frequently refers to this trade, and Roman ships called often at the port of Adulis. For part of this period Axum continued to regard Yemen as a vassal land. But by the time of the prophet Muhammad, in the seventh century, Axumite influence across the Red Sea had disappeared. The gold, ivory, and spices upon which Ethiopian wealth rested flowed down from the high plateau to Adulis and other Red Sea ports, where Persian ships seem to have dominated the trade. Ethiopian priests visited Egypt and the Holy Land, and priests from the latter places came to preach and serve in the Ethiopian church.

The report of Julian, an ambassador sent by the Emperor Justinian to Ellesbaas, king of Axum, to explore the possibility of bypassing the hostile Persian Empire with a Roman-Indian trade route through Ethiopia, provides a tantalizing glimpse of the court of Axum in the sixth century. (As it developed, Persian dominance in the Red Sea and the Indian Ocean was secure enough that Ethiopian ships could operate only under the supervision of the Persian navy.) Julian describes Ellesbaas as naked from the waist up, wearing a linen garment embroidered in gold and held with straps set with pearls. According to Julian, Ellesbaas wore golden jewelry and rode on a four-wheeled, gold-plated chariot drawn by four elephants. The king carried a small gilded shield and two gilded arrows and his councillors were similarly armed. He seems to have been a figure of considerable majesty, pleased with the prospect of closer contact with the emperor of a great Christian power.

During the seventh century Axum's history becomes somewhat obscure. The growth of Islam and the whirlwind conquest by the Arabs of much of the eastern Mediterranean littoral and northern Africa cut Ethiopia off from close contact with Christendom. Its trade came to be controlled by Arab merchant mariners. The Christian thread between the Ethiopian church and Alexandria was never severed completely, but most other contacts were.

Christian Ethiopia, though eventually surrounded by Islamic peoples, was not chronically in conflict with them. The king of Axum was one of the few rulers who responded courteously to a letter sent to the world's kings by the prophet Muhammad announcing his mission. He also provided refuge for many exiled adherents of Islam in its early struggles with the pagan aristocracy of Mecca. Although the Ethiopians never accepted the validity of Muhammad's preaching, they were sufficiently friendly and respectful that Muslim tradition long exempted Ethiopia from the hostile attitudes that Islamic nations developed toward Christian powers in Europe.

Despite the usually pacific relationship between Ethiopia and the Muslim world, there were tensions at times. In 702 Ethiopian pirates sacked Jidda, Mecca's port. This resulted in an Arabic counteroffensive, eventually eliminating Ethiopian piracy and establishing firm Arab control over the coastal areas on both sides of the Red Sea. Adulis was destroyed, and for the next few centuries Ethiopia was isolated.

During these Ethiopian dark ages, between the seventh and tenth centuries, the main energies of the kings of Axum seem to have been directed at conquering and Christianizing other Ethiopian kingdoms on the high plateau to the south. Because of the broken terrain and the comparatively balanced strength of the kingdoms the process was slow, but gradually the kingdom and the church spread south.

In the tenth century a period of comparative peace began. Control of the coastal areas was reestablished, and for a brief period Ethiopia again emerged as an important maritime power. For a time, relations between Ethiopia and Yemen and other Muslim kingdoms in Arabia were friendly, but by the eleventh century further tensions erupted between Christian Ethiopia and her coastal neighbors. Islam again began to spread among the Somali and Galla peoples who inhabited the coastal area.

During the twelfth century the long rule of the Semitic Solomonic kings, based in Axum, was broken. Non-Semitic Agau kings, based in the Lasta Mountains far to the south of Axum, founded the Zagwe dynasty. The center of power shifted from the rich plains of Axum to the wild, inaccessible mountain peaks and jagged canyons where Axumite power and culture had never been completely secure.

Although the Zagwe kings represented a resurgence of indigenous Agau peoples against Axumite rule, they were pious Christians. The greatest of their kings, Lalibela—a saint in the Ethiopian church—launched a program of church construction in the remote mountain areas. Of the hundreds of churches built under Zagwe rule, the most remarkable are the eleven monolithic churches in isolated Roha, nowadays more often called Lalibela. Each Lalibela church differs from the others in architectural style, but all were hollowed out of gigantic multicolored volcanic rocks around which deep trenches were dug.

Lofty arches and delicately carved windows reveal the consummate architectural skill and artistry of the builders. Paintings of saints and religious stories adorn many of the walls and altar areas. The largest of the churches, that of the Redeemer of the World, measures more than one hundred feet long and seventy feet wide, and is thirty-six feet high. The giant rock from which it was carved has reddened over the centuries, lending a delicate glow to the church. The small upper windows culminate in triangular shapes, closely resembling the tops of the stelae of Axum. Another of the churches, the Church of St. George, is constructed in the shape of the cross; the others are rectangular. The interiors of all the churches tend to be dark, but several are so constructed that the sun, at certain hours, casts its rays directly onto the altar.

Little is known of the architects whom Lalibela used to build these awe-inspiring monuments, nor why they chose to carve the churches out of enormous rocks rather than to build them from stone blocks. According to a fifteenth-century chronicle, almost the only available information about Lalibela and the building of the churches at Roha, Lalibela was transported to heaven to be inspired to build the churches:

> Lalibela ordered the manufacture of a large number of iron tools of all kinds, some to cut out the stone, others to hew it, as well as many others for the construction of a temple in the rock. . . . When he began to construct these churches angels came to help him in each of the operations; there were thus a company of angels at work as well as a company of men, for angels joined the workers, the quarry men, the stone cutters, and the laborers. The angels worked with them by day and by themselves by night. The men would do a cubit's work during the day, but would find a further three cubits completed on the morrow. . . . They doubted whether the angels were doing this work because they could not see them, but Lalibela knew, because the angels, who understood his virtue, did not hide from him. . . .

The exact dates of Lalibela's reign and the building of the churches are unknown. At least one other king succeeded him before the Solomonic line reasserted its power in 1270 and again claimed sovereignty

AFRO·ASIATIC

NUBIAN (SUDANI

CONGO-
KORDOFANI

SONGHAIC

CONGO-KORDOFANIAN

SUDANIC

KHOISAN

KHOISAN

Africa about 100 B.C.

over all Ethiopia. Later rulers of the Zagwe line, including those of today, have sworn fealty to the Solomonic rulers, although they are still proud of their pre-Semitic Agau heritage.

Reestablishment of Solomonic sovereignty touched off a new process of territorial expansion and continued the religious development of Lalibela's reign. Within the church an indigenous literature began to appear. Written in Ge'ez, it added to the body of writings that had been translated over the centuries from Greek, Arabic, and Egyptian. Around the beginning of the fourteenth century, new hymns, prayers, biographical and eulogistic pieces on the lives of kings, saints, and holy men, and historical documents, essays, and chronicles all began to appear.

This literary renaissance, stimulated by monks and priests, produced little change in the Ethiopian church or in its long relationship with the Egyptian church in Alexandria. The Ethiopian church is Monophysite: it shares with the Egyptian and a number of Middle Eastern churches a belief in the single, divine nature of Christ as opposed to the Roman belief in Christ as both man and God. Just as the Egyptian Coptic church uses the ancient Coptic language of Egypt in its liturgy, the Ethiopian church has long used Ge'ez. The Ethiopians, like the Egyptians, add ten extra days to Lent, observe a number of other long fasts, celebrate the Epiphany by ritual bathing, and use the Coptic calendar.

The Ethiopian church has added its own touches as well: the beating of drums and the dancing of indigenous dances in certain services; the sacrificing of animals at the dedication of a new church; the celebration of certain feasts once a month; the following of Judaic law in distinguishing between clean and unclean meats; and the observance of the Sabbath on both Saturday and Sunday. Some Ethiopian church customs derive from indigenous Agau and other ethnic traditions, others reflect the ancient infusion of Semitic ideas from the Yemeni.

The unique and durable relationship between the Ethiopian church and the Patriarch of Alexandria seems to have been bolstered by the periodic struggles between kingdoms and factions within Ethiopia. The Ethiopian throne was customarily legitimatized by alliance with the "Abuna," chief bishop of the church. The Abunas were appointed by the Patriarch in Alexandria and thus represented an important external factor in Ethiopian politics. For centuries the Abunas were Egyptians. They resided in Ethiopia but sometimes learned neither Ge'ez nor Amharic. There was little pressure from within the church or the royal lines to Ethiopianize the office of Abuna. Surprisingly, there was also little resentment of the continuing dependence on this external influence.

The first great historical work to appear in Ethiopia following the literary renaissance within the church was the *Kebra Negast* (Book of Kings). Dating to around the beginning of the fourteenth century, it tells of the legendary origin of the Ethiopian kingdom and of the glories of the Solomonic line. During the fourteenth and fifteenth centuries true historical chronicles began to appear. From the early sixteenth century on, an unbroken series of chronicles provide a continuing sketch of Ethiopian history.

Between the fifteenth and seventeenth centuries the isolation of Ethiopia was shattered. Missions of Catholic priests from Portugal, Spain, and France visited the kingdom and attempted to convert it to Roman Catholicism. These efforts were stimulated, in part, by the old legend of Prester John, the great Christian king whose powerful kingdom (whether in Africa or in India the legend did not make clear) was cut off from the rest of Christendom by the spread of Islam. The legend originated in the twelfth century and greatly excited the kings and learned men of Europe. On their first voyages to the Indian Ocean coasts of Africa, the Portuguese heard of a Christian king ruling in the interior. They assumed that he must be the mythical Prester John.

Several Catholic missions to Ethiopia had considerable success in individual conversions, and for brief periods influenced the leadership of the Ethiopian church. But the missions never succeeded in changing the basic convictions of the Ethiopian hierarchy or in swaying the mass of the church's communicants. They were also unable to use Ethiopian military power to break the grip of the Muslims who continued to control shipping along the Red Sea coasts and the northern reaches of the Indian Ocean.

By this time sizable population shifts were in motion on the hot, dry plains between the Ethiopian highlands and the coasts of the Red Sea and Indian Ocean. Muslim Somali sultans had organized small but aggressive states on the "horn" of Africa which juts into the Indian Ocean. These sultans ruled over a people who were seminomadic, moving their cattle periodically to take advantage of seasonal rains and better grasslands and practicing grain agriculture in the better-watered areas of the horn. Along the coast they traded regularly with Arab and Persian mariners, with whom they shared a deep commitment to Islam. Using their fast horses for cavalry and armed with spears, swords, and bows and arrows, they ranged far inland in search of grazing lands and power. Somali pressure against the Galla, an ethnically related people, gradually forced the Galla to move westward into Ethiopian territory.

In the sixteenth century an alliance of Somali clans under a brilliant leader, the Imam Ahmad Ibn Ibrahim al-Ghazi (whom the

Ethiopians nicknamed "Gran," meaning "the left-handed"), declared a holy war against Ethiopia. Ahmad Gran, whose ancestry included Galla, Danakil, and Somali, planned well before launching his forces against the Ethiopians. He negotiated an agreement with the Ottoman sultan in Turkey, who sent Turkish troops armed with muskets to serve with Gran's army. Gran inspired his troops by his personal qualities and by pointing to the Christian threat that he believed was emerging from contacts between Ethiopia and the Portuguese Catholics. In 1531 Gran began an eleven-year campaign of ruthless conquest and destruction in the Ethiopian highlands.

Protected by the Turkish troops and their firearms (which the Ethiopians lacked), Gran's horsemen destroyed hundreds of the ancient churches of Ethiopia, seized their gold, burned books and works of Christian art, and urged the terrorized Ethiopians to renounce Christianity and accept Islam. An Ethiopian chronicle asserts that nine out of ten Ethiopians heeded this demand.

Emperor Lebna Dengel of Ethiopia, defeated and humiliated, retreated to a monastery and died. He was succeeded by the Emperor Galawdewos (Claudius). One of medieval Ethiopia's most brilliant rulers, Galawdewos began to rally the remnants of Ethiopia's army and to instill discipline into the demoralized troops. In 1541 Portugal finally heeded Galawdewos' urgent appeals for help. Four hundred Portuguese musketeers landed at Massawa to join his command. Thus revitalized, the Ethiopian army took the offensive. Gran was beaten in a running series of battles. Finally, in the rugged mountains of central Ethiopia, Gran himself was wounded and his army destroyed. But Gran escaped to find reinforcements for one last rally. Returning with nine hundred Arab, Turkish, and Albanian mercenaries, Gran renewed his campaign, won several major battles against the Christian allies, but was finally defeated and killed in 1543. His death ended the most serious threat Ethiopian Christianity had ever faced.

During the fierce struggles with Gran's invading forces and with the Galla, who later posed a severe threat to southern Ethiopia, Galawdewos reestablished a strong measure of unity and sound organization in northern and central Ethiopia. He renewed the bonds between the rulers of the many petty states and the throne. Once again, the emperor's authority was clearly acknowledged. He assisted church leaders as they emerged from their retreats to minister to the people and begin restoring some of the damaged temples and churches. Upon his death in 1559, Galawdewos left a strong internal kingdom, although he was unable to subdue the encroaching Galla and Somali powers still aggressively challenging Ethiopian power on the kingdom's fringes.

For another two centuries relative peace prevailed in the kingdom's heartland, but periods of tension with neighbors to the south and the east erupted as Ethiopian expansion came into conflict with the Galla, Sidamo, and other peoples of the south. Missions from France and Spain, especially those of the Jesuits, continued to make determined attempts to win converts to Roman Catholicism, but in about 1645 all Catholics were expelled by an increasingly indignant Ethiopian church-state alliance. No further missions were allowed to enter the country.

In 1753, following the rule of several weak kings, the monarchy collapsed. For another century, rival dukes and princes of subordinate states and provinces struggled for power, sometimes paying lip service to a weak monarch, sometimes directly challenging his authority.

During this period of political decadence, James Bruce became the first modern European to visit Ethiopia. Bruce's highly readable *Travels to Discover the Source of the Nile,* published in 1790, sixteen years after his return to England, created a sensation, as did his personal accounts before the volumes were published. Although many English men of letters disliked Bruce or scoffed at his astounding accounts, his name became the rage. Sir Walter Scott, writing to Southey about Bruce's claim to have fought in a battle in Gondar in 1771, remarked: "A prince who left Bruce at home, if he could have brought him out, neglected the most able-bodied associate you ever saw. Pendragon was a joke to him in size and muscle."

Shortly after Bruce's return, Horace Walpole wrote to Sir Horace Mann: "Africa is, indeed, coming into fashion. There is just returned a Mr. Bruce, who has lived three years in the court of Abyssinia, and breakfasted every morning with the Maids of Honour on live oxen. . . . Oh yes; we shall have Negro butchers, and French cooks will be laid aside."

Walpole was referring to one of Bruce's most sensational tales, which, despite English skepticism, was quite true. It told how Ethiopian nobles feasted on live cattle. The raw meat was skillfully sliced from the live animal during the long interval before the cow finally succumbed to loss of blood. In this "Bloody Banquet," as Bruce described it, each nobleman fed small cubes of the quivering flesh to another after it had been doused with spices and wrapped in the moist Ethiopian bread called "injera."

Bruce's vivid reports had immense ethnographic and historical value. Court life was described in faithful detail. Customs and beliefs were recorded. Many historical notes were included, and the turbulent intrigues and conflicts of Ethiopian royal politics were set forth clearly by an acute observer who had previously been part of the drama.

During Bruce's stay in Ethiopia, the kingdom was in disorder. Con-

The seventeenth-century castle of Emperor Fasiladas at Gondor.

flicts with the forces of the Galla were frequent. Ras Michael Suhul, hereditary ruler of Tigre province, was the most powerful man in the kingdom, even stronger than the king. Ras Michael had instigated the murder of King Joas of Ethiopia in 1769, was deeply feared by the weak new king, and was engaged in a bitter struggle with the forces of Waragna Fasil, a leader of the Galla peoples and Michael's chief rival for power in Ethiopia. Michael was aging, but, as Bruce's description of him attests he was an impressive man:

> We went in, and saw the old man sitting upon a sofa; his white hair was dressed in many short curls. He appeared to be thoughtful, but not displeased; his face was lean, his eyes quick and vivid, but seemed to be a little sore from exposure to the weather. [Michael had just returned to his palace at Gondar from a grueling campaign against the Galla.] He seemed to be about six feet high, though his lameness made it difficult to guess with accuracy. His air was perfectly free from constraint, what

the French call "degagée." In face and person he was liker my learned and worthy friend, the Count de Buffon, than any two men I ever saw in the world. They must have been bad physiognomists that did not discern his capacity and understanding by his very countenance. Every look conveyed a sentiment with it; he seemed to have no occasion for other language, and indeed he spoke little. I offered, as usual, to kiss the ground before him; and of this he seemed to take little notice, stretching out his hand and shaking mine upon my rising.

While Bruce was visiting the headwaters of the Blue Nile he spent some weeks with the Agau people in that region. He was favorably disposed toward the sturdy Agau—whose power had been depleted over centuries of conflict—and left excellent descriptions of them:

The Agows, in whose country the Nile rises, are, in point of number, one of the most considerable nations in Abyssinia; when their whole force is raised, which seldom happens, they can bring to the field 4,000 horse, and a great number of foot; they were, however, once much more powerful; several unsuccessful battles, and the perpetual inroads of the Galla, have much diminished their strength. The country, indeed, is still full of inhabitants, but from their history we learn, that one clan, called Zeegam, maintained singly a war against the king himself, from the time of Socinios to that of Yasous the Great, who, after all, overcame them by surprise and stratagem; and that another clan, the Denguis, in like manner maintained the war against Facilidas, Hannes I, and Yasous II, all of them active princes. Their riches, however, are still greater than their power, for though their province in length is no where 60 miles [Bruce was wrong here; there are other groups of Agau in other parts of Ethiopia], nor half that in breadth, yet Gondar and all the neighbouring country depend for the necessaries of life, cattle, honey, butter, wheat, hides, wax, and a number of such articles, upon the Agows, who come constantly in succession, a thousand and fifteen hundred at a time, loaded with these commodities, to the capital. . . .

Though these Agows are so fortunate in their climate, they are not said to be long-livers; . . . and, though their country abounds with all the necessaries of life, their taxes, tributes, and services, especially at present, are so multiplied upon them, whilst their distresses of late have been so great and frequent, that they are only the manufacturers of the commodities they sell, to satisfy these constant exorbitant demands, and cannot enjoy any part of their own produce themselves, but live in misery and penury scarce to be conceived. . . .

Besides what they sell, and what they pay to the governor of Damot, the Agows have a particular tribute which they present to the king, one thousand dabra of honey, each dabra containing about 60 pounds weight, being a large earthen vessel. They pay, moreover, 1,600 oxen, and 1,000 ounces of gold; formerly the number of jars of honey was 4,000, but several of these villages being daily given to private people by the king [Bruce himself was given one], the quantity is diminished by the quota so alienated. . . .

Ethiopia, despite the poverty of the Agau and other subject peoples and the incessant internal strife and disunity, still maintained an enduring sense of national identity. It also maintained enough contact with the outside world, trading through the Muslim states along the Red Sea, that progress, however slow, did occur. Perhaps most significant, in view of events in the nineteenth and twentieth centuries, was the widespread introduction of firearms. While Bruce was in Ethiopia, muskets were commonly used; he noted that Tigre alone had an army of musketeers numbering in the thousands. In the decades that followed Bruce's visit, stronger kings gradually restored a measure of authority and internal harmony, culminating in the assumption of power by Emperor Menelik II in 1889. Menelik vigorously pursued deliberate modernization and involvement with the outside world. Of all the ancient states and kingdoms of Africa, only Ethiopia was able successfully to resist European conquest at the end of the nineteenth century.

5 North Africa and the Sahara

The history of the vast lands of North Africa has been dominated and intricately shaped by two geographic factors: the Mediterranean Sea on the north, linking North Africa with Mediterranean civilization, and the Sahara Desert on the south, serving as a barrier to intimate contact with the rest of Africa. Of the five modern countries that comprise North Africa, three—Algeria, Libya, and Tunisia—lie between the Sahara and the Mediterranean. Morocco borders on the Sahara and touches both the Mediterranean and the Atlantic Ocean coasts. Egypt, also bordering on the Mediterranean and sharing in its affairs, has been influenced as well by its Nile location, the Red Sea, and the land bridge across the Sinai to Asia Minor.

The Sahara is separated from the Mediterranean by the Atlas Mountains, which stretch from Morocco through Algeria and Tunisia to the Libyan border. The mountains offer protection from the heat and dryness of the desert and help to precipitate rainfall on North Africa's Mediterranean plains. Consequently the peoples of North Africa have tended to cluster in the mountains and on the coastal plains, leaving vast areas to the south to sparsely distributed nomads and shepherds.

Between the highest ridges of the Atlas Mountains and the sea stretches a long and broken chain of coastal plains, plateaus, and valleys that rarely extend more than a hundred miles inland, except along the Atlantic littoral on Morocco's west. In these areas, the soil tends to be good, and winter rains, rivers, and underground supplies for wells provide adequate water. The area has long been noted for its production of barley, wheat, olives, dates, figs, grapes, and citrus fruits.

The crops are similar to those found in the lands on the north of the Mediterranean—Italy, Spain, southern France, and Greece—which are climatically and geographically similar to this area of North Africa.

The inhabitants of most of North Africa show affinity to the Caucasoid racial type, which seems to have established itself in the region tens of thousands of years ago during the old or middle stone age. Racially, many North Africans are little different from Europeans on the northern shores of the Mediterranean, although Negroid traits are also common. Skeletal remains suggest that the Capsians of the late middle stone age, who inhabited all of North Africa, were the ancestors of the Berbers, the indigenous population of North Africa for many millennia. From the upper reaches of the Nile valley southward into East Africa, the Capsians were eventually supplanted by the vigorous ancestors of the Sudanic Negroid peoples who today inhabit all of sub-Saharan Africa. But in the heart of the Sahara, and in the coastal lands of North Africa, the Berbers were less subject to Negroid population migrations.

The language of the North African Berbers is a branch of the great Afro-Asiatic stock that stretches from Africa's western coasts into Asia Minor, and is divided into five major subfamilies: Berber, Chadic, Cushitic, Egyptian, and Semitic. All five subfamilies are spoken on the African continent. Although the Afro-Asiatic language stock is associated closely with Caucasoid peoples in northern Africa and Arabia, it includes the languages of a number of important Negroid peoples, such as the Hausa and several others of the Nigerian plateau and Bornu areas.

The Berbers, originally concentrated along the North African coasts, moved southward into the Sahara only within the last few millennia. Negroid peoples, then indigenous to the inhabitable areas of the Sahara, gradually moved eastward and southward and now are represented only by small pockets in a few Saharan oases. The Kanuric language stock, which seems to be spoken only by Negroid peoples, is scattered throughout the central Sahara, even in areas that have been under Berber rule for hundreds of years. Greek and Roman writers referred often to the peoples of the Sahara as the "Garamantes," a far-flung, warlike nation. Both the Greeks and Romans constantly had to contend with the Garamantes, sometimes sending large expeditions to battle them, at other times cementing alliances with Garamantes war chiefs in order to establish peace. Most likely the Garamantes were Berbers, perhaps often heavily intermarried with the ancient Negroid peoples of the Sahara.

Fundamentally, the history of North Africa is a history of the Berbers. They have populated that vast region for thousands of years, maintaining a high degree of cultural and linguistic homogeneity despite their wide dispersal and long periods of conquest and colonization by Phoenicians, Greeks, Romans, Vandals, and Arabs. Centuries of Arab rule and cultural imperialism had elapsed before significant numbers of Berbers allowed their own culture to be supplanted by that of the Arabs. Even today strong traces of Berber culture can be found in the more isolated regions of North Africa.

The Berbers are thought to have acquired knowledge of agriculture, metal working, and many other technological skills from the Egyptians by the beginning of the second millennium before Christ. In early neolithic times, the Berbers cultivated barley and wheat, and domesticated goats, sheep, pigs, and dogs. In these very early times North African cultures and economies seem to have borrowed little from developments in the agricultural areas south of the Sahara or north of the Mediterranean.

Throughout known history, the Berbers have remained a fiercely parochial, egalitarian people, loyal to the family, the village, and the community. They have resisted centralization except when threatened by invaders or in other times of stress. Social distinctions are minimal, especially those of class. Even though poorer Berber farmers may work for wealthier and more successful men, they are deemed equal in law and political affairs. The Berbers have traditionally ruled themselves by family and village councils, electing temporary chiefs only for war or national emergency. For thousands of years, the Berbers have struggled to retain their heritage, although successive conquests by stronger foreign peoples gradually eroded Berber tradition along the fertile Mediterranean coast.

Uprisings and resistance characterized Berber affairs under the many conquerors that invaded and settled the coastal region. Even when invaders established permanent colonies, they intermarried with the local Berber population and tended to develop an outlook colored by Berber culture. Phoenician settlement in North Africa began as early as 1000 B.C., and the coastal areas were under foreign domination almost constantly from that time on. But Berber identity, even on the coasts, was not completely submerged by seventeen centuries under Phoenicia, Greece, Rome, Byzantium, and the Vandals. Only after Arab conquest, from the late seventh century on, did the coastal Berbers finally lose most vestiges of their culture and accept the language, religion, and culture of Islamic civilization.

Yet even the Arabs found it impossible to eradicate Berber culture completely. Today strong Berber communities—numbering more than one million people—in the Kabyle highlands of Algeria consider themselves different from the Arabized Algerians of the plains. They speak

Berber at home, treasure Berber egalitarianism, and practice Berber customs. Fiercely independent Berber tribes in the Sahara battled a second wave of Arab Bedouin invaders as late as the early twentieth century. They too still practice their traditional Berber ways despite having accepted Islam as a religion.

By at least 1000 B.C., the North African Berbers had come into sustained contact with other peoples. Thus began a long process of alternate resistance and accommodation that changed the settled coastal Berbers into a different people. Gradually, the ways of the conqueror blended with those of the Berber.

The most important early contact was with the Phoenicians, who began to visit North Africa by 1000 B.C. The Phoenicians, spreading out from their Syrian homeland, established trading posts that grew into towns and important commercial cities. Carthage, near the site of modern Tunis, was established in about 800 B.C. and grew into one of the mightiest city-states in the Mediterranean world.

The Phoenicians spoke a Semitic language and were not radically different in race and origin from the North African Berbers. They were great sailors, traders, and miners. In Tunisia and Algeria, their major areas of settlement, the Phoenicians intermarried with the local Berbers, established Punic as the official language of the region, and became an integral part of the local scene. Their cities were built for trading purposes, and they confined their settlement to the lands immediately around the cities, except on the Tunisian plain. Until Carthage was destroyed by Rome in 146 B.C., the Phoenicians (or Carthaginians, more properly, since Carthage became their permanent base of operation) dominated the coasts of North Africa.

Little is known of the Carthaginian way of life, largely because the Roman onslaught and later Vandal invasions destroyed all written records. The Greek historian Diodorus, however, wrote about a Greek attempt to capture Carthage in the late fourth century B.C. His account clearly indicates Carthaginians had built an affluent civilization:

> The intervening country through which it was necessary for them to march was divided into gardens and plantations of every kind, since many streams of water were led in small channels and irrigated every part. There were also country houses one after another, constructed in luxurious fashion and covered with stucco, which gave evidence of the wealth of the people who possessed them. The farm buildings were filled with everything that was needful for enjoyment, seeing that the inhabitants in a long period of peace had stored up an abundant variety of products. Part of the land was planted with vines, and part yielded olives and was also planted thickly with other varieties of fruit-bearing trees. On each side herds of cattle and flocks of sheep pastured on the plain, and the neighbor-

ing meadows were filled with grazing horses. In general there was a mani-fold prosperity in the region, since the leading Carthaginians had laid out there their private estates and with their wealth had beautified them for their enjoyment.

All indications point to the Carthaginians as a vigorous, prosperous people who channeled their greatest talents into maritime pursuits and trade and lived affluently on the rich plains of North Africa. They devoted little effort to art, architecture, or even imperial conquest. Because of their wealth and power, they played a major role in Mediter-ranean affairs for centuries; their navy was one of the most powerful in the world. Yet the Romans, after the conquest of North Africa and the destruction of Carthage, found them a dull and uninteresting people in daily life, unrefined and even slightly barbaric by Roman standards.

Between about 600 B.C. and 300 B.C. Carthage's greatest rival seems to have been Greece, a maritime power in direct competition for the gold, silver, tin, and agricultural products that Carthaginian ships carried around the Mediterranean. Carthage sometimes formed alliances with Persia and Rome against Greece. Although Greece established her influence in Lower Egypt and adjacent Libya, Carthage prevented her from gaining a foothold in most of North Africa.

The great Carthaginian empire, encompassing most of the North African coast and parts of Spain, was a loose confederation held to-gether by common economic interests. Little effort was made to spread the Punic language, Phoenician culture, or tight Carthaginian political rule. In part, this explains why the Berbers of North Africa had little difficulty resisting Carthaginian influence. Over the years, Berbers and Phoenicians intermarried in the coastal areas, and Carthaginian civilization became uniquely North African. Inland, the Berbers con-tinued their traditional way of life.

In 264 B.C., the first Punic War between Rome and Carthage began. At its end in 241 B.C. Rome had broken the Carthaginian grip on Sardinia and much of the eastern Mediterranean. Developing a powerful new base in Spain, where they built the city of New Carthage from which the later Spanish city of Cartagena developed, the Carthaginians for the first time amassed a large land army. Hannibal, Carthage's great military hero, launched an invasion of Rome. With his famed elephant troop, he was almost successful in crushing Roman power and invading Rome itself, but Rome prevailed, and the power of Carthage dimin-ished materially. In 149 B.C. Rome declared war again and invaded Africa. The Romans ruthlessly destroyed Carthage in 146 B.C. They tore down its buildings and monuments, dismantled its harbor works, and exterminated a large part of its population. Although a Carthaginian people continued to exist under Roman rule, Carthage as an empire and a civilization disappeared forever. North Africa had become an integral part of the Roman Empire.

Roman rule extended into every cultivable part of North Africa. But, like Carthaginian rule, it failed to obliterate the basic culture patterns and customs of most of the Berber peoples. To the Carthaginians, their North African cities were homelands as well as bases for trading and commercial activity. To the Romans, North Africa was a vast colonial satrapy and breadbasket. Rome was the homeland and the permanent base of operations; North Africa was a land to be developed for the food and wealth it could provide to imperial Rome.

Under Rome North African agriculture was reinvigorated: new areas were reclaimed and irrigated; great dams and engineering works were undertaken; and splendid new cities replaced the destroyed Carthaginian cities. Troops were posted in the interior, often in powerful forts, to protect farms and caravan routes from the raids of fierce Berber tribesmen who often rebelled against Roman intrusion and domination.

Roman interest in North Africa centered on two adjacent areas: "Africa," as the Romans named Tunisia and nearby Tripolitania, and Numidia, in eastern Algeria. In these two rich provinces, Rome built some fifty strong cities, integrated them with the surrounding farmlands, Romanized the inhabitants thoroughly, and raised the provinces to a high state of civilized development.

Gradually the Berbers of these provinces, long intermingled with the Phoenicians and estranged culturally from their Berber kinsmen in the interior, became full participants in the world of imperial Rome. They contributed great leaders, including St. Augustine and the Emperor Septimus Severus, to Roman civilization.

At the peak of Roman civilization, North Africa had changed greatly. Skillfully engineered roads crisscrossed the land, long viaducts brought fresh mountain water to the farms and cities of the coasts, extensive forests were planted and cultivated in the mountains, harbors were built, and great architectural works dotted the burgeoning cities. But the single most important heritage of the Roman period was Christianity.

The Greeks and Jews of Alexandria, who so readily accepted the new faith, were among its most effective missionaries. Together with the Jews of Roman Carthage, they helped spread the new religion to much of North Africa. During the fourth, fifth, and sixth centuries, Christianity became solidly entrenched in the cities and adjacent rural areas of Roman North Africa, although it made far less headway among the un-Romanized Berbers in the mountains and the interior country.

The Romanized Berbers who accepted Christianity did so in the traditional spirit of Berber independence. As long as Christianity was repudiated by Rome, it gained wide acceptance in coastal cities and towns among the poor, who resented Roman rule and culture, but even many prominent people embraced the new religion. Later, after Roman emperors themselves accepted or officially sanctioned Christianity, the bishops of North Africa often squabbled with bishops in Rome on matters of doctrine or church administration.

In about the beginning of the fourth century, imperial authorities in Rome issued an edict ordering scriptures to be surrendered and churches dismantled. Although all Christian clergy resisted, the form and degree of resistance became a matter of great debate. The clergy in Carthage, led by Donatus, claimant to the see of that city, decided upon total resistance. A major rift developed within the North African church between the Donatists and those who preferred some compromise with the imperial authorities. For over a century the bitter controversy raged. Many clergy and laymen supported the Donatist position, but several leading bishops and other clergy argued that the Donatist position, if carried to its logical conclusion, could mean extermination of the North African church.

St. Augustine, himself a North African and proud of his origins, adopted an anti-Donatist stance. At a conference in Carthage in 411 he led the challenge to the Donatists, helping to create a better climate of cooperation between the established North African church and Rome, which by this time was itself firmly in the Christian camp. Donatism eventually died out in North Africa. It never led to permanent doctrinal schisms, but it effectively symbolized the tendency of even very cosmopolitan North Africans to espouse the ancient Berber spirit of independence.

Roman rule in North Africa, if not Roman civilization, was broken by the Vandals in 429. The century of Vandal rule that followed was one of the most colorful in North African history, although it left no permanent mark there. The Vandals were a central European tribe related to the Germanic peoples. After decades of warfare with the Franks, Gauls, and other European tribes, the Vandals migrated to Spain where they established a new homeland. Chronically quarreling with Rome and the chiefs of various Spanish tribes, the Vandals of Andalusia, numbering about 80,000, moved their entire people into North Africa. They had apparently been invited by North Africa's rebellious rulers, who saw them as allies in the resistance against Roman rule.

Within a year the Vandals, led by their king Genseric, who for the next fifty years was the scourge of both Rome and Constantinople, had taken control of every important city and town in North Africa, except Carthage, Hippo, and Cirta. Rome signed a treaty surrendering all North Africa except these cities to Genseric. In 439 Genseric marched against Carthage, defeated its pro-Roman defenders, and became master of Roman North Africa.

From Carthage, Genseric rapidly created a navy that pirated the heavily laden ships bound to and from Rome and Constantinople and became a more serious threat to Rome than even his seizure of North Africa. For a few decades the Vandals, apparently with some Berber support, maintained a North African confederation, based on their naval strength and audacity. Weakened Roman rulers in Rome and Constantinople were powerless to eradicate it.

The Vandals left little literature by which we can gain a vivid picture of the life they brought to North Africa, but at the peak of their power, they must have been a unique group of immigrants. Genseric himself was lame, but was a man of great courage, physical strength, and cunning. For about two weeks his Vandal warriors and their Berber allies occupied Rome itself, with support from an amphibious force of marines and warships. They killed many leading Romans, pillaged jewels and works of art, and destroyed many statues and monuments so savagely that their name has become a common term for wanton destruction and defacement. In North Africa the Vandals cruelly persecuted Romans and Romanized Berbers in the towns and cities, although they maintained much friendlier relations with the independent-minded Berbers of the countryside and mountains and with urban Berber chiefs who shared Vandal hatred of Rome.

As the decades wore on, however, Vandal leaders gradually succumbed to the ease and luxury of civilized life in North Africa's fertile plains. Many intermarried with Berbers and the urban peoples of mixed Berber, Punic, and Roman blood. The fierceness that had made the Vandal name one to be feared began to erode. Meanwhile the new Roman empire of Byzantium, centered at Constantinople, was strengthening. One of the major objectives of its emperors was to eliminate the Vandal threat and recapture the Roman territories of North Africa. In a combined land-sea operation in 535, Carthage was recaptured. In three months every city and town in Vandal Africa had been recovered, and the Vandals disappeared from history, politically destroyed and racially and culturally absorbed into North Africa's melting pot.

Byzantine rule attempted to restore much of what the Vandals had destroyed. The Orthodox bishops and clergy, exiled by the Vandals because of their pro-Roman sentiments, were returned to power. In the cities, churches were built or rebuilt and were richly decorated in the

Byzantine style. Lands and houses that had been seized by the Vandals were returned to Romanized loyalists. Latin underwent a renaissance among the learned classes, and the upper classes adopted a civilized life in the luxurious Byzantine style. North Africa was brought back into peaceful intercourse with the Mediterranean world.

Yet anti-Roman forces in North Africa resisted Byzantine rule. Byzantine control was often confined to the cities. Even the areas near the major cities were hostile, and religious conflicts continued. In the towns, local clergy and laymen struggled against the dictates of bishops appointed by Constantinople. Outside the towns, defiance became commonplace.

By the time of Byzantine rule in North Africa, the camel had been introduced into the Sahara from Asia Minor. Camels gave the semi-nomadic Berbers a new mobility that made them even more troublesome. Camel caravans, carrying larger quantities of goods than had been possible with donkeys, crossed the Sahara in search of trade with the affluent Negro peoples of the western Sudan. And fierce Berber camel cavalry, able to move with lightning speed, swept almost at will into the fertile plains where they harassed Byzantine farmers and their North African collaborators. Byzantine North Africa soon became a series of fortified urban strongholds, isolated from each other except by sea. This stormy period endured throughout the sixth and seventh centuries. Even after Arab rule had supplanted that of the Byzantines in the cities, the Arabs regarded the Maghrib, as they called the North African lands west of Libya and Egypt, as the wildest and least secure part of their dominions.

The invasion of superbly trained Arab forces toward the close of the seventh century brought Byzantium's North African rule to an abrupt end. Despite enduring Berber resistance to Arab conquest, the Arabs fashioned deeper, more extensive changes in North Africa than had any other group. Yet more than fifteen hundred years of pre-Arab colonization had left its mark on North Africa, and the civilization into which the Arabs thrust was a patchwork of varied cultural influences.

Egypt and eastern Libya, the area of Cyrenaica named for the Greek colony of Cyrene in Libya, had become markedly Hellenized. Greek language, writing, literature, science, medicine, and art were all firmly entrenched among the Greek colonists, the upper- and middle-class Egyptians and Libyans, and the many Jews, Persians, and others who had flocked to such wealthy and civilized centers as Cyrene and Alexandria. Life among the peasants had changed little, except that Greek political control and law maintained a system of justice and order that made life more serene. Greek irrigation encouraged good agricultural production, and Greek commerce helped keep foreign goods flowing into the region and ensured a good market for local produce.

Greek influence never penetrated much farther west than Cyrenaica. In Tripolitania, the western part of modern Libya, and the rest of North Africa westward to the Atlantic coasts of Morocco, Phoenician and Carthaginian influence had long given way to that of Rome and her Byzantine successors. Latin was widely spoken among the educated and was the official language of commerce. Most of the upper- and middle-classes spoke only Latin at home. Christianity was widely practiced, even by the farmers living around the Romanized cities and by the poorer classes in the towns.

After more than seven hundred years of Roman rule, under Rome itself and then under Constantinople, life in Carthage and in the other great North African cities and the towns and villages surrounding them was deeply Romanized. Vandal culture had left hardly a trace, and the Vandals themselves had gradually become Romanized. Yet ancient Berber ways persisted among both the urban and rural lower classes. The Berber language was still spoken at home by many farmers and even by some townspeople.

During tranquil times, life was good in North Africa. The region's benign climate and fertile soils produced excellent harvests of wheat, barley, olives, grapes, and vegetables. Intricate irrigation systems guarded the farms against frequent periods of drought and unpredictable rainfall. The fundamental conditions of life remained generally placid except when the farmers were raided by angry Berber hill people or vengeful conquerers, and turbulent changes in culture and government were felt much more keenly by the urbanites.

But during the century and a half of Byzantine rule, even the humble people in the towns and countryside were subject to warfare, reprisals, and persecution. In the hill country and in the Sahara, Berber tribes began to form alliances and confederations under the leadership of military heroes. These alliances were kept in force for long periods, despite the traditional Berber preference for local freedom and independence. Time and again Byzantine troops were forced to march out of the cities to battle bands of Berbers. But usually the Berbers, mounted on camels, retreated into the desert or mountains when faced with superior Byzantine strength. Guerrilla warfare became a chronic activity. Such was the state of affairs in the late seventh century, as the holy crescent of Islam and its ambitious Arab proselytizers erupted out of Arabia into Africa.

Between 610 and 620, in the city of Mecca in Arabia, Muhammad had begun to preach a new set of admonitions and revelations. Just as Christ had done six centuries earlier, the wealthy merchant quickly attracted a band of loyal followers, many of them poor and oppressed. Ultimately Muhammad found himself the leading force in a small theocratic state, built around the cities of Mecca and Medina. Muhammad's influence was further bolstered by the support he received from Arab chiefs of the desert. In return for this support, Muhammad and his followers promised a uniform code of law and just administration, fair ethics in commerce, and equitable taxation. In the revelations that he expressed in the holy Koran, Muhammad provided a comprehensive code of ethical behavior, just government, and individual salvation through piety, charity, and good works. The new faith spread rapidly among the proud, fierce Arab tribesmen and soon provided them with a unifying national ethic they had never before possessed.

After Muhammad's death, his followers had to resort to arms to restore rule over the Arab tribesmen, who regarded their involvement in the common cause as a compact between them and Muhammad himself. Muhammad's chief disciples successfully rebuilt the state he had initiated and agreed that one of their number, Abu Bakr, should succeed Muhammad under the title caliph, or deputy. Abu Bakr possessed even greater administrative and political ability than Muhammad. He soon turned his army against the wealthy Byzantine-ruled towns of Syria and Iraq. Aggressive, nomadic Arab tribesmen had descended from the arid lands of the Arabian desert to raid the towns and rich farmlands of Syria and Iraq before, but never had they been so effectively united under a strong general and a religious faith that was fast becoming a national ethic. Under Abu Bakr's inspired leadership and fired by the zeal of Islam, Arab cavalry drove all Byzantine rulers and their armies from Syria, Iraq, and Lower Egypt. Now the Arabs effectively controlled the vast and enormously wealthy region from the Euphrates to the Nile. By 641, Abu Bakr had risen from the leader of a small, disorganized state to the master of an empire. Both Byzantium and Persia trembled as aggressive Arab armies established military rule over many lands that had so recently been part of their own dominions.

Because of Byzantine unpopularity with the local populations, Arab conquest of Egypt, especially the delta, lower and middle Egypt, and the adjacent Libyan region of Cyrenaica, took little time and met with little resistance.

Coptic Christianity had become established in Egypt and Libya and was considered a heresy by the orthodox Byzantine church. Although Byzantine persecution failed to eradicate the Coptic faith, it led the Egyptians and Libyans to welcome the Arabs as deliverers. The local populations rose up against their Byzantine overlords and the local nobles who supported them.

Christian historians have traditionally portrayed Islam as a fanatical faith, spread by cruel and intolerant zealots. This view, largely developed as a result of the Crusades, grossly misrepresents both the Muslim faith and its early Arab disseminators. Although there were zealots who showed intolerance and persecuted infidels, much of Islam's history reveals a great capacity for tolerance and accommodation. More often than not, the Arabs were hailed as deliverers by the persecuted peoples of the Byzantine and Persian worlds. Arab conquerers, though eager to win converts for Islam, rarely forbade Christianity or persecuted Christians. Arabs and converts to Islam were accorded tax and land preferences under the Muslim administrative code, but Arab land reforms and religious tolerance more than compensated for these privileges in the eyes of the oppressed and persecuted peoples of the conquered territories.

The Arabs were early to recognize the importance of local cooperation, for there were relatively few Arabs among the vast populations of the empire. Converts were given status equivalent to that of pure Arabs, and formed the nucleus of a new elite that cemented and perpetuated Arab conquests. In the empire, zealous converts and the descendants of Arab-local marriages outnumbered those of pure Arab origin. This helped maintain the atmosphere of tolerance that followed initial conquest.

In the first centuries of the empire thousands of Arabs—soldiers, officers, holy men, and administrators—left Arabia to settle into key positions in the conquered lands. Yet many Arabs, especially those of the nomadic and seminomadic desert tribes, preferred to remain in their ancestral lands, and many of the Arab soldiers who settled in North Africa soon left the unfamiliar pursuits of urban life to settle in more remote areas where they could follow a more congenial way of life.

Islamic civilization was united through the religion, language, and the philosophy that the Arab conquerers spread. But Islam was merely a foundation, a common thread, upon which a hybrid civilization was built. The Arabs blended their language, religion, and sense of historic mission with the accomplishments of other civilizations. From Persia, Greece, Turkey, Mesopotamia, Egypt, and North Africa flowed ideas that gradually became integral components of Islamic civilization, including Greek science and philosophy, Persian poetry and literature, and naval and commercial ideas from Syria, North Africa, and Greece. Even elements of art and science from China and India were incorporated into the new culture. Within a few centuries, a new civilization had spread throughout the lands south of the Mediterranean, over the entire Near East and Arabia itself, into Turkey and Persia, and even into India. It produced great mathematicians, poets, physicians, architects, military strategists, historians, geographers, and philosophers.

North Africa eventually became a major segment of Islamic civilization and for brief periods was its leading part, but the process of conquest and acculturation was long and difficult. For several decades, the desert, inhabited by warlike Berbers, slowed the Arab westward advance. The Arabs had insufficient naval strength for major amphibious operations and their generals questioned the prudence of marching over-land from Cyrenaica to face hostile Berbers who used horses and camels in much the same fashion as the Arabs, knew the desert intimately, and had built a reputation as skilled and courageous warriors during Byzan-tine days.

Finally, in 670, an Arab army set out from Cyrenaica across hun-dreds of miles of desert and invaded Tripolitania and Tunisia. In both countries most of the Romanized cities and the farmlands immediately adjacent to them were quickly captured, but raiding Berber cavalry from the hills, too elusive for even the swift Arab cavalry, restricted the Arabs to the cities. Evidently the urban peoples, whom the Arabs called Roums because of their Roman ways, hardly resisted Arab entry so thankful were they to see the last of Byzantine rule.

Under the Arab general Uqba ibn Nafi a powerful task force of troops, too strong for any Berber or Byzantine army, pushed the initial wave of Arab conquest of the Maghrib to the Atlantic shores of Morocco. Building several powerful garrisons, including the great town of Kairouan near the present city of Tunis, Uqba simply bypassed those few cities still in Byzantine hands, but even these fell to him in short order. When he reached the Atlantic, Uqba is said to have cried out to his troops that only the boundless sea prevented him from conquer-ing more lands for Allah's glory. But as Uqba and his many successors were to learn, the conquest of the Maghrib was far from complete. For more than a century Berber cavalry continued to descend onto the Arab-held plains, destroying farms and towns and then quickly retreat-ing into the wild mountains and the trackless desert. Previously formed alliances allowed Berber war chiefs rapidly to assemble large forces for raids or for defensive purposes.

In the cities and plains, however, Arab rule was more easily estab-lished. Arabic gradually replaced Latin; Islam inexorably won converts at the expense of Christianity; and the ruling class of Arab governors and administrators was soon augmented by the large number of local people who accepted Islam. Through intermarriage, the thinly spread Arab population further blended with the North Africans. Under the leadership of the new class of Arabized North Africans, the cities and towns began to prosper. As great ideas and talented men from the conquered dominions were infused into Arabic civilization it became a thing almost apart from the Arabs. Neither the Arabs nor leaders from the dominions were powerful enough to exercise strong central control over the empire's vast territory, except for brief periods. Yet, for many centuries, the vigor of Islam and the Arab language provided a bond stronger than most central governments could have offered.

Weak central controls and the basically egalitarian qualities of Islam and the Arabic system proved deeply attractive to the Berbers and their cosmopolitan relatives in North Africa. Berber tribes that had stubbornly fought off the Arab armies gradually accepted Islam. The unifying bonds of Islamic civilization reached wider in North Africa than did the political control of the rulers in the cities. Although it took several centuries, North Africa slowly developed a sense of Islamic destiny, and even the fierce Berbers of the desert helped fight holy wars to spread Islamic civilization. Armies of Arabs and Berbers crossed the straits of Gibraltar from Morocco and conquered Spain and Portugal. The Moors, who for so long formed a part of the history of those countries, were Berbers from Morocco and other North African lands.

Within two centuries of the initial Arab invasion, North Africa had grown into one of the most powerful centers of the Arab Empire. At times, caliphs and governors based in Tunisia controlled all of North Africa, Spain, Portugal, Sicily and other islands in the western Mediterranean. For many centuries, North Africa was virtually independent of the Baghdad-based Arab Empire in the east, paying only the barest of lip service to the caliphs, who were recognized as Muhammad's spiritual successors. Great cities developed in Morocco, Algeria, and Tunisia—Fez, Marrakesh, Kairouan, Tunis, Sfax, Sousse, Mahdia—replete with ornate mosques, universities, vast palaces, libraries, and swimming baths.

Life in North Africa's great cities and towns reached a peak of affluence around the eleventh century. Vast irrigation systems brought the fertile lands of the plains to high productivity, and long periods of peace protected the daily lives of the farmers. The worship of Allah and the administration of Islamic law helped give the lives of ordinary men new meaning and tranquillity. Into the bustling ports flowed luxury goods from the Mediterranean world, and out of them poured the grains, wines, ivory, fruits, olives, and gold of Africa. In the cities, arts and fine crafts were encouraged. North African leatherwork, jewelry, knives, swords, daggers, and glass found ready markets in the Islamic world as well as in Europe and in Black Africa.

Yet even in the best of times, North Africa was not totally tranquil. The Berbers of the Sahara, increasingly Muslim in religion and conscious of their ties with the Islamic world, had become more dependent upon the urban centers for trade, but wars broke out when the more ambitious city rulers attempted to extend their control into the desert and the mountains. The Berbers came to play an ever more active role in North African political affairs, allying themselves with one urban ruler to bring down another who threatened Berber interests. By the tenth century, Berber leaders began to initiate wars of their own, aiming to seize control of urban governments, and in the eleventh century, a Berber religious leader, Ibn Yasin, led a victorious campaign that brought great changes to Black Africa as well as to North Africa.

The conditions leading to Ibn Yasin's movement were part of a tragic period in Islamic North Africa. The Maghrib's rulers recognized the caliph at Baghdad, thus defying the rival caliph in Egypt, who regarded all North Africa as subject to him. The caliph of Egypt, not strong enough to punish the Maghrib with his own forces, persuaded the chiefs of several nomadic Arab tribes—the Beni Hilal, Beni Sulaim, and others—to move from Egypt into North Africa. Led by the Beni Hilal, these formidable Arabs moved across Libya into Tunisia. According to Ibn Khaldun, the greatest Islamic historian, they so ravaged North Africa that they destroyed its civilization. Writing some two centuries later, Khaldun described them as:

> . . . a savage nation, fully accustomed to savagery and the things that cause it. Savagery has become their character and nature. . . . Arabs need stones to set them up as supports for their cooking pots. So, they take them from buildings which they tear down to get the stones. . . . Wood, too, is needed by them for props for their tents and for use as tent poles for their dwellings. So, they tear down roofs to get wood for that purpose. . . . Wherever their eyes fall upon some property, furnishings, or utensils, they take it. . . . There no longer exists any political power to protect property, and civilization is ruined.

Having disrupted the peaceful life of the plains, the Hilalians moved into the desert where they severely mauled several Berber tribes. As Berber groups pressed westward to find new lands safe from the raids of the savage Hilalians, a chain reaction covering much of the western Sahara set in.

Ibn Yasin, a holy man who had recently returned from his pilgrimage to Mecca, attempted to instill in the Berber Sanhaja nation a new sense of holy purpose and morality. At first rebuffed, Yasin established a mystic retreat on an island in the mouth of the Senegal River far below the Sahara. There he spent several years in ascetic worship and contemplation, joined by a constantly growing band of disciples, at first curious about the reputed holiness of Yasin, then fired by his call for creation of a new polity in which all men worshiped Allah with zeal and piety.

In 1042, Yasin and his followers, now numbering about a thousand, left their island monastery and embarked on a campaign to force the impious and heretical Berbers of the western Sahara to return to pure

Islam. Now called Almoravids, from the Arabic for al-Murabitun, or people of the "ribat" (monastery), Yasin's followers met with success. Within a year or two, Yasin commanded an army of more than thirty thousand zealous troops, drawn largely from a confederation of Sanhaja Berber tribesmen in what is now Mauritania and southern Morocco.

One wing of Yasin's troops swept north into the Atlas Mountains of Morocco, another moved south into the great Soninke Empire of Ghana. Before the close of the eleventh century, the Almoravid campaign had established both a renaissance of Islam and firm political control over an empire that stretched from northern Spain to modern Senegal and across the Mediterranean coast of North Africa through all of Algeria and Tunisia.

For several generations, this territory was maintained under successive Almoravid emirs. But the fanatic zeal and religious purity that had carried them into power was soon dissipated by the soft life in the cities from which they ruled. In the twelfth century, the Almohads, a movement springing from the Zenata Berbers of Morocco, swept the weakened Almoravids from power, but after less than a century, Almohad rule collapsed, and North Africa disintegrated into a group of emirates and petty states.

If Ibn Khaldun's history is correct, the seeds of North Africa's imperial decline lay in the Hilalians' savage depredations. During the several decades of their ravages, much of North Africa's agricultural production suffered irreversible harm. Irrigation systems were destroyed, and those villages lying some distance from the security of the fortified cities were abandoned. Intercity commerce and farm life were disrupted. Neither the Almoravids nor the Almohads seem to have possessed the strength or the persistence to reconstruct the fabric of the formerly prosperous North African system.

The crumbling of the great North African political system was accompanied by a loss of Muslim possessions in Europe. The Normans, under King Roger I, had captured Sicily in the eleventh century, and the Spaniards and Portuguese drove the Muslims from their Iberian territory, except Granada, in the thirteenth century. By the fourteenth century all the lands in the central and western Mediterranean, both in Africa and in Europe, were divided into small kingdoms, principalities, and city-states, each with its own pretensions to power.

In North Africa the post-Almohad centers of power roughly coincided with the modern states of that region. One sultan claimed the cities and valleys on Morocco's Atlantic and Mediterranean coasts, another claimed the Tunisian plain. The caliphate held Egypt, and Libya was divided into Tripolitania and Cyrenaica. Algeria was divided into small units, composed of individual towns and adjacent farmlands. Strong Berber chiefs prevented the coastal sultans from effectively controlling the mountains and steppes. In Tunisia, long the most racially mixed region of North Africa, the rulers and leading men retained little of the Berber heritage. Even when Berber chiefs assumed control, founding new dynasties, they gradually became acculturated. In Morocco, traditionally more isolated, Berber ties remained stronger, as they did in Algeria. In both these countries large Berber populations maintained their traditional ways of life in the mountains.

For centuries North Africa continued in this way, the peak of civilization having passed by about the twelfth century. Spain and Portugal, having grown in power since the expulsion of most Muslims in the thirteenth century, frequently invaded Morocco. On several occasions, European forces from Italy and France invaded Tunisia and Algeria, remaining for short periods before being ejected by resurgent North African rulers. Much of North Africa came under the control of the Ottoman Empire in the sixteenth century, but Ottoman rule brought few changes of significance.

Despite decline of the political bonds of the earlier Arab empire and Islamic civilization, life in North Africa between the thirteenth and nineteenth centuries remained generally prosperous. The major cities continued to trade with each other, with the Berbers of the interior, and with the growing economic centers in Europe, especially Venice and Genoa. North African wool was added to the olives, dates, wines, grains, and leather goods exported to the Mediterranean world. Near the important cities, the farms on the plains and valleys continued to prosper. But the irrigation systems of Carthaginian, Roman, and Arab times fell into disuse in the more remote regions. Few great new mosques, palaces, gardens, engineering works, and public buildings were built after the thirteenth century, but many of those built in former years continued to be used and were kept in good condition. Emirs, sultans, merchants, and government officials maintained an opulent existence, affluent from rarely failing tax revenues, customs duties, trade profits, and booty from privateering which they controlled. A tradition of education persisted and was even enriched for a time when the expelled scholars and nobles of Spain settled in Tunis and other North African cities in the thirteenth century.

The North African cities of the medieval period were cosmopolitan. In each could be found communities of Jews, which swelled after thirteenth century persecutions in Spain, Portugal, and Italy. Islamic scholars commonly traveled from one part of the Islamic world to another, spending months or years in cities as judges, religious philosophers, administrators, and teachers of the children of the wealthy. Some Europeans trickled in as representatives of the great commercial houses of Europe. Other Europeans were captured in wars and privateering ventures and became slaves of the sultans, often serving as officers and soldiers in the palace guard. Slaves from Black Africa, usually purchased from Berber caravaneers who brought them from Mali, Songhai, and Kanem-Bornu south of the Sahara, were also brought into the region.

The North Africans themselves were either wealthy nobles or commoners. Although a North African middle class of artisans, clerks, petty officials, traders, small landowners, and craftsmen remained in existence, some of the positions normally held by them were filled by European and Black African slaves and mercenaries. The average North African was a peasant farmer living just outside a city. Occasionally he owned a small plot of land, but often he tilled the soil on the estates of large landowners. He practiced his traditional way of life—Arabized, he still retained traces of the Berber heritage—and remained as aloof as possible from city affairs. In the cities, the commoners engaged in the myriad tasks necessary for maintenance of urban life: brickmasonry, carpentry, garbage collecting, petty trading, tailoring, shoe repairing, stevedoring, barbering, food vending, and laboring.

During the medieval centuries, the quality of North African government varied. Some sultans effected lighter tax burdens, more equitable laws, and better economic conditions; others were harsh, ineffective, or unjust. Decades of peace alternated with years or decades of war, either with foreign powers, Berber war chiefs of the interior, or neighboring North African states. Throughout the long medieval period, even after Ottoman rule was imposed, no reigns restored North Africa to the greatness of earlier days. Yet there were no reigns of incompetence and despotism long or harsh enough to destroy the fundamentals of civilized life. Sometimes troubled, sometimes tranquil, neither relapsing into barbarism nor moving forward into new greatness, North Africa maintained itself at roughly the same level until conquest by Europe imposed a new form of colonial rule in the nineteenth century.

6 The Sudanic Civilization

Southward from the barren center of the Sahara Desert, the annual rainfall gradually increases and the desiccated wastelands of rock and sand give way imperceptibly to steppes dotted with patches of wiry grasses. Still farther south grass begins to grow more abundantly, and stunted trees, widely separated one from another, appear. This grassy plain, called the Sudan, stretches up to a thousand miles southward from the edge of the desert and rims it nearly all the way from the Atlantic Ocean on the west to the Indian Ocean and Red Sea on the east.

The Arabs of the seventh and eighth centuries were dimly aware of this land from reports they received from camel caravans that crossed the Sahara. They called it the Bilad-as-Sudan, or land of the Blacks. The Sudan was a fabled land to these early Arabs, for the Berber caravans brought from it rich shipments of gold and awed reports of the power and wealth of its kings.

In the Bilad-as-Sudan, which is largely isolated from the rest of the civilized world by the Sahara on the north, the Atlantic Ocean on the west, and sheer distance on the east, a great drama of civilization, virtually unknown to the outside world, unfolded between 1000 B.C. and A.D. 1500. Dozens of small states grew slowly into larger states, producing great works of art and sophisticated political organizations. In a few cases, these states expanded into wealthy empires that covered vast territories and lasted for centuries.

The greatest of these empires—Ghana, Mali, Songhai, and Kanem-Bornu—were the glowing achievements of a Black African civilization that covered more than half the continent. This civilization was created by a people who migrated from their aboriginal center in the southern Sahara and the Sudan to almost every part of sub-Saharan Africa. They produced many other great states and even empires, many of which approached the four great empires in impressiveness. They are the Black Africans, the predominantly Negroid population that much of the outside world associates with Africa.

The Sudanic civilization (which is not associated with the Sudanic languages) takes its name from the Sudan region where it originated and where its great heights of development and common characteristics were first identified. But it spread into the great rain forests of West Africa, and then across the rain forests of the Congo River basin into the dry woodlands and savannas of central, eastern, and southern Africa.

It was once fashionable—and still is in some quarters—to define civilization in such a way as to identify it primarily with the developments from which the civilization of modern Europe stems. According to this view, the widespread use of writing, a tradition of science and a scientific technology, and an abundance of great buildings and monuments are essential attributes of civilization. This narrow definition limits the creation of civilized societies to the ancient peoples of the white and yellow races, leaving blacks as the only racial group that lacked sufficient genius to raise itself from barbarism.

Nowadays all but the most conservative thinkers believe that civilization should refer equally to societies that developed advanced forms of government, complex philosophies, traditions of gifted art, and technologies that enabled people to cope skillfully with their environment. Under this more fundamental definition, the Black Africans of the Sudan and their kinsmen who migrated to the West African forests and below the equator, produced a great civilization which spanned millions of square miles of diverse sub-Saharan environments.

Up to about 3000 B.C., the Africans of the Sudan lived in many areas of the Sahara that today are either uninhabitable or are thinly populated by Berber nomads. But at that time, many parts of the Sahara were much better watered. Rainfall may have been slightly greater; shallow lakes dotted a wide area; seasonal rivers and streams flowed; and grasses helped retain moisture in the soil. In this more hospitable environment, Negroid Africans hunted, fished, and grazed domesticated animals long before gradual desiccation dried out the Sahara's interior regions and pushed its borders southward.

So little archaeological investigation has been conducted in either the Sahara or the Sudan that the clues about this period are scanty. Until very recently it was thought that the Black Africans were a very primitive people prior to the state of Ghana's emergence from the stone age.

By the kindest interpretation of fact and legend, Ghana's origins could be stretched back no further than the third or fourth century of the Christian era. Recent excavations of the Nok culture in central Nigeria, however, indicated that a flourishing agriculture, iron-working and art-producing culture predated Christ, thus providing the first clue that the history of Sudanic civilization began a good deal earlier than had been imagined.

In 1969, Patrick Munson, a young American archaeologist, returned from an expedition on the edge of the desert in central Mauritania. Munson reported that he had found evidence of an agricultural society dating back to before 1000 B.C., over a millennium before the founding of Ghana. Other findings at Munson's sites north of the Mauritanian town of Dar Tichitt indicated that the early residents of the area had settled there at least as early as 1200 B.C. In this first phase of development, they built large villages of stone houses, using a dry stone type of construction. Fragments of pottery from these earliest villages contain impressions of wild grains that had presumably been gathered for food.

The second phase of development began in about 1000 B.C. The number of towns increased and were fortified by tall stone walls. In these ruins, Munson found seeds of cultivated varieties of millet mixed in with wild millet grains: apparently wild grains were still gathered, but food supplies were supplemented by the revolutionary agricultural practices of sowing and reaping.

In 800 B.C., a third phase of development began. At least two hundred towns stretched along a two hundred-mile escarpment in now uninhabited desert. Some of these towns were large enough to have housed several thousand people. Fortifications around the towns had virtually disappeared, implying that the agricultural people of the area had become numerous enough to deter harassment, probably from Berber nomads pressing south in search of better pastures for their flocks.

In a fourth phase, dated 600-300 B.C., the ancient Mauritanian peoples lived in fewer and smaller towns. These were mostly located in heavily fortified natural rock formations, as if the inhabitants were hiding from an enemy who had become too powerful to allow safe farming by large numbers of peaceful people. The ruins of these towns show no further signs of being inhabited after about 300 B.C. It was during this final phase that Herodotus wrote of the Garamantes of the desert, who used chariots and hunted the "troglodyte Ethiopians" who lived in holes. Rock engravings in the Mauritanian sites show wheeled carts, presumably those used by their desert enemies.

It could be speculated that these sedentary agriculturalists gradually disappeared after 500 B.C. But the still inhabited central Mauritanian

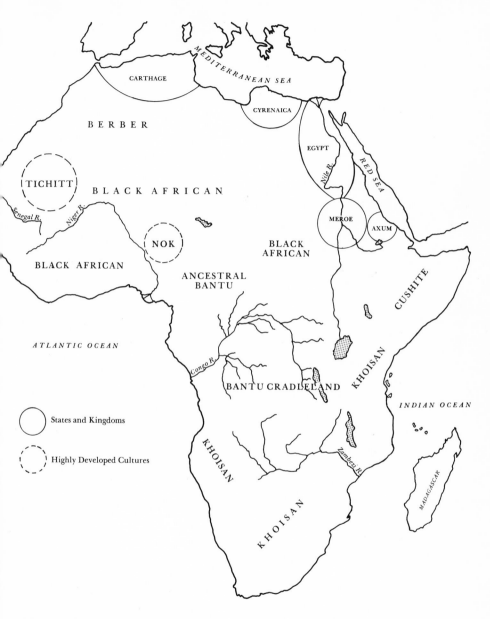

Africa's Major Language Families

town of Tichitt, used by Munson as a point of departure for exploring the ruins that lay around it, stands upon a midden, or refuse accumulation, about ten meters deep. This indicates continuous habitation for at least a thousand years before the present town, which is mentioned in an Arabic source of 1152 A.D. as a northern caravan center of the empire of Ghana, was built. Probably Tichitt was originally settled before the Christian era by the southward-retreating agriculturists from the stone ruins and was eventually incorporated into Ghana.

Munson argued that the ruins he surveyed were sufficiently numerous to imply the existence of some kind of state organization. And, because of their contiguity to the later Soninke Empire of Ghana, they may represent a much earlier ancestor state which preceded Ghana's formation. The Negroid farmers who today inhabit the oases in the vicinity of the ruins speak Azar, a Soninke language, but evidence is much too scanty to prove conclusively that Munson's Mauritanian ruins housed a large Soninke state that eventually spawned Ghana. The ruins do show that a highly developed society of Black Africans prospered in the western Sudan a thousand years before Ghana was born.

More than a thousand miles southwest of Tichitt lies the plateau of central Nigeria, a relatively fertile and cool highland where numerous artifacts of the Nok culture have been unearthed. The Nok peoples left relics—dating to around the same time as the stone ruins north of Tichitt—that indicate another root of Sudanic civilization.

In 1936, tin miners in the village of Nok, near the city of Jos, discovered a small terra cotta head of a monkey. It showed considerable artistic merit and was found at a depth that suggested it dated back to antiquity. But it attracted no serious attention until a larger and stylistically similar terra cotta human head was found in 1944 in Jemaa, some miles away. This second head was found at a depth of twenty feet.

Many terra cotta figures have since been found in an area three hundred miles long and a hundred miles wide. Burial sites, fragments of pottery and stone tools, and traces of iron smelting have also been unearthed. The Nok people had learned to work iron as early as about 400 B.C., although they also continued to make tools of stone throughout the period covered by their artifacts—from about 900 B.C. to A.D. 200.

The numerous terra cotta figurines, done in a realistic style, are often of very high technical and artistic quality, and the people who made them must have lived in a culture that placed considerable value on art work. Many of the figurines are of animals, including monkeys and elephants; others show people wearing necklaces and bracelets, and beads of tin and quartz have been found with them at a number of sites.

The Nok people cultivated grains and there is some hint in the terra cotta figurines that they herded cattle. Not enough archaeological work has yet been done to speculate about their population density and standard of living, but the long tradition of high-quality art suggests that they could afford to spend time on the creation, and presumably enjoyment, of beauty.

Scholars have found a close stylistic resemblance between the ancient Nok terra cotta figures and the early terra cotta works of Ife, which were produced more than a thousand years later in Yoruba country far to the south of the Nigerian plateau. The earliest roots of Ife and Yoruba culture have not been explored, but the kinship of the terra cotta works suggests the possibility of connections between Yoruba and Nok traditions.

The discovery that at least two agricultural societies flourished in the Sudan centuries before the birth of Christ provides some evidence about the origins of Sudanic civilization. Modern African languages yield another type of evidence. The majority of peoples living in the Sudan and southward speak languages that are closely related within two large linguistic stocks—Congo-Kordofanian and Sudanic.

The languages of these two great stocks (comparable in their diversity to the great Indo-European stock, which comprises all the languages of modern Europe and part of India and Asia Minor) are spoken in nearly all of Africa from the Sahara to the Cape. Sudanic speakers tend to inhabit the southern Sahara and eastern Sudan, including Nubia. Congo-Kordofanian speakers range from the western Sudan all the way to southern Africa. About 175 million Africans speak languages of the Congo-Kordofanian stock, and perhaps 40 million speak Sudanic languages.

Similarities among the languages within Congo-Kordofanian and Sudanic stocks suggest that they derived from a common mother tongue at some very ancient time, perhaps more than ten thousand years ago. But today they bear only distant relationships to each other. The approximately three hundred languages of the Bantu branch of Congo-Kordofanian, which has been the subject of much research, seem to have differentiated from a language spoken either in the Cameroun highlands or adjacent Nigeria. This differentiation took place over a surprisingly short period, some two thousand years. Since the other languages, branches, and subfamilies of both stocks show a much greater differentiation, it is reasonable to assume that they have been differentiating for thousands of years.

The vast area in which Congo-Kordofanian languages are spoken and throughout which Sudanic civilization has spread covers roughly half of Africa and includes more than half the population. It is spoken almost exclusively by Black Africans, and far more Negroes speak Congo-Kordofanian languages than Sudanic or Afro-Asiatic languages.

Sudanic civilization, despite its name, springs primarily from Congo-Kordofanian-speaking peoples. Sudanic languages were spoken by the ancient Nubians and their neighbors; the Egyptians spoke a language derived from the Afro-Asiatic stock. Yet many elements of both Nubian and Egyptian civilization were also characteristic of Sudanic civilization. These common characteristics—such as the concept of divine kingship and various religious beliefs—suggest some ancient, but not fully understood, connections between the Nile and Sudanic civilizations.

Although it is risky to identify one area as the place of origin of the Sudanic peoples, the western Sudan, east and northeast of the Niger River, is a possibility. This country is now inhabited by the numerous and highly developed Mande-speaking peoples, including the Soninke, the principal people of ancient Ghana. From somewhere in this general area, there has long been population expansion and migration, probably dating back as far as the third or fourth millennium B.C. This movement of people pressed ever southward to the forests along the coast of West Africa, to the Sudanic savannas of modern Nigeria and Cameroun, and from there, still southward, to the Congo, eastern, and southern Africa. But, wherever its precise location, there is evidence to suggest that such a point of common origin did exist. The Black Africans who speak Congo-Kordofanian languages are almost entirely an agricultural people and have been so for at least two millennia. Indigenous Sudanic food crops originated in the relatively dry, sandy soils of the savanna and include pearl millet, sorghum, cow peas, earth peas or Bambara groundnuts (somewhat similar to the American peanut), Guinea yams (in the forest areas), okra, calabash, watermelon, cotton, and sesame. A people growing one of these crops tended to grow them all, thus forming what is known as a complex. Individual foods—the watermelon, for example—have spread over many parts of the world, yet the complex itself is limited to sub-Saharan Africa.

With the original plants of the complex, the peoples of the Sudan could spread themselves and their pattern of agriculture over much of sub-Saharan Africa, but in the humid rain forests of West Africa and the Congo basin where environmental conditions were unsuited to the basic food complex, development was slow. The African forests provided a few plants that could be domesticated or used in the wild state—the Guinea yam and the oil palm, for example—but these were not sufficiently high yielding or nutritious to support a dense population. The scanty archaeological research conducted so far indicates that the forests have been continuously inhabited for many thousands of years,

but there is no evidence of dense populations or highly developed societies before the Christian era.

The higher development of the forest peoples seems to have been
made possible when several East Asian plants, notably the yam, the
banana, and the coco yam (or taro), were introduced during the first
millennium of the Christian era. These plants, native to warm, humid,
rain-forest lands in Malaysia, are all more nutritious than the indigenous
African plants domesticated by the forest peoples. They are also capable
of supporting large populations without excessive labor or complex
technology. The Sudanic peoples adopted the Malaysian plants and
used them to form the basis of a more productive agricultural economy
in the forests.

How the plants of Indonesia reached West Africa is not fully understood. It is highly unlikely that West Africans sailed to Indonesia or that
Indonesians sailed to West Africa. Neither group possessed the naval
technology for such long and perilous voyages against prevailing winds
and currents, nor did they have any reason to attempt them. But Indonesian mariners are known to have visited the coasts of East Africa
from at least a century or two before Christ to about the end of the first
millennium after Christ. These Indonesian mariners included the Maanyan of Borneo, or a very closely related group from whose language
Malagasy, the dominant language of Madagascar, seems to be descended.

The Maanyan developed a far-flung sea trade centuries before the
Christian era. Their maritime adventures took them both to Madagascar
and to the East African coast. Their presence in East African port cities
has been documented in several Arabic works written late in the first
millennium of the Christian era, and the *Periplus of the Erythraean Sea*
(first century B.C.) strongly suggests that they had reached East Africa
by the time of Christ. The *Periplus* refers to coconuts, which derive from
Malaysia, and two kinds of boats of Indonesian origin—dugout canoes
and boats of logs "sewn" together. Today, there are many other signs of
Indonesian influences in East Africa: flat bar zithers not found elsewhere
in Africa, coconut graters, lobster pots, and a peculiar method of catch-
ing turtles using sucking lampreys.

The commodities the Indonesians traded on the East African coast
in this early period are not known. Presumably they fished, acquired
provisions to continue their voyages, and bargained for minor quantities
of goods that may have found their way to the coast from the interior.
But they must certainly have introduced their own food plants (the
banana, yam, and taro), which must have been welcomed because of their
superiority to most indigenous African plants.

These plants could have spread across Africa by several routes. It is unlikely, however, that they spread via Meroe westward across the Sudan, for in this area the people still depend on the ancient Sudanic complex of plants, along with Egyptian additions. A route inland from the coast is a more likely possibility. This route would have extended somewhere between southern Somalia and southern Mozambique to the great lake country between Uganda and Zambia, then westward to the area between Lake Chad and the Cameroun. The Indonesian plants must have reached central Africa very early in the Christian era. The great population expansion of the Bantu peoples, which was certainly aided by the adopted Indonesian plants, seems to have originated in this area at about this time.

Acquisition of these valuable Indonesian plants enabled the Sudanic peoples of the rain forests to attain a greater prosperity than had been previously possible. During the first thousand years of the Christian era, they developed a new way of life in the forest country and expanded southward so rapidly that they had settled almost all of sub-Saharan Africa before the end of the millennium.

Agricultural innovations were not the sole cause of higher development in Sudanic societies. Also of vital importance were a knowledge of mining, smelting, and forging iron. These skills were acquired by the Sudanic peoples several centuries before Christ (the earliest smelting site so far unearthed dates to about 400 B.C.). In these very early times, iron must have been too precious for use in large quantities, but it was soon sufficiently available to provide points for spears, heads for axes, and blades for hoes. The chief advantage that iron gave the early Sudanic farmers was a superior ability to fell trees. With iron axes, the rain forests and the dry woodlands that blend with the savannas of much of central Africa were cleared for soil cultivation. Once trees were felled and the dead trunks and branches were burned away, iron hoes afforded easier working of the soils. Iron weapons and tools, as well as superior food-producing techniques, enabled the Black Africans to supplant the ancient Bushmanoids who inhabited most of Africa south of the Sudan before the Sudanic peoples usurped the land. Today, the only traces of Bushmanoid inhabitation are a few isolated groups of Pygmies deep in the Congo forests and the artifacts of stone and bone, characteristic of Bushmanoid industry, that archaeologists are beginning to unearth.

The Sudanic peoples who expanded their civilization in the forests and central and southern areas of Africa at the beginning of the Christian era were not a primitive stone age people. As suggested by the Tichitt and Nok archaeological evidence, they had begun, in at least two areas of the Sudan, to build a complex and prosperous civilization early in the first millennium before Christ. They possessed an evolving technology that had mastered agriculture and metal work and a political organization that provided the basis for higher development.

The ways in which the Sudanic peoples worked out their destinies, especially during the past millennium, have varied greatly. Environmental and historical factors have ensured that no two Sudanic societies developed in precisely the same way. Yet, amid this variegated development, there were underlying uniformities and common characteristics. Even the few Sudanic civilizations built by peoples whose languages do not derive from either Congo-Kordofanian or Sudanic language stocks (the Songhai and Hausa groups) have shown agricultural, political, and cultural similarities to the millions of Sudanic peoples bound together into the two major language stocks. The Indonesian plant complex represents the only major variation from the common Sudanic agricultural pattern.

Perhaps the most striking pattern of commonality among the Sudanic peoples is political structure. Most Sudanic peoples developed elaborate states, usually headed by an emperor or a king. Even in those societies that lacked such state organization, there was often a similarity in political ideas and practices. Almost all Sudanic kingships shared dozens of common characteristics. The king enjoyed absolute power, at least in theory. He claimed ownership of all land, livestock, and game in the state and could levy taxes or tribute on them. He was believed to be divine, or to have unique access to divine powers, and was customarily isolated from contact with ordinary persons. He resided in a capital town and was at the center of an elaborate royal court with pages, guards, entertainers, chamberlains, and personal attendants.

The king normally was assisted by a council of ministers, including usually a prime minister or vizier, a military commander, a chief justice, a royal executioner, and a supervisor of the royal princes and princesses. The state was always divided into provinces or districts, each with officials responsible for maintaining order, collecting taxes, and levying troops and labor. Succession to the throne was usually in the hands of a committee of ministers who were not legally bound to follow the king's wishes in appointing his successor.

This political pattern required certain environmental and historical conditions to develop fully. The most important condition was enough wealth to support the ornate court, the state's administrative apparatus, and the military force upon which both king and state depended. This wealth could come, as it did so abundantly in ancient Egypt, from a highly productive agricultural base. In the more fertile parts of the Sudan and the forest, certain states—Ghana, Mali, and Asante (or Ashanti)—seemed to derive some of the necessary wealth from their own

farm productivity; but in most of Sudanic Africa, slim domestic agricultural productivity meant that wealth had to be derived from other
products, or from the control of access to these products. Virtually all
the greater Sudanic states owed most of their growth and well-being to
commerce. They traded in gold, ivory, spices, hides, cloth, iron,
and slaves. Where there was insufficient wealth from agricultural
produce or from trade, the development of a strong state was impossible.

Sudanic states could rarely support rapid and continuing development of the entire society. Much of the wealth flowed into the central
coffers of the king or emperor and was used to maintain the state
structure and the luxuries of the court. At best, the masses, especially
the peasant farmers, benefited from the reflected glory of the court, more
just government, greater tranquillity and order, and protection against
the ambitions of adjacent kings. Of all Africa, only Egypt produced,
over a long period of time, sufficient wealth to support construction of
costly edifices and to maintain a large cadre of priests and learned men
who had the time and resources to produce major scientific and technological advances.

Still, the life of the Sudanic peasant was neither barren nor
stagnant. Over many centuries, his agricultural technology developed to
a point where it could wrest from the land the best living it afforded.
Starvation was extremely rare, and there were few poor. Many states
provided wise and equitable government. In those states with the greatest
access to wealth, such as the Hausa and Songhai states, formal education
was established and gradually spread outward from the court. In many
of the more affluent states, religion and the arts were encouraged, and an
atmosphere of culture and refinement became part of a national ethos.
Even in the poorest states, the peasant's life was tolerable and the arts
and crafts developed to high standards.

The Sudanic state almost universally began as the political organization for a single ethnic group, in which all the peoples spoke the
same language, shared a common culture, and traced their origin to a
real or legendary common ancestor. The peoples of the state usually
inhabited contiguous territory, but borders were usually not precisely
demarcated. Disputes between states often grew out of encroachments
by the peoples of one state onto the lands of another. Such encroachments were common because of the frequent use of "slash-and-burn"
farming practices, in which trees were felled, the debris burned, and the
land tilled until its fertility was exhausted. The farmers then shifted to
adjacent fields to repeat the process, returning to the original plots
after as much as ten or fifteen years.

Cyclical farming was supplemented by pastoral practices that also
required occasional moves to find better grazing lands. These agricultural

practices necessitated that each village be surrounded by a comparatively large area, much of which was unused for several years at a time.
Encroachments onto these surplus lands—prompted by droughts, simple
covetousness, or the need of displaced groups to relocate—led to disputes
between states.

Only rarely, in the very largest states, were armies professional
or standing. Normally they were formed from the men of each village,
clan, or vassal state who were called up when needed and sent home
when a campaign ended. Soldiers usually did not wear uniforms and each
bore the arms he preferred (spears and bows plus leather shields were
usual). Troops were normally not deployed according to professional
ideas of strategy and tactics.

Customs of warfare tended to be dictated by each campaign and
battle, and the dogged total-warfare practices of today's professional
soldiers were uncommon. Both the troops and their leaders often preferred retreat, even rout, to last-ditch stands. For them, war lacked the
glamour or deadly aura of modern times. The objectives of war
were to defend or seize territory and material possessions, not to win
victories for their own sake or to exterminate populations.

The needs of the Sudanic kings for wealth may have led to the
frequent conquest of neighboring states, and such conquests led in
turn to the formation of empires. The Sudanic empire was thus composed of several states, under the suzerainty of a strong conquering state.
The vassal kings (or appointed governors in some cases) were required
to pay tribute to the emperor, usually a portion of the state's taxes.
Other obligations included road maintenance and provision of troops for
the emperor's army and labor for special projects. Occasionally vassal
states provided the emperor with special goods, such as gold, copper, or
gems. In return, the emperor provided protection from aggression,
assistance in maintaining law and order, guarantees of trading rights
and safe passage for goods. Failures on the part of either party to abide
by his obligations were not infrequent and resulted in tensions, reprisals,
and occasionally, revolt.

Generally, Sudanic imperial systems did not require that conquered
states accept the language and culture of the ruling state. The empires
were thus enforced confederations. Their internal stability and longevity
depended upon many varying factors: the strength and leadership of
the emperor, the ambitiousness of vassal kings, the onerousness of tribute,
and the appeals and blandishments of rival imperial powers. Some
empires endured for long periods. Ghana, for example, seems to have
maintained internal cohesion for at least six centuries. Others were almost ephemeral, with strong vassal states successfully breaking away
from the empire within a few years of their conquest.

The states and the empires developed as opportunities for acquiring wealth increased and as new ideas and techniques of war, government, or commerce were adopted, either from internal innovation or from other peoples. Systems of professional government, under which tributary states were declared provinces, evolved in both Mali and Songhai. Administrators, appointed by the emperor because of their loyalty and ability, governed the provinces.

Islam—which brought with it new concepts of law, learning, and commerce—made its way into the Sudan across the great trans-Saharan camel caravan routes. Individual traders, usually of Berber or North African origin, established small settlements in the major trading towns of the sub-Saharan countries. Occasionally Arabs from the North African cities accompanied the caravans. As early as the tenth century, communities of these traders were established in several parts of the Sudan, especially in Tekrur and Ghana, in the west, and Kanem, in the east. A number of resident merchants lived in the communities with their wives (often local women) and slaves (usually purchased locally). Here, too, transients rested for weeks or even months after the arduous crossing of the Sahara.

Yet these Berber communities did not foster the immediate establishment of Islam. Many of the merchants who initially lived in them were not Muslims, for the Berbers themselves were slow to accept Islam. Besides, the Sudanic rulers carefully regulated the communities, and their people probably would have been barred from very energetic proselytizing even had they wished to seek converts. Islam's cultural and religious impact was thus limited and slow to develop. Probably the first Black Africans to accept Islam were slaves, attached to the merchants almost as family members. An occasional Negro merchant saw commercial advantage in accepting Islam or was genuinely persuaded of the efficacy of the new faith.

By the eleventh century, however, the kings themselves began to accept Islam. They employed Islamic merchants to advise them on ways of dealing with the traders and perhaps to keep records. The kings were impressed by the sophistication of these able aides. Once a king, accepted Islam, it often spread to his numerous relatives, his large household of slaves, and his leading lieutenants and vassals. Where Islam was adopted in such states as Tekrur and Kanem-Bornu, it seems to have been the religion of the court. The ordinary townspeople and the farmers of the countryside continued to practice the traditional religions of their own cultures. In the more powerful Sudanic states, there were often serious tensions between the traditionalists and the urban Muslims, with the kings torn between loyalties to their wealthy town supporters and the desires of the rural majority.

Even though Islam was introduced gradually, rarely penetrating into the ranks of the majority, its precepts had considerable influence on government. Kings who adopted Islam eventually altered the political structure under which they administered both their own and vassal states. Under Islamic influence, the kings appointed governors and local administrators, generals, judges, and tax collectors. Often coming from the ranks of foreign settlers or slaves, these officials owed their offices to the king and presumably had less opportunity or reason to organize revolts or to build up local support than did the hereditary kings, chiefs, and headmen of prior imperial governments. Law, drawn from the Koran and from centuries of Islamic experience elsewhere, was conveyed to the Sudanic kings by learned Muslims. It supplanted traditional law in the towns.

Many early visitors attributed all Sudanic achievements to Berber and Arab conquerors and to Islam. They were unaware, however, that many equally impressive states of the Sudan had had virtually no contact with Islam. And most states that had visible Islamic ties began to develop long before the advent of the new religion. Islam introduced many changes into a number of Sudanic states and empires, but it had nothing to do with their origins or their basic viability.

Islam had no effect on Sudanic art. The Sudanic tradition of sculpting in stone, bronze, clay, and wood extends back thousands of years. Islam's prohibition against making images of God has long carried over into a hostility toward sculpture, but this scarcely affected the tremendous productivity of Sudanic sculptors in every part of Africa. From their huts and benches have come a profusion of masks, figurines, statues, and abstract forms.

This artistic tradition spread as the Sudanic peoples settled new lands. As the cultures of each group differentiated so did the technique and inspiration of the art. Yet the basic preference for carving and molding wood, stone, or metal has persisted, as has the tendency to express the artist's conception of the subject rather than a detailed representation. Art was valued and appreciated by whole peoples, who saw it as an integral part of religious life and cherished belief systems. Several of the best modern European artists, such as Picasso and Modigliani, have acknowledged the inspiration they have received from Sudanic African sculpture.

The cultural characteristics of the western Sudan's Mande-speaking peoples, among whom so much of Sudanic civilization originated, provide a useful backdrop for a survey of the states that spread over sub-Saharan Africa. Originally the Mande-speaking peoples inhabited the area now covered by southeastern Mauritania, eastern Senegal, western Mali, and the inland regions of Guinea, Sierra Leone, and Liberia.

Over the past millennium, they migrated into many other parts of the Sudan. A few groups even established settlements in the forests of Sierra Leone, near the coast.

One of the most numerous peoples of the Sudan, the Mande-speakers are now dispersed over an enormous territory, extending far beyond their original homeland. In some areas they established their own cultures and autonomous states. In others, they adopted the cultures and languages of the peoples among whom they settled. But in both instances they spread Mande ideas of agriculture, religion, warfare, and political organization, further deepening the basic cultural homogeneity of the Sudanic peoples.

Mande-speaking peoples are more divided than those of some other language groups, largely because of extensive Mande conquest and settlement of new territories during the centuries of the Mali Empire. The most prominent Mande-speakers are the Malinke (sometimes called Mandinka or Mandingo), the Mende (who moved far to the south, in modern Sierra Leone, in the 16th century), the Soninke, the Susu, the Bambara, the Dyula, and the Dialonke. These groups speak separate Mande languages, although many are so closely related as to be nearer dialects than distinct tongues. Rarely do the Mande speakers differ from one another more than do the Spanish and Portuguese or the Norwegians and Swedes, and their cultural homogeneity is as great as their linguistic ties. Yet each of these tribes (later we shall see that the term "tribe" rather inaccurately describes the peoples in most of the western Sudan) has long had its own distinctive political structure, beliefs, traditions, and national consciousness.

The Mande peoples are Negroid. However, Berber intermixture with some groups, especially the Soninke, has produced some hybrid physical characteristics. In the areas where Berbers intermarried with the Soninke, one finds individuals with thinner lips, longer and sharper noses, wavy rather than tightly curled hair, and bronze complexions.

In many parts of the Sudan, people live in small villages or dispersed homesteads. The Mande, however, usually live in large villages and sizable towns each surrounded by fields that are tilled each day. Perhaps because of the wars that have wracked their lands over the past millennium or more, the Mande have long surrounded their towns with sun-dried brick or mud walls up to nine or ten feet high. Houses cluster together in compounds, each organized around a family head and his married sons. The houses are generally round with walls of sun-dried brick or mud and conical roofs of thatched straw. In some areas, especially in the northwest where the Soninke live, rectangular houses long ago replaced the more typical Mande round houses, and mud or brick roofs, supported by horizontal pole beams in the Berber and Arab style, replaced the thatched roofs.

Many Mande towns housed as many as ten to twenty thousand people, but villages and small towns with populations of five hundred to three thousand were more typical. A few of the towns that were strategically located to control large trading systems served as state capitals and had populaces of thirty to forty thousand. (See pages 303-04 for a description by Mungo Park, an eighteenth-century British explorer, of Segu, the Bambara capital.) The larger villages and towns became strong fortresses in times of war. Moats and pits lay outside the town walls. From parapets and towers, bowmen and spear throwers could defend the town against hostile armies.

The material possessions of the farmers and traders of the towns were limited. Furniture consisted of cots, rugs, and stools. Wooden or woven chests were used to store the better clothing and personal ornaments as well as the essential tools of Mande life. These included bows and arrows, spears, axes, hoes, scythes, baskets, a variety of household pots, and such utensils as grinding stones for making meal from millet and sorghum.

Despite his limited possessions, the average Mande was generally prosperous and sophisticated. The Mande (and most of the other peoples of the Sudan) wore skillfully woven cotton breeches in ancient times when the less prosperous peoples of the coast went naked or wore bark breech clouts. Tunics and sandals were common. Famine was almost unknown, and the diet of even the poorest farmer was adequate though plain. Millet, rice, or sorghum were the basic foods, with peppers and indigenous spices added for flavor. Among some Mande, milk from cattle and goats was drunk fresh or made into cheese. Kings, chiefs, the nobility, and the wealthy ate the same staples, but enjoyed more meat as well as imported delicacies such as dates and citrus fruits.

Class distinctions based on wealth and hereditary rank were a prominent feature of Mande society. The wealthier, higher-born Mande clearly lived better than the common farmers or craftsmen. They wore more expensive clothes, ate better foods, carried more and better weapons, and owned objects of art, imported books, timepieces, swords, daggers, copper utensils, and other locally or foreign-produced articles that the commoner could not afford.

The noble classes included the royal family (which was often numerous because polygyny was widely practiced) and a hereditary class from whose ranks were chosen kings, court officials, military leaders, and administrators of provinces and dominions; these, as well as members of subordinate royal families, owed fealty to the king. Added to this

Africa about A.D. 1000

hereditary hierarchy were others who achieved their positions by superior merit in trading, war, craftsmanship, or service to the king. Occasionally, slaves achieved freedom and superior status since they were frequently able to render distinguished service to the king or to leading nobles.

Like virtually all African peoples, the Mande-speaking peoples had a complex religious and belief system. They believed in a god who created both the universe and man and who laid down basic laws for natural and human behavior. But like most other Africans, they regarded the supreme being as relatively remote from daily affairs. Prayers and rituals were usually addressed to ancestors or unseen spirits as intermediaries between man and God. To the Mande, an ancestor, especially one who had lived a distinguished and pious life, was revered because he was thought to be closer to God than his living descendants could be. Yet the departed ancestor was considered still of the family and therefore able to understand the problems of his survivors.

Praying to deceased ancestors was a vital element in both religion and morality. A man who failed to live up to family obligations was thought to have betrayed trusts sanctified by his ancestors. If displeased, these ancestors could punish the offender, causing his crops to fail, his business to suffer, and his relations with his family and friends to deteriorate. If pleased, ancestors could direct good fortune into the affairs of the morally correct descendant.

The Mande peoples also believed that God had appointed a variety of spirits who dwelt in, or often visited, certain mountains, trees, rocks, and rivers. These spirits, it was believed, sometimes appeared in human form, especially in dreams. Usually, prayers and offerings were made to these spirits on special occasions, such as before crops were planted.

In general, the Mande peoples had a comparatively pragmatic philosophy of life. They believed that good behavior, prayer, and dutiful observance of rituals and offerings were the important substance of religion. Yet the more reflective and curious individuals pondered fundamental questions about human origins and the nature of the universe. The disdain shown toward African "paganism" by early Muslim visitors, and later Christians, was, and is, unjustified. The African religious systems are no less complex or intellectually sophisticated than those of other parts of the world, and there are many similarities between African and other religions. Mande and most other African religions rest on a very complex set of beliefs about God, the universe, the nature and destiny of man, the natural order, the stars, and the cosmic forces that God created.

The Mande have long been skilled farmers. They learned to cultivate millet and sorghum as long as three or four millennia before

Christ. The Mande long ago ceased to depend upon hunting and fishing. With their hoes and much patient labor, they built and sustained a good standard of living for themselves. As their skills developed, and especially as they learned to build dikes and earthen dams for irrigation, they were able to produce an agricultural surplus that supported kings and courts, specialized traders and artisans, and small standing armies that could be expanded during times of national need.

Before the introduction of corn and other foods from the New World, the chief Mande crops were millet, sorghum, cotton, groundnuts, rice, cow peas, okra pumpkins, watermelons, kola nuts, sesame seeds, and shea nuts (from which a kind of butter has long been produced). Supplemented by leafy vegetables and several wild fruits, these products provided an ample diet for the farmers of the Sudan. Some crops, such as cotton, kola nuts, sesame, and shea butter, were sought in trade by the Berbers of the desert and the peoples of the rain forests.

In Mande society, the work of farming is done primarily by the men. The women, however, harvest the crops and grow vegetables on small plots near the village. Each day during the season when the soil must be readied, the men march to their individual or family plots where they work until late afternoon. They clear the wild grasses and weeds, turn the topsoil, prepare ditches for drainage and irrigation, and plant seeds. Later, as the plants are growing, daily field work is unnecessary. During these periods, the men busy themselves building or repairing houses, making tools, performing labor or military service for the state, and closely following or participating in local government and village affairs.

Mande women have traditionally been hard workers. Their labors are more constant than those of the men since they must keep house, cook, tend children, trade for foodstuffs and domestic articles, tend the gardens, make pots and baskets, as well as harvest and process the crops. Though the men tend the cattle, sheep, and goats, the women care for the poultry which provides meat for the Mande diet.

Since soils in most parts of the western Sudan are easily depleted, the Mande shift plots after a year or two, leaving exhausted land to lie fallow. In some areas, both animal and human fertilizer are used to prolong soil fertility, but until modern times only a few groups rebuilt soils by crop rotation. Thus each Mande village must be surrounded by considerable acreage if it is to survive permanently. Land encroachment has been a traditional source of dispute and even war.

Few Mande villages can produce all the food and articles that their inhabitants use. Dried fish, fish oil, salt, lumber, kola nuts, and slaves have flowed for centuries into the busy village and town markets, while millet, sorghum, shea butter, cloth, stoneware, and other local products flow out in exchange. All but the smallest villages have areas set aside for markets. In the smaller towns, markets are open every six or seven days, but in the larger towns and cities they operate daily. In the smaller markets most sellers and buyers are Mande-speaking peoples of the locality; in the large, cosmopolitan markets both goods and merchants come from many parts of West and North Africa.

Until the twentieth century most of the buying and selling of goods in the village markets was on a barter basis; but in the large markets of the great trading cities, cowrie shells, bars of copper or iron, standardized weights of gold, strips of cotton, and even written drafts were often used as currency.

The trading proclivities of the Mande peoples were known throughout the Sudan. The Dyula, a Mande-speaking group composed of clan brothers from other Mande tribes (the Soninke are among the most numerous), established Sudanic trading routes that linked Tekrur in the far west to the Songhai and Mossi countries farther east. Individual Dyula traders and small trading associations carried goods of all kinds to all parts of the Sudan. As their trading system developed in the twelfth and thirteenth centuries, they acquired slaves in the various kingdoms with which they traded. The Dyula then purchased land and set their slaves to work on it. Thus Dyula caravans had their own bases in foreign kingdoms. Here they rested in homes tended by their slave settlers, secured provisions, and stored goods. These bases allowed the Dyula to operate their far-flung trading system in relative comfort and without total dependence upon local chiefs and farmers.

Both the short-distance, domestic trading systems of the Mande and other Sudanic peoples and the long-distance systems that the Mande helped to extend throughout the Sudan were connected with and stimulated by the great trans-Saharan system, which the Mande were also in a unique position to dominate. The several caravan routes that led across the Sahara, from oasis to oasis and waterhole to waterhole, brought large quantities of foreign goods into the Sudan and allowed large quantities of African goods to move from the Sudan into North Africa. The kings into whose markets these goods flowed, all along the southern edge of the Sahara, found both an opportunity for reaping profits, in customs duties and taxes, and a challenge in building strong governments and armies to protect the trade. Thus, it was in the western Sudan that great states first developed.

7 The Western Sudan

The western Sudan stretched from the Atlantic Ocean on the west, where modern Mauritania and Senegal are located, some thousand miles to the great bend of the Niger River in the east, in modern Mali. It includes the territories of the Songhai people and their once great cities of Gao, Jenne, and Timbuktu.

On the north the western Sudan stretches to the Sahara, and on the south, to the edges of the West African rain forest. Not an unusually vast region as African distances go, the western Sudan nevertheless includes more than one million square miles of sweeping grasslands. Nowadays its population numbers some fourteen or fifteen million and it encompasses Senegal, Mali, and Upper Volta, and major portions of Mauritania, Guinea, Sierra Leone, Liberia, Ivory Coast, and Ghana.

The peoples of the region speak many languages and dialects and are divided into dozens of tribes and ethnic groups. Their languages represent three quite different subfamilies of Congo-Kordofanian: the Atlantic, Mande, and Voltaic. In Mauritania and Mali intrusive small settlements of Berbers, owing fealty to the Negro states of the area, further add to the linguistic diversity.

Yet for all the diversity, there is considerable cultural and economic homogeneity in the entire western Sudan, and for centuries much of the region was unified under one or another powerful empire. All the peoples base their livelihoods on the Sudanic agricultural complex. Trade routes, for centuries an important factor in the area's economy, bind linguistically diverse people into a large and complex commercial system. Although each tribe or state is strongly conscious of its own unique heritage and identity, similar patterns of kinship, political organization, technology, and even religious belief add to the cultural homogeneity.

Several millennia of migrations, state expansion, and movements of small groups have created a patchwork of peoples. Mande speakers inhabit areas of the Songhai, Voltaic, and Atlantic peoples, and groups of these people have settled in Mande territory. Yet in general, people speaking Atlantic subfamily languages are found in the far west of the Sudan. The Mande speakers are found in the territories next to the east; the Songhai, east of the Mande on the Niger River; and the Voltaic peoples are centered on the headwater area of the Volta River and its tributaries, south of the Mande and Songhai.

In the far west, both in the grasslands of the western Sudan that reach the Atlantic in southern Mauritania and Senegal and in the forests near the coast in modern southern Senegal, the Gambia, and Guinea, live numerous ethnic groups who speak languages of the Atlantic subfamily. Among the most prominent are the Tukulor and their close kinsmen, the Fulani, the Wolof, the Serer, and the Temne.

Southeast of the Mande-speaking peoples live the peoples of the Voltaic language subfamily. They are divided into several states and a number of clans and tribes whose languages are related, sometimes closely, but who also cherish local traditions and affiliations. Among the most prominent are the Mossi, the Senufu, the Bobo, the Gurma, the Dagomba, and the Borgu.

Along the Niger River, north of the Voltaic peoples and east of the Mande peoples, live the Songhai people. The Songhai language is of a completely separate stock, the Songhaic, and the Songhai form one relatively homogeneous nation. Within the nation, people recognize the importance of their own clans and extended family groups, but they are also conscious of their Songhai identity.

Sudanic civilization early reached its flowering, aided by trans-Saharan trade, among the peoples of these linguistic and cultural divisions. In the international, long-distance trading system that developed between the Sudan and North Africa, two items stood out: gold from sub-Saharan Africa and salt from North Africa. In the Sudan and the forests to its south there is virtually no natural salt. Coastal peoples made salt from sea water, but this supply was distant and expensive. Slabs of salt, however, could be mined from plentiful natural deposits in the Sahara and transported by camel southward to the markets of the Sudan. Several important gold-producing areas were located south of the Sudan. The most productive of these were in modern Ghana and Guinea. In these areas, the indigenous Negroid peoples learned to mine the gold, digging shafts as deep as fifty feet, and to wash out nuggets from the sands of streams. The earliest gold miners may have been Mande-speaking peoples or peoples speaking Atlantic languages, but by the days of the Mali Empire, Ghana's successor, the Mande peoples controlled at least the production of gold. The exact locations of the gold mines, as well as information about who mined them and how, were closely guarded secrets.

By about the eighth century, when the earliest written records appear, a thriving trans-Saharan trade system had been developed. It centered on the great market towns of the Mande of the western Sudan and the Berber of the southwestern Sahara. To Walata, Tichitt, Kumbi Saleh, Awdoghast and many other towns that have long since vanished streamed dozens of Berber camel caravans each year. The caravans, sometimes up to ten thousand camels strong, carried slabs of Saharan salt, finely wrought daggers, timepieces, silks, jewelry, and fine cloths of the Mediterranean world. Into these cities came traders and artisans of the Sudan. They brought gold, leather, cotton, kola nuts, pots of shea butter, baskets of millet and sorghum, bars of iron, and slaves. Mande kings developed strong states, to regulate the brisk and voluminous trade.

Thus the fabled empire of Ghana began. Within a few centuries after Christ, Soninke kings, inhabiting the grasslands in the far west of the Sudan, gradually accumulated the power and the wealth to regulate the rich trade in their great market towns.

In all the western Sahara, caravans could follow only two consistently reliable routes and still find occasional oases. One such route originated in the city of Marrakesh in Morocco and terminated in the city of Tekrur, on the Senegal River, roughly two hundred miles inland from the Atlantic. This route crossed only a few small oases. The other route, much more heavily traveled, led through a part of the Sahara that had more frequent and reliable water holes. It originated in the Moroccan town of Sijilmasa, on the northern edge of the desert, and terminated in the great Berber market towns of Awdoghast and Walata. From these towns roads led to other trading centers throughout the land of Ghana. This route passed through the salt mining town of Taghaza, in Berber country, where heavy loads of salt were added to the goods from Morocco. A few hundred miles south of Taghaza, it was joined by another caravan route which originated in Tripoli and led through the central oasis of Tuat, in modern Algeria.

The route between Marrakesh and Tekrur ended in the land of the Tukulor peoples, who built a powerful state known to the ancient Arabs as Tekrur. Arabic sources from the eighth and ninth centuries refer to Tekrur with considerable respect, and as frequently as they refer to Ghana. The kingdom probably began between about the third and sixth centuries of the Christian era, at about the same time as Ghana. By the tenth century, Tekrur had lost its independence to Ghana and the kings of Tekrur were required (probably very unwillingly, judging by later events) to pay tribute to the emperor of Ghana. In the eleventh century, when the Almoravid army invaded Ghana, the king and most nobles of Tekrur had already accepted Islam. They eagerly allied themselves with the Almoravids against their Ghanaian overlords, and the troops of Tekrur probably played a significant role in Ghana's defeat and destruction.

After Ghana's collapse, Tekrur regained an independence that it maintained until the late thirteenth century. Then the Malinke peoples, building their Empire of Mali, invaded Tekrur, bringing it again into a tributary status.

Located in modern Mauritania, Tekrur was on the edge of the Sahara, and its people were in close contact with the Berbers of the desert and its steppes. Early in the Christian era, if not before, Berber cattle herders crossed the Senegal River to settle in the grasslands to the south. They accepted the rule of the Tukulor kings. The Tukulor, a Negroid people who have traditionally preferred grain farming to herding, developed a symbiotic relationship with the Berber pastoralists, exchanging their grains and farm products for Berber meat and cattle products. Eventually the immigrant Berber were absorbed into Tukulor culture, and a great deal of intermarriage took place. Thus originated the great Fulani peoples. For a thousand years or more, the Fulani divided into two closely related groups—the town Fulani, sedentary farmers and traders of ancient Tukulor stock, and the cattle Fulani, herders who stem from the ancient Berber-Tukulor merger. Among the Fulani, especially the cattle Fulani, Caucasoid racial influence can often be detected, even though they are a predominantly Negro people. The Fulani share a common language and culture and recognize their common origin and ties of kinship.

Tekrur was one of the earliest states of Black Africa to accept Islam. The town Fulani, who have for centuries migrated eastward across the Sudan, eventually became the Sudan's leading propagators both of Islam and of writing and learning. The cattle Fulani accepted Islam more slowly and have been less aggressive in spreading the faith.

Early in its history, Tekrur absorbed groups of Wolof and Serer peoples, themselves related culturally and linguistically to the Tukulor. For many centuries, these two groups seemed to live as willing subjects of Tekrur. But between the eleventh and fourteenth centuries, probably because of disagreements with both the Tukulor and the Malian governors of Tekrur, they began to migrate to the east and south. By the mid-fourteenth century, the Wolof had occupied a large area near the coast, between the Senegal and Gambia rivers, and had organized four small but powerful states that were able to resist the forces of Mali, still the most powerful imperial system in the Sudan. These states, Jolof, Walo, Cayor, and Baol, never united into a closely knit federation or empire, but their relations were sufficiently cordial so that they could aid each other against external threat. Jolof was considered the senior of the four states, and its king had precedence over the other three.

The Serer people had earlier settled on the plains of the highland of Futa Toro in modern Senegal. They lived side by side with the Tukulor and were ruled by them until the eleventh century. At that time, perhaps because of growing Islamic influence among the Tukulor, the Serer—who refused to accept Islam—migrated to an area between the Sine and Salum rivers in what is now southeastern Senegal. The Serer conquered the Mande-speaking tribes then inhabiting the Sine-Salum and settled the area. Within a century, however, powerful Malinke invaders also moved into the Sine-Salum, settling among the Serer as a ruling class. Gradually the Malinke were assimilated into Serer culture. They abandoned their own language but continued to form a ruling caste within the newly-created hybrid society. Between the thirteenth and fifteenth centuries the Serer-Malinke peoples prospered. Kings appeared as rulers of two small, highly structured but strong states, Sine and Salum.

Tukulor, Wolof, and Serer societies were highly stratified. Among the Serer, for example, there were a number of castes, some of which were subdivided into clearly delineated categories. At the top of the structure was the ruler-warrior caste, composed largely of the descendants of the Malinke immigrants. This caste, called the tiedo, subdivided into the "guelowar," or the nobles eligible for the kingship (only Malinke or the descendants of Malinke-Serer marriages were included); the "domibur," from which came minor chiefs of both Malinke and Serer descent; the warriors, who were part of the entourage of the king and chiefs; and the crown slaves, whose leader was a close adviser and aide to the king. Below the ruling caste came the freemen. They were the most numerous of all the castes and included mostly Serer farmers, followed by smaller groups of blacksmiths, leather workers, weavers, wood carvers, and griots (historians and bards). At the bottom of the social hierarchy were ordinary slaves.

Some Serer slaves were included in the ruling caste because they were considered affiliates of the king's family and thus under his direct protection. Most slaves were captives, taken in the wars with surrounding states or presented by these states to the kings of Sine and Salum as tribute. Slaves were not a despised group. They had clear rights, especially if they had attained high position in the king's service. Children born to slaves were still part of the slave caste, but they had more legally recognized rights than did their parents. They could not be sold, for example. In some of the Serer, Wolof, and Tukulor states that had long and successful military histories, the number of slaves increased more rapidly than the freeborn group, and slaves constituted a majority of the population. Slaves thus became more like serfs or bonded peasants, tilling the lands of the king and the nobles, maintaining their households, practicing various crafts, and undertaking business or diplomatic ventures for the king. Armies were often led by slave commanders or corps of elite and well-trained slave troops. In many cases, kings came to depend so heavily on talented and favored slaves that they were installed as governors and tax collectors in conquered territories.

The highly stratified Serer, Wolof, and Tukulor societies were not unique in the Sudan. Many Mande peoples, especially the Malinke and Soninke, were similarly organized. French visitors to Malinke country in the early nineteenth century reported that slaves outnumbered freeborn Malinke nearly three to one.

The histories of the Serer, Wolof, and Tukulor are closely interwoven, and even after the Wolof and Serer migrated out of Tekrur, intermittent contacts were maintained, sometimes amicable and sometimes hostile. All three peoples developed a formidable military capacity, based largely on swift-moving horse cavalry. They occasionally warred with each other as well as with strong parties of invaders. The histories of the Wolof and Serer are confined to the general area they inhabited, but the Fulani offshoots of the Tukulor played a role in the entire Sudan.

Although the Tukulor and their Wolof and Serer kinsmen had fashioned highly developed social, political, and economic systems, the Soninke people, who lived in the region where the most important trans-Saharan caravan route terminated, achieved a lustrous ascendancy through their great empire of Ghana. Even today Ghana inspires African intellectuals and political leaders as a crowning achievement of ancient Africa. The modern nation of Ghana, far distant from ancient Ghana's locale, chose its name to symbolize the resurgence of Black Africa to a new age of glory.

Actually, the Soninke kingdom that became Ghana was named Aoukar. Its kings were called ghana, meaning "war chief" in Soninke. Visiting Arabs, Berbers, and peoples from other parts of the Sudan used the king's title to refer to his kingdom, and by the ninth century, Ghana was recognized as the name of the great Black Kingdom below the Sahara.

Aoukar was situated on the grasslands north of the headwaters of the Senegal and Niger rivers. Its people inhabited the land as far north as the arid steppes of the Sahara's edge. There, no crops could prosper, and cattle, goats, and sheep of Berber pastoralists grazed each year after the rains had coaxed the sparse, wiry grasses into greenness. Farther south in Aoukar's territory, where rainfall was sufficient to support the cultivation of millet, sorghum, and other crops of the Sudanic complex, the Soninke developed their civilization.

Soninke country, not especially fertile compared to some more favored parts of the Sudan, supported a population that must have been at least several hundred thousand. It covered an area of some fifty to sixty thousand square miles in what is today the southeastern part of Mauritania, eastern Senegal, and western Mali. The Soninke, like most Mande peoples, lived in villages and towns rather than in dispersed homesteads. These settlements tended to cluster near the streams, lakes, and ponds that held water for some months after the annual rains. Because of the skill with which the Soninke preserved scant water supplies and raised good crops through the use of irrigation ditches, the kingdom was generally prosperous, if not bountifully favored. But strategic trade location added increments of wealth that early gave Ghana an advantage over other peoples of the western Sudan.

Salt, cloth, metalwork, silk, and other goods of North Africa flowed into Walata and Awdoghast, where teeming markets hummed with the bargaining of Berbers, Soninke, Dyula, Malinke, and other traders from both the Sahara and the Sudan. Into these two great markets, from smaller markets throughout Ghana, came smaller caravans of donkeys, each loaded with gold, pepper, kola nuts, elephant tusks, millet, sorghum, iron bars, and leather.

Astride the whole system of trade sat the king of Aoukar, the ghana, and his army of officials and tax collectors. Goods entering or leaving the kingdom were subject to carefully specified customs duties. In return for payment of duty, the palace troops and provincial conscripts protected the merchants against brigands and thieves. Cheating in the markets was forbidden, and royal edict required debtors to pay their creditors according to the terms of loan agreements.

Not all the products that passed through Ghana originated in the kingdom. Goods came from as far south as the forest region and from as far east as Songhai country, around Timbuktu and Jenne. Gold, Black Africa's most important product in those times, came from the land of Wangara, located in what is now the interior of Guinea. The local people mined the gold and traded it to Ghana's merchants through the ancient system of "dumb barter," described as early as the fifth century B.C. by Herodotus, who had heard of its use in other parts of the world. Soninke and Malinke merchants would arrive in Wangara, their donkeys laden with grains, leather, and cloth. Then they would set out their wares in neat piles along a stream or at the edge of a thicket. Beating their drums to announce their presence, they would then retire to some distance, while the Wangarans (probably a people related either to the Mande or to the Atlantic-language group) came out to inspect the goods. Beside each pile of goods the Wangarans would place the quantity of gold they were willing to exchange. If the merchants were satisfied, they would gather the bags of gold and withdraw. If the merchants felt the gold was insufficient, they would again retire, and the Wangarans would again come out and make a counteroffer.

In later times, long after the dissolution of the Ghana Empire, Malinke rulers established closer contact with the Wangarans and supervised the mining of gold on behalf of the emperor of Mali. But for centuries the source of the gold was kept secret. In Guinea, modern archaeologists have discovered numerous mining shafts, some as deep as fifty feet. Despite their avoidance of close contact with foreign merchants, the Wangarans were obviously a capable people, knowing both the value of their gold and how to mine it.

Although Ghana's rulers must have maintained accounts for the duties that flowed into the king's coffers, the empire never developed a system of writing. Thus, Ghana's history comes to us from carefully transmitted oral histories and from writings by early Arab historians and geographers, dating from the eighth century on.

The writings of the eighth-century Arab astronomer al-Fazari contain the earliest definite reference to Ghana. Al-Fazari called Ghana "the land of gold." The ninth-century Egyptian historian al-Hakan also mentioned the land of gold, and Ghana is found on the first important Islamic world map, which was produced in the ninth century by Mohammed Khwarizmi, a Persian geographer. Another Arab geographer, al-Ya'qubi, was the first to offer a description of Ghana. According to al-Ya'qubi's ninth-century account, "there is the kingdom of Ghana. Its king is mighty, and in his land are gold mines. Under his authority are various other kingdoms—and in all of this region there is gold."

References to Ghana appeared more frequently in books by Muslim scholars and travelers in the eleventh and twelfth centuries. The most helpful account that has been found is in al-Bakri's *Kitab al Masalik wa'l Mamalik,* written in Moorish Cordoba in 1067. Al-Bakri, regarded by modern researchers as an accurate reporter of his times, provides extremely useful information on Ghana's economy, its system of government and taxation, the magnificence of its court, and its trade and relationship with North Africa.

From al-Bakri's description and from linguistic and ethnological analysis, preliminary archaeological studies, oral histories, and information about trade in North Africa, historians have outlined Ghana's characteristics and history.

By the end of the tenth century, Ghana had conquered Tekrur, extending its territory all the way to the Atlantic Ocean. It had also incorporated a number of other states of the Mande-speaking peoples to the south and east of the Soninke state into the empire. In 990 Ghana captured the important Berber city of Awdoghast on the edge of the Sahara and thus established control of the caravan trade. During this period, when Ghana was at its peak of imperial expansion, it controlled a population of several million and a territory of roughly 250,000 square miles. It was a power no other African state was capable of challenging.

Although Ghana was in close contact with Muslim civilization, its culture remained purely Sudanic. Its capital, Kumbi Saleh, accommodated a large Muslim population concerned with the trans-Saharan trade, and Muslim ideas and skills were of great use to the kings of Ghana. But both the kings and the mass of people remained true to their own religion and way of life. The most vivid account of imperial Ghana at about the mid-eleventh century comes from al-Bakri:

> Ghana consists of two towns lying in a plain. One of these towns is inhabited by Muslims. It is large and possesses twelve mosques in one of which the people assemble for the Friday prayer. There are imams, muazzins and salaried reciters of the Koran as well as jurists and learned men. Around the town are wells of sweet water, from which they drink and near which they grow vegetables.

> The town in which the king lives is six miles from the Muslim one and bears the name Al Ghaba. The land between the two towns is covered with houses. The houses of the inhabitants are made of stone and acacia wood. The king has a palace and a number of dome-shaped dwellings, the whole surrounded by an enclosure like the defensive wall of a city. In the town where the king lives, and not far from the hall in which he holds his court of justice, is a mosque where pray the Muslims who come on visiting diplomatic missions. Around the king's town are domed buildings, woods, and copses where live the sorcerers of these people, the men in charge of the religious cult.

Al-Bakri also provides a classic portrayal of the pomp and majesty of the typical Sudanic kingship:

> The king adorns himself like a woman, wearing necklaces and bracelets, and when he sits before the people he puts on a high cap decorated with gold and wrapped in turbans of fine cotton. The court of appeal is held in a domed pavilion around which stand ten horses with gold embroidered trappings. Behind the king stand ten pages holding

shields and swords decorated with gold, and on his right are the sons of the subordinate kings . . . all wearing splendid garments and with their hair mixed with gold. On the ground around him are seated his ministers, whilst the governor of the city sits before him. On guard at the door are dogs of fine pedigree, wearing collars of gold and silver adorned with knobs . . . the royal audience is announced by the beating of a drum which they call "deba" made out of a long piece of hollowed-out wood. When the people have gathered his co-religionists draw near upon their kneees, sprinkling dust upon their heads as a sign of respect, whilst the Muslims clap hands as their form of greeting.

Al-Bakri also attests to the might of the king:

. . . The king who governs them at present . . . is called Tenkaminen; he came to the throne in A.H. 455. . . . Tenkaminen is the master of a large empire and a formidable power. . . . The king of Ghana can put 200,000 warriors in the field, more than 40,000 being armed with bow and arrow.

Al-Bakri's information on the size of the king's army is probably correct. But the king's forces were certainly not a standing army. More likely, the king had a thousand or so troops at his palace. These troops, drawn from slave ranks, were well armed, thoroughly trained and disciplined, and completely loyal to the king. They wore a kind of uniform that consisted of sandals, loose-fitting cotton breeches reaching to the knees, a sleeveless tunic, and a headdress of either cotton or leather, decorated with one or more feathers. Their weapons included iron-pointed spears, daggers and short swords, wooden battle clubs, and bows and arrows. By the ninth century, before al-Bakri's time, the king would also have had a small horse troop, armed with long lances.

These royal troops, whose only duty was to protect the king and lead his wars, trained rigorously and maintained themselves in peak physical condition. They were organized into companies and lived in special soldiers' compounds. Their commanders were close confidants of the king and often represented him on diplomatic missions to conquered and tributary rulers. In time of war, palace troops were augmented by the forces of lesser chiefs and vassal rulers and by slave and freemen conscripts from Soninke towns and villages; thus it was that the king could field the impressive army of which al-Bakri wrote.

The imperial might of Ghana was maintained for centuries on gold and other products of the empire, revenue from the trans-Saharan trade, and the considerable army the king had at his command. The kings of Ghana also probably controlled the empire's iron supply. There is no information available concerning the amount of difficulty the Soninke kings had in keeping restive subject kings quiet, but it is reasonable to suppose that occasional revolts and conspiracies took place. During the long centuries of Ghana's existence, there must also have been sporadic external threats, either from the Berbers to the north or from Sudanic states to the east. But until late in the eleventh century, no force was strong enough to threaten Ghana's power and territorial integrity.

Al-Bakri makes no mention of the war against Ghana that was commencing while he was writing his accounts. It was this war that sounded the death knell of the empire. In 1076, a powerful army of Almoravids, the desert Berbers who waged one of the greatest holy wars of the Muslim era, captured and sacked Kumbi Saleh, then the capital of Ghana.

Ghanaian seizure of Awdoghast in 990 and Ghana's subsequent control of the Saharan trade had resulted in a burning Berber hatred of Ghana. The Berbers, under Almoravid leadership, captured their city in 1054. Then, in alliance with the forces of rebellious Tekrur, they launched a determined campaign against the heartland of the great empire. It took twenty-two years to destroy the seat of empire, but Ghana was dealt a blow from which it never recovered.

The Almoravids spent their fervor in the conquest of Ghana, and were able to control the empire for only a few years. In 1087, their leader, Abu Bakr, was killed while attempting to suppress a revolt. The empire fell apart, never again to recover its former territory. For the next hundred and fifty years, the kings of various formerly subordinate states struggled against each other to pull the empire under their control. None succeeded.

Ghana, the first and most illustrious of the great Sudanic empires, lasted nearly a thousand years. It was eventually followed by Mali and Songhai, both even wealthier and larger in area, but these states never achieved the incredible longevity that was Ghana's greatest achievement. Today Ghana lives in the legends of the Sudan, but few great ruins mark its former glory.

Modern archaeologists have discovered the ruins of Kumbi Saleh, likely the great Ghanaian capital described by al-Bakri, about two hundred miles north of modern Bamako in Mali. The town that has been unearthed covers approximately one square mile; it contained a mosque, several large tombs, and a number of stone houses. Two square miles of cemeteries surround the town, attesting mutely to both its large size and its longevity. It may be the Muslim community of al-Bakri's account.

About ten miles from Kumbi Saleh, another site has been discovered. As yet it has not been explored, but it apparently lacks stone structures and thus may be the ruins of the indigenous town al-Ghaba described by al-Bakri.

Although the great empire of Ghana had broken into numerous

petty states of Soninke, Malinke, and Atlantic peoples by the early thirteenth century, Sudanic civilization was still very much alive. Other Sudanic states and empires were developing as far as two thousand miles from ancient Ghana in the Lake Chad-Nigeria regions. And in the western Sudan one of the petty Mande states was on the verge of creating the fabled empire of Mali, an even greater empire than Ghana.

Mali's history is better known than that of Ghana, partly because of the excellence of oral histories that the Mande griots handed down from generation to generation and partly because of fuller descriptions in the works of Arab scholars and travelers.

The empire of Mali was launched from the state of Kangaba, a small kingdom of the Malinke people. Their territory lay several hundred miles to the south of Ghana, in the western end of modern Mali near the modern Mali-Guinea border. The people of Kangaba were closely related to the Soninke of Ghana in language and culture. They had long been part of Ghana's empire, and Kangaban traders were closely involved in Ghana's gold trade. (Kangaba lies very near the ancient gold mines of Wangara.)

After Ghana's dissolution, Kangaba was independent for a brief period. Then, it was conquered by the kingdom of Kaniaga, a state of the Mande-speaking Susu people, located farther west between Kangaba and the country of the Tukulor and Wolof. Kaniaga, though a kingdom of peoples closely related to the Soninke and Malinke, was ruled by a dynasty of Tukulor origin. This dynasty stemmed from Tukulor warriors who left Tekrur after the Almoravid conquest of Ghana. They moved eastward and established control over several kingdoms of Mande speakers who had been loyal to Ghana. Under the leadership of these Tukulor conquerors (who soon were assimilated into Susu culture, as so often happened in Sudanic societies), Kaniaga itself began to expand. Its kings and nobles were eager to reunite the former parts of Ghana's empire under their own command.

The most powerful Kaniaga leader was King Sumaguru, who was also the hereditary ruler of Diara, another small Susu state adjacent to Kaniaga. In 1203, Sumaguru conquered Kumbi Saleh, the former capital of Ghana and still the most important Sudanic market center for the trans-Saharan trade. Sumaguru was soon frustrated in his attempts to cement his imperial successes by controlling the trans-Saharan trade. The Arab and Berber merchants, who had for so long traded in Kumbi Saleh, moved northward to the oasis city of Walata on the southern edge of the Sahara. There, beyond Sumaguru's reach, they built a new center of trade that soon eclipsed Kumbi Saleh. Nevertheless Sumaguru's conquests enabled him to exercise some degree of suzerainty over a number of states in the western Sudan. Among these was Kangaba, which had a serious interest in the Saharan trade because of its strategic position adjacent to the southern gold-producing lands.

Surviving legends portray Sumaguru as a harsh master, levying heavy taxes and ruthlessly disposing of members of royal families whom he regarded as potential threats to his imperial control. Mali legends mention, as a special source of resentment against Sumaguru, his capricious seizure of girls from the Malinke royal line as concubines, without respect to traditional marriage arrangements and guarantees. Probably Sumaguru's need for revenues, following the decline of Kumbi Saleh's importance, forced him to demand stiff taxes from his vassal kingdoms, and the growth of independent Kangaba power may have caused him to be especially harsh where that state was concerned.

A few years before 1230, Sumaguru led his armies against Kangaba, which was then ruled by Nare Famaghan, a member of the long-lived Keita dynasty. Sumaguru defeated Nare Famaghan, killed most of his sons, and drove him into exile. Two sons were spared: the lame and scorned Sundiata Keita and his half brother Dankaran Tuman, who was installed as king. Sudiata apparently had a stronger claim to the throne but was rejected. The young man fled the capital and went into exile outside Kangaba.

Eventually Sundiata returned to Kangaba, formed alliances with relatives and friends, and claimed the throne. As king he immediately launched successful campaigns against small surrounding states. Between 1230 and 1234, he built Kangaba into a powerful and burgeoning force, and declared it independent of any form of fealty to Sumaguru. Recognizing the threat to his fragile empire, Sumaguru marched against Sundiata, vowing to destroy him.

The two powerful forces met at the town of Kirina and fought a battle that is still celebrated in Sudanic legends. Sundiata's forces defeated Sumaguru's army and a few days later, Sundiata killed Sumaguru. This decisive encounter ended attempts to restore the empire of Ghana, and cleared the way for the even more renowned empire of Mali, as the kingdom of Kangaba later came to be known.

After seven centuries, Sundiata's triumph at Kirina is still recounted by the oral historians of the modern nations of Mali and Guinea. D. T. Niane, a modern Malian, has recorded Sundiata's story "as told by an obscure *griot* from the village of Djeliba Koro . . . in Guinea." The griot's account of the battle makes a moving story:

> The sun had risen on the other side of the river and already lit the whole plain. Sundiata's troops deployed from the edge of the river across the plain, but Soumaoro's [Sumaguru's] army was so big that other sofas remaining in Krina had ascended the ramparts to see the battle. Soumaoro

was already distinguishable in the distance by his tall headdress, and the wings of his enormous army brushed the river on one side and the hills on the other. . . . Sundiata did not deploy all his forces. The bowmen of Wagadou and the Djallonkes stood at the rear ready to spill out on the left towards the hills as the battle spread. Fakoli Koroma and Kamandjan were in the front line with Sundiata and his cavalry.

With his powerful voice Sundiata cried, "An gnewa." The order was repeated from tribe to tribe and the army started off. Soumaoro stood on the right with his cavalry.

Djata and his cavalry charged with great dash but they were stopped by the horsemen of Diaghan and a struggle to the death began. Tabon Wana and the archers of Wagadou stretched out their lines towards the hills and the battle spread over the entire plain, while an unrelenting sun climbed in the sky. The horses of Mema were extremely agile, and they reared forward with their fore hooves raised and swooped down on the horsemen of Diaghan, who rolled on the ground trampled under the horses' hooves. Presently the men of Diaghan gave ground and fell back towards the rear. The enemy center was broken.

It was then that Manding Bory galloped up to announce to Sundiata that Soumaoro, having thrown in all his reserve, had swept down on Fakoli and his smiths. Obviously Soumaoro was bent on punishing his nephew. Already overwhelmed by the numbers, Fakoli's men were beginning to give ground. The battle was not yet won.

His eyes red with anger, Sundiata pulled his cavalry over to the left in the direction of the hills where Fakoli was valiantly enduring his uncle's blows. But wherever the son of the buffalo passed, death rejoiced. Sundiata's presence restored the balance momentarily, but Soumaoro's sofas were too numerous all the same. Sogolon's son looked for Soumaoro and caught sight of him in the middle of the fray. Sundiata struck out right and left and the Sossos scrambled out of his way. The king of Sosso, who did not want Sundiata to get near him, retreated far behind his men, but Sundiata followed him with his eyes. He stopped and bent his bow. The arrow flew and grazed Soumaoro on the shoulder. The cock's spur no more than scratched him, but the effect was immediate and Soumaoro felt his powers leave him. His eyes met Sundiata's. Now trembling like a man in the grip of a fever, the vanquished Soumaoro looked up towards the sun. A great black bird flew over above the fray and he understood. It was a bird of misfortune.

"The bird of Krina," he muttered.

The king of Sosso let out a great cry and, turning his horse's head, he took to flight. The Sossos saw the king and fled in their turn. It was a rout. Death hovered over the great plain and blood poured out of a thousand wounds. Who can tell how many Sossos perished at Krina?

After Sumaguru's defeat, Sundiata added many states to his empire and put the imperial economy on a sound footing. Although Sun-

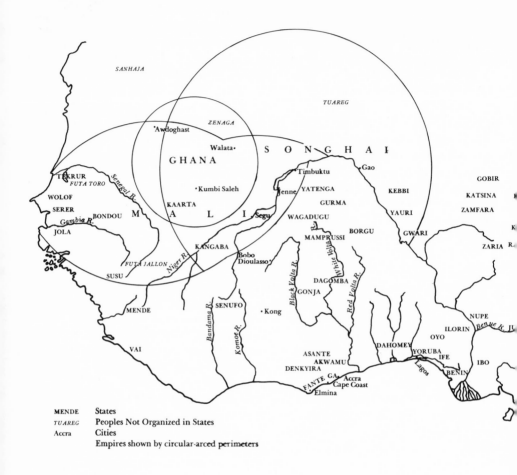

SANHAJA

TUAREG

ZENAGA

'Awdoghast

Walata·

GHANA

S O N G H A I

Gao

GOBIR

TEKRUR
FUTA TORO

·Timbuktu

WOLOF

·Kumbi Saleh

Jenne

YATENGA

KEBBI

KATSINA

SERER

KAARTA

GURMA

ZAMFARA

Gambia R.

BONDOU

M   A   L   I   Segu

WAGADUGU

YAURI

JOLA

BORGU

GWARI

MAMPRUSSI

ZARIA R.

KANGABA

Bobo
Dioulasso·

FUTA JALLON Niger R.

SUSU

DAGOMBA

GONJA

MENDE

SENUFO

·Kong

NUPE

ILORIN Benue R. II

VAI

OYO

DAHOMEY

YORUBA

ASANTE
AKWAMU

IFE

IBO

DENKYIRA

GA Accra

BENIN

FANTE Cape Coast

Elmina

MENDE	States
TUAREG	Peoples Not Organized in States
Accra	Cities
	Empires shown by circular-arced perimeters

West African States, Empires, and Cities, 1000-1800

diata founded Mali, his royal line, the Keitas, had ruled Kangaba for three centuries before him. And the Keita dynasty continued to rule Mali for at least two centuries after Sundiata's death.

The first Keita king about whom anything is known was Barmandana Keita. Legends claim that he accepted Islam in 1050 when, after a long drought, he was told that rains would come if he acknowleged Allah. According to tradition Barmandana's acceptance of Islam did end the drought, and the people of the kingdom became convinced of his divine attributes.

Little is known about the Keita kings after Barmandana. They were evidently Muslims, and at least a few are believed to have made the pilgrimage to Mecca. Their reigns were uneventful until the time of Nare Famaghan and his son Sundiata. But from that time onward, the Keitas distinguished themselves in West African history.

Sundiata reigned from 1230 to 1255. He established firm control over the flow of gold across the Sahara and made himself master of the trans-Saharan trade. His capital, Niani, became an important trading and financial center, and trade routes through the empire again became safe. By the time of Sundiata's death, Mali stretched securely as far as Tekrur in the west to the great bend of the Niger in the east, and from the desert's edge on the north to the Mossi states of the Voltaic peoples on the south. The cities of Timbuktu and Jenne were part of the empire, and were already emerging as important trading centers.

Following Sundiata's death, his son Mansa (emperor) Uli reigned for fifteen years. He not only held the empire together but expanded its borders and strengthened it internally. Mansa Uli completed the conquest of Songhai by capturing Gao, its capital city, which was located farther down the Niger from Timbuktu and Jenne. Within fifty years, however, Songhai forced its Malinke governors out of Gao.

Mansa Uli's death in 1270 was followed by fifteen years of weak rule by several kings of the Keita line, during which only the strength of the slave-led standing army kept the empire intact. Slave army commanders (ranked, as in Serer society, with the highest class of men in the kingdom) grew tremendously powerful, and in 1285 one of them, Sakura (whose origins are unknown), deposed the Keita king and seized the throne. Sakura was a man of strong resolution and was popular enough in Malinke circles to exercise vigorous leadership. During his reign, a number of rebellious vassal chiefs were punished, bringing relative quiet to the empire, and Mali's forces marched into Tekrur, forcing its Tukulor king to swear fealty to Mali. Sakura's troops also marched into Berber territory in the Sahara and established garrisons at several mines that were the chief suppliers of copper in the trans-Saharan trade.

Sakura was assassinated in 1300 while returning from his pilgrimage to Mecca, and a new Keita was elected to the throne. The Malinke, like most Sudanic peoples, "elected" their kings. Selection was made from one or another leading class or clan. Several powerful nobles, acting officially as kingmakers, met and agreed upon the claims of one candidate, usually from a field of several contenders. In Malinke society, the successful contender was widely accepted by noble and commoner alike. In some other Sudanic societies, however, the election of a king often touched off a bitter armed struggle, during which the named contender was expected to prove his right to the throne by defeating his rivals.

The most illustrious Keita king came to the throne in 1312, when Mansa Kankan Musa was chosen to rule. In a relatively brief reign, between 1312 and either 1332 or 1337, Mansa Musa made Mali into one of the world's largest empires. He spread its fame beyond the Sahara, as far as the capitals of Europe. Musa sent a powerful Malian army into Tekrur because the king there had failed to pay the required tribute. He subdued not only that state but most of the Tukulor and Wolof areas to its south. With this campaign, Mali's frontier stretched to the Atlantic Ocean. Musa also recognized the vital importance of the great northern Berber trading towns to Mali's economic prosperity. After a campaign of several years, most of the important Berber cities of the western desert were under Mali's control: Agades, Arawan, Tichitt, Tadmekket, Walata, and Takedda. Mali garrisons were established in several of these cities, giving Musa and his successors tighter control over the lucrative Saharan trade than Ghana had ever had. Mali's northern frontier, during Musa's reign, extended into much of modern Mauritania and southern Algeria.

In the east, Mansa Musa squelched threatened rebellions in the Songhai cities of Timbuktu and Gao and sent armed parties down the Niger beyond Gao to establish trading contacts with the prosperous Hausa states, located in modern Nigeria. The peace and security that he was able to guarantee within his vast empire, which during Musa's time was roughly twice as extensive as ancient Ghana and had a population that numbered somewhere between five and ten million, became one of Musa's most lauded accomplishments.

By the fourteenth century, Islam had become deeply entrenched among the nobles of many states of the Sudan, and the Mali Empire, despite its remoteness, was known far and wide in the Islamic world.

Twelve years after Mansa Musa's death, Ibn Battuta, a Berber from North Africa, visited Mali and described the state of affairs there. Ibn Battuta easily rivals Marco Polo as a world traveler. He left vivid accounts of his experiences in West Africa, India, China, and the lands in between. After describing the arduous and dangerous crossing of the

Sahara, Ibn Battuta summarizes his impressions of life in Mali's capital (probably Niani):

My stay at [the capital of Mali] lasted about fifty days; and I was shown honor and entertained by its inhabitants. It is an excessively hot place, and boasts a few small date palms, in the shade of which they sow watermelons. Its water comes from underground waterbeds at that point; and there is plenty of mutton to be had. The garments of its inhabitants . . . are of fine Egyptian fabrics. Their women are of surpassing beauty, and are shown more respect than the men. The state of affairs among these people is indeed extraordinary. Their men show no signs of jealousy whatever; no one claims descent from his father, but on the contrary from his mother's brother. A person's heirs are his sister's sons, not his own sons. This is a thing which I have seen nowhere in the world except among the Indians of Malabar. But those are heathens; these people are Muslims, punctilious in observing the hours of prayer, studying books of law, and memorizing the Koran. Yet their women show no bashfulness before men and do not veil themselves, though they are assiduous in attending the prayers. Any man who wishes to marry one of them may do so, but they do not travel with their husbands, and even if one desired to do so her family would not allow her to go. . . .

The Negroes possess some admirable qualities. They are seldom unjust, and have a greater abhorrence of injustice than any other people. Their sultan shows no mercy to anyone who is guilty of the least act of it. There is complete security in their country. Neither traveler nor inhabitant in it has anything to fear from robbers. . . . They do not confiscate the property of any white man who dies in their country, even if it be uncounted wealth. On the contrary, they give it into the charge of some trustworthy person among the whites, until the rightful heir takes possession of it. They are careful to observe the hours of prayer, and assiduous in attending them in congregations, and in bringing up their children to them. On Fridays, if a man does not go early to the mosque, he cannot find a corner to pray in, on account of the crowd.

Mansa Musa's greatest fame outside Mali arose from his pilgrimage to Mecca in 1324. This expedition excited the attention of the entire Islamic world because of its size, pageantry, and enormous wealth. Musa's arrival in Cairo was preceded by five hundred slaves, each carrying a six-pound staff of gold. Next came Musa and his retainers, followed by a caravan of one hundred camels, each carrying three hundred pounds of gold. Hundreds of other camels carried food, clothing, and other supplies.

Mansa Musa made a great point of refusing at first to call on the sultan of Cairo, as protocol required. Visitors were required to prostrate themselves before the sultan, and Musa claimed this would be impossible for an emperor of his rank and power. He finally agreed to a face-saving compromise in which he prostrated himself before the sultan as the agent of Allah, not as a mundane ruler. The wisely appreciative sultan immediately recognized Mansa Musa as an equal and had him sit beside him for a long discussion.

Mansa Musa's generosity in Cairo won him much esteem, but his largesse was so rich that his gold caused a severe period of inflation. Some twelve years later al-Omari, a Cairo administrative official, offered a vivid description of the effect of Mansa Musa's visit:

> This man [Mansa Musa] spread upon Cairo the flood of his generosity: there was no person, officer of the court, or holder of any office of the Sultanate who did not receive a sum of gold from him. The people of Cairo earned incalculable sums from him, whether by buying and selling or by gifts. So much gold was current in Cairo that it ruined the value of money. . . . Let me add that gold in Egypt had enjoyed a high rate of exchange up to the moment of their arrival. The gold mitqal that year had not fallen below twenty-five drachmas. But from that day onward, its value dwindled; the exchange was ruined, and even now it has not recovered. The mitqal scarcely touches twenty-two drachmas. That is how it has been for twelve years from that time, because of the great amounts of gold they brought to Egypt and spent there.

Perhaps because of his trip to Egypt and Arabia, Mansa Musa also had an appreciation of the world beyond the lands he had so regally brought under his rule. From his travels, he brought back to sub-Saharan Africa many scholars and men of talent, including as-Saheli, an architect who was commissioned to build new mosques at Gao and Timbuktu and a palace for the emperor. Musa also sent ambassadors to Morocco and Egypt and had agents in several North African cities.

Mansa Musa had brought Black Africa to the attention of the Mediterranean world more vividly than any other Sudanic ruler. European scholars and traders of the day were very much aware of his empire. European maps of Africa, from at least 1375 onward, carried a large drawing of Mansa Musa in the area of western Africa, and the whole western Sudan was labeled "Rex Melli" or "Musa Mali." Excited by the tales of Mali's gold, Portuguese sailors visiting the Atlantic Ocean coasts of West Africa in the fifteenth century eagerly sought contact with the empire, unaware that even Mali had never developed direct contact with the kingdoms of the dense forests near the coast.

Mansa Musa's reign was followed by a very brief reign by his son Maghan. Maghan was succeeded by Musa's brother, Suleiman, another able and successful leader. Suleiman kept the empire intact, except for Songhai. He continued to attract Muslim scholars and learned men to Mali and refined the systems of law, government, and economics, He reigned until 1359, and was the last of the Keita dynasty to achieve glory for Mali.

Mali continued as a strong empire until about 1400. Then a process of irreversible decline began. Gao seceded from the empire, clearing the way for the growth of the Songhai Empire. The Berbers and their kin, the Tuaregs, soon recaptured their cities of the desert and eventually captured Timbuktu and Walata. Tekrur and its Wolof neighbors rebelled and regained their freedom, and the Wolof began to build a strong group of states that could withstand future imperial ventures. Mali's deterioration was gradual, continuing throughout the fifteenth century and into the sixteenth. In 1546 the Songhai, who had been steadily absorbing chunks of Mali's empire, entered the capital, Niani, and sacked it. By the early seventeenth century, Mali was dead as an empire. Its king ruled only a small area around the village from which the empire was launched.

Just as Mali had begun as a small state within the great empire of Ghana, the powerful and wealthy empire of Songhai grew from what had once been part of Mali. Songhai, covering a vast territory at its peak of growth, was in many ways the pinnacle of development for Sudanic civilization.

The heart of the Songhai Empire was its capital city of Gao and the surrounding area southeast of the great bend of the Niger River. Fertile and well watered, Songhai also lay at the southern end of several important trade routes from North Africa. From its founding it was a strong state and Songhai successfully resisted conquest for centuries, except for a fifty-year interlude under Mansa Musa's reign.

The Songhai people are not closely related to their neighboring Sudanic peoples, and their language is of a different stock. They moved to the lands they now occupy in the seventh and eighth centuries, coming from a considerable distance down the Niger from what is now Hausa country. Their first capital was a town called Kukya. From here, in the seventh century, groups of Songhai fishermen ventured northward and colonized Gao. In the eleventh century, the southeastern Songhai, who were farmers, conquered their own fishermen kin in Gao, and made that city the capital of a consolidated Songhai state.

According to Songhai legend, the king who established the capital at Gao was named Kossoi. He is said to have been the first Songhai Muslim king. Kossoi, the legends hold, was the fifteenth king of the Dia line, which was founded at Kukya by a Berber chieftain whom the Songhai accepted as king. Some of the Songhai legends, including the story of Dia Kossoi's conversion to Islam, have been corroborated by the discovery of several ancient tombstones of Spanish marble. Arabic inscriptions on the tombstones indicate clearly that by the eleventh century Gao was ruled by Muslim kings, and was in trade contact with North Africa.

Ghana and Mali had benefited enormously from control of the

trans-Saharan trade in the western part of the Sudan. The Songhai profited from trade located farther east. A great caravan route originates in the city of Gao and makes its way through the central Saharan oasis cities of Tamanrasset, Ghat, and Murzuk to Cyrenaica in Libya. From there, other routes lead eastward to Egypt and westward to Tripolitania. Gao, along with its sister city of Timbuktu, early became the entrepôt for goods from a vast African region that now is covered by portions of Sierra Leone, Liberia, Ivory Coast, Ghana, Upper Volta, Mali, and Nigeria. In Gao, the Dias set up their rule.

The Dia dynasty continued to rule Songhai until the fourteenth century, and Songhai grew strong and prosperous under them. The only setbacks were the subjection of Timbuktu and Jenne to Mali rule and the conquest, by Mansa Musa, of Gao and the rest of the Songhai state in 1325. Perhaps because of Songhai resentment at the loss of their independence, the Dia line was deposed in 1335. A new king of the Sunni (from the title assumed by the new king) dynasty was elected. Like the Dias, the Sunnis were Muslim. They must have been acceptable to Mali, but events soon showed that they possessed both the will and the popular support to reassert Songhai independence. In 1375, after several years of growing tension, the troops of Suleiman-Mar, the second king of the Sunni line, expelled the Malinke from Gao and drove them out of most of Songhai's territory.

For nearly a century after it cast off Malian domination, Songhai had intermittent conflicts with neighboring peoples, but no serious defeats or territorial expansion occurred. Then, in 1464, Sunni Ali Ber came to power, and Songhai rise to greatness began.

Sunni Ali ruled Songhai for twenty-eight years, until 1492. During most of his reign he was on the march with his troops, consistently defeating all who challenged his might. He built Songhai's military strength around a cavalry force, using horses imported from North Africa. He conscripted troops from the Songhai and vassal states and organized a navy of war canoes that plied up and down the Niger.

Ali waged his first campaigns against the Mossi peoples of Yatenga, to the south, who had for years terrorized Timbuktu and the Songhai agricultural peoples along the Niger. He defeated the Mossi in a series of battles and pushed them relentlessly back into Yatenga. He then turned his attention to the fierce Tuareg (a Berber nation of the central Sahara), who had raided the Niger territories for years, and who had occupied Timbuktu. Ali drove the Tuareg from Timbuktu, and executed or exiled many of the Muslim leaders of the city for their compliant collaboration with their Tuareg overlords.

A scholar of Timbuktu, as-Sadi, in his work the *Tarikh al-Sudan*, depicts Sunni Ali as a brutal and harsh tyrant. Ali's treatment of the leaders of Timbuktu was cited as proof of his cavalier attitudes toward Islam, and his disdain of Islamic law and civilized behavior. It is more likely, however, that Ali's ruthlessness was deliberate. Firmly, he attempted to unify the peoples of Songhai, upon whom he depended for his strength, and who were neither Muslim nor friends of the cities.

By the time of his death in 1492, Ali had converted Songhai into a true empire, greatly expanded in territory, unified and at peace within, and strong enough to defend itself easily from external threat. All this was a great accomplishment, especially since Songhai had been internally divided when he assumed power.

Sunni Ali had been able to win the strong support of the common people and the lesser leaders of the rural areas, while still maintaining a measure of cooperation with the urbane townspeople. It is unlikely that he could have unified the kingdom and expanded the empire so greatly without support from both the urban Muslims and the rural farmers and fishermen who clung to traditional religious beliefs. He was unable to abolish the differences that brought disunity, but he was able to submerge them in his drive for a great imperial destiny for Songhai.

Sunni Ali's son, Sunni Baru, came to the throne after his father's death, but refused to accept Islam, instead proclaiming his allegiance to Songhai's own God and religion (which had many similarities to the Mande faith). The Muslims of the cities regarded him as a dangerous tyrant and began almost immediately to plot his downfall.

Sunni Baru was deposed after only 14 months of rule by Muhammad Touré, a soldier who was to become the most brilliant ruler in Songhai's history. Touré, who assumed the title "askia" (general), was a Soninke who had distinguished himself in military service to Sunni Ali. He was a devout Muslim, a famed general, and a great favorite among the learned and wealthy urban peoples of Gao, Jenne, and Timbuktu. Their support enabled him to depose the despised Sunni Baru and claim the throne on behalf of a new dynasty, rooted firmly in the cities.

Askia Muhammad Touré was both an inspired administrator and a brilliant general. He quickly adapted the tenets of Islamic law and administration to Songhai. The country was divided into a new series of provinces, each with a professional administrator as governor.

Muhammad gathered around him a group of distinguished Islamic legal experts and judges ("cadis") to ensure that Islamic law applied uniformly to the entire kingdom. Even non-Muslim Songhai received just and equal treatment under the new legal system. Taxes were adjusted to reduce the burden on the commoners, and provincial administrators were required to govern justly and fairly.

With the renaissance of Islam and the peace that soon was established in Songhai, Islamic scholars and visitors flocked to the state's three

great cities. At that time Gao was the largest Songhai city and had a ·
population of around 40,000, Jenne's population was perhaps 20,000,
and Timbuktu had about 25,000 residents. The Islamic scholars who
affiliated with the numerous mosques of the cities used them as schools
for teaching reading, writing, philosophy, medicine, law, and government. By the sixteenth century the mosques had become universities,
in the medieval sense.

With internal unity reestablished, Askia Muhammad turned his
attention to territorial expansion and pacification efforts. His first campaigns were successfully directed against the Tuareg nation of Berbers.
Muhammad's cavalry was the backbone of his formidable army. It consisted of at least four or five thousand horses, mounted by soldiers who
were mostly slaves of high status with long years of experience under
Muhammad. Swift and disciplined, the Songhai cavalry, which had been
feared throughout the Sudan under Sunni Ali, seemed undefeatable.

After the conquest of the Tuareg lands, and the installation of loyal
Songhai governors and troops there, Muhammad turned his attention
against another old enemy, the Mossi states of Yatenga and Wagadugu,
located in what is today Upper Volta. As early as 1338 Mossi troops
had sacked Timbuktu. Although Sunni Ali had driven them back into
Yatenga, within a few years their rapidly charging horsemen were again
raiding the peaceful farms and herds along the Niger. Inexorably, the
Songhai army drove the Mossi horsemen back into their own country.
Muhammad's Songhai were the first foreign troops known to have
fought successfully in Yatenga territory. They contented themselves
with ravaging a part of the countryside, then marched back to the Niger.
The Mossi, though not destroyed, avoided the Songhai territory along
the Niger for decades.

Askia Muhammad built the Songhai Empire into the largest and
most powerful force in the western and central Sudan. His armies pushed
the borders of the declining Mali Empire back to the Malinke heartland. It is believed that Songhai troops seized Niani, Mali's capital,
at least briefly. In the east, they conquered several Hausa states, and
fought a few inconclusive battles with the only Sudanic force that could
match their strength, the army of the great Kanem-Bornu Empire, based
far away in the Lake Chad region. Control of the lands along the Niger,
from Malinke to Hausa country, freedom from raids by Tuareg and
Mossi, and the rule of Songhai governors stationed far into the Sahara,
made the Songhai Empire a vast commercial power as well as a political
and military force.

Askia Muhammad made the traditional pilgrimage to Mecca, where
he was officially recognized as Caliph of the Western Sudan by the sharif
of Mecca, the spiritual ruler of all Islam. By virtue of this appointment,

Muhammad was able to claim the allegiance of all Muslims from Songhai westward to the Atlantic. The military conquests he had made in much of the region were thus cemented.

In 1528, when he was about 80, Muhammad was deposed by his son, Musa, who secluded him from contacts with Songhai leaders. Sadly and ignominiously, Muhammad, now blind and feeble, ended a long career as one of the most brilliant and enlightened rulers ever to appear in Black Africa.

The Askia dynasty continued throughout the sixteenth and seventeenth centuries. Most of its rulers were relatively undistinguished. The only Askia who approached Muhammad greatness was Askia Dawud, who became king in 1549. In a thirty-three-year reign, Dawud did much to restore the luster of the empire. When he died, the borders of the empire were extended as far as those set by Muhammad. Administration of the provinces had been strengthened, and new respect for Islamic law was instilled in the land.

A combination of weak leadership on the throne and growing rebelliousness in the conquered states caused Songhai to suffer ill fortune almost immediately after Askia Dawud's death. The Hausa states rebelled and regained full independence. The Tuareg again raided Songhai towns and villages and eluded the attempts of Songhai troops to punish them. And the Mossi, no threat for a century after Askia Muhammad's campaigns against them, again began to harass Songhai from the south.

In 1591 an army set forth from Morocco on a long march across the Sahara to attack Songhai and seize the vast stores of gold it was thought to possess. Led by a Spanish Christian named Judar, the army consisted of some six thousand ill-assorted but effectively armed men: Spanish Muslims, captured Christians from Europe, and Moroccans. Armed with arquebuses, primitive guns that were the most powerful weapons of the day, and even a few cannon, the men of the Moroccan army knew that they must conquer or perish when they reached Songhai. Only a thousand of them reached the Sudan in condition to fight, but with their weapons this was enough.

The Songhai emperor, Askia Issihak, assembled a force that was numerically far superior to the Moroccans. He marched to meet them as soon as word of their coming reached him, but the firepower and discipline of Judar's little army forced the Songhai army to retreat. In battle after battle the Songhai suffered heavy casualties. Judar captured Timbuktu and then Gao. Issihak's weakened army was reduced to a fugitive force seeking safety far down the Niger.

Although Judar eventually dispatched some gold to Morocco, the vast riches that had been expected never materialized. Morocco gained

Timbuktu, with the great mosque of Sankore in the background.
(From a midnineteenth-century drawing by Heinrich Barth.)

little from its daring conquest, but Songhai suffered much. Judar and his successors were able to maintain control over the main Songhai towns and the former empire's heartland. But they were unable to restore its full territory or its internal cohesion. Songhai troops, operating as guerrilla forces, continued to raid their conquerors from the countryside for many years. Gradually, Songhai degenerated into city-states, while the ruling group from Morocco slowly was absorbed into the local population.

The Voltaic peoples and their strong and prosperous states of Mossi, Yatenga, and Gurma, were the only polities of the western Sudan that successfully resisted absorption into Ghana, Mali, or Songhai. The homeland of the Voltaic peoples lies largely in what is now Upper Volta. From Timbuktu and Gao to the beginning of Mossi country is only two to three hundred miles. But the intervening country is dry and steppelike, inhabited mainly by nomadic Berber herders. About two hundred miles southeast of Timbuktu, the land rises gradually to a low plateau, which is just high enough to benefit from slightly heavier rainfalls and to support both natural grasses and cultivated grain. From this plateau, the two streams that combine to form the Volta River originate. Here the Mossi peoples, the most numerous and best organized of the Voltaic peoples, made their home.

Today the Voltaic people number about seven million, and are more populous than the Mande. Their ranks, however, have been swelled over the centuries by immigration of Mande-speaking peoples, as well as other Black Africans, from the rain forests to the south. It is difficult to estimate whether they or the Mande peoples were more numerous in the past. Whatever the case, the Voltaic people are evenly spread over about 100,000 square miles in what is one of the western Sudan's more densely populated regions.

Although the languages and dialects of the Voltaic subfamily are quite distinct from the Mande subfamily, the cultures of the two groups are broadly similar. Both practice similar agricultural methods and grow the same crops. Generally, Voltaic and Mande dress is the same. Cotton is widely used for the breeches and tunics of the men and the long shifts of the women. Both peoples have traditionally built round houses of dried mud with thatched roofs. Both cluster their houses in compounds. Typically, the Voltaic peoples live in dispersed homesteads rather than in towns and villages and even the villages where the kings resided were small by Mande standards.

For defense, the Voltaic peoples depended more on mutual aid than on fortified towns. When an enemy threatened (a rarer occurrence than in Mande country), the call went out to a large number of compounds. From miles around, the men, both on foot and on horse, hastily assembled to repel the intruders. As the Songhai invasion of Askia Muhammad proved, this system was a good one. Sudanic troops found it difficult to deal with an enemy that rose up from every homestead, determined to defend homes and crops with as much will as professional soldiers.

Not all the Voltaic peoples were organized into states, as was the fashion in most of the western Sudan. Five states arose among them: Yatenga and Wagadugu of the Mossi, Gurma of the Gurma people, Mamprussi of the Mamprussi people, and Dagomba of the Dagomba people. Of the five, the first three were in the area that now constitutes Upper Volta, while the latter two were located in the northern region of modern Ghana. These states were small. Their populations consisted only of the peoples of the king's own ethnic group. As much as half the Voltaic peoples lived outside the borders of the states and were governed mostly by local headmen, with an egalitarianism not usually found in the western Sudan. There is no record of aggressive expansionism on the part of the states, nor of major wars among them. Both the Voltaic states and the decentralized clan and family rules were remarkably stable and enduring. Yatenga and Wagadugu were founded in 1170 and 1050, respectively. They maintained their governments intact until French conquest at the beginning of the twentieth century, and even today the kings command the deep respect of their people within the modern government of Upper Volta.

In keeping with decentralized and egalitarian patterns of government, there was relatively little social stratification among the Voltaic
peoples. Although slavery was widespread, only those Voltaic peoples
who developed strong monarchical states—the Mossi, Gurma, Mamprussi,
and Dagomba, most notably—also developed castes and hereditary no-
bilities. In those states, whose kings were considered divine rulers of the
characteristic Sudanic pattern, social stratification was pronounced, especially around the court.

The Mossi kings of Wagadugu and Yatenga, like those of other
Voltaic states, headed elaborate courts. Well-organized and thoroughly
trained slaves guarded the king, the royal family, and the household.
The kings had numerous wives, but most of them were dispersed
throughout the kingdom in subpalaces, each surrounded by eunuchs.
Several provincial governors and a number of district chiefs, most of
whom were trusted slaves, acted as tax collectors and intermediaries with
the hereditary local chiefs and headmen. District officers were appointed,
but governors inherited their posts. Each governor also had responsibilities in the capital: one, acting as prime minister, headed all the palace
slaves and eunuchs, another the cavalry, another the infantry, another
the royal tombs, etc.

These governors, despite the fact that many of them were of slave
origin, also acted as kingmakers. Upon the death of the king, they sat as
an electoral college to choose his successor from among his numerous
sons. Sons who were eligible for the throne were forbidden to live in the
central palace, and instead grew to manhood with their mothers in the
district palaces.

Trade was highly developed among the Voltaic peoples, despite
their comparative remoteness from the termini of the great trans-
Saharan caravan routes. Much of the trade was in the hands of Mande
traders, especially the great Dyula companies, and large Mande settlements grew in various Voltaic locations.

Although the Voltaic peoples were able to resist incorporation
into the great empires, they maintained contact with them both in
trade and in war. On numerous occasions, troops of the Mossi fought
with parties of Mali cavalry, each time successfully preventing invasion. The power of the Voltaic peoples proved too great for any
serious aggression by either Mali or Songhai. Thus the long security of
the Voltaic homeland was preserved. Not until the eighteenth century
were invaders, from the powerful Asante Empire to the south, able to
breach the sturdy Voltaic defenses of professional soldiers and eager
conscripts.

Today the Voltaic peoples form a majority of the population of
Upper Volta. Many of the Mande and Atlantic peoples of the Sudan

have scattered far beyond their homelands, sometimes merging into the local populations, sometimes establishing separate alien communities. But the Voltaic peoples have tended to cling to their traditional lands and their long political and cultural heritage. Today Ouagadougou, the modern capital of Upper Volta, stands near the site of the ancient capital of Wagadugu, symbolizing the depths of its peoples' roots.

8 The Eastern Sudan

From Songhai country and the Niger's great bend, the grasslands of the Sudan stretch eastward across the basin of Lake Chad to the Nile valley. For convenience of description, the eastern Sudan is here defined as the area between the Niger and the Nile. Its greatest concentration of population lies between the Niger and the Lake Chad basin, also the site of the most impressive historical events of the eastern Sudan.

The Sudan's grasslands dip deep to the south along the Niger's banks. Past the land of the Songhai, the grasslands follow the river to the rain forests of southern Nigeria. This is the territory of the populous Hausa peoples. The Hausa are a Negroid people whose culture is typically Sudanic except for their language, which forms a branch of the Chadic subfamily of the Afro-Asiatic stock, to which Berber and Egyptian also belong. The Hausa peoples probably originated in the Sahara, in an area near the Berber. They later moved into the Sudan where they mixed with other Black Africans who practiced basically Sudanic culture.

South of the Hausa live other Black Africans who practice Sudanic cultures and speak a variety of Congo-Kordofanian stock languages. Among the more prominent are the Nupe, Jukun, Tiv, and Yoruba. Most of these groups live around the Nigerian plateau, a highland region east of the Niger River and west of the Benue. Culturally and linguistically, the plateau is one of the most heterogeneous regions in all of Africa. Within its several thousand square miles live people of dozens of different tribes and ethnic affiliations. Some of these people achieved powerful and highly developed states, while others long remained economically and culturally stagnant. Even today several of the plateau's least developed groups go naked, a rare phenomenon in Africa.

To the north and northeast of the Hausa live numerous peoples of the Kanuric language family, a major segment of the Sudanic stock. The Kanuric languages are spoken only in the southern Sahara and eastern Sudan. From the central Sahara, these peoples have spread their hegemony southward over the past two or three millennia. They have conquered a number of Chadic-speaking groups east of the Hausa in the Bornu region, just as the Chadic groups there and in Hausa country subordinated the original peoples. Blending in with the Chadic and other groups in the Lake Chad country, the Kanuric peoples became linguistically dominant and established the great empires of Kanem and Bornu, which rivaled the empires of the western Sudan in size, wealth, and longevity.

Beyond Lake Chad and the country of the Kanuric peoples live several groups that, for the most part, speak languages of the Sudanic family. They are grouped in the countries of Bagirmi, Wadai (in which languages of still another language stock, Maban, is widely spoken), and Darfur. Darfur lies just west of Nubia and the Nile region.

All the peoples in the vast region of the eastern Sudan are Black Africans, except in those areas where Arabic or Berber intermixture has occurred in recent times. Between Lake Chad and the Nile, the Sudan is somewhat more arid than to the west of Lake Chad, and a smaller volume of trade was borne on the Saharan caravan trails that terminate in this region. With comparatively sparse populations and with less trade than in the western Sudan, Hausaland, and Kanem-Bornu, the peoples of Bagirmi, Wadai, and Darfur did not enter the mainstream of African history until recent times. And because of their inaccessibility and general unattractiveness to the European conquerors of the nineteenth and twentieth centuries, they have been studied less than other Sudanic peoples.

The Hausa peoples of the eastern Sudan are closest to the great tides of history in the western Sudan. Today they are one of the most numerous populations in all Africa. Although the most recent censuses in Nigeria are the subject of dispute, it is estimated that as many as fifteen million people belong to the Hausa nation. Like the Voltaic peoples, the Hausa live far enough south to enjoy relatively high annual rainfall. In its most fertile parts, their country supports as many as five hundred people per square mile, a dense population by Sudanic standards. The Hausas supported a dense population by growing the crops in the Sudanic agricultural complex, and they produced the surplus necessary to support the administration of states. More than this, however, several Hausa states, Kano and Katsina especially, had a large enough crop production to support a substantial class of artisans. These craftsmen produced goods that added to a high standard of living in Hausaland and provided exports that were known as far away as southern Europe. Cotton cloth, particularly dyed indigo, and processed leather for a variety of uses including sandals, scabbards, seats and cushions, were among Hausaland's most profitable products.

Even though the leading Hausa cities were too far south to compete with Gao and Timbuktu as primary termini for the trans-Saharan trade they were an integral part of the trade from early times. Up to about 1600 several Hausa cities attracted camel caravans that separated from the larger caravans crossing the desert to Timbuktu, and Hausa goods flowed into the large markets of their competitors. With the Moroccan invasion of Songhai, the peace of the Niger bend was shattered, and the markets there suffered. Many large caravans traveled directly to Katsina, Gobir, and Kano, three of the most important Hausa cities, and Hausaland enjoyed an even greater prosperity.

The Hausa peoples are believed to have migrated into what is now northern Nigeria and southwestern Niger during the first millennium of the Christian era. They conquered the prosperous Negro farmers who had earlier settled there, mingled with them, and superimposed the Hausa language and perhaps political ideas onto them. In the process, the Hausa themselves accepted most of the customs and religious beliefs of the Sudanic farmers they conquered. Perhaps because of warfare between the bands of Hausa invaders, who had migrated southward to escape both Berber encroachment and the Sahara's desiccation, fortified towns began to develop at least as early as the eleventh or twelfth century. They grew up in the midst of the dispersed family homesteads and small villages that still dot the countryside. Around these fortified towns emerged what was to become a distinctively Hausa political characteristic—the strong, feudal city-state.

According to Hausa tradition, Bayajidda, son of the king of Baghdad, fled to Bornu after a quarrel with his father. He entered Bornu in around A.D. 1000 with a number of his followers and plotted to overthrow the king. But Bayajidda was outwitted. The king let Bayajidda marry his daughter, then lured away the prince's followers by making them chiefs in newly conquered towns. Realizing that he had been bested, Bayajidda fled westward into Hausa country. He left his Bornuese wife in the town of Biram, where she bore a child who founded the state of Biram. Bayajidda went on to Daura, where he killed a dreaded serpent that had terrorized the town. This feat won him the hand of the queen of Daura, and they had a son who ruled that state. The queen and Bayajidda then had six more sons. These sons ruled Daura, Kano,

Rano, Katsina, Gobir, and Zaria. With Biram, these states form the Hausa Bakwai, or seven sister states of Hausaland.

Nowadays few well-educated Hausa accept this colorful legend as anything more than a condensation of history. Bayajidda, if he existed at all, probably was a leader of Bornu origin. Sultan Bello of the modern Hausa state of Sokoto, a great ruler of the nineteenth century, wrote that Bayajidda was a slave commander who had risen to high position in the Bornuese court and was sent to conquer Hausaland. But Bayajidda may be a legendary figure symbolizing the process through which a number of military commanders from the north and east gradually migrated into Hausaland and established their suzerainty there. Bayajidda's supposed Middle Eastern origin probably crept into the legend after the fifteenth century, when Islam became a prestigious influence in Hausa affairs.

Hausa history is better known than that of many of its neighbors to the south because of the visits of many Berber and Arab Muslims to Hausa cities after the fourteenth century and because of the later development of literacy in Hausaland itself. Virtually all the records and treatises that are believed to have been written from about the fifteenth century on have been lost or destroyed, but there are accounts of Hausa history, written later in the nineteenth century, based on these earlier writings. Originally all the writing in Hausa country was in Arabic. Probably in the late sixteenth or early seventeenth century, Hausa itself developed a modified Arabic script. The history of Kano is better known than that of the other Hausa states. The Kano Chronicle is the most complete and descriptive of any Hausa records, but even Kano's history is dim before about the fourteenth century. Written records for both Kano and Katsina refer to events that date to approximately the eleventh century, but these are too vague to be very helpful in reconstructing events. Certainly Kano and Katsina existed by the eleventh century, but better understanding of what they were like at the time awaits proper archaeological study.

The Hausa cities began as small fortified towns, somewhat like those found so extensively in the western Sudan among the Mande. As the cities grew, they attracted farmers, artisans, and merchants, and city walls were rebuilt to enclose larger areas. When the largest areas were enclosed, perhaps in the twelfth or thirteenth century, farmland was included so that some grain and vegetable crops could be grown within the safety of the walls. These great walls, built of dried mud, were as thick as ten to twelve feet at base and up to fifteen feet high. They were as long as eight of nine miles in circumference, and were broken at intervals by huge wooden gates, bound with iron, that stood open for

The Hausa city of Kano. (From a
midnineteenth-century drawing by Heinrich Barth.)

normal commerce but could be closed when attack threatened. The
populations of the Hausa cities were large: Kano had somewhere near
75,000 people in the seventeenth and eighteenth centuries, and Katsina,
Zaria, and Gobir could hardly have been much smaller.

Into the Hausa cities came goods from the surrounding prosperous
countryside: millet, sorghum, cow peas, shea nuts, meat and skins from
goats, sheep, and cattle, honey, cotton fiber, bars of iron, and pottery.
Inside the cities, thousands of artisans plied their trades, turning out
articles for export across the Sudan and the Sahara as well as for internal
consumption. Weavers made blankets and cloaks from wool and cotton; leather workers cut, tanned, and fashioned animal skins, especially
those of the brown goat, into a variety of products. Even today Moroccan leather, known all over Europe, comes mostly from Hausaland's
leather workers. Smiths forged iron into weapons and tools and copper
and gold into ornaments and utensils. Although the industry of the
Hausa cities would nowadays be classed as "cottage industry" carried on
by individual artisans and guilds in small houses, the Hausa cities
were the leading manufacturing centers of the Sudan.

The location of the Hausa cities, despite the strong competition
from Timbuktu, Gao, and Bornu, proved to be a unique factor in their
rise to wealth. Their proximity to the dense populations along the

Niger and Benue rivers and in the forests of southern Nigeria enabled the cities to trade with the largest concentration of people on the continent. The fifteen to thirty million people who several centuries ago lived in what is now Nigeria provided the Hausa cities with a far larger economic hinterland than could be found in any other comparable area of the Sudan.

At the time of the founding of the earliest Hausa cities, the land must have already been a rich and well-settled farming region. The influx of Hausa invaders from the north probably started as early as the eighth century and began to pull the clans and extended families into a series of small states by 1000. The fortified towns in which the ruling nobility lived became the nuclei of the great cities and the capitals of these states.

By the fourteenth century the Hausa cities were becoming prosperous. They were in close contact with the imperial governments and commerical systems of both Mali and Bornu. Mansa Musa of Mali is known to have sent ambassadors to Hausaland, although he never felt strong enough to attempt to conquer it. In the middle of the fourteenth century, during the reign of Sarki (king) Yaji of Kano, Muslim missionaries from Mali converted the king and many of his court to Islam. The Kano Chronicle records the conversion and some of the difficulties Yaji experienced because his subjects were reluctant to give up their Hausa religious faith:

> . . . In Yaji's time the Wangarawa [men from Mali] came from Mali, bringing the Mohammadan religion (about forty in all). The name of their leader was Abdurahaman Zaite. . . . When they came they commanded the Sarki to observe the times of prayer, and he complied. . . . The Sarki commanded every town in Kano country to observe the times of prayer. So they all did so. A mosque was built beneath the sacred tree facing east, and prayers were made at the five appointed times in it. The Sarkin Garazawa [a powerful provincial ruler] was opposed to prayer, and when the Moslems . . . had gone home, he would come with his men and defile the whole mosque and cover it with filth. Dan Bujai was told . . . to patrol round the mosque with well-armed men from evening until morning. He kept up a constant halloo. For all that the pagans tried to win him and his men over. Some of the men followed the pagans and went away, but he and the rest refused. The defilement continued until Sheshe said to Famore, "There is no cure for this but prayer." The people assented. They gathered together on a Tuesday in the mosque at the evening hour of prayer and prayed against the pagans till sunrise. They only came away when the sun was well up. Allah received graciously the prayers addressed to him. The chief of the pagans was struck blind that day, and afterwards all the pagans who were present at the defilement— they and all their women. After this they were all afraid. Yaji turned the

chief of the pagans out of his office and said to him, "Be thou Sarki among the blind."

From the fourteenth century on Islam persisted as the favored religion among most Hausa kings and nobles, although its spread in the countryside was very slow, as was the case elsewhere in the Sudan. As late as the early nineteenth century, non-Muslim sentiment was strong enough to weaken the practice of the religion. Many traditional rituals, incantations, sacrifices, and beliefs—especially the belief in the ancestor spirits—were retained alongside Islam even in court circles. Yet Islam set the tone in the cities and around the courts, and holy men and learned Muslim scholars from other parts of the Sudan and North Africa increasingly visited the growing Hausa cities. By the sixteenth century, Katsina and Kano had become centers of learning, with numerous mosques and hundreds of literate and scholarly Muslims, both foreign and Hausa. Each city developed a university, along the lines of the school in Timbuktu, where scholars instructed the young men of Hausaland in writing, reading, ethics, philosophy, mathematics, government, and religion. The development of Katsina and Kano as centers of learning, as well as major centers of commerce, was stimulated greatly by the upheavals in Songhai that began with the Moroccan invasion late in the sixteenth century. Most merchants and scholars fled Jenne, Timbuktu, and Gao, attracted by the peace and the civilized quality of life in Hausaland. The once great cities of Songhai degenerated into dusty market towns, while the prospering Hausa cities supplanted them. Today Timbuktu is a large village of mud huts, almost deserted and forgotten. But Kano and Katsina still thrive with industry and trade.

The Hausa states, even though they shared common origins, language, culture, and tradition, never embarked on an imperial course. Indeed, they never federated with each other except in ephemeral alliances when faced with mutual threats from foreign invasion. More often than not they were jealous of each other's power and prosperity and frequently warred with each other or allied with foreign powers to war against rival Hausa states. The relatively equal power of several of the Hausa states and their neighbors made it difficult for one to establish long rule over the others. The proximity of powerful imperial systems on either side—Songhai and Mali to the west and Kanem-Bornu to the east—added to the difficulty of conquest.

Though they were wealthy and powerful, the Hausa states were unable to prevent foreign conquest. Askia Muhammad's Songhai forces invaded Hausaland in the early sixteenth century. For several years the rulers of Katsina, Kano, and Gobir were forced to pay tribute and acknowledge Songhai supremacy. Songhai power in Hausaland was broken by the one man in Hausa history who is known to have attempted, with partial success, to create a Hausa empire—Kotal Kanta, king of Kebbi.

Kebbi borders on Songhai to the west of the main Hausa states. It is one of the states the Hausa call the Banza Bakwai, or "bastard seven," a group of independent adjacent states where the Hausa language was widely spoken. These states played integral roles in Hausa history, but retained pre-Hausa cultural traditions and considered themselves distinct from the Hausa states. The Banza Bakwai includes Zamfara, Kebbi, Nupe, Gwari, Yauri, Yoruba, and Kororofa, or Jukun.

Kotal Kanta came to the throne of Kebbi between 1500 and 1505, when he was about forty years of age. Tradition describes him as a large man, inclined to be fierce, strong-tempered and strict in his rule. He was unusually energetic in his personal habits as well as in his role as king. He constantly moved about, seeking ways to improve his kingdom and his army. When he came to power Kebbi was subject to Songhai, then ruled by the great Askia Muhammad.

For several years Kotal Kanta served Askia Muhammad with loyalty, aiding him in his campaigns against the Tuareg of Aïr. In the process, however, Kanta built his own army into a formidable force. On campaign, the Kebbi army depended on a well-organized troop of cavalry. For defense, however, Kanta relied on foot soldiers and boatmen. Kebbi has many areas of marshland and Kanta is said to have built a huge canoe, sheathed with copper and propelled by fifty paddlers, in which he toured his country during the season when rains flooded the marshes.

Following the Songhai conquest of Aïr, Kanta quarreled with Askia Muhammad over the spoils and declared Kebbi's independence. A powerful Songhai army was assembled to punish Kanta for his disloyalty. The troop marched on Kebbi in about 1516. Kanta's seasoned, disciplined, and inspired army met the Songhai at a town called Tara, there inflicting upon them one of the worst defeats ever suffered by that mighty empire and sending them in rout back up the Niger into the safety of Songhai country. This great military accomplishment is still one of Kebbi's most cherished events. The victory made Kanta the most powerful man between Songhai and Bornu, and he turned his attention almost immediately to the imperial expansion that his former mentor, Askia Muhammad, had pursued with such dazzling success.

In the next twenty years Kanta's armies conquered much of Hausaland and Aïr, exacting tribute from the rulers of Aïr, Gobir, Kano, Katsina, Daura, and Zaria. He established a new capital at a village named Surame and fortified it heavily. In most of the states he conquered, Kotal Kanta allowed the native rulers to continue to govern, so long as they paid him tribute and supplied the troops and labor that his adventures required. Several states, including Zamfara, Ader, and Wangara (a small state in Hausaland, unrelated to the more famous Wangara of Mali), were completely incorporated into Kebbi and were ruled by Kanta's trusted lieutenants.

The Kebbi empire fell apart after Kotal Kanta died, either in battle or in an accident following a war with the Kanuri of Bornu, in 1545-50. At his death Kanta was about eighty, still vigorous and driven by the energy that had marked his forty years of brilliant rule.

Several times, the Hausa states were conquered by the emperors of Kanem-Bornu, that powerful and durable empire to the northeast. Relations were traditionally close between Bornu and the Hausa states, since there was considerable trade between them and no natural boundaries separated them. Until the beginning of the seventeenth century, however, Songhai seems to have acted as a countervailing force, so that the Hausa states acted as buffer states between the two powerful empires, neither empire attempting to incorporate Hausa territory for fear of reprisals from the other. Askia Muhammad briefly broke the pattern at a time when Kanem-Bornu was relatively weak. In the seventeenth century, however, with the collapse of Songhai and the growth of Kano and Katsina as centers of trade and wealth, Bornu was free to turn its attentions toward Hausaland with impunity. Throughout the seventeenth and eighteenth centuries the chronicles of both Bornu and the Hausa states refer to the payment of tribute by Kano, Katsina, Zaria, and other Hausa states.

During the late sixteenth century, another threat to the Hausa states came from Kororofa, the capital of Jukun, which seems to have been an aggressive power from that time until the early eighteenth century, when it declined and disappeared without a trace. The few scattered Jukun peoples today live in an inaccessible area south of the Benue and east of the Niger. Their oral traditions contain little hint of the power they possessed three centuries ago, a power that is amply documented in the written records of Bornu and the Hausa states. On numerous occasions between about 1580 and 1700, a large and fast-moving cavalry force swept out of Jukun into Hausaland, ravaging the countryside around Kano and Zaria, and on a few occasions entering and sacking these cities.

The Jukun people, who today number perhaps no more than fifty thousand, are Negroid and practice many elements of Sudanic culture and agriculture. But they speak a language of the Bantoid subfamily of Nigritic and are thus classified quite differently from the Hausa, Nupe, and others with whom they interacted in medieval times. What occasioned the sharp decline of their once powerful kingdom is unknown and their history is so poorly known that even the location of Kororofa, which must have been a substantial town when it was the capital, has never been ascertained.

The failure of the Hausa states to develop into empires or even into a confederation and the frequent invasions and exaction of tribute by Songhai, Kebbi, Bornu, and Jukun did not halt the growing prosperity of the country. Katsina and Kano, between the early fifteenth and late seventeenth centuries, constantly rivaled for preeminence and for the control of the rich trans-Saharan and trans-Sudanic trade in which both cities participated. Generally Katsina seems to have had the edge, but in the late fifteenth century Kano began to develop a military prowess that eventually evened the balance somewhat. In 1463 Muhammad Rimfa, the greatest king in Kano history, commenced a program of dynamic development in both civil and military affairs.

The Kano Chronicle tells little of Rimfa as a man, but from the glowing tales of his works he must have been a brilliant and energetic leader. As a devout Muslim he welcomed Muslim travelers to his country, and during his reign the first inflow of learned Fulani preachers and scholars from the empire of Mali arrived. They established themselves peacefully enough, in view of the dynamic force they were to become some centuries later. Rimfa introduced the great public feast period of Id-al-fitr, which follows the month-long fast of Ramadan, during which the devout Muslim eats nothing between sunrise and sunset.

Rimfa reorganized his state's system of administration and eliminated some of its feudal remnants. He ceased relying on hereditary chiefs for administration and substituted an Islamic system based on non-hereditary governors, many of them talented slaves. Rimfa also commissioned one of the most cherished writings in Hausa history, a treatise by a learned Algerian theologian, preacher, and politician, Shaikh Muhammad al-Maghili. Entitled *The Obligations of Princes*, the treatise may have stimulated Rimfa's creation of a strong council of state. Included on the council were several prominent leaders of the slave caste, one of them a brilliant eunuch.

True to the Arabic pattern, Rimfa built a vast palace, the largest of any in Hausaland, and created a harem that the Kano Chronicle says included more than a thousand wives who were guarded by eunuchs. Conscious of the need to dignify the crown, he introduced regalia such as great ostrich feather fans.

But it was in construction and military matters that Rimfa's innovations gave Kano its greatest thrust forward. He enlarged the walls around the city, completing portions that had lain vacant, and built a large new market site to accommodate the growing commercial activity of his capital. He enlarged and reorganized the army and enforced a new discipline. Rimfa also introduced the tactic of sending foot soldiers into battle in the midst of the cavalry so that they could hide among the horses when hard pressed by the enemy. Having developed his army, he declared war on Katsina, and fought against that city for eleven years. According to the Kano Chronicle this was the first war ever waged against Katsina. It was by no means the last. Hostilities erupted repeatedly between the early sixteenth and late seventeenth centuries, until at last Kano emerged as the militarily stronger city.

During the eighteenth century, only one other Hausa state prospered and expanded its influence. This was Gobir, the youngest and most northerly of all the Hausa kingdoms. Gobir was located near the modern border of Nigeria and Niger, very near the edge of the Sahara. Gobir was never able to compete with Katsina and Kano, which were more easily reached by both Sudanese and Saharan traders, but it grew in military strength in its constant battles with the Tuareg, who frequently tried to find new grazing land in Hausa territory. In the early eighteenth century Gobir invaded and exacted tribute from the productive regions of Kebbi and Zamfara, and by the end of the century Gobir was as powerful as the more civilized and established states of Kano and Katsina.

The sturdy Hausa commoners benefited little from the growth in wealth and learning that the Hausa states experienced during the seventeenth and eighteenth centuries. Most were still non-Muslims, content to farm their lands and live their traditional way of life. They were aware of but aloof from the luxury of the large courts and the cosmopolitan lives of the noble and commercial classes of the cities. This gap between the kings and their urban supporters and the people of the countryside slowly widened. Despite the region's prosperity, the eighteenth century was a period of degeneration in Hausaland. Rulers became captives of an effete style of life that developed in the cities. They governed and lived in the manner of oriental potentates. Two groups of people in Hausaland came to resent the rule of the kings: the heavily taxed farmers and the more deeply devout Muslims of the cities. These Muslims saw signs of heresy in the careless and selfish quality of the court life and the growing superficiality with which Islam was practiced.

By the late eighteenth century the most devout large group of people in Hausaland were the town Fulani. These people had begun to arrive during the reign of Muhammad Rimfa and had settled in every Hausa town and city. They were scribes, theologians, administrators, court advisers, and traders. The growing despotism of the Hausa kings offended the Fulani religious sensibilities grievously. It also threatened the livelihoods of the large number of Fulani who served as professional administrators, committed to government under the Koran. At the beginning of the nineteenth century, under the inspired leadership of one Usman dan Fodio of Gobir, they rose against the Hausa kings and in a few years revolutionized the entire Hausa political system.

The Fulani originated in Tekrur, where they were among the first Sudanese Africans to become Islamized. After the Almoravid invasion of Ghana they began a long series of migrations toward the east, always split into the two closely related but very different communities of town Fulani and cattle Fulani. The latter were less fervent Muslims, eschewed town life, and showed a tenacious devotion to cattle herding.

Most of the peoples among whom the cattle Fulani settled were grain farmers who found the Fulani useful partners from whom to buy meat, milk, and manure for fertilizer. In later times, in areas where cattle were valued, as was the case in Hausaland, the Fulani often tended the herds of kings and wealthy farmers in return for a share of the wealth thus produced.

The town Fulani, similarly, were usually welcomed for their learning, their administrative abilities, and their wide experience in long-distance trading. As devout and learned Muslims there were especially sought after by the Sudanic kings who had accepted Islam.

The two groups of Fulani, worlds apart in religion and way of life, maintained cordial contact as each moved ever farther to the east. Both groups recognized their common origin and felt the kinship that fellow countrymen so often feel in a foreign land. Through the inveterate travels of town Fulani traders, ties of clan kinship were kept active, and the Fulani of one country had a good knowledge of what was occurring among their Fulani kin in other countries.

While great Muslim kings reigned in the Sudanic states and empires, the Fulani prospered through the high connections and favored positions of many of their members. But when non-Muslim kings reigned, or when the Islamic patterns of government deteriorated, the Fulani were often considered an alien minority. Thus it was in the western Sudan in the late seventeenth and early eighteenth centuries, after the collapse of Songhai and the Islamic system to which its emperors were committed. Many ancient kingdoms in Mandeland gradually came to be ruled by dynasties that were not Muslim and that regarded Islam as an alien force. Many of the Mande-speaking peoples, who had lived under the Islamic rulers of Mali and Songhai, were ruled by the kings of the Bambara, a Mande group that had never accepted Islam and that regarded the lingering Islamic power in Timbuktu and Jenne as a threat to its own imperial ambitions.

During the seventeenth century, an Islamic spiritual renaissance, which was part of a puritanical resurgence throughout the Sahara and northern Africa, began to emerge. Led by a number of brotherhoods, each composed of disciples who committed themselves to preach the pure and rigorous concepts of Islam, this movement called for an organized effort to proselytize the hitherto pagan masses as well as to seek governments committed to administration in accordance with the best principles of the Koran. Among the most fervent members of the brotherhoods were the town Fulani, especially those of the Torodbe clan, itself a kind of brotherhood of Fulani who were professional clerks, administrators, and teachers in countries stretching from Tekrur to Bornu.

In the early 1700's the Torodbe of the western Sudan revolted against the non-Muslim rulers of their homeland in Futa Toro, a part of ancient Tekrur still inhabited by the Tukulor kinsmen of the Fulani. Conquering Futa Jallon, the highlands to the south in what is now modern Guinea, the Torodbe Fulani set up two theocratic states. From these states they proselytized and campaigned in Wolof, Serer, and Malinke country. Nearly fifty years were required for this Islamic movement to secure a base in Futa Toro and Futa Jallon, but by the end of the eighteenth century, Islam had been accepted by most of the peoples of these states and many areas to their south and east.

The successes of the Islamic revival in the far west were well known to the Fulani of Hausaland, where the Torodbe were strongly represented. Usman dan Fodio, a devout Torodbe who had followed the struggles of his kinsmen in the west with keen interest, became the leader of the movement in the Hausa kingdoms.

Dan Fodio resided in Gobir, which by that time was at the peak of its military power and was ruthlessly governed by its Hausa king. Dan Fodio was a close adviser to the king, having established a fine reputation as a teacher and administrator. But he grew increasingly disgusted at the harsh taxation, lavish courts, and pagan practices that the king tolerated. Already highly respected by his Torodbe colleagues and other Fulani, dan Fodio attracted Muslim well-wishers and disciples from both the Hausa and the foreign communities. The king, irritated by dan Fodio's outspoken criticisms and concerned at the support his views were winning among the wealthy and educated, dismissed him from his state appointments and forced him to retire.

Up to this point Usman dan Fodio had been a reformer. With exile, however, he soon became a rebel. Thousands of followers gathered around him at Gudu, the small town to which he had been exiled, and thousands of others from all over Gobir and other Hausa kingdoms sent messengers to offer their support. In 1804, dan Fodio's assembled followers elected him caliph for Hausaland. He then proclaimed a jihad against the corrupt and apostate government of Gobir.

As dan Fodio's fervent warriors marched against Gobir's army, substantial additional support began to appear. The neighboring state of Zamfara, which had its own quarrels with Gobir, signed a treaty with the Fulani and sent an army. The cattle Fulani, though unmoved by the religious zeal of their town kinsmen, sent warriors, and a surprisingly large number of Hausa commoners, most of them non-Muslims angered by the harsh taxes and corruption of the king's government, provided armed men, as well as support and shelter to the Fulani troops. Dan Fodio was able to attract wide support because there was a deep need for political reform and because the jihad was not an anti-Hausa ethnic war. Dan Fodio conquered Gobir with ease, and his victorious forces, joined by ever larger numbers of Fulani and Hausa in the other Hausa states, expanded the war to all Hausaland.

In less than four years Usman dan Fodio and his Fulani troops were masters of every Hausa state, although pockets of resistance continued until 1820. Dan Fodio himself took little part in the fighting, which was directed by his brother, Abdullahi, and his son, Bello. After securing Hausaland itself, Bello and Abdullahi encouraged Fulani revolts in the south, eventually conquering Nupe, Jukun, and the Yoruba state of Ilorin. In the east they attempted to seize power in Bornu, but after initial Fulani successes, the king of Bornu prevailed, losing only a portion of his imperial territory. To the southeast, in what is now northwestern Cameroun, the state of Adamawa was brought under Fulani rule. This completed the creation of a widely scattered, loosely knit Fulani Empire.

The Fulani Empire lasted until British conquest in the early twentieth century. For the first time in history, all of northern Nigeria was united under a common system of law and government. All Hausaland, together with many surrounding territories, became part of a coherent polity. Although the Fulani conquest involved a certain amount of brutality and vandalism, it established a rule of law with a fair measure of justice. The emirs (commanders) of the states in the empire, autonomous in certain matters, were clearly bound by Islamic law and codes of good government. They rarely disputed the authority of the sultan of Sokoto.

Under Bello, who became sultan of Sokoto after the death of dan Fodio, there was a burst of scholarly and literary activity. Bello also enforced the uniform practice of Islamic law, helped to reform government and administration throughout Hausaland, and instituted a more just system of taxation. Clearly the chief architect of the Fulani Empire, Bello was one of the truly great leaders to arise in the Sudan.

Following Bello's death in 1837, some of the zeal for reform began to wane. Gradually some individual emirs grew materialistic and harsh, and the effectiveness of the sultan of Sokoto diminished. Nevertheless,

Square in the town of Kukawa, site of the Mai of Bornu's residence. (From a midnineteenth-century drawing by Heinrich Barth.)

Hausaland continued to prosper. Throughout the nineteenth century, internal trade expanded, wealth increased, and the lot of the commoner remained better than it had been before the Fulani conquest.

During the nineteenth century the Fulani rulers of Nigeria pushed vigorously ahead with the missionary effort that had begun nearly two centuries before. Koranic schools were established in every village and town of consequence, and Muslim teachers labored to convert commoners and slaves to Islam. By the end of the nineteenth century, Islam had become a popular religion, practiced by millions of people in the countryside as well as in the towns.

In the regions where Fulani power was greatest, such as northern Nigeria and the Mande countries that now lie in interior Senegal, Guinea, and western Mali, the Fulani missionary campaign was so successful that Islam became the majority religion. The traditional religions survived only in the more isolated and inaccessible areas. Fulani suzerainty stretched from the Atlantic Ocean to the eastern borders of Hausaland. But the sway of Islam continued eastward far beyond Fulani influence, especially in Kanem-Bornu, where native rulers had long espoused its tenets.

The long history of Kanem-Bornu begins in the seventh and eighth centuries when a nomadic people, the Zaghawa, arrived from the southeast part of the Sahara and settled to the east of Lake Chad. Lake Chad is in the heart of Africa, roughly equidistant from the Atlantic Ocean and the Red Sea, and almost as far from the Guinea Coast as from the Mediterranean Sea. Moderately fertile, the lands around Lake Chad afforded a reasonable standard of living from grain agriculture and grazing, and the lake itself supplied fish. The indigenous people of the area lived in small villages and were not centrally organized into states. This made it comparatively easy for the nomadic Zaghawa to assume control after they had settled in sufficient numbers.

In the eighth or ninth century one group of the Zaghawa, the Beni-Saif, set up the state of Kanem to the east of Lake Chad. The Beni-Saif founded the dynasty known as the Sefewa, which ruled the state and empire of Kanem for a thousand years. Late in the eleventh century Mai Ume (Mai is the title by which all Sefewa kings were known) accepted Islam, indicating that the kingdom was in regular contact with Muslim traders from North Africa at least by that time.

In view of Kanem's strategic location, it is likely that it early became an important trade center. Several routes across the Sahara from Tunisia, Libya, and Egypt all converged in the Kanem region, as did the routes from the forest lands of modern Nigeria and the Cameroun. In contact with Fezzan and Darfur to the east and northeast, Kanem also sat astride routes between the Nile country and the western Sudan lands of Ghana, Mali, and Songhai. These great empires channeled the gold, ivory, slaves, hides, and kola nuts from south to north in the western Sudan. Kanem performed the same function in the eastern Sudan.

Because of its trade, Kanem gradually grew powerful, and as its power expanded so did its territory. The people of Kanem were blocked in their efforts to acquire more land by the Tuareg of Aïr and Fezzan to the north, and by the Bulala to the east. Thus, they spread gradually to the west and south, into the country of Bornu, homeland of the So people. The So resisted bitterly, but by the middle of the thirteenth century the Kanuri ruled Bornu as well as Kanem. Their holdings constituted an empire that surrounded Lake Chad and stretched north into the Sahara.

The Bulala, long-time enemies of the Kanuri, continued to press Kanem, and occupied that country during the fourteenth century. In about 1391, the Sefewa family transferred its court wholly to Bornu and set up a new capital at Kaka. In later years Kanem was recaptured and forced to swear fealty to the Sefewas.

The empire of Kanem-Bornu flourished between the fourteenth and eighteenth centuries. Trade was the basis of its strength during these centuries of greatness. Kanem-Bornu's trade was similar to that of the other Sudanic empires, except for gold, which was not as plentiful in the eastern Sudan as in the west. But Kanem-Bornu, lying to the north of a vast territory of weaker peoples, made up for its lack of gold by exporting numerous slaves. For centuries slaves flowed by the thousands out of Kanem-Bornu to Egypt, Libya, Tunisia, and the oases in the Sahara.

The Sefewa dynasty produced many Mais whose names have been celebrated in legend and written history, but the most famous was Mai Idris Alooma, who ruled Kanem-Bornu from 1580 to 1617. In the half century before Idris Alooma came to the throne, Kanem-Bornu had apprehensively watched the growing power of the Songhai Empire. Although no Songhai army ever seriously threatened Bornu, and no Kanem-Bornu army ever intruded into Songhai, the two empires were involved in serious rivalries over Aïr and the Hausa states. When Songhai's Askia Muhammad invaded Aïr in the early sixteenth century, the Tuareg of that country owed fealty to Bornu. And when the Songhai

Mounted bodyguard of the Mai of Bornu. (From an early nineteenth-century drawing by Major Dixon Denham.)

At his court the Mai of Bornu is protected by a screen
from physical contact with his subjects, who were also
not supposed to look directly at him. (From an early
nineteenth-century sketch by Major Dixon Denham.)

launched their campaign against the Hausa states, their troops reached
the borders of Kanem-Bornu. Perhaps fortunately for Kanem-Bornu,
which had other powerful enemies as well, the Songhai suffered their
defeats at the hands of the invading Moroccans before a real contest between the two empires crystallized.

Mai Idris Alooma came to power only a few years before Songhai's
defeat. Comparable in many of his accomplishments to Askia Muham-

mad, Idris distinguished himself in both the military and political fields. He reorganized the army of Kanem-Bornu almost as soon as he took the throne and intitiated a series of campaigns designed to restore the shaky foundations of his empire. He subjugated a number of small states to Kanem-Bornu's south, establishing peaceful frontiers in that direction. He then marched into Kanem, which had challenged his authority, and, in a long campaign, defeated the Bulala forces. By the time of his death in 1617, Kanem-Bornu had recovered all the territory it had ever possessed.

Like Askia Muhammed, Idris Alooma was a brilliant head of state. He established Islamic law on a common footing throughout his empire and introduced many reforms in government and administration. He professionalized the army, much as Askia Muhammad had done before him in Songhai, and imported muskets and Turkish military instructors for his soliders.

After Mai Idris Alooma, fifty years of peace and prosperity followed for the people of Kanem-Bornu. But in 1667 Bornu was successfully invaded by Tuareg warriors from Aïr and by an army from the state of Jukun in the south. Mai Ali, the ruler at the time, was defeated by both, and was besieged in his capital at Gasreggono. Although both forces were subsequently driven out of Bornu, the empire suffered grievously and never regained its former vitality.

Shrinking gradually in size, it remained just strong enough to repel invaders, but no more. Finally, in 1808, Fulani forces drove Mai Ahmad from Gasreggono. He was later rescued by a powerful army from Kanem, and when he died, in 1846, the throne of Bornu passed to Kanem's Shaikh Amin, thus ending the thousand-year reign of the Sefewas. Kanem-Bornu continued to exist as a state until the colonial conquest, but its imperial days had ended.

9 States of the West African Forests

The vast plains of the Sudan have tended, until the last few centuries, to dominate Africa's history as they dominate its geography. South of the Sudan, in much of West Africa, lies a long and relatively narrow belt of rain forests. These dense forests discouraged penetration into West Africa by the troops and traders of the great Sudanic states and empires, just as they helped confine Europeans to the coasts. Yet in the midst of these forests, comparatively isolated from direct outside contacts, live millions of Africans who have produced a vigorous variation on the Sudanic civilization. The sculpture and music of this forest civilization have had a profound influence on the art and music of modern Europe and America.

The West African forest stretches from modern Senegal to the Congo basin, with one brief interruption in Togo and Dahomey, where the grasslands of the Sudan sweep down to the shores of the Atlantic. In the forest grow giant hardwood trees, whose lofty foliage often prevents the sun's rays from reaching the ground. In some areas, especially in the coastal lowlands of Guinea, Liberia, and Nigeria, the forests nurture dense swamps and jungles. More typically, however, the forests grow in hilly and upland areas, beginning a few miles inland from the coast, where the rivers and streams flow rapidly down to the ocean.

The rain forest was not quite the idyllic habitat suggested by the stereotype of the happy savage plucking bananas and fruits from the nearest branch. On the contrary, it originally offered very few indigenous plants, either wild or cultivated, that were sufficiently nutritious to support a population. Nor do the forests contain large numbers of animals that can serve as a substantial supply of food. The great herds of antelope, zebra, elephant, and other meaty animals live far away, in the grasslands and plains. Monkeys, reptiles, birds, and small rodents, and tiny deer live in the forests.

It seems probable, judging by the scanty archaeological evidence available, that the West African forests were not densely populated before the latter part of the first millennium A.D. But that they were populated is certain: one excavation, at Akure in the forests of southern Nigeria, has unearthed more than half a million stone artifacts that date back to about 9000 B.C. Before the time of Christ the people of the forests fished, hunted, and harvested the few tubers, roots, and fruits that were native to the forests. Very probably they also possessed a knowledge of agriculture, since their relatives on the savannas of the Sudan had long been industrious grain farmers. But the grains that grew on the plains could not be grown in the forests; in this region the Guinea yam tuber was probably the major crop, but it had to be supplemented by nonagricultural food procurement.

Probably several millennia before the Christian era, the forests were settled by peoples who were of the same stock as the Negroid peoples of the Sudan. It is likely that these Negroid peoples replaced Pygmoid or Bushmanoid peoples, who were widely settled in the Congo basin and eastern and southern Africa, and who may have spread into West Africa many tens of thousands of years earlier. There is some evidence of this in the Bushman-type stone tools that have been unearthed, but linguistic evidence indicates that Negroid peoples have inhabited the Sudan and the forests for at least three or four millennia. Judging by the oral tradition among many forest peoples and the familial affinity between the languages of many savanna and forest peoples, major new migrations of peoples from the savannas bordering the forests took place between the time of Christ and about A.D. 1200, adding fresh Sudanic infusions to the Sudanic peoples already there.

It is not clear whether the indigenous forest peoples were completely absorbed by the migrations of whole societies, or whether smaller conquering forces established cultural and political hegemony over the indigenous peoples. Whatever the case, many of today's forest peoples seem to have emerged as identifiable societies between about 1000 and 1300.

Importation into the forests of several highly nutritious Malaysian crops, which improved the region's economy, occurred during the first millennium. During this period the yam, coco yam (taro), and banana, all East Asian plants, appeared in the forests, making it possible for larger numbers of people to support themselves. They permitted a major surge forward in the development of the forest peoples, who already possessed a technology that encompassed a good knowledge of mining and smelting metals, including iron. By the end of the first millennium the population density of the forests was increasing rapidly and soon enough surplus food was being produced to support the division of labor upon which states and civilizations can be built.

By the fifteenth century, when European ships began calling at West African shores, there were numerous small states that evidenced considerable stability, complex and effective political organization, and enough military competence to make a strong impression on the European visitors. European accounts during the fifteenth, sixteenth, and seventeenth centuries make it clear that they regarded the West Africans as a comparatively civilized, well-developed people. Not until the eighteenth century, when Europeans became increasingly imbued with a chauvinistic sense of the growing industrial and. technical potency of their civilization, did they begin to regard the Africans as less than equals.

Soon after the first Portuguese ships visited West Africa, they brought another complex of food plants. These crops, which came from the New World, included corn, tobacco, tomatoes, pineapples, manioc, and peanuts.

These new crops, as well as the guns and manufactured goods that formed the basis of West Africa's growing trade with Europe, provided further stimulus to the vigorous development of the forest peoples. By the seventeenth century, West Africa's expanding affluence supported the growth of several new states. Empires began to appear, and the power, prosperity, and political organization of the forest peoples began to rival that of the earlier peoples of the great Sudanic states and empires.

Even before the advent of European goods and American crops, West Africa's forests had seen an impressive development of social organization and material conditions. The institution of kingship had appeared in many of the forest societies prior to the fifteenth century. Some kings were surrounded by an aura of divinity and taboo reminiscent of patterns in the Nile valley and the Sudan. Classes and castes of nobles, artisans, freemen, and slaves, were firmly established. Important market towns and political and religious centers had developed. The forest peoples were increasingly involved in trade with the Hausa states, Songhai, Mali, the Mossi states, and Kanem-Bornu. Both kings and traders were growing rich on the profits. The Mande Dyula traders had even established trading towns, such as Kong and Bobo Dioulasso in the northern Ivory Coast, as entrepôts for their trade with the forest peoples.

Art, religion, and music also flourished. Masterful wood carvings were widespread, and some societies, Ife and Benin most notably, were producing sculptures in bronze and clay. Surviving sculptures from this pre-European period portray spiritual themes that attest to the complex religious thought of the times.

The religions of the forest peoples were generally similar to the Mande religion. They recognized a supreme being as creator and worshiped through the spirits of deceased ancestors and the spirits of nature. The latter were charged with responsibility for regulating winds, rains, crops, river flows, fire, and other natural phenomena. Shrines at which offerings and sacrifices could be made were common in the forest towns and villages and in many family compounds. Typically the ancestor shrines were adorned with wood or stone sculptures that symbolized the ancestor's spirit.

Crafts were also flourishing when Europeans first arrived on the West African coast. Early Portuguese reports note that fine quality cotton cloth was plentiful along the coast. In 1556 an English ship captain wrote of the fine iron work made by the peoples of the West African forests, listing "spears, fish-hooks, farming tools, and swords that are exceedingly sharp on both edges." Special castes of workers produced houses from clay.

The societies of the forests differed from each other in many respects, but the basic similarity of the forest environment and the widespread use of the same crops and of Sudanic agricultural techniques made for a certain measure of homogeneity. A sketch of the histories of several notable forest peoples is, therefore, a convenient way of examining events in the rain forests of western Africa.

The Akan people, who now inhabit most of southern Ghana and part of the neighboring Ivory Coast, all speak Twi, a branch of the Kwa subfamily of the Congo-Kordofanian stock; there are a number of distinct Twi dialects. The Akan are divided into a number of ethnic groups—Akyem, Kwahu, Akwapim, Gomoa, Assin, Twifu, Denkyira, Nzima, Asante (Ashanti), and Fante. Of these, the Asante produced the best-known and most illustrious polity, but the customs, religions, and political systems of all Akan peoples are closely related. Most Akan societies consist of eight matrilineal and eight patrilineal groups; a Denkyira who belong to a particular clan regards an Asante of the same clan as a clan brother or sister, despite the fact that they belong to different states.

The origins of the Akan peoples are obscure. A modern Ghanaian historian, A. Adu Boahen, contends that they originated in the savannas of the Sudan in what is now northern Ghana, moving into the forests between A.D. 1000 and 1300. The high productivity and nutritiousness of East Asian crops underlay the population growth and affluence of the

Akan peoples in the early centuries of the second millennium, although it is not certain whether they settled the forest area because they had learned to grow East Asian crops or were attracted into the forest because of the growing prosperity East Asian crops had already brought. Probably pressures from the expanding peoples farther north and west in the Sudan, in the areas that produced the empires of Ghana and Mali, also influenced the southerly migrations of the Akan into the forest.

Whatever the case, the Akan peoples were well settled in the forests of southern Ghana (the modern state) by the late thirteenth century. By the time the ships of the Portuguese explorers began to call in the late fifteenth century, they had formed a series of small states along the coast and in the interior. At least a century, possibly several centuries, before the arrival of the first European ships the Akan were involved in a regular trade system, through which salt and cloth from the coasts and kola nuts, gold, and slaves from the forests moved northward. Saharan salt and many manufactured goods from the Mediterranean area moved south in exchange.

Because of the arduous labor involved in cutting and clearing the massive trees of the rain forests, Akan settlements were grouped almost exclusively into compact villages and towns. In these settlements the population normally ranged from five hundred up to several thousand, and towns with tens of thousands were not (and are not now) uncommon. The Yoruba, a forest people in modern Nigeria, have built towns with populations in excess of 100,000. Their largest city, Ibadan, is now the largest all-Black city in Africa, with more than 700,000 people. Inside the towns of both the Akan and the Yoruba there are numerous quarters in which people of differing clans or ethnic affiliation live. Smaller compounds of extended families radiate outward from market areas, or commons, along narrow streets.

Each day, the farmers go out from the towns to till their gardens. The tuberous crops of the rain forests are grown in small clearings in the midst of the towering trees, and it is rare to find large areas of cleared fields. If the town is large, the farmers may have to walk several miles to reach the gardens and they sometimes erect small shelters in which to spend a night or two in order to avoid the long daily walk from home. Today, some farmers even commute by bus from the larger forest cities to plots many miles away, returning home every few days to rest and be with their families.

Depleted plots lie fallow over a period of several years, while successive adjacent plots are cultivated. The hoe is universally used in the forests, as it is in the Sudan. Although men traditionally clear the plots of trees and underbrush, prepare the soil, and plant and weed, both men and women often carry the heavy loads of yams, taro, cassava, and other products from the fields to the towns. There, crops are stored for home use, as well as sold and exchanged for other products. No beasts of burden are used in the forests, in contrast to the Sudan where the donkey carries goods of every description.

Despite an almost complete absence of Islamic influence, urban and court life was as rich and civilized, in its own way, as it was in the great states of the Sudan. There was no knowledge of writing, yet priests and intellectually curious men often debated religious and philosophical questions. Oral historians could recount for hours the adventures and achievements of the great kings. In many Akan and Kwa societies (the latter living in Nigeria, and including the Yoruba) a form of theater developed several centuries ago. Professional actors and musicians traveled from town to town performing plays based on popular moral and religious themes. A rich "oral literature" produced thousands of proverbs, parables, morality tales, and humorous stories, each diligently memorized and recited to audiences by semiprofessional storytellers. From this cherished tradition came Brer Rabbit and other tales that were borne by slaves from the rain forests and were gradually added to the folk literature of America.

Few people who have come to know the drama, poetry, folktales, music, and sculpture of the forest peoples are left unmoved, and many regard their art as the finest in Black Africa. Benin and Ife bronze busts are highly prized by many great museums of Europe (as well as those of modern Nigeria). The music of the forest peoples, spread by slaves to the New World, has formed the basis for jazz and some of the most popular modern music in the United States and the Caribbean. In the political realm, the forest peoples showed the same mastery of the art of state building and government as their cousins of the Sudanic grasslands.

Between about 1350 and 1650 a complicated and little-known process of state formation occurred among the Akan. By about 1400 the small but powerful state of Bono was established. It served as the focus for Akan trade with the Sudanic states and North Africa. Located in the Takyiman region of central Ghana and inhabited by the Brong group of Akan, Bono attracted frequent visitors from the Sudan. A number of Dyula traders from Mali settled in Bono-Manso, the capital town. Controlling the large and important source of gold that is still mined in modern Ghana, the kings of Bono for several centuries maintained a state that at times was strong enough to resemble a small empire, with vassal kings paying tribute to it.

Although Bono seems to have been the first Akan state to achieve sufficient power and wealth to overshadow its neighboring kingdoms, two others became prominent in the early seventeenth century. Akwamu, in the southeast of Ghana, had developed into a small empire by the end of the seventeenth century. It claimed hegemony over a number of other states that stretched between central Ghana and modern Dahomey. At its peak, in the early eighteenth century, Akwamu's armies roamed as far east as Ouidah in Dahomey. The other Akan state, Denkyira, controlled most of southwestern Ghana in the late seventeenth century; among its vassals were the several tiny states of the Asante in central Ghana.

Trade seems to have played a key role in the development of Akwamu and Denkyira, just as it had in Bono, but the trade upon which these two small empires prospered was the European trade, which was growing extensive during the sixteenth century. The Europeans along the coast—Portuguese, British, Dutch, and Danes most notably—maintained treaties with the kings of the coastal states and traded under their supervision. Profits accrued to these kings, especially in the Fante states and Ga (around modern Accra), but their ties with the Europeans curbed imperial expansion. A state with Dutch support, for example, would find that neither the Dutch nor their European rivals were willing to support wars of expansion. Peace was essential to trade. The states of the interior, on the other hand, were not subject to such protection or limitation. As guns and gunpower were added to other goods these interior states received in exchange for their gold and slaves, some established overlordship over neighboring states. Denkyira and Akwamu, close to the coastal trade centers but free from direct European influence, were notably successful.

While Akwamu and Denkyira were in their ascendancy, events were transpiring farther north that would lead to the creation of one of the greatest empires ever to appear in the forests of West Africa, the Asante Empire. In the mid-seventeenth century a large number of petty Asante states and kingdoms had developed in the vicinity of the modern city of Kumasi. These kingdoms were little more than large villages with clusters of smaller ones surrounding them, but the peoples of the area had evolved beyond decentralized rule by autonomous village and compound headmen. They had formed state systems, each with a king or chief who had established sovereignty over the villages and family heads of his territory.

Closely related to the Denkyira, the Asante seem to have moved northward from lands controlled by the "denkyirahene" (king) in the late fifteenth and early sixteenth centuries, but were soon brought under Denkyira control again. In about 1670, a chief of the Oyoko clan of the Asante, Obiri Yeboa, became king of one of the small states, Kwaaman. Either through conquest or diplomacy he persuaded the chiefs and ruling families of several other small states to merge with his clan and to accept him as chief. According to tradition, Obiri Yeboa was killed in the late 1670's in a war against the Domaa, who ruled another small state in the area.

Yeboa, in a sense the father of the Asante nation, was succeeded by Osei Tutu, who built the nation into a tightly knit superkingdom, endowed it with a deep sense of nationhood, and launched it on an imperial career. Osei Tutu was closely supported by a politically sagacious priest named Okomfo Anokye, who seems to have had a genius for political organization and tactics. According to stories that are told and retold today by the proud Asante, Osei Tutu organized a strong alliance of the several Asante clans against the detested power and taxes of Denkyira. Summoning the leaders of most of the little Asante states, Osei Tutu persuaded them to proclaim him "asantahene" through a brilliant performance by his friend and adviser, Okomfo Anokye. Tradition says that Anokye brought down from the sky, "in a black cloud and amidst rumblings," a golden stool (the beautifully carved stools of the Asante serve as symbols of the throne), which came to rest on Osei Tutu's lap. Anokye announced that the Gold Stool should, from that day forward, embody the soul and unity of the Asante people and should be considered sacred. He also said Osei Tutu and his lineage should head the Asante union.

Osei Tutu was then proclaimed asantahene. With the close support and counsel of Anokye, he began to build the Asante into a strong nation. Kumasi was declared the national capital and became the seat of the asantahene's throne. A compact, in reality an unwritten constitution, was formulated, requiring that every man conceive of himself solely as an Asante. The compact also acknowledged the spiritual unity of all Asante and the divine significance of the asantahene. With this compact several hundred thousand Asante, who had previously given their primary allegiance to the family, the clan, and the petty state, proclaimed their common nationality and accepted the legitimacy, the laws, the commands, and the mystical authority of one king. This process, which in most Sudanic societies took centuries of gradual development, was apparently condensed into one great national event.

Within a few years Osei Tutu had organized a national army. Athletics and constant practice in the use of arms became almost a national pastime. By this time a number of companies were armed with guns, mainly muskets with muzzle-loaded balls and flintlocks which had begun to trickle into Asanteland from the European trade along the coast. Other soldiers used the more traditional iron-tipped spears and wooden shields.

One of the first Europeans to visit Kumasi, the Englishman Thomas

Bowditch, wrote an account of that city in 1817. His description would not have differed too much from the scene in Osei Tutu's time, a little over a century before:

> We entered Coomassie at two o'clock. . . . Upwards of five thousand people, the greater part warriors, met us with awful bursts of martial music. . . . The dress of the captains was a war cap, with gilded rams horns projecting in front, the sides extended beyond all proportions by immense plumes of eagles feathers and fastened under the chin with bands of cowries. . . . Their vest was of red cloth, covered with fetishes and [scraps of Moorish writing] in gold and silver. . . . They wore loose cotton trowsers, with immense boots of a dull red leather, coming half way up the thigh. . . .
>
> Our observations . . . had taught us to conceive a spectacle far exceeding our original expectations; but they had not prepared us for the extent and display of the scene which here burst upon us: an area of nearly a mile in circumference was crowded with magnificence and novelty. The king, his tributaries, and captains, were resplendent in the distance, surrounded by attendants of every description. . . . More than a hundred bands burst out at once on our arrival, with the peculiar airs of their several chiefs; the horns flourished their defiances, with beating of innumerable drums and metal instruments, and then yielded for a while to the soft breathings of their long flutes which were truly harmonious. . . . At least a hundred large umbrellas, or canopies, which could shelter thirty persons, were sprung up and down by the bearers with brilliant effect, being made of scarlet, yellow, and the most shewey cloths and silks, and crowned on the top with crescents, pelicans, elephants, barrels, and arms and swords of gold. . . .
>
> The caboceers, as did their superior captains and attendants, wore Ashanti cloths, of extravagant price from the costly foreign silks which had been unravelled to weave them in all the varieties of colour, as well as pattern; these cloths were of an incredible size and weight, and thrown over the shoulder exactly like the Roman toga; a small silk fillet generally encircles their temples, and massy gold necklaces, intricately wrought, suspended Moorish charms, dearly purchased, and enclosed in small square cases of gold, silver, and curious embroidery. . . .
>
> Coomassie is an oblong of nearly four miles in circumference. . . . Four of the principal streets are half a mile long, and from 50 to 100 yards wide. I observed them building one, and a line was stretched on each side to make it regular. The streets were all named. . . .
>
> The Ashantis persisted that the population of Coomassie . . . was upwards of 100,000. . . .
>
> What surprised me most . . . was the discovery that every house had its cloasae [toilet], besides the common ones for the lower orders without the town. They were generally situated under a small archway in the most retired angle of the building, but not unfrequently upstairs, within a separate room like a small closet. . . . The holes are of a small circum-

Courtyard in the palace of the Asantahene.
(From a drawing by Thomas Bowdich, 1819.)

ference, but dug to a surprising depth, and boiling water is daily poured down, which effectually prevents the least offense. The rubbish and offal of each house was burnt every morning at the back of the street, and they were as nice and cleanly in their dwellings as in their persons.

Osie Tutu's constitution provided not only for the office of asantahene, but also for a strong advisory council, on which sat the kings of the several original Asante states, which had become provinces of the nation. Each former king had to swear allegiance to the asantahene, renouncing the right to make war on his own. He also had to agree to provide troops and supplies for the national army when the asantahene declared war. A judicial system, which legitimized traditional law, was also provided. Cases would be decided by the traditional village headmen and chiefs, but were subject to review, upon appeal by a citizen, by a national court in Kumasi.

Following national unity, Osei Tutu concentrated on building his military organization. By 1680 he had launched a ten-year program of small wars that brought all the states in a wide circle around Kumasi under his rule and drove from the territory those peoples who could not become absorbed into the union. Asante armies then turned to their greatest foe, Denkyira. In a series of battles between 1699 and 1701, Asante crushed the power of that formerly great state. With the defeat of Denkyira, Asante inherited its suzerainty over a number of states in southwestern Ghana including Elmina, where the Dutch centered their flourishing trade. By about 1716, Osei Tutu's forces had firmly established his control over Denkyira's vassal states, and the Dutch sent a full diplomatic mission to Kumasi in recognition of his sovereign status.

In 1717, Osei Tutu was killed in a revolt by the Akyem state. The Asante Empire he left was too new and too violently created to be either united or peaceful. Revolts usually came within a year or two after the Asante armies moved on to conquer other foes, and constant punitive action and statesmanship were required to hold the restive dominions together. If a weak ruler had succeeded Osei Tutu, his pioneering work would very likely have been undone. But Osei Tutu was succeeded, after a period of bitter dispute over the succession, by his grandnephew Opoku Ware, who proved himself a worthy ruler in every respect.

If Osei Tutu cemented the national union and built the framework of empire, Opoku Ware brought both to vigorous fruition. He became asantahene in about 1720 and ruled through thirty years of constant expansion and conquest. Opoku Ware distinguished himself as an empire builder, a great general and master tactician, yet he began his career as asantahene by deepening the national spirit that Osei Tutu had nurtured. He proclaimed the anniversary of Osei Tutu's death as a time of national reaffirmation. Each Asante swore a solemn oath to

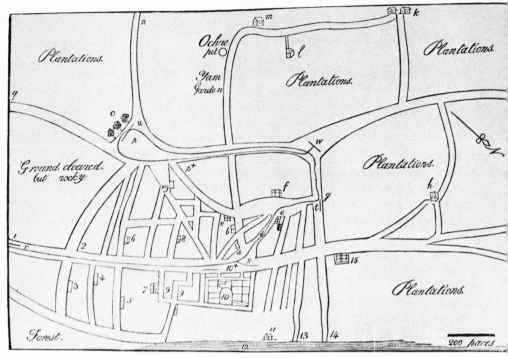

Earliest known map of Kumasi, sketched by Thomas Bowdich, 1819.
Points of interest: *1* (middle left), road leading to Fante
and Assin; *10*, the royal palace; *p*, the main marketplace.

conduct himself in a manner worthy of that great king, especially in
battle and military affairs. The quasi-militaristic tradition that Osei Tutu
had introduced was declared a matter of national honor. The destiny
of the Asante nation, as revealed by God through Osei Tutu, required
every Asante to uphold this honor, never to retreat before the enemy,
and always to press the foe relentlessly.

After revitalizing the sense of national mission, Opoku Ware
turned his attention to the suppression of revolts by Akyem, Denkyira,
and Akwapim. These three states had united to throw off Asante control. They then allied with Sefwi, an adjacent state that feared conquest.
Opoku Ware's armies dealt the rebellious allies a crushing defeat, then
marched beyond their territories into other states in the south and
southwest of modern Ghana. For twenty years, the Asante extended and
maintained their empire, which stretched in the southwest to the
Atlantic shore and included the vital trading centers of Elmina, built
late in the fifteenth century by the Portuguese, and Appollonia, built
in the seventeenth century by the Dutch. At both Appollonia and
Elmina, the Dutch quickly recognized Asante ownership, and paid
rents to them rather than face war with this formidable new power.

The several states of the Fante people lie in the center of modern

Ghana's coast. During Opoku Ware's campaigns, they were closely allied in trade with the Dutch and the English. Asante made no attempt to invade their lands, having established satisfactory outlets to the sea farther west. Instead Asante moved against the Ga peoples to the east, whose capital and chief trading center was Accra, the large and thriving capital of modern Ghana. In 1742 Opoku Ware entered Accra and accepted vows of fealty from the leaders of the Ga and their close relatives, the Adangbe. This victory gave Asante direct connections with the coastal trade and access to European arms and gunpowder. Both were essential to the maintenance of power. In return for European weapons and manufactured articles, Asante exchanged gold and slaves.

After establishing its jurisdiction at Accra, Elmina, and Appollonia, Asante determined to expand to the north where, just beyond Asante's borders, there was additional gold, as well as slaves, gums, kola nuts, grains, and livestock. In the forests, where the Asante army had forged its strength, the absence of large clearings had demanded a form of warfare based on infantry, which infiltrated toward the enemy under cover of the great trees and underbrush. In the Sudan, however, little cover was available, and the enemy had long possessed strong cavalry. Yet the Asante quickly defeated the forces of the peoples near the forests and added their horse-borne warriors to the Asante army in order to even the odds with the stronger states that lay farther north—Gonja, Dagomba, and Mamprussi.

In 1744 Opoku Ware marched against Gonja and the small neigh-

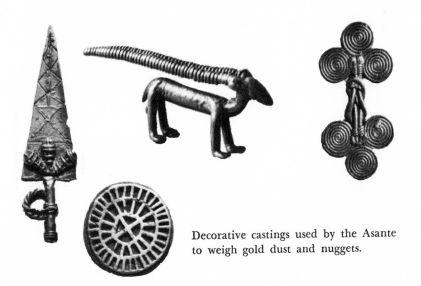

Decorative castings used by the Asante to weigh gold dust and nuggets.

boring state of Krache. Both were subdued and annexed in less than two years. The armies of Dagomba were defeated almost immediately afterward. Opoku Ware declared a protectorate over that nation, and exacted tribute from its northern neighbor, Mamprussi. By now he had acquired a large force of horsemen from the conquered states, and these, when added to the famed Asante infantry, made him more than a match for the armies of the grassland states.

The rapid adaptation of their military strategy to differing needs reflected an ability the Asante often showed in subsequent times. They were able to incorporate alien ideas, techniques, and personnel into their own system without diluting it. During the nineteenth century Asante is known to have employed scribes, military trainers, commercial advisers, and artisans from Hausaland, the Voltaic states, and even Europe, to assist it in governing the vast domain it ruled.

By the time of his death in 1750, Opoku Ware had expanded the Asante Empire almost to its greatest limits. For thirty years he had led Asante armies from victory to victory. His awe-inspiring reputation is perhaps best expressed by the author of the *Tarikh Gonja* (history of Gonja, written in Arabic): "May God curse him, may He take his soul and cast it into the fire. He it was who troubled the people of Gonja; continually and at all times did he trouble them. He seized their possessions. Whatever he wished, so he did, for he was all powerful in his rule."

During the nineteenth century, Asante had many periods of weak rule, disputes among the noble families, and revolts by vassal kings, but in general the empire remained vigorous and viable, except for the increasingly debilitating effects of its struggles with the Fante and their allies, the British. Throughout the eighteenth century Asante had pursued its imperial expansion without major confrontations with the prosperous Fante states on the central coast of Ghana. There were disputes and tensions, and occasionally serious incidents, but generally Asante's need for coastal trading access was satisfied by its control of Elmina and Accra. The Fante were divided into numerous small states (nineteen are recognized today), which seem to have originated during a Fante population expansion in the seventeenth century. So long as Asante's access to coastal trading was secure, it had no reason to undertake any expansionist campaign against the Fante.

During the early nineteenth century the relationship between Asante and the Fante states took a turn for the worse. It seems likely that the Asante became apprehensive that the Fante would deny them access to the sea. In 1806 the Asante invaded Fante territory and won a major victory. From this time forward the asantehene regarded the Fante as a conquered people. But neither the Fante nor their British allies were willing to recognize the asantahene's authority. Decades of tension followed. Fante troops occasionally attacked Elmina or threatened Accra; fugitives from Asante vassal states were given refuge in Fante; and Asante traders were insulted or interfered with in Fante country. In 1811, 1814-16, 1823-24, 1826, 1863, 1869 and 1873 there were Asante-Fante wars. In each, Asante forces invaded Fante territory. An uneasy peace followed each war. Finally, in 1874, a Fante-British army invaded Asante and inflicted a crushing defeat that ended any further Asante threat to the Fante.

The Asante-Fante wars developed, especially after 1820, into a conflict between the Asante and the British. Increasingly British arms, money, military advice—and eventually British troops—threw back the Asante threat to Fante-British territory on the coast. From the 1823-24 war onward, each conflict resulted in Asante defeats that were accompanied by the freeing of one or another of the Asante vassal states. By 1874 the territory of Asante had shrunk almost to the territory of the original union. Asante's imperial career was ended by the growing power of British imperialism in the Gold Coast, although as a state Asante remained strong. In 1896, when a talented new asantahene, Prempeh I, showed signs of effectiveness in rebuilding the old empire, he was seized by British troops, deposed, and eventually sent into exile.

If the British had not been committed to curbing Asante influence during the nineteenth century, all of modern Ghana would probably have become part of the Asante Empire. Had this happened, the political talent of the Asante, and their ability to use European arms and ideas, might have created a very different modern history for the Gold Coast.

Beyond the Volta River, east of modern Ghana, lie the small countries of Togo and Dahomey. There, the towering trees of the rain forest give way to savanna country. In Togo and eastern Ghana live the numerous Ewe people, who, although cultured and prosperous, never developed a large and powerful state system. To their west, in Dahomey, another group of Ewe peoples, the Fon, did develop a state system that attained considerable power and affluence during the seventeenth, eighteenth, and nineteenth centuries.

On the coast of Dahomey, which Europeans named the Slave Coast because of its importance as a source of slaves, the first European ships found a number of small, well-organized city-states. The peoples of these states spoke a language of the Ewe cluster of languages, which were part of the Twi branch of the Kwa subfamily of the Congo-Kordofanian stock. The Ewe-speaking peoples are related to the Akan-speaking group, and seem to have settled in Togo and Dahomey at about the same period as the Akan settled Ghana. The Fon group occupied central Dahomey and other Ewe groups settled along the coast.

In the fifteenth century, while the coastal peoples were living in well-organized small states, the Fon lived in much more loosely organized societies. During the growing slave trade of the sixteenth and early seventeenth centuries, the Fon were often captured by raiding troops of Ardrah and Ouidah, two of the most powerful kingdoms on the coast. The Fon were subject to the king of the Yoruba state of Oyo, whose dreaded cavalry periodically swept into Dahomey for slaves or to suppress revolts among the Fon.

In about 1650 the Fon formed a national union, based on the need for mutual protection, under King Wegbaja. By 1725 the state, called Abomey (or sometimes Dahomey), was strong enough to push beyond its own borders. It sent an army against Great Ardrah, near the coast, and sacked the city. In 1728 Abomey troops moved against the small coastal states of Savi and Ouidah, conquering both. From that time on Abomey was the master of central Dahomey, and controlled most of the coast and the European slave trade. After 1740 the king of Abomey appointed a high-ranking official who resided in Ouidah and dealt directly with the European traders there.

In order to protect itself against its many threatening neighbors, Abomey was organized along military lines from its inception. The king was granted total power by his people and also served as the nation's high priest. He appointed chiefs as well as army officers and administrators. All citizens and appointed officials owed the king unswerving loyalty and service. Through this system the king soon became one of the most powerful monarchs along the West African coast, a notable development in view of the small size and poverty of his country.

Because Abomey was relatively poor and had a comparatively small population, perhaps less than 200,000, its elaborate court and government were too costly to be supported by local wealth or wealth from normal trade. Wars of conquest became ever more frequent. As the Englishman Brodie Cruickshank reported when he visited Abomey's King Gezo in 1848:

> The state which he maintained was great; his army was expensive; the ceremonies and customs to be observed annually, which had been handed down to him from his forefathers, entailed upon him a vast outlay of money. These could not be abolished. The form of his government could not be suddenly changed, without causing such a revolution as would deprive him of his throne, and precipitate his kingdom into a state of anarchy.

Abomey's need for wealth provided a constant stimulus to slave raids and pillaging expeditions. It also created two internal effects that were most striking to European visitors of the nineteenth century—large numbers of human sacrifices and widespread use of women in government and the army.

Human sacrifice, although not unknown in Sudanic societies, was not a usual phenomenon. In Abomey it represented a means of offering more precious gifts to the spirits of the ancestors, in order to ensure their aid in the ceaseless search for wealth. Criminals within Dahomey and slaves captured in raids were used in the sacrifices. As the nineteenth century wore on, Dahomey's position became increasingly insecure, due to the great growth in power of the Yoruba states to the east. More and more slaves were sacrificed. A few European visitors reported sacrifices of several hundred lives on the great annual ceremonies when supplications were made for the next year's fortunes.

In Abomey, women were paired with men in most government offices. They advised the men and served as their replacements in times of war. This practice was especially important in the court and the central government. Sons of the king were very numerous because of the king's many wives and were prohibited from holding public office, lest they use their position to intrigue in favor of their claims to the throne. The king appointed hundreds of his wives and daughters to serve as co-officials with men, partly to ensure that the functions of office would be carried on when the men were away and partly to ensure that the women, presumably loyal because of their relationship to him, would guarantee fair and unselfish performance by their male co-officials.

The women's military corps was a fully functioning unit. Its women —often termed "Amazons" by visiting Europeans—fought alongside corps of male soldiers in both offensive and defensive action. They had their own female commanders, underwent rigorous training, and were regarded as the equals of men in combat. One can do no better in describing these unusual troops than to quote Sir Richard Burton, the great English explorer who visited Dahomey in 1863. Burton's account is usually regarded as objective, apart from its anti-Negro bias:

1. The Agbarya or blunder-buss women, who may be considered the grenadiers. They are the biggest and strongest of the force, and each is accompanied by an attendant carrying ammunition. With the blunder-buss women rank the Zo-hu-nun, or carbineers, the Gan'u-nlan, or Sure-to-kill Company, and the Achi, or bayoneteers.

2. The elephant huntresses, who are held to be the bravest. Of these women, twenty have been known to bring down, at one volley, with their rude appliances, seven animals out of a herd.

"Amazon" warriors of Dahomey, as conceived by a
nineteenth-century European artist.

3. The Nyekplo-hen-to, or razor women, who seem to be simply an epouvantail.

4. The infantry, or line's-women, forming the staple of the force, from whom, as in France, the elite is drawn. They are armed with Tower muskets, and are well supplied with bad ammunition; bamboo fibre, for instance, being the only wadding. They have but little ball practice. They "manoeuver with the precision of a flock of sheep," and they are too light to stand a charge of the poorest troops in Europe. Personally, they are cleanly made, without much muscle; they are hard dancers, indefatiguable singers, and, though affecting a military swagger, their faces are anything but ferocious—they are rather mild and unassuming in appearance. They fought with fury with Gezo before Abeokuta because there is a jealousy between them and their brother soldiers, and because they had been led for many years by that king to small but sure victory. They fled, however, with the rest, when a little perserverance would have retrieved the fortunes of the day.

5. The Go-hen-to, or archeresses, who in Gezo's time were young girls —the parade corps, the pick of the army, and the pink of dancers. They were armed with the peculiar Dahoman bow, a quiver of poisoned light cane shafts—mere birdbolts, with hooked heads, spiny as sticklebacks— and a small knife lashed with a lanyard to the wrist. They were distinguished by scanty attire, by a tattoo extending to the knee, and by an ivory bracelet on the left arm. Their weapon has naturally fallen in public esteem. Under Gezo's son they are never seen on parade; and when in the field they are used as scouts and porters; like our drummers and doolee-bearers, they also carry the wounded to the rear.

The use of female troops was due, at least in part, to an acute shortage of manpower. With its total population of less than 200,000, Abomey often bested enemies with five or ten times as many people.

Abomey prospered for a century and a half. When the state union was formed, it was subject to the king of Oyo, but Oyo's power over Abomey weakened progressively. In 1726, and again in 1728, 1729, and 1730, the cavalry of Oyo swept into Dahomey, defeated the troops of the Fon, and spread devastation. After each invasion, however, the Fon recuperated rapidly and they never lost control of their coastal vassal states. During the nineteenth century, Fon troops seized some of the more westerly Yoruba territory, and came to regard the ancient power of Oyo as a dead issue.

Abomey's growth never included serious attempts to expand into Asante territory on the west, and eastern expansion was limited to relatively small parts of Yorubaland. During the mid-nineteenth century Dahomey occasionally threatened Egba, Abeokuta, and Ibadan in Yorubaland, but its troops were not numerous enough to support a large imperial growth. The affluence of Dahomey stemmed mostly from the slave trade, and the kingdom possessed little wealth apart from the slaves it could capture from weaker peoples.

After the abolition of slavery, and the suppression of the slave trade by European naval forces, the prosperity of Dahomey declined. By 1893, when Dahomey was declared a French protectorate, it was in a general political and economic depression.

As the thinly wooded savannas of Dahomey give way to the great rain forests on its east, one soon enters the country of the Yoruba, one of the most highly organized peoples of Africa. Living in both villages and cities that frequently number well over 100,000, the Yoruba are spread over the forests of southwestern Nigeria and a large expanse of savanna country to the north of the forest. The Yoruba people speak a language of the Kwa subfamily of the Congo-Kordofanian stock, indicating that the Yoruba are not too distantly related to their neighbors in Dahomey, Togo, and Ghana.

The Yoruba seem to have entered southern Nigeria before A.D. 1000, splitting into two main groups: one on the savanna in the Oyo region, another in the forest in the region of Ife and Ijebu. Each of these groups has differentiated into distinct subgroups. Long before 1000, the Yoruba had mastered agriculture and iron working; evidence of iron smelting in their area of Nigeria has been traced back as far as 400 B.C. Like the Akan, however, their prosperity in the forest country cannot have been very substantial until sometime in the first millennium A.D., when East Asian plants were introduced.

Yoruba tradition locates the origin of the Yoruba peoples at Ife. One myth maintains that all mankind was created at Ife, and spread across the world from there. Another, much more modestly, holds that Oduduwa, the ancestor of all the Yoruba, arrived in Ife from somewhere far to the east, and established the Yoruba people. Whatever the case, all Yoruba still regard Ife as a hallowed city. Modern archaeologists are in the midst of extensive excavations in modern Ife, a difficult task in view of the dense clustering of its houses and the large number of sacred places that cannot be touched by the archaeologist's shovel. The numerous busts and statues of stone, terra cotta, and bronze that have so far been found date back before 1300 and indicate a high level of wealth and stability.

Most Sudanic societies lived within one or another geographic environment; not so the Yoruba, who played a role both in the grasslands of the Sudan and in the rain forests. Major groups of Yoruba have long inhabited the areas of Ilorin and Oyo south of Nupe and Hausaland. Around Oyo they built a powerful small empire whose known history goes back at least to 1400. Other groups of Yoruba and closely related peoples in the forests of southwestern Nigeria, around the cities

Audience with a central Nigerian king, the Ata of Igala.
(Drawing by Commander William Helen, 1832–33).

of Ife, Ilesha, Ibadan, Lagos, Ijebu-Ode, Akure, Ondo, and Abeokuta, built highly-structured states and a culture rich in art, music, religion, drama, and oral literature.

The lives of the Yoruba of the savannas, in Ilorin and Oyo, were closely related to the widespread Sudanic pattern. Their economy, like those of the other peoples of the Sudan, was based on the production of millet, sorghum, cow peas, and other Sudanic crops. The Yoruba of the forest and those of the savanna speak the same language, acknowledge common origins, share a similar social and political organization, and wear similar dress. Yet the forest Yoruba, like the Akan and other forest dwellers, live in large villages, towns, and cities and devote themselves to the cultivation of tuberous crops.

The unique achievement of the forest Yoruba, like that of the related Edo peoples who created the empire of Benin to the east of Yorubaland, was their art. Oyo, on the other hand, seems to have turned its attention more to politics and government and never achieved the greatness in art that its sister peoples just to the south reached.

Still, the Oyo Empire was the crowning political achievement of the Yoruba people. At least as early 1400 the Yoruba of Oyo were organized into a state, under the rule of the "alafin" (king). According to tradition, which is heavily blended with national religious myths, Oyo was founded by Oranmiyan, a son or grandson of Oduduwa, who came from Ife. Forty-three alafins are said to have descended from Oranmiyan in a dynasty that may be as old as six hundred years. The third alafin, Sango, brought several surrounding small states under Oyo's control; legend has so glamorized Sango that he is now revered as the Yoruba god of thunder and lightning.

Oyo traditions speak of frequent early contact, and conflict, with Nupe, Hausa, and Borgu. Oyo must early have occupied a key trading position as the southern terminus of a trade route connecting the forest and coastal peoples with Nupe, Hausa, and the Sudan. Nupe and Oyo were rivals, and the earliest verifiable date for Oyo is when Nupe's great king, Tsoede, destroyed Old Oyo in about 1531.

Throughout the late sixteenth and seventeenth centuries Oyo extended its territory northward to include the Yoruba of Ilorin, and inflicted major defeats on Nupe. To the south it gradually incorporated other Yoruba states. But Oyo's cavalry never succeeded in establishing firm control in the hilly forests of the Yoruba states to the south and southwest. Oyo concentrated its expansion to its southwest and west. It established suzerainty over the Yoruba state of Egbado and the Fon of Dahomey. Through Egbado it gained direct access to the coast, where it could take part in the trade with Europe.

The political system of Oyo was very complex. The alafin had broad powers, and, in typical Sudanic fashion, was held to be semidivine. His power was balanced by a council, the Oyo Mesi, which was headed by an official called the bashorun. In times when the alafin was strong and judicious, the Oyo Mesi served to strengthen his administration. In times of weak alafins or strong bashoruns, the Oyo Mesi tended to reinforce internal divisions and tensions. Yoruba political theory tends to question the wisdom of having a ruler whose power cannot be readily checked. The Oyo Mesi, which served as a check on the alafin, was itself under the surveillance of the Ogboni, a secret society that included many religious and political leaders. The strong alafins constantly struggled to buttress their power by building a personal following among military and provincial leaders. The Oyo Mesi, and sometimes the Ogboni, tried to curb such efforts. The Oyo Mesi had one ultimate power in this struggle: it could, and frequently did, require a tyrannical or unethical alafin to commit suicide.

Under this system Oyo prospered between the early seventeenth and late eighteenth centuries, reaching the zenith of its power between about 1650 and 1750. In 1754, following a period during which the powers of the alafin had grown, a ruthless bashorun, Gaha, came to power. Gaha undermined the powers of the next several alafins, until one Abiodun came to power and murdered Gaha and his family. During Abiodun's rule, from 1774 to 1789, important tributary states in the Oyo Empire rebelled and regained their independence. This marked the beginning of a long process of decline in the empire's fortunes. During Abiodun's reign, or within a few years after his death, Borgu, Egba, and Nupe threw off Oyo control, and Dahomey, while still acknowledging Oyo's overlordship, several times refused to pay its customary tribute. In 1818 Dahomey formally declared its independence; Ilorin allied itself with the expanding Fulani Empire of northern Nigeria; and war broke out between Oyo and Owu. After this war, Owu became independent.

At its zenith Oyo had controlled a huge territory that stretched from the Niger River to the Atlantic, and from inside the forest region across the savannas to the border of modern Togo. For at least two centuries Oyo prospered on the trade and tribute of its imperial system. After becoming a powerful empire, Oyo began to participate in the slave trade with European agents along the coasts of Dahomey and western Nigeria, but this trade seems to have had more negative than positive consequences for Oyo. Nupe and Borgu were both sources of slaves in the trade through Dahomey, but as they grew strong enough to break away in the late eighteenth century, Oyo turned toward the Yoruba states of the forest as a supplementary source. As the Oyo slave raids increased, so did the resentment and retaliation of these Yoruba states. Early in the nineteenth century the situation developed into a civil war, which was to wrack Yorubaland for more than half a century.

Several factors were important in causing and perpetuating the Yoruba civil wars. An interest in throwing off and destroying Oyo's power certainly was an initiating factor. The slave trade, marked by Oyo raids and then by raids of one Yoruba state on another, greatly exacerbated the wars. The southward thrust of the Fulani jihad, borne by the Islamized Yoruba state of Ilorin, also played a key role, especially during the mid-nineteenth century.

As a consequence of the civil wars, Oyo was reduced to impotence. Old Oyo was totally destroyed in 1835. Refugees from Oyo and other states streamed through the countryside seeking safety. Abeokuta and Ibadan, two of the largest modern Yoruba cities, stem from settlements of large groups of these refugees. Ibadan, now numbering well over half a million Yoruba, grew rapidly and came to serve as the most effective bulwark against Fulani domination of southern Yorubaland. Abeokuta became the focal point of British Christian missionary activities in Nigeria, as well as the Yoruba stronghold that defeated a powerful Dahomeyan army, in 1851, thus preventing further conquest of Yoruba territory by the Fon.

By 1893 the Yoruba civil wars, no longer aggravated by the slave trade, had ended. The British played an important role in the peacemaking efforts. With the end of the civil wars came the beginning of colonial rule in Yorubaland.

East of Yorubaland live the Edo peoples, who produced the great empire of Benin. Benin was for a long period the most powerful and highly developed state in the forests of the Guinea coast. To the European visitors of the fifteenth and sixteenth centuries it clearly outshone any other kingdom in West Africa.

In the mid-seventeenth century, when Benin was at the height of its power, a Dutch geographer, Olfert Dapper, published a geography of Africa. It devoted a good deal of space to Benin City, as well as to the state and its government:

> Fourteen or fifteen leagues from Gotton, as one travels north, lies a town which the Dutch call Great Benin, because in fact there is no town so great in all those regions. The palace of the Queen alone is three leagues round, and the town five; so that the town and the palace taken together have a perimeter of eight leagues. The town is enclosed on one side by a wall ten feet high, made of a double palisade of trees, with stakes in between interlaced in the form of a cross, thickly lined with earth. On the other side a marsh, fringed with bushes, which stretches from one end of the wall to the other, serves as a natural rampart to the town. There are several gates, eight or nine feet high and five feet wide: they are made of wood, all of one piece, and turn on a stake like the hurdles which enclose meadows.
>
> The King's palace . . . is a collection of buildings which occupy as much space as the town of Harlem, and which is enclosed with walls. There are numerous apartments for the Prince's ministers and fine galleries most of which are as big as those on the Exchange at Amsterdam. . . .
>
> The town is composed of thirty main streets, very straight and 120 feet wide, apart from an infinity of small intersecting streets. The houses are close to one another, arranged in good order; they have roofs, verandahs and balustrades, and are covered with leaves of palm-trees and bananas—for they are only one storey high. . . . These people are in no way inferior to the Dutch as regards cleanliness; they wash and scrub their houses so well that they are polished and shining like a looking-glass. . . .
>
> . . . These Negroes are much more civilized than others on this coast. They are people who have good laws and a well organized police; who live on good terms with the Dutch and other foreigners who come to trade among them, and show them a thousand marks of friendship. . . .
>
> . . . The arms of these people consist of pikes and shields, assegais, bows, and poisoned arrows. Gentlemen who are on their way to take part in

Benin bronze of a mounted soldier.
(Courtesy of the British Museum.)

a campaign, and who want to display themselves, wear a fine scarlet coat, a necklace of elephants' and leopards' teeth, and a red furred turban trimmed with leopard or civet skin, from which hangs a horse's tail. . . .
. . . He is a powerful Prince, the King of Benin: he can mobilize 20,000 soldiers in a day, and raise in a short time an army of 80,000 to 100,000 men. Thus he is the terror of his neighbors, and an object of fear to his own peoples.

According to Edo tradition the state of Benin was founded in about A.D. 900 by the Bini people who migrated from Egypt. Neither the date of founding nor the view that the people came from Egypt can be taken literally. The state was more likely founded in about the eleventh or twelfth century and its founders, like the founders of many other forest states, were peoples of the savanna who moved into the forest and merged with the indigenous peoples there. The Edo language is a branch of the Kwa subfamily of the Congo-Kordofanian stock and is closely related to the Yoruba and Ibo languages.

Whatever the origins of the founders of Benin, the state takes second place only to Ife in antiquity of development. The magnificent bronze castings of Benin artists and craftsmen (clearly related in style to those of Ife) date back almost as far as those of Ife. They were being produced as early as the late fourteenth century, if not earlier.

The history of Benin, particularly as it has been handed down in oral tradition, has been most authoritatively written by the modern historian Chief Jacob Egharevba, himself a member of the Benin nobility. According to Egharevba, the rulers of the first dynasty were called ogiso. From the supposed founding of Benin in about 900, there were thirty-one ogisos. Benin grew gradually and included within its political system the Bini group of Edo peoples and a few closely related Edo groups. A few years before 1170 a serious dispute about the legitimacy of succession of a new ogiso occurred. The disgusted Bini people sent a delegation to Oduduwa, the great legendary king of Ife who is regarded as the father of the Yoruba peoples, to ask him for a new ruler. Tradition holds that Oduduwa sent his son Oranmiyan, the same Oranmiyan who later founded Oyo, as the first "oba" (the Yoruba word for ruler) of Benin. Oranmiyan is said to have ruled for several years. He then returned to Yorubaland, asserting that Benin could not be properly ruled by an outsider. He appointed his son by a Bini wife to be his successor. This son, Eweka I, was the first native-born oba.

This legend is almost certainly a symbolic representation of the vital role that the Yoruba city of Ife played as a center for new ideas and talent. Historical speculation provides a slightly different account.

Just before A.D. 1000 Black Africans of the Sudanic stock must have been settled in the forest region of modern Nigeria as well as in the adjacent grasslands, as far north as the Niger River. An agricultural people, they may have begun to add the East Indian plants to their economies by 1000. Very probably they were descended from the Nok peoples. The people in the vicinity of Ife must have taken the lead in developing a state, as well as in iron working, bronze casting, and techniques of art.

Probably there was a comparatively rapid increase in the forest population at about this period. Extended families or groups of adventuresome men, with their relatives and friends, must have left the increasingly crowded Ife area to seek their fortunes in adjacent regions. The king of Ife may have sent out these parties of settlers, and they may have been able to establish themselves in positions of prestige and authority by virtue of his support.

These Ife bands would have been quickly absorbed in the Yoruba areas to which they migrated. Ife presumably was not able to sustain the power to incorporate the adjacent Yoruba areas into its own political system. In those early times the difficulties of moving armies through dense forests certainly discouraged the creation of empires.

In Benin, itself located in the great forests, the Ife settlers, even if they were conquerors, may have been unable to maintain easy contact with Ife itself, and would have become absorbed in the local culture. The leading Ife settler might have found it impossible to establish himself as a ruler of a strong non-Yoruba people and may have departed voluntarily or been expelled. In this case his son, born of a local princess, could easily have succeeded to the throne. Such a dynasty would not have represented a complete break with the past, yet it could have enhanced its prestige by asserting its relationship with the powerful and advanced kingdom of Ife. In such a situation, Ife would no longer have posed a direct threat to Benin. The two states could have maintained peaceful intercourse and Ife techniques in arts and crafts could have made their way into Benin quite naturally.

Benin tradition is in accord with such speculation. It reveres Ife for supplying its modern dynasty of rulers and for developing its famous bronze industry. Historians find no evidence that Benin has ever been politically subject to Ife. On the contrary, it is clear that Benin early became a militarily powerful state and established political suzerainty over a number of Yoruba kingdoms. Its empire between the fifteenth and eighteenth centuries stretched across the southern tier of Yoruba states to Lagos and Badagry, near the western edge of modern Nigeria.

The great longevity of the Benin state under the obas seems to have been made possible, at least in part, by the fact that the oba acceded to the throne under a clear constitutional provision that provided for hereditary rule by the oba's eldest son. The Uzama, or state council of noblemen, installed the new oba and had certain constitutional powers in state affairs, but had no power to remove the oba. The tensions that so often characterized relations between the alafin and Oyo Mesi in Oyo were effectively precluded in the Benin system. Some obas were strong and creative, while others were weak and ineffectual, but their sacred right of tenure helped to provide continuity and to discourage internal plotting and disunity.

Eweka I, the first native oba, was the founder of the state and the oba under whom the Uzama is thought to have begun. After him the state grew stronger and gradually expanded its territory under obas of varying quality. In about 1440 one of the greatest obas in Benin history came to the throne: Ewuare. Ewuare, celebrated in tradition as a great magician, healer, and military leader, undertook a major expansion of the empire. Tradition maintains that Ewuare battled and defeated 201 towns (many of which were tiny states) of. the Yoruba and Ibo and spread Benin authority to the Niger River on the east and well into Yoruba country on the north and west. According to tradition, he raised Benin City to the status of an important metropolis. During his reign a Portuguese named d'Aveiro became the first European known to have visited the country.

Benin's position, not far from the sea on navigable rivers, exposed it to direct European contact from 1485 on. In the early years of the sixteenth century d'Aveiro, on his second visit to Benin, is said to have urged the oba to establish relations with Portugal. Benin sent an ambassador to Portugal, and Portugal sent traders and missionaries to Benin. A church was built and Portuguese missionaries, with the support of the oba, baptized thousands of Bini. When the first Englishman visited Benin, in 1553, he found that the oba himself could speak Portuguese.

The Portuguese presence and Christianity in Benin eventually faded. The traders found the climate and health conditions unsatisfactory and soon abandoned their trading stations in the country. By the seventeenth century little trace of Portuguese influence had survived, and Benin's contacts with Europe depended largely on visiting British and Dutch traders. Most European trade shifted to Dahomey in the west and to the new "river states" that began to develop at the mouths of the Niger: Bonny, Brass, Kalabari, and others. Benin, though by no means isolated, became an area of secondary importance as far as the European and African trade was concerned.

During the eighteenth century, the Benin Empire began to shrink. The empire of Oyo, at the zenith of its power, limited Benin's influence on the north and west; the growing strength of the Yoruba states of Ekiti and Egbado permitted them to break away from Benin, and Benin's former trading primacy waned.

At several periods during the nineteenth century the old power of Benin reasserted itself, and former territory was recaptured. But Benin's long-stable political system had begun to deteriorate, and civil wars and factional rivalries became frequent. With each new internal dissension, territories under the empire would break away again. In Yorubaland, Akure and a number of Ekiti towns rebelled, and the growing power of Ibadan expanded eastward into Ilesha and other Yoruba areas formerly under Benin control. By the 1890's Benin's territory included only the Edo heartland and western Iboland. British influence, now well established in the Niger delta and east of the Niger, effectively precluded any imperial expansion by Benin. In 1897, after a British mission was massacred on its way to Benin, the oba was arrested by a British force and exiled. Thus the empire of Benin came to an end, after a career of over six centuries.

10 The Bantu States and Peoples

From West Africa the savannas of the Sudan and the rain forests nearer the coast bend southward toward the equator. In a great arc, they curve around the Gulf of Guinea and continue southward through the modern states of Cameroun, Gabon, and Congo (Brazzaville), merging with the great rain forests that blanket the Congo River basin on both sides of the equator. The Sudan's savanna extends southward through Chad and the Central African Republic, but to the east, in the neighborhood of East Africa's Great Lakes, it begins to break up into patches. Moister highland areas and spots of moderately dry woodland mix in with the grasslands. This mixed topography is characteristic of much of eastern and central Africa. South of the Congo basin there are no more large areas of rain forest, nor are there any large areas of savanna.

This vast region covering all of Africa south of the equator is inhabited by peoples of the Bantu language group, which is divided into more than three hundred languages and dialects. When the first European scholars studied the Bantu-speaking peoples, they assumed that their languages and cultures were unrelated to those of other Black Africans. Racially, too, the Bantu seemed to represent a divergent variety of African, differing considerably from each other and from the Black Africans of West Africa. Among the Bantu there are groups with brownish skins, as well as black; many are tall and others are rather short.

Twentieth-century research has found that the Bantu-speaking peoples are fundamentally related to one another and to the peoples of western Africa. The hundreds of Bantu languages are only one branch of the Congo-Kordofanian language stock.

Several major facts help provide a broad outline for Bantu history. First is the linguistic kinship of the Bantu languages with other African languages farther north and northwest. Second, the Bantu-speaking peoples created numerous states and small empires that shared the fundamental features of the Sudanic states. Third is the almost universal use by the Bantu-speaking peoples of the Sudanic agricultural complex. Fourth, methods of mining, smelting, and forging among Bantu peoples are similar to those of western Africa. Fifth, the Bantu-speaking peoples are a Negro people, though in many areas they have absorbed, within the past millennium or two, sizable populations of Bushmen or Cushites, the latter an Afro-Mediterranean people who long ago migrated into modern East Africa. And sixth, the Bantu-speaking peoples share with their West African cousins common fundamental attitudes about God, religion, kinship, the nature of the world, and life. Clearly the Bantu-speaking peoples, widespread and diversified though they may be, form an integral part of the Sudanic civilization of Black Africans.

Today Bantu-speaking Africans form the majority of the populations of every country south of the equator, and extend north of the equator into Cameroun, Nigeria, the Central African Republic, Kenya, and Somalia. They fall into some three hundred "tribes," although they are almost as difficult to describe with this term as the West Africans. Bantu societies range from tiny units of only a few thousand people to nations of several million people. In some modern countries of Africa, such as Lesotho and Swaziland, one Bantu nation has formed a modern state. In most others, however, a number of formerly separate ethnic groups live together in the modern polity. In still others non-Bantu immigrants have mixed with the earlier Bantu inhabitants. In southern Africa, alien minorities rule over Bantu majorities. But with the exception of southern Africa men of Bantu origin head the governments of most of the modern nations of the region: Congo, Zaire, Kenya, Tanzania, Zambia, Gabon, Malawi, Botswana, Lesotho, and Swaziland.

Nowadays many immigrants from other parts of Africa and from Europe and Asia live within the countries of the Bantu. From various parts of Europe millions of settlers have come to South Africa, Rhodesia, Angola, Mozambique, South West Africa (Namibia), Kenya, and Tanzania. From Asia, especially from India, perhaps a million settlers have come to Kenya, Uganda, Tanzania, Mozambique, Rhodesia, Malawi, Zambia, and South Africa.

In South Africa, South West Africa, and Botswana live the last few thousand survivors of the aboriginal Khoisan or Bushman population,

Typical house among the northwest Bantu. This is a
ceremonial meeting house of the Bimbi in Tiko, Cameroun.

which was once distributed over a larger part of Africa than the Bantu.
Today, the diminutive, yellow-skinned Bushmen live almost entirely in
the most arid and inhospitable deserts and steppes of southern Africa.
They hunt and gather in nomadic bands of a few dozen people, although gradually they have begun to settle as laborers on the European
farms.

Just as the Black Africans from the Sudan absorbed or exterminated
the indigenous inhabitants of the West African forests many thousands of
years ago, their southward moving relatives absorbed, displaced, and
sometimes killed indigenous Bushmen. But this process began as recently
as the time of Christ and numerous Bushmanoid racial traits can be
found in some of the Bantu-speaking peoples of southern Africa. In a
few societies, such as the Dorobo of Kenya and the Hadzapi of Tanzania,
the people speak Bushmanoid languages, though racially they are little
different from the Bantu among whom they live. These peoples, until very recent years, made their living by hunting; they retained an

original Bushmanoid language and culture, yet through intermarriage have become indistinguishable from the Bantu.

The first Bantu probably entered the southern third of the African continent at about the time of Christ. They seem to have originated in the savanna near the modern Nigeria-Cameroun border. By the time of Christ a buildup of population in the grasslands adjacent to the West African rain forests was likely resulting in a shortage of land. The extensive pattern of Sudanic cultivation, where grains were sown over a large area in one year and then over an adjacent area in the next year, necessitated hundreds of acres to support even a few hundred people.

As land pressure mounted, parties of explorers ventured from the Cameroun highlands and the grasslands farther east in what is now the Central African Republic down the numerous streams that flow southward into the Congo River. After hundreds of miles, the Congo rain forests and swamps begin to give way to grasslands. And in the modern Katanga Province of Zaire, the terrain is again very much like the savannas and highlands of Cameroun and north-central Nigeria.

Into the familiar savannas of Katanga, the ancestors of the Bantu migrated, some time around the beginning of the Christian era, or perhaps a century or two earlier. There they felled the sparsely scattered trees, cleared the brush and the wild grasses, hoed the soil, and sowed their millet and sorghum seeds. The new homeland must have been settled in the beginning by only a few hundred or a few thousand pioneers, arriving over a period of decades or even centuries; perhaps large canoes loaded with several brothers, their wives, children, tools, and seeds arrived at one site or another, two or three at a time. Many must have given up long before Katanga was reached, landing their boats at the likelier looking spots along the river's banks, clearing the trees for a small settlement, there to eke out a living by hunting, fishing, gathering wild fruits and tubers, and probably cultivating the indigenous forest tubers. But eventually a few parties reached the new homeland, and the expanding Sudanic civilization began to sink new roots far from its center in the West African Sudan.

The culture of the new settlers in Katanga would not have been very different from that of the Nok peoples of the Nigerian plateau. The early Bantu migrants came from a region only a few hundred miles east of the Nok peoples, and began their migrations at roughly the same period as the Nok people were smelting iron, making terra cotta figurines, shaping stone tools, and sowing grains. Linguists who have studied modern Bantu languages comparatively have found that Luba, together with Bemba, spoken only a few hundred miles to the west of the Luba territory, is one of the very oldest Bantu languages: the farther one goes from the Luba-Bemba country of Katanga and adjacent

Zambia, the more divergent the Bantu languages become in root words, for example. This divergence is found approximately equally in the far north and the far south of the Bantu territory, adding more evidence to the hypothesis of dispersion outward from the original Katanga homeland.

Within a century or two the settlers had grown sufficiently numerous to expand over the grasslands and dry forests that stretch across what are today Angola, Zambia, Rhodesia, and Mozambique. Between about A.D. 100 and 400, they reached the Indian Ocean coast of Mozambique on the east. Soon thereafter they came to the Atlantic Ocean coast of Angola on the west. Thus within a few centuries, the early Bantu had created a new Black African population center and had expanded in a long ellipse to the eastern and western coasts of central Africa.

The Bantu were clearly superior to the Khoisan peoples in weapons, organization, and spirit. A strong people with a long history of expansion, conquest, and development behind them, the Bantu probably met little Khoisan resistance. The Khoisan and Bantu ways of life were not especially competitive. Gradually the Bantu absorbed the weaker indigenous Khoisan, driving those who had a less assimilationist spirit into drier and less hospitable areas. The Bantu occupied the lands suitable for their agriculture. Their crops and the abundant game and fish of central Africa enabled their population to grow.

In the region of East Africa's Great Lakes, however, the early Bantu met another agricultural people who had long before migrated southward from the Ethiopian area. These people were the Cushites, an ancient mixed Caucasoid-Negroid people related to the aboriginal Ethiopian and Somali peoples. They had filtered into eastern Africa a millennium or more before the first Bantu arrived, and had established scattered settlements in the moister plateaus on the eastern side of the Great Lakes, in what are now Uganda, Kenya, and Tanzania, and in a few sites along the Indian Ocean coast of Kenya, Tanzania, and possibly northern Mozambique. The Cushites were skilled farmers. They built irrigation systems and terraces for their crops, and cultivated a group of plants of Ethiopian origin, including eleusine millet and a variety of sorghum different from that cultivated in the Sudan. Despite the Cushite skills in agriculture and in stone working, they apparently did not know how to use iron.

The Cushites evidently lived in towns perched on hillsides and on high mountainous plateaus. The infiltrating Bantu probably surrounded these settlements, establishing their villages on drier and lower land. One finds evidence in East Africa that the Bantu eventually absorbed the Cushites. Today several Bantu groups, such as the Wachagga of Mount

Kilimanjaro, show faintly Caucasoid racial traits, and practice an agriculture that shows Cushitic influences. And near the stone ruins of the now-deserted town of Engaruka, in western Tanzania, the Iraqw peoples along with several other smaller tribes, still speak a language of the southern Cushite branch of the great Afro-Asiatic stock. These tribes are the lone survivors of the ancient Cushite farmers, most of whose relatives have long since been absorbed into the Bantu peoples.

As the Bantu-speaking peoples expanded outward from the Katanga area, they were changed by the indigenous peoples they absorbed and supplanted. The Negroid racial type predominated, but many Bantu-speaking peoples throughout eastern and central Africa came to show a racial heterogeneity that resulted from intermarriage with the Cushite and Khoisan peoples. Culturally, too, the Bantu benefited from contact with different peoples. From the Cushites they learned to cultivate the Ethiopian eleusine millets and sorghum, which in many parts of Bantu Africa supplanted Sudanic millet and sorghum. The Bantu who first reached the Indian Ocean, probably in the area where the Zambesi River flows into the ocean in modern Mozambique, found small settlements of Indonesian mariners. From them, they learned to cultivate the banana, the East Indian yam and coco yam, and the coconut. The yams and bananas enabled the Bantu to expand into rain forest areas throughout southern Africa and into the Congo basin. Almost certainly, these invaluable crops found their way into West Africa via the Bantu and enabled the Sudanic peoples to build much denser and more productive societies in that region's rain forests.

Within three or four centuries expanding pioneer bands of Bantu had moved out from Katanga in an east-west pattern. They finally reached the shores of the Indian and Atlantic Oceans by the third or fourth century. Their movements to the north and south were somewhat slower. To the north lay the comparatively moist lands of the Great Lakes, where the crops of the Sudan and Ethiopia could not grow well. This region became more attractive as soon as the Bantu learned to cultivate bananas and yams from Indonesia. By the ninth or tenth century Bantu migrants were settling in what is now eastern Zaire, western Tanzania and Kenya, and Uganda; by about the tenth century they had reached the farthest point of their northern expansion, the river valleys of southern Somalia. The new Indonesian crops were used to move into moister areas that had previously been by-passed. These included the lower Zambesi valley in Mozambique and the southern highlands of Tanzania.

Also by the tenth century, the Bantu had begun moving into the rain forests of the Congo basin. These forests were sparsely inhabited by bands of Pygmies, who were distantly related to the Khoisan and by Negro peoples who lived in scattered small villages. Many of the Negro

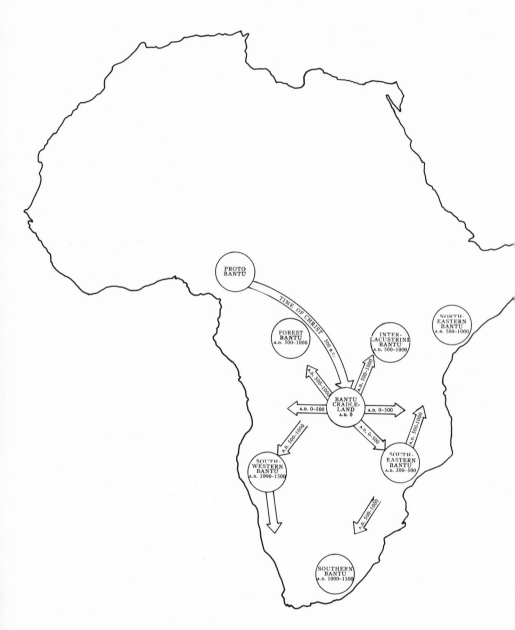

PROTO
BANTU

TIME OF CHRIST 500 B.C.

FOREST
BANTU
A.D. 500–1000

INTER-
LACUSTRINE
BANTU
A.D. 500–1000

NORTH-
EASTERN
BANTU
A.D. 500–1000

A.D. 500–1000

A.D. 500–1000

BANTU
CRADLE-
LAND
A.D. 0

A.D. 0–500

A.D. 0–500

A.D. 0–500

A.D. 500–1000

SOUTH-
WESTERN
BANTU
A.D. 1000–1500

A.D. 500–1000

SOUTH-
EASTERN
BANTU
A.D. 300–500

A.D. 500–1000

SOUTHERN
BANTU
A.D. 1000–1500

Bantu Origins and Migrations, 500 B.C.—A.D. 1500

peoples were related to the early Bantu and were culturally similar to them, but before the arrival of the northward-migrating Bantu, the forest Negroes cultivated indigenous crops that could not support a large and expanding population. With the arrival of new immigrants and the better plants they brought, trees were felled, villages were built, and large gardens were planted. By the twelfth or thirteenth century Bantu-speaking peoples were settled in every part of the great Congo rain forests.

South of Katanga, all the way to the southern tip of Africa, lie vast plains, often located on plateaus several thousand feet above sea level. Before the Bantu began to settle this region, it was inhabited by the Khoisan people. The Khoisan peoples of what are now Rhodesia, southern Zambia, Botswana, and South Africa knew how to tend cattle. Thus their economy was sufficiently similar to that of the Bantu that the two were in competition for land. The Bantu advance to the south was therefore slow, compared with their rapid movements to the east, west, and north.

In the more southerly parts of this region the Bantu may not have become predominant until as late as the fourteenth or fifteenth century, although there was considerable intermarriage between Bantu and Khoisan. The Zulu and Xhosa peoples of South Africa, both Bantu, borrowed from Khoisan the unusual practice of making clicking sounds while speaking. Presumably the Khoisan wives of Bantu-speaking men adopted their husband's Bantu language but added click sounds to it.

The gradual rate at which the Bantu pushed southward gave rise to a European historical fallacy, still used by the dominant minority of South Africa to justify its rigorous system of white supremacy. They maintain that the Black Africans arrived in South Africa at about the same time as the Europeans, and that the two alien peoples met for the first time in the early eighteenth century when Dutch farmers settled the territory to the south of the Fish River. The Fish River, located to the east and northeast of Cape Town, did mark the limits of Bantu expansion in South Africa's southeast corner. But the European view ignores the fact that the very dry country between the tip of South Africa and the Fish River was inhabited by Khoisan pastoralists. The southward migrating Bantu were content to leave this country, with its poor soils, to the Khoisan; the Dutch exterminated the Khosian and appropriated their lands.

The Bantu conquest of central and southern Africa was one of the truly great population movements of human history, comparable to the Polynesian settlement of the Pacific islands, the Indian settlement of the Americas, and the movements of Europeans into new lands after the discoveries of the fifteenth and sixteenth centuries. In about a thousand years Bantu speakers had established themselves in the entire southern third of the African continent, an area some 2,500 miles long and up to 2,500 miles wide. During this period, the Bantu population multiplied many hundredfold. By about the eleventh century there were between one million and six million Bantu people. Today, there are seventy to eighty million.

Both the archaeological record and oral and written history suggest that the Bantu followed the same lines of development that their relatives in the Sudan are known to have pursued. The Bantu population grew rapidly in the more fertile areas. In those areas where land resources were sufficient to maintain a reasonable level of food production and there were products to use in developing a trade system, the Bantu built kingships and states along Sudanic lines.

In Katanga, northern Angola, southern Zaire, and on the Rhodesian plateau—all settled by the Bantu during the first five centuries of their migrations—an intra-African trade developed as early as the seventh or eighth century. Strong states developed in these areas by the thirteenth or fourteenth century. To the north, in the Great Lakes region of eastern Zaire, western Tanzania and Uganda, and in Burundi and Rwanda, a similar Bantu development took place at about the same period or a century or two later.

The earliest archaeological evidence of this development comes from Katanga, where Belgian archaeologists discovered a vast cemetery along the shores of Lake Kisale, dating to the eighth and ninth centuries. They found tens of thousands of graves, stretched along a ten-mile site; although no attempt has been made to count the graves (the political upheavals in Katanga after 1960 prevented full investigation), it is estimated that the cemetery may contain several hundred thousand. The people who buried their dead in this veritable "city of the dead" must have been a populous society, clustered densely along the fertile shores of Lake Kisale, probably for a period of many centuries. Only a high agricultural productivity could have supported such a population.

Also striking is the comparatively great wealth buried with each corpse. Only a few dozen graves, selected at random, were excavated, and presumably they were those of ordinary citizens of the society. Yet in grave after grave the archaeologists found quantities of copper bars, long used in that area as currency, finely wrought copper bracelets, bangles, pendants and necklaces, and a number of beads made of glass and cowrie shells from the Indian Ocean. The copper work and many fine pots provide mute testimony to the wealth of the people.

The beads in the Kisale graves indicate the existence of trade that reached over a thousand miles from the Indian Ocean to central Africa.

The prosperous people of Kisale likely traded their one outstanding form of wealth, copper, for these beads. In many parts of the Angola-Katanga-Zambia-Rhodesia ellipse mine shafts have been found, boring down into lodes of copper, iron, and gold, and there is definite evidence from Arabic sources that these metals were bought at trading towns along the coast of Tanzania, Kenya, and Mozambique as early as the ninth century, if not before.

In modern Katanga, in the Kisale region, the Luba are the founders of one of the first empires in subequatorial Africa. Even in modern Zaire, the Luba are leaders in trade, the professions, and government. Luba oral history begins with the year 1500. It makes no mention of any earlier developments, although the archaeological evidence suggests that Luba history may have begun nearly seven centuries before. Little is known of these seven hundred years, but some trade and the evolution of a state system must have occurred. According to Luba oral history, the Lake Kisale region of Katanga was the birthplace of the Luba people, and Kongolo, a charismatic chieftain from a nearby but unidentified country, was the founder of the first important Luba kingdom.

A number of societies in Lubaland and adjacent regions were politically well developed by 1500. During Kongolo's reign a powerful and prestigious hunter named Ilunga Mbili arrived in Kongolo's kingdom. He stayed for some time and married one of Kongolo's daughters, who bore a son, Kalala Ilunga. After a time, Ilunga Mbili tried to point out to Kongolo that he possessed power but little skill in government and the two men quarreled. This implies that Ilunga Mbili was probably a son of a king in some neighboring kingdom that was older than Lubaland and regarded itself as more cultured and civilized. Following the quarrel, Kongolo drove his nagging son-in-law from Lubaland.

Kongolo's grandson, Kalala Ilunga, was a distinguished warrior. He led parties of warriors to subdue rebellious vassals and conquer new villages on the periphery of the kingdom. He was so successful at war, and so popular with the Luba, that the aging Kongolo grew jealous and drove him into the land of his father. Kalala Ilunga, as a member of that state's royal line, was able to add to his small force of followers and create a powerful army. In about 1520 or 1525, he invaded Lubaland, defeated and killed his grandfather, and became king of Luba.

Under Kalala Ilunga, Luba prospered. The kingdom grew rapidly into a small empire as his armies conquered a number of surrounding peoples. The empire that Kalala Ilunga created did not include all the Luba peoples, who by this time were constantly sending forth small bands of pioneers to settle among neighboring peoples, occasionally absorbing them into Luba culture. To the west and southeast of the central Luba state were at least three other Luba kingdoms, established at roughly the same time as the state of Kongolo. None of these states showed the expansionism of the central state. Many of Kalala Ilunga's conquests were to the south, east, and northeast, among non-Luba peoples. Only a few years after his reign, additional conquests were made to the southwest, among the closely related Lunda peoples. It is estimated that Kalala Ilunga enlarged his kingdom from some 40,000 square miles, which were inhabited almost entirely by Luba peoples, to about 75,000 or 100,000 square miles, inhabited by at least three or four other major ethnic groups. In the process he crystallized a distinctive Luba political system, which persisted for centuries among the Luba and was also adopted, in whole or in part, by the Lunda, Bemba, Lozi, and several other groups in central Africa.

In the Luba state, each village headman was appointed by the king, but probably with the consent of the leaders of the village's lineage. Groups of villages formed chiefdoms, headed by a territorial chief called the kilolo. Several chiefdoms constituted a province, and all the provinces made up the kingdom.

The king was assisted by several title holders—a war leader, a keeper of the sacred emblems, another who ruled during an interregnum, and several others—many of whom were his close relatives. In theory the king, who ruled by divine right, was an absolute monarch, but there was a practical check on his authority: members of his lineage possessed the quality of "bulopwe," the sacred right of leadership, and could legitimately organize a revolt if the king became unpopular.

The central Luba political system set the pattern for the empire. Conquered chiefs continued to rule their villages, but were under the clear control of Luba immigrants. The conquered chiefs were not considered to have bulopwe and were heavily taxed. Perhaps because of this political inflexibility, the Luba kingdoms never grew into widely extended empires. The four Luba states—each with its own tradition of founding and royal line—were never able to coalesce or confederate in any way.

In most of the heartland of central Africa the low fertility of the soil made it impossible for the Bantu to create dense populations over large areas. Villages in many parts of the region number one hundred people or less, and these people move every few years as the fertility of the soil is exhausted. In parts of Lubaland, however, the topsoils are deeper and less susceptible to exhaustion. Populations are dense in restricted localities, with as many as three hundred people per square mile. Yet even in Luba country, villages usually included only a few hundred, or perhaps a thousand, people. Only capital towns, established by the kings, had several thousand residents. Unlike the towns and villages of many parts of the Sudan, those of the Bantu were rarely fortified by walls or ditches. They were simply large areas of houses among which market areas were interspersed. Permanent markets were opened for trade every fifth day.

Mostly local produce was bought or sold, including millet, sorghum, yams, vegetables, chickens, and goats. Some craftsmen specialized in making pots, which they traded for foodstuffs. Others mined and smelted copper and iron. These metals were made into tools, weapons, jewelry, and bars, which were often used for currency. The Luba were not given to long distance trading, but were willing to exchange their metals for the cloth, beads, tools, and, eventually, guns that traders from neighboring states brought to Lubaland.

The religious beliefs of the Luba and most Bantu peoples were similar to those of the Sudan. A supreme creator was recognized. The Luba believed that God could be prayed to directly, without the use of intercessor spirits, yet they saw God as distant from man's affairs. Numerous nature and ancestor spirits were believed to have more relevance to the occurrence of natural phenomena and to individual fortunes. Whether prayers were addressed to God or to the various spirits, they usually involved offerings, sacrifices, and complex ritual. As in the Sudan, medicine men, priests, and sorcerers existed in central African societies. They were believed to be especially efficacious in offering prayers and sacrifices, as well as in healing.

Life in Luba society was generally more prosperous than in many central African societies, yet less so than in some of the more affluent and sophisticated kingdoms of the Sudan and the West African forests. With smaller towns and villages and more sparsely scattered populations, the central Africans tended to be more isolated and parochial. With less productivity per farmer, less specialization into class and craft associations, and less trade, the central Africans lived a simpler material life than their Sudanic kinsmen.

To the south and southwest of the Luba kingdoms live the closely related Lunda peoples. According to tradition, Luba noblemen married into Lunda noble families in the fifteenth and sixteenth centuries. These Luba transmitted the sacred quality of bulopwe into the Lunda political system. Soon thereafter the Lunda commenced a process of empire building that, over the next several centuries, resulted in the formation of several very large kingdoms. Lunda political ideas spread to surrounding peoples in what are now the modern countries of Zaire, Angola, and Zambia. The main Lunda kingdom lay in eastern and central Angola, but as it grew into an empire, usually referred to as the empire of Mwata Yamvo (which was the title of the king), it extended from western Angola to northern Zambia.

The lands of Mwata Yamvo were most extensive during the eighteenth century, but another Lunda kingdom, that of the Kazembe, rivaled the main Lunda state in power and area by the mid-eighteenth century. The Kazembe—located around the Luapula River in eastern Katanga—paid tribute to the Mwata Yamvo but were independent in every other respect.

The Lunda system of power and Lunda institutions, although they stemmed from the Luba, spread with relative ease. Small groups of Lunda conquerors settled in new areas, recognized the local ruler, and served mainly as tax collectors and legitimizers of local power. Local customs and political beliefs were little affected and were often incorporated into the great Lunda imperial system. With this flexibility the loosely knit Lunda empire expanded gracefully and was able to maintain itself for more than two centuries.

During the Lunda hegemony, the influence of the Portuguese was strategic. Trading through intermediaries, Lunda kings secured guns and manufactured goods from the Portuguese in return for copper, gold, ivory, and slaves. The Portuguese also introduced into central Africa American plants, notably maize, manioc, tobacco, peanuts, tomatoes, and pineapples. These quickly spread to Lunda and Luba farmers and increased the ability of the Bantu to support themselves in various environments. Probably the introduction of these plants helped to stimulate migratory movements of bands of Luba, Lunda, and other Bantu peoples during the seventeenth and nineteenth centuries.

During the first three centuries of trade between Portugal and the Bantu states of central Africa, no Portuguese are known to have visited Lundaland. In the nineteenth century, however, several Portuguese traveled the thousand miles that lay between the Portuguese forts on Mozambique's Indian Ocean coast and the capital of the Mwata Kazembe, the ruler of the eastern and smaller of the two Lunda empires. Captain Antonio Gamitto, a member of a party that visited there in 1831-32, left an account that provides a vivid impression of this great inland capital and its emperor:

> . . . I made solemn entry into what is perhaps the greatest town of Central Africa.
> Continuing our march we entered . . . a long street of enclosures made with posts fixed into the ground and interlaced with grass to a height of ten or twelve spans. . . .
> Arriving at the Musumba [the Mwata Kazembe's residence] we found the great square filled with a throng of people. . . .
> The warriors in the square were the Lunda army, which would comprise some five or six thousand men, all armed with bows and arrows, Mpok, and spears. . . . The Mwata was seated on the left side of the eastern gate of the Musumba; many leopard skins served him as a carpet . . . over these

was an enormous lion skin, and on this a stool covered with a big green cloth. On this throne the Mwata was seated, in greater elegance and state than any other Mambo [African king] I have seen.

His head was ornamented with a kind of miter, pyramidal in shape and two spans high, made of brilliant scarlet feathers; round his forehead was a dazzling diadem of beads of various kinds and colors. Behind his head a band of green cloth, supported by two small ivory needles, fanned out from the back of his neck. . . .

Mwata Kazembe looks fifty years old but we were told he is much older. He has a long beard, already turning gray. He is well built and tall and has a robustness and agility which promises a long life; his look is agreeable and majestic, and his style splendid in its fashion. We certainly never expected to find so much ceremonial, pomp, and ostentation in the potentate of a region so remote from the seacoast, and in a nation which appears so barbarous and savage.

The surprise of the Portuguese at this royal display reflected the low opinion Europeans had formed of Africans, especially in the Bantu areas of central and southern Africa, after several centuries of the degrading slave trade and European conquests along the coasts. But it also mirrored the fundamental European ignorance of this part of Africa. Gamitto's surprise might have been even greater had he known that the Mwata Kazembe was at least nominally subordinate to the Mwata Yamvo, far to the west in the interior of Angola, and that comparable pomp could also be found in the capitals of the Lozi, Luba, Bemba, and several other Bantu nations.

One of the most illustrious polities of Bantu Africa was the kingdom of Kongo, whose history has been heavily influenced by Portuguese contact. Situated well to the west of Luba and Lunda territory. Kongo covered the plateau south of the Congo River down into northern Angola. At its peak, Kongo reached from the Atlantic Ocean to beyond Stanley Pool (the present location of Kinshasa and Brazzaville) and included numerous chiefdoms north of the Congo River.

Before the kingdom of Kongo was founded there were a number of small states of Bakongo (people of Kongo) on both sides of the Congo River, from Stanley Pool to the sea. In the fourteenth century, Wene, the son of a king of the small Bakongo state of Bungu, led a party of migrants into the lands of the Ambundu and Ambwela peoples (both related to the Bakongo). Marrying into the local ruling lineage, Wene began to conquer surrounding kingdoms. Other kingdoms voluntarily accepted his rule. Soon he adopted the title of "manikongo" (king of the Kongo) and ruled a kingdom that united at least six of the small states south of the Congo between the Atlantic and Stanley Pool. A similar process of state growth was underway at roughly the same time in the related Loango and Tyo areas north of the Congo River and in

Okango much farther to the east of Kongo territory. But by the late fifteenth century, when the first Portuguese mariners arrived, Kongo was the largest and strongest of the coastal states.

The Kongo political system, like those of the Luba and Lunda, was based on the village unit, with a headman who was the senior man of the lineage. Villages were organized into districts, headed by titled chiefs who were appointed by the king. The districts formed six provinces—Soyo, Mpemba, Mbamba, Mpangu, Mbata, and Nsundi—which represented the states before Wene's consolidation. Each province was headed by a titled governor who was appointed by the manikongo. At the head of the state was the king, assisted by a number of titled officials each of whom had departmental responsibilities.

The king was both an absolute monarch, appointing all officials down to village level, and a semidivine and sacred personage; he could not be observed eating and drinking, for example, on pain of death. The complex administrative structure under him depended on the king's pleasure. There was no clear rule for succession and customarily there was an actual or a ceremonial battle among pretenders following the king's death. All pretenders had to be descended from the line of Wene, but this eventually included thousands of eligibles. After the death of King Affonso I, in 1540, only his descendants could inherit the throne, but these eligibles became so numerous by 1700 that they formed a separate social class.

Although Wene was the traditional founder of the Kongo nation, its greatest ruler was Affonso I, who launched a grand strategy of modernization centuries before any comparable effort in any other part of Black Africa.

Nzinga Kuwu was king of the Kongo during the time of first Portuguese contact. Diogo Cão, the first Portuguese captain to visit the Kongo, arrived in 1482. He returned in 1485, left four missionaries, and brought four Kongo nobles to Portugal. Diogo made several visits, each time carrying a group of Kongo nobles back and forth. In 1491 Nzinga Kuwu was baptized, along with most of his family, and took the Christian name of John I. He and part of his family drifted away from Christianity after a few years, but the queen mother and one son, Affonso, remained faithful to the Church. When Nzinga died in 1506, Affonso, after a pitched battle with a non-Christian half-brother, took control of the kingdom.

Affonso saw in Christianity a means of ennoblement and progressive development for his people. He believed that the pagan members of the nobility and the traditional religious leaders of Bakongo society were antithetical to the progress he sought. Affonso solicited priests and technicians from King Manuel of Portugal to help him convert his people and to bring technological progress. He began to weave Christianity and Western concepts into the official fabric of the Kongo political system. He sent many young nobles, especially his sons and close relatives, to Lisbon to acquire a Portuguese education. Schools for the nobility were established in Kongo itself. As befitted a king who was proud, and who regarded himself (and was accepted) as a peer of the Portuguese monarch, he paid for these educational services by sending slaves, copper, and iron to Portugal. Affonso intended to make of Kongo a Christian nation, equipped fully with Western knowledge and technology and capable of playing a dignified role in the world, as well as in Africa.

Affonso's grand design suffered difficulties almost from the beginning. A letter he wrote to Portugal's King John in 1526 eloquently states his problems:

> Sir, Your Highness should know how our Kingdom is being lost in so many ways that it is convenient to provide for the necessary remedy, since this is caused by the excessive freedom given by your factors and officials to the men and merchants who are allowed to come to this Kingdom to set up shop with goods and many things which have been prohibited by us, and which they spread throughout our Kingdoms and Domains in such an abundance that many of our vassals, whom we had in obedience, do not comply because they have the things in greater abundance than we ourselves. . . .
>
> And we cannot reckon how great the damage is, since the mentioned merchants are taking every day our natives, sons of the land and sons of our noblemen and vassals and our relatives, because the thieves and men of bad conscience grab them wishing to have the things and wares of this Kingdom which they are ambitious of; they grab them and get them to be sold; and so great, Sir, is the corruption and licentiousness that our country is being completely depopulated, and Your Highness should not agree with this nor accept it as in your service. And to avoid it we need from those your Kingdoms no more than some priests and a few people to teach in schools, and no other goods except wine and flour for the holy sacrament. . . . it is *our will that in these Kingdoms there should not be any trade of slaves nor outlet for them.* [These words were emphasized in Affonso's original letter.] Concerning what is referred above, again we beg of Your Highness to agree with it, since otherwise we cannot remedy such an obvious damage. . . .

The merchants who were creating such difficulty for Affonso were operating from the major Portuguese trading base on the island of São Tomé, off the coast of modern Gabon. There, wealthy Portuguese merchants and sea captains had built a vital entrepôt for the African trade and a base for their naval forces. When Affonso wrote, their power was already great enough that Portugal was not fully able to

Antonio of Nigritia, who was
appointed ambassador to the
Vatican by King Affonso I, who
sought Vatican recognition
of the Kongo nation.
Bust is in the church of
S. Maria Maggiore in Rome.

control them. On numerous occasions they seized cargo sent by Kongo
to Portugal. They feared free communication and gift exchange between Affonso and the Portuguese crown because they felt it might
weaken their stranglehold on the West African trade.

Even the missionaries sent to Kongo eventually became corrupted
by the slave trade. They owned slaves themselves and sold them to the
eager merchants from São Tomé. Affonso barely held his kingdom together, as priests and merchants conspired with ambitious vassals of his
kingdom to enslave and sell Kongolese, as well as neighboring peoples.
He and successor kings found honest and cooperative Portuguese who
were committed to the development of a Christian nation under Kongolese rule. But there were constant tensions between the Kongo kings and
their Portuguese supporters, on the one hand, and the São Tomé-
Kongolese vassal arrangements, on the other.

Affonso I was one of the truly great yet tragic figures in African
history. As a child he had been tutored by Portuguese priests who told
glowing stories of the brilliance of Portugal and Christian civilization.
Probably a genius, Affonso was inspired by a vision of a great Christian
kingdom in the heart of Africa. The Portuguese who met him recognized
in him the qualities of royalty and command, and to his Kongolese
supporters, especially those who accepted Christianity, he was a revered
leader. But to his vassals he was a man to be feared and plotted against.

In the grand mosaic of African history, Affonso ranks with Mansa Musa, Askia Muhammad, Osei Tutu, and Usman dan Fodio. In his quest for Christianizing and modernizing his kingdom, he would not seem out of place in the company of the many great modern African leaders who have inspired their peoples to throw off the yoke of colonialism and make the sacrifices necessary to regenerate and modernize Africa.

Affonso's tragedy was to watch his dream gradually eroded by greedy Portuguese slave merchants, eager to buy Africans for the slave markets of Brazil. Even the Portuguese crown was eventually swept along by the irresistible tide of Portuguese world conquest and the concomitant lust for gold and profits. Affonso was nearly assassinated by Portuguese in his own capital of San Salvador in 1539, and one of his chief aides was killed. Between 1541 and 1543 Affonso died. By then he was so little regarded by his former Portuguese royal brothers that no record was even made of exactly when and how his death occurred.

Between 1545 and 1561 Kongo was ruled by Diogo I, an able man

Kongo's King Alvare II receiving Dutch envoys.

and a grandson of Affonso. Diogo began his reign with strong popular support and the help of the Portuguese faction that favored Lisbon rather than São Tomé. Diogo seems to have had a shrewd sense of how to deal with the Portuguese, but his reign was marked by increasing internal division, and by the beginning of direct Portugese relations with the kingdom of Ndongo, Kongo's southern neighbor. These relations were to lead to the founding of the Portuguese colony of Angola.

Diogo I died in 1561. After several brief reigns by short-lived kings, Alvare I came to the throne in 1567. He began to pull the distintegrating kingdom back together, but almost immediately suffered a catastrophe. The Jaga, a fiercely militaristic central African people about whom little is known, expanded westward, conquering Kongo with lightning speed in 1568. They drove Alvare into refuge on an island in the lower Congo and destroyed San Salvador, the Kongo capital. Alvare appealed to Portugal for help, and finally, in 1571, a Portuguese troop of six hundred soldiers arrived. A two-year campaign drove the Jaga out of the kingdom, but by no means destroyed them. They continued to ravage other kingdoms for decades and played a major role in central African politics for at least half a century.

After Alvare I was restored to the throne, a period of peace returned to Kongo. Internal dissension was never quelled permanently, but the kingdom held together. Portuguese influence grew, and Portuguese food, manners, and court etiquette became deeply established. In 1614 Alvare I's successor, Alvare II, died, and a long period of internal disorder began. Not until the reign of Garcia II, beginning in 1641, was internal cohesion restored. In the same year a group of Italian Capuchin missionaries arrived in Kongo. The Capuchin effort represented the first serious attempt to expand Catholicism beyond the court and the nobility, and it met with considerable success, considering the basic instability of the kingdom and the gradual disintegration of central authority from about 1665 on.

The Portuguese, based in Angola, invaded Kongo in 1665 with the support of troops from several African kingdoms. Many nobles and their families were sold into slavery. The ensuing period of desperate internal disorder permanently ended the basic unity and central control of Kongo. The chief factor that prevented the reuniting of the kingdom was the lack of a clear rule for succession to the throne. Each of the numerous pretenders could expect a measure of royal privilege, and each tended to build a small base of power and support. None of Affonso's many descendants was willing to surrender full power to the throne. The result was a central system that existed only in theory. No one questioned its basic legitimacy, but no one was prepared to grant it power.

Until the beginning of the colonial era, this almost lifeless, dream-like political system survived. Under Portuguese cultural influence of the seventeenth century, dozens of dons, donas, princes, dukes, lords, and ladies maintained the royal system. But most exercised power only at the village level. These nobles continued to come together in shifting alliances to elect kings. They then returned to their local power bases to rule their local fiefs. Gradually the influences of Portugal disappeared; Christianity faded away; and the grand strategy of Affonso I and the several modernist kings after him was forgotten. The idea of Great Kongo lingered on, but with no substance to give it reality.

By the end of the nineteenth century, when the Congo was conquered by Belgium's Leopold II and converted into a vast colony, the central political system of the once great Kongo state was only a memory. The economic life of the Bakongo people was in the hands of numerous European trading companies, that, after the abolition of the slave trade, sought ivory, copra, palm oil, peppers, gold, copper, and other products. Not until the 1950's would a modern, Belgian-educated Bakongo politician and nationalist leader, Joseph Kasavubu, attempt to reunite the ancient kingdom of Kongo, but by that time the modern state of Zaire, including most Bakongo, as well as Luba, Lunda, and other Bantu peoples, had become a more compelling political institution.

Typical Congo house. This is one of the houses of the king of the Bakuba in Kasai, Zaire.

11 Zimbabwe, Mwene Mutapa, and the South

In the Rhodesian highlands, the Bantu speakers early formed another center of their civilization. From this secondary center, they expanded more slowly into what is now the Republic of South Africa. The Bantu gradually absorbed and pressed ever farther south the Khoisan pastoralists of southern Africa. By about the year 1000 the Bantu were established in what is now South Africa's Transvaal and northern Natal provinces, and they were sending parties into the Orange Free State province, eastern Bechuanaland (now the Republic of Botswana), and the northern portions of the Cape Province.

In the Rhodesian plateau and adjacent southern Mozambique the predominant group was the Shona nation, a large population that was broken into several clans, branches, and subgroups (notable among which were the Rozwi and Karanga). To their southeast were the Nguni-speaking peoples, another Bantu group which includes the Swazi, Zulu, Xhosa, and several other ethnic and linguistic subdivisions. The Tswana peoples and the Basuto, as well as a number of smaller tribes, comprised the widely dispersed Sotho group located to the Shona's southwest and south.

All these peoples speak Bantu languages that are clearly related to those of the Kongo, Luba, and Lunda peoples. Perhaps the greatest difference between the southern Bantu peoples and those of the central region is that strong kingdoms were less prevalent in the south. Only the Shona nation produced a state-empire that was clearly in the same league with those of Kongo, Luba, and the Sudanic states. This difference is mainly due to two factors: the dispersed pattern of settlement and the high incidence of cattle herding in the south, and the relative recency with which most of the southern Bantu peoples settled southern Africa.

More archaeological investigation has been conducted in the Zambia-Rhodesia-South Africa region than in any part of Africa except the Nile valley. Much of this investigation has been devoted to the spread and development of the iron-age culture that was the hallmark of the expanding Bantu. Yet, paradoxically, the fact that the soils of the region decompose skeletons quickly has made it far easier to trace the development of the culture than to be positive who was practicing it. The reason for this uncertainty is that some of the very few skeletal remains that have been found, in earlier dated sites, show strong affinities with the Khoisan peoples. This has given rise to the hypothesis that Bantu culture was frequently adopted, at least in part, by their Khoisan Hottentot neighbors, who gathered wild foods, herded cattle, and conceivably even mined gold, iron, and copper, for a few centuries before being absorbed by their expanding and stronger Bantu neighbors.

This confusion is especially notable at the rich excavations at Mapungubwe, a flat-topped hill that rises sharply from the surrounding land in the far western Transvaal near the Botswana border, a few miles from the confluence of the Shashi and Limpopo rivers. Several hundred feet high, the walls of Mapungubwe are so steep that it is impossible to ascend them except by a secret route that only the local inhabitants knew (but almost never used, since they regarded the hill as sacred) until the 1930's. When explorers learned the secret access and reached the top, they found evidence of complex house ruins, numerous graves, and considerable wealth. For centuries the top of Mapungubwe was probably a sacred place, where chiefs and priests lived and practiced religious ceremonies.

In the lowest levels of excavation, pottery and other artifacts that resembled the culture of most of the Transvaal were found; at levels that were dated to about A.D. 1000, however, a new and much more refined style of pottery was found, together with abundant iron tools, and heaps of daga, a clay material used for building throughout southern Africa, which showed that there were several large houses with courtyards and verandas. Between 1000 and 1600 the royal and priestly personages who inhabited the lonely hilltop, and who were buried there, left in and near their graves hundreds of artifacts: points for spears and arrows made of iron as well as of stone, hoes, axes, and whorls for spindles, indicating a knowledge of weaving, perhaps of wool or goat hair as well as cotton. From about the middle level of the excavations, dated to about 1380-1420, the objects left in the burials became more numerous and more costly, when increasing quantities of jewelry, especially of gold, were buried with the deceased; necklaces and bangles of various kinds, and a quantity of gold foil and gold tacks, for hammering the foil onto wood, were added to the iron and pottery artifacts of Mapungubwe.

This increased wealth indicates the existence of some kind of trade system that became important during the fourteenth century and afterward, until the seventeenth century, when Mapungubwe seems to have been abandoned. It cannot be determined whether the trade was purely intra-African or whether it involved the seacoast and foreign merchants, but certainly the accumulation of gold, iron, and copper was brought to Mapungubwe by chiefs and priests who received it from a wide area, probably in trade.

Mapungubwe is one of the very few African excavations that has contained skeletal remains sufficiently intact to study and gain an idea of the people of the area; several of the skeletons show Khoisan-Bushmanoid characteristics, in height, skull size and shape, configuration of the facial bones, etc. Yet the culture that Mapungubwe represents is clearly that of the Bantu-speaking peoples. There can be only two explanations for the presence of Bushmanoid remains there: either Khoisan peoples in the area had borrowed the agriculture and metalworking skills of neighboring Bantu, or Bantu rulers had established suzerainty over a population of Khoisan peoples in the Mapungubwe area. The pottery and metal objects of the more affluent phase of the Mapungubwe site are clearly Shona in type, indicating that the Shona nation began to assume dominance in the area, several hundred miles from the main center of Shona development in northeastern Rhodesia, from about the fourteenth century on.

The archaeologically based picture of the iron age in southern Africa begins within a century or two after Christ, when the Gokomere culture began to spread over the Rhodesian plateau and to the south, beyond the Limpopo River. First evidence of Gokomere culture was found in the 1930's during an excavation in the village of Gokomere near modern Fort Victoria. Gokomere culture is best known for its pottery. Comparatively simple in design, decoration, shape, and technique, Gokomere pots frequently show bands of channeled or incised decorations around their necks. Despite many variations in design, the Gokomere tradition was deeply enough rooted that its products all show a basic kinship.

The Gokomere people knew agriculture. Remains of storage granaries and numerous remnants of slag and the small clay furnaces in which iron was smelted have been unearthed. Sheep bones that have been found in Gokomere culture excavations suggest that some domestic animals were kept. Probably the Gokomere people fished, hunted, and gathered for some of their diet and planted small plots of millet, sorghum, cow peas, and vegetables in areas that required relatively little clearing. They do not seem to have produced iron tools in much quantity, relying to a larger extent on bone and stone. Gokomere culture appears to be ancestral, in its pottery styles and tool-making techniques, to contemporary cultures in Zambia, Botswana, and the northern Transvaal.

By about the year 600 a slightly different, and somewhat more advanced, culture began to supplant that of Gokomere. It is known by the intriguing name of the Leopard's Kopje culture, from the small hill ("kopje," in South Africa's Afrikaans language, means hill) on which its artifacts were first discovered. Clearly based on the Gokomere culture, but showing development from it, the Leopard's Kopje culture produced abundant pottery that was generally more refined than that of the Gokomere people. The Leopard's Kopje people also mined, smelted, and worked iron, making arrow and spear heads, hoe blades, and ornaments, chiefly rings and beads.

They practiced the typical Bantu grain agriculture and herded cattle and sheep of several varieties. Their small villages were built in well-watered valleys, on the crests of ridges, and among rocky hills. Stone barriers to help protect both the people and their domestic animals from predators were formed by piling rocks atop each other in fence rows, a practice still in use among some of the Bantu peoples of the Rhodesian plateau and adjacent areas. Their huts were circular, built of pole walls plastered with daga, and averaged ten to twelve feet in diameter.

The Leopard's Kopje people were a small immigrant group who moved into Rhodesia from the north and soon established dominance over the Gokomere peoples, themselves Bantu and Khoisan intermixed. The Leopard's Kopje culture appeared as early as about 600 and continued to be practiced in a few areas as late as the eighteenth century, according to the archaeological record. Its people were Negroes, although they sometimes intermarried with the remaining Khoisan elements whom they found on the Rhodesian plateau. The language they spoke is unknown. Very probably they were the advance parties of the Shona people, who appeared in the region as early as the end of the first millennium. The Shona peoples began moving into Rhodesia as early as about 850, coming from the north, somewhere near Lake Tanganyika. This would relate them to the Luba and Bemba peoples who both lived to the west and southwest of Lake Tanganyika. The main Shona group was the Karanga nation, whose center of strength, by the time Shona history began to take reasonably clear shape in the fourteenth century, was on the eastern and northeastern portions of the Rhodesian plateau between the Zambezi and Limpopo rivers and is in the mountains and valleys on the east of the plateau.

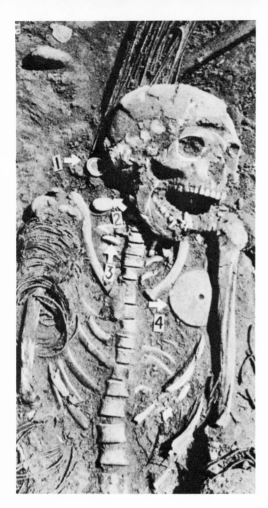

Skeleton of a woman buried at Ingombe Ilede, *c.* the tenth century. The bangles on the arm are of copper. Arrows point to gold ornaments.

The culture of the Karanga people was basically the same as that of the Leopard's Kopje and Gokomere peoples, whom they first ruled, then completely absorbed. But the Karanga had long been in touch with the most sophisticated and culturally developed Bantu peoples of Katanga and central Africa and had direct contact with Arabs and Swahili Bantu along the Mozambique coast. From the former they had learned comparatively advanced mining, metal-working, and perhaps political techniques. From the latter they had acquired an interest in trade. Armed with a wider knowledge of different peoples, the Karanga fanned out over the Rhodesian plateau and learned to exploit its indigenous population and its mineral wealth more effectively than their predecessors. They employed the indigenous people as cattle herders, miners, potters, and craftsmen, instructing them in the superior methods of the Karanga.

The Karanga located new sources of gold, copper, and iron on the

Rhodesian plateau. Both the Gokomere and Leopard's Kopje people had mined small quantities of copper and gold, but they evidently used these metals only in trade for iron, beads, and cloth from the people to the north. As the Karanga moved south on the plateau, mining output increased and gold and copper were used for making ornaments for wealthy and noble Karanga leaders, as well as for trade.

The Karanga seem to have been middlemen or overlords in the plateau's mining operations. They either forced or persuaded the indigenous miners to produce more gold and copper. Mining was an ancient industry among the indigenous peoples, and it was extensive. Over seven thousand shafts and pits have been found on the plateau, some as deep as 150 feet. The miners commonly used open-pit techniques, simply digging trenches as deep as the water table, ventilation, and the depth of the reef permitted. Some shafts were used, mainly in the northeast of Rhodesia, but they were not common. As the miners dug into the veins, they extracted the ore with iron bars about the size of a cigar. Stone wedges were employed to help split off large segments of ore.

The ore was then pulverized in stone mortars and panned in a nearby stream to remove the gold dust and nuggets. Often the dust was stored in porcupine quills, which were handed over to traders in exchange for salt, beads, cloth, iron, and other goods. Several young female skeletons have been found in mine sites, from which archaeologists have surmised that girls did much of the underground work in the mining operation.

The extensive mining industry of the Rhodesian plateau began in the early centuries of the first millennium. It seems to have ended almost completely in the political and military upheavals that beset Rhodesia in the nineteenth century, just before settlement of the country by Europeans.

The Karanga people moved into this rich mining territory as traders and overlords. Probably they came in small parties at first, building small villages near the villages of the indigenous inhabitants. Soon the Karanga were employing indigenous people in other capacities than mining, especially cattle herding. Additional Karanga families moved into the region. They were attracted by trade, the superior positions that the Karanga enjoyed, and the possibilities of acquiring wealth and power. Gradually the Shona language and culture were accepted by the indigenous people and within a few centuries the entire Rhodesian plateau had become a Karanga homeland. Few identifiable traces of the earlier peoples survived.

The archaeological record shows this progressive establishment of Karanga culture, its new and superior ideas and techniques blending with the broad culture base that the Karanga and the indigenous Leopard's Kopje people shared already, by the appearance of increasingly refined pottery, more iron tools and weapons, and considerable quantities of gold and copper ornaments and jewelry buried in some graves. Thus the richest levels of Mapungubwe, itself far to the southwest of the main Karanga center, show Karanga influence: pottery sherds dated to between 1380 and 1420 are of unmistakably Karanga-Shona design, iron tools in the same level are abundant, spindle whorls for weaving appeared for the first time, and the ornaments and jewelry already described appear in larger quantity.

At the other extreme edge of Karanga influence, on the middle Zambezi River near the present site of the great Kariba Dam, excavations at Ingombe Ilede reveal another part of their expansion. There, on a long, low ridge overlooking the river, archaeologists found evidence of habitation over a period of about three centuries, or a little more, by a people who were intimately involved in the long-distance trade up and down the Zambezi which helped to motivate the Karanga expansion across the Rhodesian plateau. The earliest level at Ingombe Ilede is dated at about 680, while the latest is roughly three centuries later. In the earliest level potsherds reveal a relatively simple pottery industry, generally resembling that of the Batoka plateau of Zambia, which lies north of the Zambezi. In the lower level there are numerous elephant bones, indicating that the people who lived at Ingombe Ilede hunted elephants, almost certainly for their ivory—a very prized commodity in the Zambezi-Indian Ocean trade. The people cultivated millet and sorghum, and kept cattle, goats, and dogs. Their houses were probably built of wood and grass straw, materials still commonly used there by the Tonga peoples (distantly related to the Shona).

At each higher level at Ingombe Ilede the refinement of the pottery increased, until, by the last level, dating to the tenth century, the pottery had become some of the best produced in southern Africa: made in a variety of shapes, it was fired with great skill, and often carefully burnished and painted. And with the increasingly refined pottery was found a growing store of trade goods, imported from some distance away. In some of the most richly stored burials were found traces of several varieties of cotton cloth and spindle whorls of pottery. The arms and legs of skeletons were encased in copper and iron bangles, which were covered with several layers of cotton cloth. (Traces of cloth were preserved—a rare thing in African archaeology—because of the preservative effect of the copper ornaments adjacent to them, which helped to neutralize the destructive properties of the soil.) Around the necks of some of the skeletons were strings of gold and glass beads and of shells imported from the Indian Ocean; one of the shells had a backplate of hammered gold. Numerous copper artifacts were in the graves, rivaling those at Lake Kisale in Katanga: copper crosses, sheaves of copper trade wire, and several sets of wiredrawing tools, including hammers, tongs, and drawplates. With two of the bodies were found welded copper gongs, a common symbol of royalty in the Luba-Bemba regions farther north.

The upper levels of Ingombe Ilede attest to the presence of comparatively great wealth and to the existence of trade: with the exception of iron, the area around Ingombe Ilede is poor in metal deposits, hence the gold and copper must have been procured in return for the ivory and salt which the Ingombe Ilede people produced. There are salt deposits only a few miles away, which were exploited as late as the nineteenth century.

There is nothing about the Ingombe Ilede region to suggest that it was an area of great natural wealth: as just noted, it is deficient in metal ores, and its agricultural productivity is no better than average for southern Africa. The burials at the excavations therefore represent those of a privileged group, either native chiefs or foreign overlords. Since the pottery of the latest levels shows strong kinship to Karanga styles found elsewhere throughout the Rhodesian plateau, it is very probable that Karanga traders, supported by armed parties, began to establish a position of wealth, and perhaps political influence, over the Ingombe Ilede people in the ninth and tenth centuries, at about the same time that they began to move into the Rhodesian plateau.

The role of the Zambezi trade in Karanga expansion and conquest and in their great political achievements was considerable. The Karanga early settled around the Zambezi, especially to the south of the river, in a region that lies three to four hundred miles inland from its mouth. The Zambezi can be traveled by canoe all the way to the sea. Arab and Indonesian mariners and traders visisted its mouth as early as the time of Christ, and by the end of the first millennium A.D. had established small colonies all along the Indian Ocean coast of Africa, from southern Mozambique up to Somalia. Probably they and the ancestors of the Karanga, or other Shona peoples, were in contact by the third or fourth century and engaged in a growing trade during the first millennium and the early centuries of the second.

The Arabs and their Swahili allies eventually became the exclusive agents of the coastal trade, establishing trading posts in African communities far up the Zambezi River. It is estimated that there were as many as 10,000 Arab and Arab-African mixed peoples in the Rhodesian area by the beginning of the sixteenth century. They were settled in small groups in most parts of Karanga-Shona country, as well as in sizable communities along the Zambezi from the town of Tete down to the sea. They seem to have had little cultural influence over the Karanga, but their economic influence was considerable. The trade they brought encouraged the Karanga to spread out over a vast area in search of ivory, gold, copper, and slaves.

At least partially because of their trade connections, the Karanga chiefs and their followers fanned out over the entire Rhodesian plateau by about the fourteenth century. At about this time one of their most powerful chiefs, whose name has disappeared even from oral history, established his authority over other chiefs and created a kingdom similar to those in the classic Sudanic system. When the Portuguese arrived in the area early in the sixteenth century, they called this kingdom Monomotapa, a corruption of its proper name, Mwene Mutapa. The kingdom may have been in existence as early as the fourteenth century, but its known history begins in about 1420-40, when its king, Mutota, began a process of expansion that resulted in the establishment of a great empire.

Mutota was king of a Karanga group known as the Rozwi. The chiefs of many small Karanga states are known to have come from the Rozwi clan, and it is presumed that Rozwi men, by the late fourteenth century, had entrenched themselves in Karanga country as traders, military leaders, priests, and chiefs. The Rozwi elite developed a strong sense of identity: it was conscious of a common origin, believed in its destiny to rule, and spread ideas of religion, technology, and culture that were at least slightly different from those of the Karanga nation at large.

In about 1440 Mutota assembled an army that launched a campaign of conquest over other Karanga states and districts. By 1450 Mutota's army had conquered all of the Rhodesian plateau, except the eastern mountainous country. The various Karanga kings and chiefs, Rozwi and non-Rozwi alike, were forced to swear fealty to him. In several cases Mutota appointed chiefs of the Rozwi clan to governorships over conquered kingdoms in order to solidify his rule. Mutota soon was lauded as Mwene Mutapa, which means "Master Pillager" in the Shona language. From this his empire took its name.

The religion of the Karanga people played a special role in their political affairs and helped the Rozwi to widen their control over the countryside. Like most religions of the Sudanic civilization, it acknowledged a supreme being, named Mwari, who was believed to have created the world and man, and, like the Sudanic religions, it held that Mwari was relatively aloof from the day to day affairs of man and nature. But the Karanga believed that ordinary men were totally unable to communicate directly with Mwari, who had to be worshiped and supplicated through the spirits of ancestors. Ancestors were most efficaciously reached through community-wide prayer, led by nobles who served a priestly role. Thus the Karanga people looked to their most powerful chiefs and nobles (especially to the Rozwi) for leadership in religion. When there was a drought, only the chief, acting on behalf of the entire community, had the necessary power and prestige to influence the ancestor spirits to intervene with Mwari and the appropriate nature spirits. The first Karanga kings were thus able to heighten their political and economic positions with this religious role.

To facilitate worship of Mwari, Karanga chiefs established special shrines where they and their chiefs could live and pray for extended periods. These shrine-towns were private and inaccessible, often located on hilltops or in large natural rock formations and surrounded by stone enclosures in areas where this was necessary to ensure privacy. Thus the aloof hilltop of Mapungubwe, developed by people related to the Karanga if not by the Karanga themselves, was an ideal location for the houses and shrines of a chief whose responsibility included acting as intercessor with the ancestor spirits and Mwari.

The most impressive of these shrine-towns ever built by the Karanga was at Zimbabwe in Rhodesia. The great stone ruins at Zimbabwe still attract thousands of tourists and have excited more speculation about ancient Africa than almost any other single phenomenon south of the Nile valley. When nineteenth-century European hunters and explorers first saw Zimbabwe's sixty acres of massive walls, buildings, and houses, they quickly concluded that they had found evidence of a very ancient foreign civilization. King Solomon received more votes than anyone else as the putative inspirer of Zimbabwe. Theories abounded but the one point on which there was near unanimity was that the "primitive" Bantu of the Rhodesian highlands could never have created such impressive monuments.

Located seventeen miles southeast of the modern town of Fort Victoria, in central Rhodesia, the ruins of Zimbabwe are dominated by two features. On a hill is a series of connected enclosures, with elaborate walkways, steps, walls, and hidden passages, often referred to as the "Acropolis." In the valley adjacent to the Acropolis is the Great Enclosure or temple, the highlights of which are a wall, which is eight hundred feet long with heights up to thirty-two feet and widths up to seventeen feet, and a conical tower over thirty feet high.

Zimbabwe was constructed over a long period of time, perhaps centuries. The walls of the Great Enclosure and the conical tower represent the peak of architectural achievement by the Zimbabwe builders. They are made of smooth, even layers of granite building blocks put together with great care and skill. By this phase of construction the

builders had begun to introduce intricate refinements—rounded gate-
ways, curved stepways, doors with timber lintels, platforms for statues
and monoliths, and stepped recesses.

The possibility that Africans had built Zimbabwe grew more believ-
able as it was discovered that most of the city's stone ruins were of
dwellings, defensive walls, enclosures for livestock, and other utilitarian
structures, most of which closely resembled similar structures built by
the modern Bantu-speaking peoples of the same area, albeit in different
materials. Then, in 1931, Dr. Gertrude Caton-Thompson, an eminently
qualified archaeologist who was asked to investigate Zimbabwe, systematically destroyed the several vague theories about alien builders. Zimbabwe, she declared, had been built by Bantu artisans indigenous to
the area, with skill that increased steadily over the several centuries of
construction.

Granite outcroppings are very common on the central Rhodesian
plateau, and nature itself helped to extrude slabs of granite that make
an ideal construction material. With the aid of simple tools, fire, and
water, artisans augmented the large, naturally produced supply of granite
slabs. The earliest builders simply piled convenient flat slabs one on
top of the other, usually taking advantage of huge boulders, outcroppings, or depressions, in order to form defensive enclosures shaped like
the stone or thorn kraals in which domestic animals were kept at night.
As time wore on, techniques became more refined, and more intricate
stone structures developed.

Subsequent to Dr. Caton-Thompson's study, several other excavations of the ruins at Zimbabwe revealed a fairly complete culture history
that exemplifies, in microcosm, the broader sequence of cultures on the
Rhodesian plateau. The first iron-age inhabitants of the Zimbabwe site
were the Gokomere people, who seem to have abandoned it around A.D.
400. Then there is a gap, shown by soil layers in which no artifacts
have been found, of several centuries' duration. In deposits from the
ninth and eleventh centuries, a second layer of soil and debris with
artifacts appears. Judging by the pottery, the second-stage inhabitants
were related to the Leopard's Kopje people.

In about the latter part of the eleventh century, perhaps in about
1075, the third phase of occupation of Zimbabwe began. A new group,
with different pottery styles, moved in and established supremacy over
the peoples of the second phase. In both the first and second phases, the
pottery consisted primarily of gourd-shaped, simply decorated pots and
hemispherical bowls. During the second period numerous clay figurines
of humans and cattle, much in the style of the Leopard's Kopje people
elsewhere in Rhodesia, were left.

The third phase represents the Karanga period. It began in about

Zimbabwe: section of the Great Wall.

1075 and lasted until about 1440. During this period much more refined and better decorated pottery—all in typical Karanga-Shona style—appeared, as did spindle whorls and ornaments of copper and gold. Huts, larger in diameter and with thicker, stronger walls, were built.

During the third phase the first stone was used for building the great shrine complex. In about the middle of the period, probably in the thirteenth century, the south wall of the Acropolis was begun. Roughly shaped slabs of unequal thickness and length were piled up to form the lower section of the wall. The stone work was crude, compared with later work, but effective. By the fifteenth century a strong wall of irregular slabs and natural rock formations encircled an area on the Acropolis hill. The ruins show that the chief, or perhaps, by this time, a Karanga king, had established his residence-temple complex. In about 1440 a fourth phase, lasting until 1833, began. As this phase began Mutota was forming his empire.

When Mutota invaded the lands around Zimbabwe he found a Karanga kingdom named Butua there, and incorporated it into his empire. Modern Shona history does not make it clear whether he appointed a Rozwi vassal to rule Butua for him, but the fourth phase of occupation at the ruins of Zimbabwe show that Rozwi cultural influence began during Mutota's reign. The first definite historical evidence of the Rozwi rule of Zimbabwe comes, however, a few years later in about 1450, during the reign of Mutota's son, Mutope.

Mutope succeeded to the Mwene Mutapa throne in 1450, and immediately embarked on a process of pacification and conquest that greatly extended the territory of the empire. During his thirty-year reign he conquered other Shona peoples in the highlands and mountains of eastern Rhodesia and in central and southern Mozambique. During his reign the empire of Mwene Mutapa stretched some six hundred miles from west to east, from the Ingombe Ilede area at the edge of the Batoka plateau to the Indian Ocean, and another six or seven hundred miles north and south, from the Zambezi River at least to the Limpopo.

Mutope continued his father's system of appointing Rozwi vassals. Early in his reign he appointed a strong Rozwi chieftain, Changa, as governor over the kingdom of Butua. Changa ruled Butua from Zimbabwe, which was already a great religious and political center for the south-central portion of the Rhodesian plateau. Changa served Mutope faithfully and effectively as governor over a province that was at least as extensive and as wealthy as the main center of Mwene Mutapa. By the time Mutope died, in 1480, Changa had come to be regarded with as much respect as the Mwene Mutapa himself. Around this time Arab and Swahili traders flocked onto the Rhodesian plateau. They were lured by the hope of profit from the region's ivory, gold, and copper. Obviously respectful of the great power exercised by Changa in this mineral-rich region, they came to refer to him as "amir," or "prince," and to pay him special homage in order to facilitate their trade in his province. Changa, apparently, was pleased and impressed with this adulation and formally changed his name to Changamire, from the Changa-amir of the Arabic.

When Mutope died in 1480, he was succeeded by his son, Nyahuma. Changamire refused to accept the overlordship of the new Mwene Mutapa, and Nyahuma declared war, after vowing to force Changamire to pay tribute. A series of battles resulted in complete victory for Changamire. Nyahuma was killed in 1490, and Changamire became Mwene Mutapa. But the Rozwi of the central kingdom resented Changamire, and rallied behind Nyahuma's son. In 1494 the great Changamire was himself killed, and the Mwene Mutapa throne reverted to the royal line founded by Mutota.

The empire was permanently split by Changamire's struggle for power. The kingdom he had ruled was no longer known as Butua, but was referred to as Changamire. The empire of Mwene Mutapa had assumed the name of its founder. Changamire's son, Changamire II, succeeded his father as ruler of the kingdom. He successfully resisted the new Mwene Mutapa's efforts to reunite the former empire. Changamire II drove the Mwene Mutapa's forces from eastern Rhodesia and adjacent Mozambique, winning that territory as a permanent part of the Changamire Empire and giving Changamire access to the sea.

The greatest period of development of the great stone structures at Zimbabwe began at about the time of Changamire's assumption of power and continued for nearly four centuries afterward. Construction of the Great Wall began in the early sixteenth century under the Rozwi nobility. As the centuries of Rozwi rule at Zimbabwe wore on, the techniques of construction showed progressive improvement. By the eighteenth century the stone masons employed by the Rozwi kings were able to fashion smooth, even slabs of stone that could be fitted together with great accuracy and permanence. Artistic patterns of stone-laying came into use, especially in portions of the Great Wall and Temple. By the time the Conical Tower was built, probably in the seventeenth century, the stone masons had achieved a high level of sophistication. Stones were laid with great precision. Although no mortar was used, a solid, highly durable structure—tapered from bottom to top with geometrical precision—resulted.

The great stone edifices at Zimbabwe were not the only creations of the Shona peoples. Over the Rhodesian plateau, and in adjacent areas of northern Transvaal, more than a hundred stone ruins of the same general type have been found. Although none was as elaborate as Zimbabwe, many were impressive in size and skill.

The Rozwi empire of Changamire continued into the nineteenth century. Mwene Mutapa, however, gradually declined, due as much to close Portuguese influence as to any other factor. Many Portuguese traders had settled along the Zambezi, especially at Tete and Sena, and the Portuguese controlled the coasts. Bit by bit the Mwene Mutapa became a client of the Portuguese. Relations between the Mwene Mutapa and the Portuguese were not always amicable. During several periods of marked hostility, Portuguese residents were killed and Portuguese power was restricted to its stronghold at Tete. The Arabs, who were the natural competitors of the Portuguese for the trade of the area, encouraged and assisted African efforts to resist Portuguese power. But eventually most Arabs were driven from the area during a period of Portuguese ascendency.

The Portuguese maintained intermittent trade relations with Changamire's Rozwi rulers but were not allowed to establish large trading stations in the empire. In 1693, the Changamire ruler, Dombo, was persuaded by the Mwene Mutapa to assist in driving the Portuguese from the interior. Dombo launched a ruthless military campaign that not only cleared the country of the Portuguese but allowed Dombo to add much of Mwene Mutapa to his domain. By the time the war ended in 1695, Dombo and his army were supreme over the Rhodesian plateau and most of the Zambezi valley. The Mwene Mutapa's territory was reduced to a small area surrounding the strong Portuguese bases at Tete and Sena.

Dombo's successors continued to rule this large empire until the mid-nineteenth century. The Portuguese made no effort to invade the Changamire heartland and confined their power to the coast and to the area around Tete and Sena. Not until the 1880's, when the general European drive to acquire African territory became feverishly competitive, did the Portuguese reestablish wider control in the interior areas of Mozambique.

The Changamire Empire, and the power of the illustrious Rozwi clan, ended in the nineteenth century at the hands of another African power, the Zulu nation. The Zulus are but one of several ethnic groups of the diverse Nguni language group. Today probably six million or more people speak one or another of the closely related Nguni languages, with Zulu and Xhosa being the most prevalent. Although the origins of the Nguni-speaking groups are obscure, they seem to have settled in what are now Swaziland, Natal Province, the Transkei, and the eastern Cape Province of South Africa at least as early as the fifteenth century, and probably several centuries earlier. In this region they maintained long contact with the Khoisan peoples who preceded them there and absorbed the several click sounds that are distinctive Khoisan language traits.

The Nguni-speaking peoples, like other Bantu speakers, learned to cultivate American crops during the sixteenth and seventeenth centuries. By the nineteenth century, although sorghum and millet were still cultivated, corn had become the chief grain among most Nguni peoples. Unlike some of the Bantu of Katanga, Zambia, and Rhodesia, the Nguni peoples have long tended large herds of cattle, goats, and sheep. In many of the less fertile regions in which the Nguni peoples live their herds have overgrazed the soils, helping to deplete their fertility and cause erosion.

During the eighteenth century the Nguni peoples were spread over the area that now covers Swaziland, Natal, and the eastern Cape. In the more fertile parts of this area, especially in Natal, there was significant population pressure during the eighteenth century. But the northward movement of European settlers from the Cape prevented Nguni expansion to the south and southwest. During the 1770's the advancing Boer farmers, descendants of the earlier Dutch settlers of the Cape, began to move their large herds of cattle into the lands of the eastern Cape along the Great Fish River. There they found large settlements of Nguni peoples, including the Xhosa, who herded cattle and grew corn much as the Boers did. For a century the two groups raided each other across the river, stealing cattle, burning fields, and occasionally fighting pitched battles. The Xhosa, who had acquired a few guns by this time, were able to defend themselves successfully against the tough Boer frontiersmen.

But a line had been drawn. The Bantu-speaking peoples, who for centuries had pressed southward, were at last stopped by a powerful foe. A similar situation obtained to the west, on the high plateau that forms most of what are now the Orange Free State and Transvaal provinces of South Africa. This area had long been inhabited by the Sotho peoples. Into their lands pushed the hardy Boer farmers with their cattle and covered wagons. Slowly they dispossessed the Sotho people of bits and pieces of their land through bribery, trickery, or outright conquest.

With expansion thus stifled, the Nguni peoples in northern Natal soon began to overpopulate the land, and by the beginning of the nineteenth century the situation had become acute. In about 1800 a half century of conflict and upheaval began. Originating in the Natal region, it was termed the Mfecane, or time of troubles, by the Nguni and Sotho peoples. During this period, clan fought against clan and tribe fought against tribe, in a struggle to gain control of the best lands for grazing cattle and growing corn.

The outstanding event of the Mfecane was the emergence of the great war chief Shaka, who created a powerful nation of the Zulu people and an empire that covered a vast region of southern Africa.

When Shaka was born in 1787 the Zulu were ruled by a king, but their political system was relatively decentralized. District chiefs and heads of lineages exercised great authority in the name of the king, and controlled such vital matters as land allocation. When Shaka became old enough to serve in the army, the Mfecane was just beginning. The Zulu king was Dingiswayo, a man of considerable talent and vision. Under Dingiswayo the Zulu began to develop a strong sense of national pride, and their military regiments fought those of neighboring peoples with courage and skill. Shaka very quickly emerged as a warrior of unusual ability.

While serving under Dingiswayo, Shaka developed a military innovation that was to become his most distinctive contribution—the formation of regiments of professional soldiers, grouped by age. The regiments fought with the assegai, or short stabbing spear, instead of with the long throwing spear that was traditional in Bantu warfare. As young men came of age they were obliged to join the appropriate regiment.

Shaka, King of the Zulus, who shortened the
long spear to produce the famed stabbing assegai.
(From an early nineteenth-century drawing.)

Soldiers underwent rigorous physical and military training, and served in garrisons wherever they were ordered. They were forbidden to marry until their regiment reached a certain age and had seen a certain amount of military service. Even after marriage, soldiers were in reserve units that could be called up when needed.

When Dingiswayo was killed in 1818, Shaka, a military hero who had already led Zulu armies to many victories, was his logical successor. After Shaka assumed the throne, his real genius flowered. Shaka declared himself divine, usurping from the Zulu priests many of their most sacred functions. As a divine king he demanded absolute, unquestioning obedience from his subjects, especially from the rigidly disciplined army. He is said to have once commanded a troop to march over a precipice to their deaths, simply to demonstrate their total loyalty to his authority.

Shaka's "impis," as his regiments were called, marched in close formation against a foe, much in the manner of the Roman legions. They fended off the thrown spears of the enemy with large shields and never faltered in their determined advance. As soon as they made contact with the enemy, they would stab with their assegais while still moving in close formation. Invariably the enemy would flee from the apparently nerveless, death-dealing impis. Within a few years the reputation of Shaka's Zulu impis had become so formidable that some opposing armies fled at sight of them.

With this military power Shaka embarked on a campaign of imperial conquest, destroying whole populations if they opposed him. Survivors were absorbed into the Zulu nation, as were whole conquered peoples. When Shaka died in 1828, after only ten years of rule, the Zulu nation had grown to nearly one million people, and its territory extended from southern Mozambique to central Natal and into portions of modern Transvaal and the Orange Free State.

Shaka's detractors, African and foreigner alike, have pictured him as a bloodthirsty tyrant and a conqueror without mercy. But merciless and death-dealing as he may have been, Shaka was a genius in both military and political affairs, comparing more fairly with a Genghis Khan than an Adolph Hitler. He created a great nation from what had been a small tribe, and ruled firmly and effectively through wisdom and justice as well as fear. His troops were fanatically loyal to him, inspired to greatness by his leadership and his dream of a great Zulu empire. The hundreds of thousands of conquered peoples who were absorbed into his Zulu nation remained Zulu, and revered his name with as much sincerity as the Zulus who formed the tribe before Shaka's time.

The consequences of Shaka's imperial conquests and of the internal upheavals that attended his assumption of absolute power were felt far beyond the Zululand that Shaka created. Several gifted Zulu leaders, unable to accept Shaka's rule but equally unable to resist his power, led their own regiments—organized along lines that Shaka had originated —in campaigns of conquest in distant lands. These several militaristic migrations brought fundamental political and cultural changes to most of southern Africa.

One such Zulu chieftain, Zwangendaba, led his regiments and camp followers to the north, crossing the Limpopo River in about 1822. Zwangendaba devastated the country through which he passed. He seized corn and cattle and took many captives. Male captives were used to reinforce his regiments and the females to swell the size of his tribe. Several times he settled attractive areas, only to move on again in the face of constant harassment from the indigenous people. In about 1827 or 1828, another Zulu war chief named Nxaba pressed Zwangendaba so hard that he moved north of the Limpopo onto the Rhodesian plateau. There he clashed with the peaceful Karanga peoples of the Changamire Empire. By this time the Rozwi nobility had lost the military energy that had enabled them to create and expand their empire. They were no match for the lean, seasoned warriors of Zwangendaba.

In about 1830 Zwangendaba and his Nguni impis reached the great holy shrine at Zimbabwe. They ruthlessly sacked and pillaged it, seizing gold and copper articles that were easily portable and killing large numbers of Rozwi nobles. For several years they roamed the peaceful lands of the Karanga, seizing food, animals, and captives at will. In 1835 they crossed the Zambezi, moving north, and continued to plunder the peoples of Mwene Mutapa and the Luangwa River region, in what is now the nation of Malawi.

Zangendaba died in 1845, and his horde split into several groups. One segment settled in southern Malawi, where their descendants still live, while others continued to move north toward the Great Lakes of East Africa, eventually reaching and settling in western Tanzania. A third major group, under the leadership of Zwangendaba's son, Mpezeni, roamed for several years through eastern Zambia, destroying crops and people, but finally blending in with the indigenous Bantu-speaking peoples and settling there.

Within five years after Zwangendaba's departure, another Zulu war king appeared, and settled his regiments in the western part of the Rhodesian plateau. This new conqueror was Mzilikazi, whose people had, during the course of their long march from Zululand, acquired the name "Matabele," or "those who disappear behind their immense Zulu war shields of stout cow hide."

Mzilikazi, as a young commander serving under Shaka, had distinguished himself in a campaign against the Sotho peoples in the

Transvaal but then defied Shaka. Since Shaka brooked no defiance from his lieutenants, Mzilikazi was forced to flee back into the Transvaal, under pursuit by Shaka's more powerful troops. Mzilikazi commanded the same devoted loyalty from his men that Shaka required from his own forces. In flight, Mzilikazi led a strong force of Zulu impis ambitious for conquest and pillaging. Settling in the central Transvaal, the Matabele became strong and wealthy from their conquests. They were not, however, safe for very long. Zulu forces under Dingaan, Shaka's successor, continued to harass them, and soon the Boer frontiersmen began to battle them as well.

By about 1825 the Matabele began retreating northward, seeking more booty and less harassment from strong enemies. They made their way into western Rhodesia, where the Rozwis still ruled a peaceful portion of the former empire of Changamire, in the late 1830's. In about 1840 the Matabele settled permanently in the Matopo Hills of Rhodesia, killing most of the Rozwi nobility and absorbing the Shona survivors into the Matabele kingdom. To this day the western portion of the Rhodesian plateau is known as Matabeleland, and the eastern portion as Mashonaland.

Other Zulu chieftains, in every case having quarreled with the fierce and vengeful Shaka, led regiments on long journeys into other parts of southern Africa. The modern kingdom of Swaziland (the Swazis are an Nguni people closely related in culture and language to the Zulus) owes its origin to the war chief Sobhuza, one of whose descendants, King Sobhuza II, today rules the independent nation of Swaziland. Another Zulu war chief, Soshangane, marched northward into eastern Mozambique and established the Gaza kingdom. All adopted the military organization and the methods of training and fighting developed by Shaka.

The military upheavals that emerged during the Mfecane and Shaka's reign were not confined to the Nguni peoples. In two notable cases, the neighboring Sotho peoples acquired similar military capabilities and caused far-reaching changes in other parts of southern Africa. One Sotho king, Sebituane, led a strong party of warriors on a campaign of conquest through eastern Botswana, just to the west of the route followed by Mzilikazi at about the same time. He eventually entered the prosperous Lozi kingdom in southwestern Zambia, far up the Zambezi River. During their long trek of conquest Sebituane's people had come to be known as the Kololo. Sebituane and his Kololo regiments quickly conquered the Lozi rulers and their troops.

Sebituane's Kololo and Mzilikazi's Matabele frequently clashed with each other. Their enmity persisted after they settled in their respective homelands in Zambia and Rhodesia. When the noted missionary David

Livingstone began his missions in Africa he worked in Lozi territory for a time and became a friend of Sebituane. His journals noted the sporadic clashes between the Kololo and the Matabele to the south.

A few years after Sebituane's death, the Lozi nobility rebelled against his successor and regained control of their lands. The Kololo were largely absorbed into Lozi culture, and the kingdom survives to this day under Lozi rule as a province of the Republic of Zambia. It is no longer sovereign, yet it is firmly committed to the continuation of the centuries-old kingship, now a powerless constitutional monarchy in a modern larger state.

To the south, the Matabele established themselves permanently on the western part of the Rhodesian plateau. Under Mzilikazi's successor, Lobengula, they maintained a formidable military kingdom, but they were not sufficiently powerful to conquer and rule all of Shonaland. Many individual Shona chiefs offered effective resistance to the Matabele even though the central power of the Rozwi rulers of Chagamire was destroyed by the initial Matabele invasions. But the creative impulses that had sustained Rozwi rule and development for over four centuries died with the Matabele invasions. The great shrine at Zimbabwe was abandoned, as were virtually all the shrines and stone enclosures that had been built over the Rhodesian plateau.

The destruction of Changamire was due to causes that were deeper than the Matabele invasion, although this was certainly the specific act that crushed the empire. More fundamental was the decline of the trading system upon which the Rozwi had built their wealth. During the nineteenth century the Portuguese, who controlled the coasts of eastern Africa, especially in Mozambique, had themselves lost most of their former power. They paid scant attention to the trickle of ivory, gold, copper, and other goods that flowed down to the Mozambique coast from Changamire country. As the slave trade ended Arab traders along the Indian Ocean coasts of eastern Africa shifted their attention to other goods, but the presence of the Portuguese in Mozambique prevented any large-scale Arab commercial activity that far south. Changamire thus suffered an economic depression during the nineteenth century.

Whether the Rozwi, or some other Shona lineage, might have created a new central political system after the misfortunes of the nineteenth century will remain an unanswered question. By the 1880's and 1890's the European conquest of southern Africa was in full force. European farmers and mineral prospectors, under the auspices of the British South Africa Company, established themselves in force on the Rhodesian plateau. The Portuguese, after centuries of inactivity, were busily colonizing Mozambique. Shona and Matabele power was ineffectual against the repeating rifles and machine guns of the Europeans.

The Mfecane, which encouraged the brilliant rise of Zulu power under Shaka and set into motion the far-reaching conquests of so many other Zulu and Sotho war chieftains, produced one other great hero of the Bantu peoples of southern Africa: King Moshesh, the founder of the Basuto nation. As the Zulu impis marched westward onto the plains of the Transvaal, small Sotho tribes and clans were at first easy prey for the fierce and brilliantly led Zulu troops. But farther south, in what is now Basutoland (the modern nation of Lesotho) and the eastern Orange Free State, the Sotho clan led by Moshesh began to organize forces that were sufficiently powerful to resist the marauding Zulu.

Moshesh was a leader of great vision and possessed immense political talent. Partly by conquest, but mainly by persuasion and personal example, he began to unite the scattered Sotho clans and tribes. By 1830 he had created a strong and closely knit kingdom. The northward migrating Boers by then had reached the southern and western borders of his kingdom, so that he had to maintain constant military vigilance against their encroachments, as well as against the Zulus to the north. On the east his kingdom was protected by the high mountains of the Drakensberg chain, which rise gradually from the plains of the Orange Free State on the west but fall sharply in great escarpments to the Natal plains along the Indian Ocean on the east.

Recognizing that he could protect and develop his new kingdom only by creative leadership, Moshesh invited European missionaries to come and teach his people. He acquired guns and encouraged his people to learn to use them, but Moshesh consistently followed a policy of persuasion and kindness. It is said that as a young man he was deeply affected by the advice of an elderly Sotho chief who told him that he had been instructed by God to rule with love. Moshesh later maintained that this precept was his constant guide. His method was effective. In 1822, when the Zulu war bands began ravaging Sotho country, Moshesh ruled an estimated two thousand people. He led this small group to safety on top of a large hill some miles to the south and added new followers by his "rule of love." His kingdom had grown to some twenty-five thousand by 1836, and to more than eighty thousand in 1848.

But Moshesh was no pure pacifist; a man of gentle personal qualities, genuinely inspired by humanitarian ideals, he was nevertheless a shrewd politician and, when need arose, a formidable warrior. In his younger days he was reputed to be one of the most audacious fighters of all the Basuto, and his policy of encouraging his followers to arm themselves showed clearly that he recognized that love and pacifism had limits in the stormy days of the mid-nineteenth century. Between about 1830 and 1855 his warriors fought numerous minor engagements with armed Boer farmers, who eagerly eyed the fertile Basuto lands at the foot of the Drakensbergs. For a time, Moshesh's forces prevented the Boers from seizing more than small slices of his territory. In 1856, however, the Boers formed a large force, and full-scale war broke out. Although they gave a good account of themselves, Moshesh's warriors were defeated in a series of battles and were gradually pressed back into the foothills of their mountain stronghold. Thousands of acres of the best lands of Moshesh's kingdom were lost to the Boers, and he found himself master of a mountain kingdom that offered great military protection but little good farmland.

In 1868 Moshesh asked for British protection. In order to preserve what little good land and freedom he had left, he placed his kingdom under the rule of Britain. Basutoland, which became the new nation of Lesotho in 1966, was able to cling to that critical small thread of political freedom lost by virtually all other Bantu-speaking peoples in southern Africa, as they were conquered and made servile to the swelling advance of European settlement.

The powerful kingdom that Shaka had created among the Zulus became something of a superpower compared to other southern African polities, but it failed to achieve the permanence that Moshesh built into his Basuto nation and that King Sobhuza, another Nguni war chieftain, achieved in the Swazi nation. (Swaziland, like Basutoland, accepted British protection and administrative control to avoid being swallowed up by European settlers. In 1968, it became independent.) In 1828, only ten years after he had become king of the Zulus, Shaka was assassinated by an alliance of fearful and jealous nobles, including his own brothers. King Dingaan, his successor, proved to be a less able ruler than the great Shaka; but the political bonds that Shaka had forged proved to be strong ones. The Zulus under Dingaan fought one important war with the Boers. Although they were defeated, the Zulus slowed the pace of relentless Boer encroachment into their lands, and the nation survived. Dingaan was killed, during the battle of Blood River, in the war he fought against the Boers. He lost this war because he had alienated many of his own subordinates (as Shaka had done before him), and several of these rebels, under the leadership of Chief Mpande, allied themselves with the Boers in order to crush Dingaan's power.

When Dingaan was defeated and killed at Blood River, in 1840, Mpande succeeded him and proved far more able in reuniting the Zulu kingdom. He did not regain any of the lands that Dingaan had lost to the Boers, but he was able to maintain peace with them and halt further seizure of Zulu territory. He attracted numerous small clans and families of peoples related to the Zulus into his kingdom, so that its population at his death in 1872 had grown to about half a million.

One other king, Ceteswayo, followed Mpande before the Zulu kingdom was finally humbled by European power. Ceteswayo inherited a large, closely knit, and generally peaceful kingdom from Mpande, but times were changing rapidly. In addition to the Boer farmers who were settled in the plains of the Transvaal to Zululand's west, the British had begun to settle many areas of coastal Natal, on Zululand's eastern borders. In 1879, less than seven years after he had succeeded to the throne, Ceteswayo found himself at war with the British. In 1880 a powerful British force invaded Zululand, deposed Ceteswayo, and established British rule over the Zulu kingdom. The bonds of language, culture, and traditions that Shaka had established have survived British rule. Today there are more than two million Zulus, deeply conscious and proud of their common heritage and history. But the strong political system that Shaka created was swept away by British conquest, and there has been no way for a great Zula king to rebuild it.

12 The East African Coast and the Interior

In central and southern Africa the Bantu-speaking peoples shared an essential commonality of culture. As they migrated into eastern Africa, however, the Bantu peoples entered a cultural melting pot in which significant variations from their basic common cultural traditions evolved.

In the present states of Tanzania, Kenya, Uganda, Burundi, and Rwanda, together with adjacent parts of Mozambique, eastern Zaire, and southern Somalia, the vast majority of people are of Bantu origin. But in many areas they have come into long and intimate contact with other groups. Along the coast, and on the numerous small islands that lie just off shore, the Bantu had nearly two thousand years of contact with explorers, traders, settlers, and military adventurers from Indonesia, India, Arabia, Persia, Portugal, and even China. This contact helped to create the distinctive Swahili civilization, which is a fascinating mosaic of various cultures, languages, religions, economies, and even racial traits.

Far into the interior, in the fertile lands that lie between the numerous great lakes and on both sides of these lakes, northward-migrating Bantu encountered and blended with the ancient Khoisan and Cushite peoples. But as soon as the Bantu sank their roots into the more northerly portions of this huge lake region, they suffered invasions of southward-migrating African peoples of the Nilotic language group. This encounter between Bantu and Nilote, between the fourteenth and the nineteenth centuries, produced another complex blend of cultures and peoples that added numerous new elements to the basic Bantu cultural pattern.

Before the beginning of the Christian era, the Greeks, Romans, and Egyptians of the eastern Mediterranean had some knowledge of eastern Africa and often referred to it as Azania. East Africa was distinguished in their minds from Ethiopia, which was a more general term for the Black Africa that they knew from direct contact. By the beginning of the Christian era, enough was known about the Azanian coast for a maritime guidebook, the *Periplus of the Erythraean Sea,* to devote several sections to sailing directions, names of key Azanian market towns, and products that were traded along the East African coast.

The Azanian trade in these very early times was dominated by Arabs from the southern part of Arabia. These Arabs were somewhat isolated from the rest of Arabia by deserts and had developed a seafaring way of life. The Indonesians also visited the Azanian coast, and left much evidence of their presence—their rain forest plants, the use of outriggers on canoes, a musical instrument called the flat-bar zither, and, most prominently, one of their languages, which is still widely spoken in Madagascar. But except for large settlements on Madagascar, the impact of the ancient Indonesian mariners on eastern Africa was limited to these few, but important, items. The Arabs, on the other hand, continued and gradually expanded their contact as the centuries wore on. They left a strong permanent impression on East Africa.

The *Periplus* describes the trade of Azania and even mentions its people:

> . . . Some traders sail chiefly to these trading posts [around the Red Sea and Somali region], while others continue down the coast and exchange their cargoes for whatever is available. The country is not under the rule of a king but each mart is governed by its own chieftain.
>
> Imports into these trading posts consist chiefly of the lances manufactured locally at Muza, axes, hatchets, awls, and several kinds of glass. Into some places a fair amount of wine and wheat is imported, not for trade purposes but to win the friendship of the natives. Exports consist of a large quantity of ivory (but less than that of Aduli) [this is Adulis, the great Axumite trading center on the Red Sea], rhinoceros-horn, tortoise-shell which ranks next to the Indian variety, and a little coco-nut oil.

Almost certainly the people of Azania at the time the *Periplus* was written were ancient Cushites, related to the Cushitic peoples who today inhabit much of southern Ethiopia, and who are believed to have migrated to many parts of eastern and central Africa long before the Christian era. The Cushites were absorbed by the waves of Bantu migrants who entered the region between about A.D. 100 and 1000. In

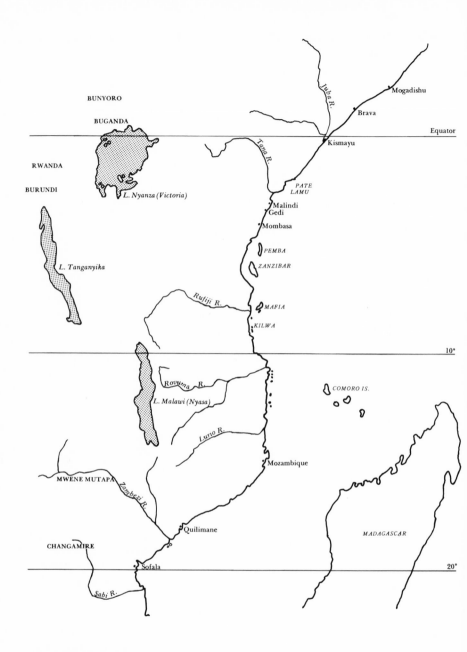

BUNYORO

BUGANDA

RWANDA

BURUNDI

L. Nyanza (Victoria)

L. Tanganyika

Juba R.

Mogadishu

Brava

Equator

Kismayu

Tana R.

PATE
LAMU

Malindi
Gedi

Mombasa

PEMBA

ZANZIBAR

Rufiji R.

MAFIA

KILWA

10°

Rovuma R.

L. Malawi (Nyasa)

Luro R.

COMORO IS.

Mozambique

MWENE MUTAPA

Zambezi R.

Quilimane

MADAGASCAR

CHANGAMIRE

Sofala

20°

Sabi R.

**East African Coast:
The Swahili Cities and Inland Sites, c. 1600**

historic times the Cushitic peoples show an admixture of Caucasoid and Negroid racial traits, much as has been the case in Egypt, and during the time of the *Periplus*, they probably resembled modern Somali and southern Ethiopian peoples. Many Cushitic peoples, especially in northeastern Africa, tend to be tall in stature and may have seemed especially tall to the relatively shorter Arab and Greek mariners upon whose descriptions the *Periplus* relied.

The *Periplus* seems to concern itself with the East African coast down to mid-Tanzania. The first Bantu-speaking peoples to reach the Indian Ocean probably did so in the vicinity of the Zambezi River mouth—at least a thousand miles farther south than the area known to the writer of the *Periplus*. Yet Bantu migrations were rapid enough to cover vast distances in a short time. Arabic sources make it almost certain that Bantu speakers had reached the coast of southern Somalia well before the beginning of the tenth century. In a period of less than nine centuries, the Bantu occupied the entire African coast from Somalia south, and they were regarded by Arabic writers of the time as its indigenous inhabitants.

Knowledge of Bantu cultural practices elsewhere allows us to surmise that the trading posts of Azania during the first millennium were villages of no considerable size, normally containing no more than a thousand or so people. Villages consisted of small square houses built of dried mud plastered over a framework of light wooden poles, with roofs thatched with either palm fronds or wild grasses.

These villages would have been headed by a chief, who was the head of the lineage to which most of the villagers belonged by descent or marriage. During the early centuries of the first millennium the trade between these villages and the itinerant mariners from Arabia, Indonesia, and other lands was not of large volume. Articles traded—such as those listed in the *Periplus*—were not of great value. Thus it is unlikely that the chiefs and their associates in the trade grew very wealthy from it.

Within a few centuries after the Bantu migrated into the Azanian coastal area, the pace of development quickened. The basis for Swahili civilization was being laid by the Bantu immigrants and their Arab trading partners well before the end of the first millennium. A vivid picture of this process of civilization building has survived in the writings of al-Mas'udi, one of the greatest of the early Arab geographers and historians. Al-Mas'udi visited East Africa and traveled frequently in the Red Sea and Indian Ocean region. In about the year 915, he traveled to Persia, India, and China. On the return voyage, he journeyed up the East African coast from a point along the central Tanzanian coast to Oman in Arabia. He never traveled to the south of Tanzania, but what he heard of Sofala (located south of the Zambezi River mouth on the Mozambique coast) obviously impressed him:

> The pilots of Oman pass by the channel of Berbera to reach the island of Kanbalu, which is in the Zanj sea. *It has a mixed population of Muslims and Zanj idolators* [Zanj was the Arab name for Black Africans in the eastern part of the continent] . . . *The aforesaid Kanbalu is the* furthest point of their voyages on the Zanj sea, and the land of Sofala and the Waqwaq, on the edge of the Zanj mainland and at the end of this branch of the sea. . . . The land of Zanj produces leopard skins. The people wear them as clothes, or export them to Muslim countries. They are the largest leopard skins and the most beautiful for making saddles. . . . They also export tortoise-shell for making combs, for which ivory is likewise used. . . .
>
> In the same way that the sea of China ends with the land of Japan, the sea of Zanj ends with the land of Sofala and the Waqwaq, which produces gold and many other wonderful things. It has a warm climate and is fertile. The Zanj capital is there and they have a king called the *Mfalme.* This is the ancient name of their kings, and all the other Zanj kings are subject to him: he has 300,000 men. The Zanj use the ox as a beast of burden, for they have no horses, mules, or camels in their land, and do not know of their existence. . . .
>
> It is from this country that come tusks weighing fifty pounds and more. They usually go to Oman, and from there are sent to China and India. This is the chief trade route, and if it were not so, ivory would be common in Muslim lands. . . .
>
> They use iron instead of gold or silver. . . .
>
> To go back to the Zanj and their kings, these are known as *Wafalme,* which means son of the Great Lord, since he is chosen to govern them justly. If he is tyrannical or strays from the truth, they kill him and exclude his seed from the throne; for they consider that in acting wrongfully he forfeits his position as the son of the Lord, the King of Heaven and Earth. They call God *Maliknajlu,* which means Great Lord. . . .
>
> The Zanj have an elegant language and men who preach in it. One of their holy men will often gather a crowd and exhort his hearers to please God in their lives and to be obedient to him. He explains the punishments that follow upon disobedience, and reminds them of their ancestors and kings of old. These people have no religious law: their kings rule by custom and by political expediency.
>
> The Zanj eat bananas, which are as common among them as they are in India; but their staple food is millet and a plant called *kalari* which is pulled out of the earth like truffles. It is plentiful in Aden and the neighboring part of Yemen near to the town. It is like the cucumber of Egypt and Syria. They also eat honey and meat. Every man worships what he pleases, be it a plant, an animal, or a mineral. They have many islands where the coconut grows: its nuts are used as fruit by all the Zanj peoples. One of these islands, which is one or two days' sail from the coast,

Zanzibar harbor. (From a drawing made in 1886.)

has a Muslim population and a royal family. This is the island of Kanbalu of which we have already spoken.

The Zanj peoples of whom al-Mas'udi speaks are clearly Bantu. Their foods, their system of government, their religious customs, even their language (the terms "mfalme" and "wafalme" are the singular and plural, respectively, of the Swahili term for a kind of chief) all attest to this fact. The Arab trade, based at Oman, was quite regular, and the exports of ivory, tortoise shells, leopard skins, and even gold (from Sofala) indicate that the trade was probably large enough in volume to allow at least some Zanj rulers to accumulate wealth. The references to Sofala, even though al-Mas'udi did not visit there, suggest that that land, which played such a vital role as a trade entrepôt for the inland kingdoms of Luba, Mwene Mutapa, and Changamire, was already beginning to develop—even allowing for the probable inaccuracy of al-Mas'udi's claim that its king commanded all the other Zanj kings and 300,000 soldiers. (This could have been true some centuries later, at the peak of Mwene Mutapa's power, but very probably was not the case as early as the ninth century.) But the fact that al-Mas'udi wrote of Sofala and its gold and ivory indicates that it was in existence and was already exporting the wealth of the interior of Mozambique, Rhodesia, and adjacent areas.

Between the first and ninth centuries Bantu-speaking peoples of many lineages and dialects migrated northward along the Indian Ocean coast from the Zambezi region of Mozambique. Settling both the mainland and the hundreds of islands, small and large, that lie along this coast, they adapted themselves to this new environment by combining their traditional pattern of agriculture (still using millet as a staple) with fishing. Presumably they found at least a few Cushite settlements along the coast, but either exterminated or absorbed them so completely that there is today no trace of the Cushite presence.

The Bantu peoples inherited the modest trade that had preceded their arrival and rich archaeological evidence suggests frequent foreign contacts throughout the first millennium and later. Coins of Persian, Roman, Greek, Arab, Indian, and Chinese origin have been found in large numbers. Pottery and glassware from China, India, Persia, and Arabia have been found all along the East African coast. Unlike the Atlantic Ocean coast of West Africa, which experienced no foreign contact before the fifteenth century, the East African coast, at least as far south as the region opposite Madagascar, was in constant contact with the Greek-Roman-Egyptian world in ancient days, and the Indian Ocean world of Arabia, Persia, India, and China in later days.

As the trade continued, enterprising merchants, both Bantu and Arab, were alert for more opportunities to export valuable goods from the interior. Thus as soon as the traders in the Sofala area found evidence of copper, gold, and ivory in the interior, they began to devote more attention to Sofala, visiting it more frequently, and bringing more goods from abroad. Although the coastal traders likely had no direct contact with the producers of these goods, they hoped to convince them, through whatever middlemen were available, to export in larger quantities.

Between the tenth and fourteenth centuries, several other centers of concentrated trading activity appeared, or became more prominent—Mozambique island, off the coast of Mozambique, Kilwa, Mafia, Zanzibar, and Pemba, along the Tanzania coast; Mombasa, Malindi, Lamu, and Pate in Kenya; Kismayu, Brava, and Mogadishu in Somalia. All of these except Mogadishu seem to have been populated by Bantu-speaking peoples, and even in that city there were (and are still) quarters with Bantu names, indicating the presence of Bantu inhabitants before the Somali settled there.

The typical development of these centers seems to have followed two courses. In one situation, the Bantu peoples took the initiative in encouraging the growth of trade. They instituted trade regulations and tax systems, guaranteed protection and fair treatment for visiting merchants, and developed their own form of government as their chiefs grew wealthier on the profits from the trade. In the other type of situation, the initiative came from Arab or Persian (from Shiraz) merchants or adventurers, who came in force to an emerging trade area, established their authority by force of arms, guile, or political astuteness, and developed a colonial city-state with the Bantu inhabitants as subjects.

Regardless of how they originated, all of the trading centers that grew up along the Zanj coast attracted permanent settlers from outside Africa, especially from Arabia. For a period, especially during the elventh to thirteenth centuries, the Shirazi Persians exercised a considerable influence on the more northerly of the trading centers. Shirazi influence eventually spread southward and today many Zanzibaris refer to themselves as Shirazis. Generally, the Arab settlers came to trade or to serve as trading factors. Often they married Bantu women and would have been absorbed into Bantu society had it not been for the fact that for centuries they arrived in such large numbers that a mixed population was produced by constant Arab infusion into the Bantu base.

The mixed population that resulted from the constant Arab-Bantu marriages was, of course, the Swahili. Its hybrid quality, together with the fact that its seamen and merchants frequently traveled up and down the coast from city to city, tended to unify the culture and language of the Swahili peoples over a long stretch of coast. Where once there may have been a dozen or more emerging Bantu "tribes," between northern Mozambique and southern Somalia, one long culture area began to take shape, and one language, Swahili, became not only the lingua franca but eventually the mother tongue.

Swahili is a typical Bantu language in every respect save one: it has borrowed a larger percentage of foreign words than most other Bantu languages. These borrowed words come from German and English, as well as from Arabic. Still, more than 80 percent of the Swahili vocabulary is Bantu in origin, and the language contains fewer foreign-originated words than does English.

Although the Bantu cultural base proved to be dominant, there was a distinct difference between the cultures of the cities, where the Arabs settled in larger numbers, and the cultures of the rural areas, where relatively fewer Arabs settled. The urban culture was confined to the islands and a few spots on the mainland where most of the cities were located. Islam soon became the dominant religion in the cities and was eventually accepted by the majority of the urban people. Its spread in the rural areas was much slower, although over a long period of time it did reach most of the coastal peoples. Today, for example, about half of Tanzania's ten million people are Muslims.

There were also some differences in government between the cities and the rural areas. In the latter, chiefs who headed clans or lineages ruled with carefully circumscribed power. They were advised by councils of elders, bound by custom and limited to relatively small areas, where members of the clan and their spouses were settled. Generally the rural areas were subject to the rulers of the main city of their area. But until very recent times, the Swahili civilization was politically decentralized;

for centuries each of the several cities was independent, exercising suzerainty over its own population and a limited surrounding area.

In the cities themselves the rulers (who came increasingly to use the title "shaikh" or "sultan") generally came from powerful families. The Arabs, like the Africans, placed great importance on family connections, and in this respect had little difficulty intermeshing with African political ideas. Inheritance of property and succession of political authority among the Arabs was through the male line, while the Bantu groups along the coast varied, some being patrilineal and others matrilineal. In the towns and cities the Arab system became the rule, while in the rural areas, where Arab influence was weaker, the Bantu culture tended to persist. Differences between Arab and Bantu inheritance rules caused little conflict except in the matter of land. Arab custom recognized individual ownership of land, while the Bantu universally regarded land as the possession of the lineage or family group. The Bantu believed that only the fruits of the land could be owned by the individual or family using the land. Usually the Arabs were allowed to continue using the land more or less indefinitely but were not allowed to sell it. In a few areas, where there were large numbers of Arabs, the land came gradually to be regarded as theirs to dispose of as they wished.

Although Islam was widely accepted among the coastal Bantu peoples, the religion's great flexibility—converts were allowed relatively wide latitude in worship so long as the essential tenets of Islam were adhered to—ensured the survival of Bantu beliefs. Sacrifices to ancestors and rituals to propitiate the spirits of various natural phenomena and to ensure good crops and good catches in fishing continued to be performed—sometimes even in the towns, where Islam and Arab influence were strongest.

Several highly visible Arab contributions became integral parts of Swahili civilization. First was the growth of large towns and cities. The coastal Bantu originally settled in dispersed family homesteads, with few villages of any size. Larger villages, towns, and even a few cities developed at those trading sites where Arabs came both to trade and to settle. Kilwa, Zanzibar, Mombasa, Malindi, and Lamu were the most prominent of these trading cities. The majority of the population in these urban centers were Bantus or Bantu-Arab hybrids, but the cities had an appearance and a quality of urban life that was very different from the traditional Bantu settlements along the coastal region. Forms of architecture and techniques of building were non-Bantu; they were imported by the Arabs and they became essential parts of the emerging Swahili culture.

Second was the Arabic style of dress, which consisted of long robes and small "skull-cap" hats for men, and cloth "kangas" for women, which covered both the body and the head. The original Bantu dress typically consisted of skin or grass robes and skirts, intended to cover the private parts of the body. Robes of bark cloth or cotton were imported by the wealthier men. As Islam was accepted by the Africans, and as Swahili culture developed, the new forms of dress spread rapidly. Even today the kanga is the typical dress of most Swahili women, and the men still wear long cotton skirts, separate jackets, and small caps.

Third was the Arabic system of writing. Swahili civilization gradually adapted Arabic characters to the Swahili language. A literature of poetry, historical legend, and religious writing developed, and writing in Swahili became an essential tool of the commercial system all along the Indian Ocean coast.

Between the twelfth and fourteenth centuries the famous commercial cities, known through the writings of both Arab and European visitors, reached their peak of development. The first good eye-witness account of these cities comes from the great Ibn Battuta, whose wide travels and excellent written accounts have done so much to enlighten modern understanding of the great states of the Sudan. Battuta visited East Africa in about 1331, calling at Mogadishu, Mombasa, and Kilwa.

Of Mogadishu, Battuta commented that it "is a very large town. The people have very many camels, and slaughter many hundreds every day. They also have many sheep. The merchants are wealthy, and manufacture a material which takes its name from the town and which is exported to Egypt and elsewhere."

Battuta was favorably impressed by Mombasa and its sultan. But a slight note of ascetcism creeps into his vivid account of that city's food and the eating habits of its citizens:

> The food of these people is rice cooked with butter, served on a large wooden dish. With it they serve side-dishes, stews of chicken, meat, fish, and vegetables. They cook unripe bananas in fresh milk, and serve them as a sauce. They put curdled milk in another vessel with peppercorns, vinegar, and saffron, green ginger and mangoes, which look like apples but have a nut inside. Ripe mangoes are very sweet and eaten like fruit; but unripe mangoes are as acid as lemons, and are cooked in vinegar. When the Mogadiscio people have taken a mouthful of rice, they take some of these pickles. One of them eats as much as several of us; they are very fat and corpulent.

His impression of Kilwa, however, makes it clear that he regarded it as the leading city on the Zanj coast:

> We spent a night on the island and then set sail for Kilwa, the principal town on the coast, the greater part of whose inhabitants are Zanj of very black complexion. Their faces are scarred, like the Limiin of

Janada. A merchant told me that Sofala is half a month's march from Kilwa, and that between Sofala and Yufi in the country of the Limiin is a month's march. Powdered gold is brought from Yufi to Sofala.

Kilwa is one of the most beautiful and well constructed towns in the world. The whole of it is elegantly built. The roofs are built with mangrove poles. There is very much rain. The people are engaged in a holy war, for their country lies beside that of pagan Zanj. The chief qualities are devotion and piety; they follow the Shafi'i rite.

Trade in the great commercial cities was not, by world standards, unusually large or lucrative. Small sailing boats, often less than thirty feet in length and carrying crews of no more than four or five, sufficed to collect small quantities of ivory, gold dust, millet, coconuts, turtle shells, skins, iron and copper bars, fibers for making rope, occasional fruits and vegetables from villages and minor markets on the mainland and the islands. Most of the gold, iron, and ivory—generally the most valuable products of the trade—seem to have come from the south, particularly from the Sofala area, which received these products from the inland regions of Mozambique, Rhodesia, Zambia, and Katanga.

Into the larger trading cities, such as Kilwa and Mombasa, came larger vessels—sturdy Arab dhows up to sixty and seventy feet long, and even larger ships from Persia and India. Occasional fleets of Chinese ships sailed westward to trade in Arabia and Africa. In about 1417-18 and 1431-32 Chinese fleets consisting of hundreds of huge ships, larger than those of the Spanish at the time of their Armada in 1588, visited several East African ports. For internal reasons, however, China retired from oceanic voyages in the fifteenth century, and afterward, as in earlier days, Chinese goods reached Africa and African goods China in non-Chinese bottoms.

The vessels that came to East Africa's ports brought a variety of goods: silks, spices, cotton cloth, swords, axes, knives, glassware, porcelain vessels, and even coins. Ruins of the East African trading cities, dating to between the twelfth and fifteenth centuries, are rich in old coins and fragments of fine glass and procelain from India, China, Persia, Egypt, Greece, and Rome. A British scholar, Sir Mortimer Wheeler, visiting the Tanganyika coast in 1955, reported that he had "never in my life seen so much broken China as I have seen in the past fortnight along the coast here and the Kilwa islands: literally, fragments of Chinese porcelain by the shovelful. . . ."

Swahili civilization developed to a higher point of affluence and civilization for two centuries after Ibn Battuta saw it. Dozens of towns and cities with gracious homes built of stone and mortar dotted the coast. These homes were several stories in height, with carefully laid out tropical gardens, fountains, and pools. Ruins of palaces indicate that a few homes were designed for the most luxurious kind of living. Small but exquisitely built mosques were scattered about the cities, and mosques of wood and mud were found in most small towns and villages. The harbors of the chief cities were busy with ships arriving and departing, and some had stone quays to facilitate loading and unloading. The cemeteries around these ancient cities, in which were buried the many wealthy merchants, court officials, and rulers, are filled with inscribed and decorated tombstones, and there are numerous large tombs with graceful stone pillars and structures.

Just as the history of other parts of Africa contains great gaps that archaeological reserach may some day illuminate, the full extent of the Swahili accomplishment remains to be determined. Something is known of a dozen or so of the urban trading centers that originated as early as the tenth and eleventh centuries, yet one eminent British scholar of the East African coast, G. S. P. Freeman-Grenville, has compiled a list of sixty-three ancient towns and cities whose ruins have been found on the Tanzania coast alone.

These numerous and highly developed towns and cities were in no sense alien implantations on a barren or passive African soil. Arab traders and settlers stimulated development of the Swahili civilization and brought it new techniques of knowledge in writing, architecture, religion, law, government, and commerce. But it was the Bantu-Arab hybrid that produced this unique civilization. Sometimes, new potentates from Oman or Shiraz would establish themselves as rulers, but within a generation or two they were absorbed, and the majority of sultans and shaikhs in cities were Swahili. This blending process was more pronounced on the Azanian coast than it was in North Africa. Although the blend between Berber and Arab in North Africa was a basic process, Arabs arrived in such numbers, maintained such close contact with other Arab centers, and so often brought their wives with them, that the Arab language and culture made a deep and lasting impression.

The Swahili way of life spread over a vast expanse of coastal mainland and islands stretching well over a thousand miles from southern Somalia to northern Mozambique. It was never one political unit. Each city was basically autonomous, and the occasional allegiance East Africans owed to rulers in Arabia or Persia was more or less symbolic. Often there were tensions between the rival trading cities and between the cities and the non-Swahili Bantu peoples in the interior, but despite these tensions, the Swahili way of life was not particularly militarized. Apart from small-scale wars between cities, which involved at most a few hundred men engaged in raids, and similar adventures with the peoples on the mainland, war was conspicuously absent from Swahili history. There were no standing armies, no wars of conquest, no efforts to expand territories, and no fleets of armed ships.

This comparatively peaceful way of life was shattered abruptly, and virtually destroyed, when the Portuguese arrived at the beginning of the sixteenth century. Vasco da Gama, with his small fleet of four ships, was the first known European to visit the thriving trading cities along the Swahili coast. In early 1498, he began to sail northward along the Indian Ocean coast after rounding the Cape. By this time the Portuguese were well acquainted with western Africa, had built their first forts on the Guinea coast, and had established contact with the kingdom of Kongo. But they were seeking, in the Indian Ocean, two things that they had failed to find in the Atlantic: the legendary kingdom of Prester John, who was supposed to rule a large Christian country somewhere in the interior of Africa or India, and direct access to the spices, gems, and reputed wealth of the Indies. Portuguese achievement of both objectives was blocked in the Mediterranean area by the remnants of Muslim power in North Africa, Egypt, Arabia, Persia, and Turkey; but the Portuguese hoped to circumvent the Muslims and perhaps link forces with Prester John to forge a Christian alliance that would remove the Islamic threat permanently. They were eager for wealth, and ruthless in their determination to obtain it.

When Vasco da Gama (and later Portuguese sailors) found Kilwa, Malindi, Mombasa, and other highly civilized cities along the East African coast, they were surprised and impressed. According to Duarte Barbosa, one of the earliest Portuguese mariners to visit the coast (he visited it several times between 1500 and 1518), it was a quite respectable land:

"Kilwa," he recorded, "is a Moorish town [the early Portuguese tended to call all Muslims in Africa Moors] with many fair houses of stone and mortar, with many windows after our fashion, very well arranged in streets, with many flat roofs. . . . It has a Moorish [we know from other evidence that the ruler at the time was Swahili] king over it. From this place they trade with Sofala, whence they bring back gold, and from here they spread all over "Arabia Felix," which henceforth we may call by this name (even though it be in Ethiopia) for all the seacoast is well peopled with villages and abodes of Moors."

Of Mombasa, Duarte notes that it "is a place of great traffic, and has a good harbor, in which are always moored craft of many kinds and also great ships, both of those which come from Sofala and of those which go thither, and others which come from the great kingdom of Cambay [in India] and from Malindi; others which sail to the Isles of Zanzibar. . . ."

The Portuguese experienced a certain respect for the civilized development they unexpectedly found in East Africa, and they noted that the local inhabitants failed to find the Portuguese especially impressive. Da Gama himself noted in his log, upon visiting a town in Mozambique which he called Quilimane, an encounter that gives some insight into the Swahili perspective:

> When we had been two or three days at this place two gentlemen of the country came to see us. They were very haughty, and valued nothing which we gave them. One of them wore a *touca*, with a fringe embroided in silk, and the other a cap of green satin. A young man in their company—so we understood from their signs—had come from a distant country, and had already seen big ships like ours.

Impressed or not, the Portuguese motivation in exploring the East African coast and the Indian Ocean was to seek wealth and to find possible allies against the "Moors." Ever since the Moorish rulers of Portugal had been expelled, there had been rivalry and enmity between the two groups. The Muslim hold on commerce between the Indies and Europe increased the Portuguese sense of hostility as Portugal began to break out of its isolation, in the fifteenth and sixteenth centuries.

In 1505, when Major D. Francisco de Almeida was sent to the Indian Ocean with a powerful naval and military force, his instructions from the throne left no doubt as to the strategic objectives of his mission:

> It is on this voyage that we intend with the help of Our Lord to build the fortress of Sofala [this was only seven years after the first Portuguese contact with Mozambique] whereto we have appointed as captain Pero d'Anhaya with the ships men and artillery and all things assigned thereto. . . .

After a detailed set of instructions specifying that Almeida was to use guile, seize all the Moors and their goods, but assure the local king that Portugal meant him no harm, the orders went on to describe the objectives and tactics for taking Kilwa:

> You shall upon leaving Sofala go by way of Kilwa . . . and having landed, you shall endeavor to take this place, and if the Moors show fight you shall see to it with that particular care that we know you to have that no man is lost in so far as it is possible, and which we hope that Our Lord will allow, and if it is taken by force or foresaken by the Moors you shall endeavor to capture and seize as many of the chief ones as you may, and the others if they surrender the place to you without fight, as may Our Lord allow, it is our pleasure that you let them go without further hurt to their persons, and you shall only endeavor to seize the riches of the place—namely—gold and merchandise, for we are assured that the King as well as the merchants there have great riches, and we trust you to use good care to see that everything is saved, and

whatever is seized shall be delivered to our factor aboard your *nao* as we ordered you to do in the exploit of Sofala.

And if by chance you find the King disposed to our service and that he has paid to the captains presently there the *paryas* and the tribute due to us every year, in this event you shall not cause him distress, but you shall tell him that it is needful to our service to have a fortress here wherein to shelter our people and our merchandise, and then you shall build it with or without his pleasure. . . . .

And we would remind you that if you have occasion to do them hurt, we have here information that there is great wealth in gold, due to the long period of time they have had the trade of Sofala, and we are told that the King is very rich, and also that there are very rich merchants, and that there is here much merchandise of profit to the trade of Sofala due to the ships that put in there to trade. And therefore be watchful and do all the things we have entrusted to you, storing away everything that nothing may be lost. . . .

This set of instructions contained one other paragraph that succinctly exposed the larger Portuguese objective:

It seems to us that nothing would be more important to our service than to have a fortress at the mouth of the Red Sea or near to it either inside or outside wherever best placed to close it and prevent any more spices from passing to the lands of the Sultan and persuade all the peoples of India to put aside the fantasy that they can ever again trade with any but ourselves, and since it is also near to the lands of Prester John whence it seems to us there may follow many gains first to its Christianity and also much increase to our treasury. . . .

As Almeida (and dozens of Portuguese captains in the decades that followed) discovered, the distinction they assumed between the "Moors" and the local people was not real. By the sixteenth century the Swahili people, all Muslim, were so intermixed with Arabs that they themselves were "Moors," in the broad sense that the Portuguese used the term. Furthermore, few of the "kings" of the merchant cities along the coast were inclined to welcome the arrogant Portuguese as rulers or to allow the wealth of their merchants and trading clients to be seized. A few town rulers initially welcomed the Portuguese as allies against rival cities, but eventually discovered that Portugal intended to enrich herself, and no more. Other cities resisted, and the Portuguese fleets took their instructions from Lisbon quite seriously: they simply sacked recalcitrant cities, seized all the gold and goods they could find, and installed garrisons to maintain a permanent Portuguese presence.

Mombasa was one such city that refused to cooperate. Almeida virtually leveled the city, killing all who tried to defend it. Mombasa's ruler, and some of the city's residents, retreated to the mainland; upon returning to their ruined city, they found utter devastation. The sultan, after surveying the damage, wrote a letter to the sultan of Malindi in which he said he found "no living thing in it, neither man nor woman, young nor old, nor child however little. All who had failed to escape had been killed or burned."

The prosperous trading cities along the Zanj coast were virtually defenseless against the cannon, the well-armed troops, and the ruthless determination of the Portuguese. For centuries they had treated warfare as a minor matter.

During the first half of the sixteenth century Portugal had little difficulty in establishing its supremacy along the coast. At first Portugal found the results profitable, but trade began to deteriorate along the coast and between the inland and the coast. In the rich hinterland from which Sofala's gold came, the struggles between the Mwene Mutapa and the Changamire continued intermittently, and the Swahili deliberately influenced the Changamire to cease sending gold to the coast. In 1506 the clerk of the Portuguese Factory at Sofala wrote a letter to the king of Portugal, telling of the struggles between the two great interior kingdoms. In this report he recognized that the arrogance of the Portuguese along the coast was already reaping its bitter fruits:

> . . . And for this reason, Sire, there is no gold coming to Sofala for one robs the other, and the gold, Sire, is all in and around the lands of the amyr [i.e., Changamire] although there is some all over the king-dom but very little. And when the land was at peace, Sire, there was taken from Sofala each year three or four *naos* with a million of gold and at times one million and three hundred thousand mitcals of gold over a million and not less. . . . And thus, Sire, I labored to find by what manner to make peace between these two the king of Ucalanga and Toloa and I was told that this could not be done save by the king of Sofala or the king of Kilwa. But that these have not done it during all this time to prevent the gold from coming to Sofala to be found there by the Christians who come thither, for they knew that when the admiral came to India, straightaway the Christians became lords of Sofala and for this reason they have not made peace.

Clearly the Swahili and Arab traders were not displeased by the civil war and the resulting cessation of gold shipments. In the absence of any way to retaliate directly against Portuguese aggression, they were using another weapon—their influence in the interior—to prevent the Portuguese from profiting by their supremacy on the coast. For this and other reasons, the Portuguese devoted most of their energies to the Indies, and their influence on the Swahili civilization and its commercial foundations was almost wholly negative. Coastal trade dwindled to a trickle as Portuguese ships transported goods directly from the Indies to Europe. Ports were virtually abandoned as fewer and fewer ships arrived. The fortunes of local families declined and then were exhausted. Great palaces were deserted when their owners lost the means of maintaining them. By the end of the sixteenth century, a hundred years after Vasco da Gama, Almeida, and the other Portuguese admirals and captains first arrived, the East African coast was desolate.

By the end of the seventeenth century, the Portuguese were driven out of eastern African north of Mozambique by the Omani Arabs, but the damage they had done was nearly fatal. Most of the once prosperous cities were in ruins or were little more than sleepy trading villages. The coastal trade consisted of little more than a small-scale exchange of local goods, and little gold, ivory, and valuable skins were exported. Apart from bringing into Africa the important new food crops of the New World, such as maize and manioc, the contribution of the Portuguese to the Swahili civilization was to wither it into impotence. It was not until the nineteenth century that an ambitious sultan of Oman, Sayyid Said, began to rebuild the commercial system and restore some of the vitality of the Swahili world.

During the thousand years or more while the Swahili civilization was developing, a very different drama was being enacted far to the west, in the interior of modern Tanzania, Kenya, Uganda, Burundi, and Rwanda. This drama was, so far as is known, almost totally isolated from coastal developments until the late eighteenth or early nineteenth century.

Bantu-speaking peoples began migrating into the interior of East Africa, around the Great Lakes (Lakes Tanganyika, Nyasa, Kivu, Victoria, Albert, Edward, and Kioga), at about the same time as the coastal Bantu were moving into the Azanian coast. Between about the sixth and tenth centuries they had reached the region of Lake Victoria, settling the lands that are now Burundi, Rwanda, western Tanzania, and southern Uganda.

The isolation between the two waves of northward-migrating Bantu peoples is due to a large belt of dry, relatively infertile country in central Tanzania and Kenya. Along the coast of both countries, the rainfall is heavy enough to sustain cultivation. This, combined with an abundance of fish and commercial opportunities, provided an environment that could support the development of the Swahili civilization, even without a very dense population or great agricultural productivity. In the region of the Great Lakes, the rainfall is good and the soils are quite fertile. This interior region, though it produced little mineral wealth and had little opportunity for lucrative trade, was able to provide for the growth of a dense population. In some of the modern areas of the region, such as Burundi, Rwanda, and southern Uganda, population density averages more than three hundred people per square mile, and is often two to three times as high in the most fertile local areas.

Between the two areas to which the Bantu migrated, lie hundreds of miles of rolling country where rainfall is low and topsoils are thin. In this central belt grow wiry wild grasses and trees of the dry-forest type. These trees can be cleared, with enough labor, but the poor soils produce low yields. There are years in which the rains are very light, causing crop failure and famine. Quite naturally the migratory movements of the Bantu farmers avoided this unattractive territory.

Bands of Khoisan hunters, however, were scattered about this semi-arid central region and followed the great herds of wild game that abound there. And in the occasional fertile spots, inside the larger dry region, there is evidence of settlements of Cushite farmers who practiced irrigation and terracing. Small bands of Bantu farmers may have begun to move into the central region as early as the tenth or eleventh century, but they did not enter in large numbers until the sixteenth or seventeenth century. Even then they spread slowly and increased in population much less rapidly than their relatives around the Great Lakes. (Oral traditions of the inhabitants of parts of central Tanzania place the arrival of their ancestors in their present locations as recently as the late eighteenth and early nineteenth centuries.)

The history of central East Africa is less well known than that of most of Africa, partly because little archaeological work has been carried out until the past few years, partly because no written accounts refer to the area with any clarity prior to the nineteenth century, and partly because the complex intermingling of peoples—Bantu, Khoisan, Cushite, Sudanic, and Nilote—over the past millennium has made oral histories useful only for the past three or four centuries at best. Prior to the sixteenth century, the most certain historical fact about the area is that the Bantu settlers had sunk roots and expanded their population considerably on both sides of the Great Lakes. They had developed enough wealth by about the fourteenth century to have begun at least some rudimentary process of state and kingdom formation.

The lakes region, and adjacent areas, contain bits and pieces of ruins that have something of the same romantic mystery about them that Zimbabwe had when it was first discovered. One great stone city, Engaruka, has been found in interior Tanzania, on the wall of the great Rift Valley.

Engaruka consists of about six thousand houses, built of stone without mortar. It stretches along man-made terraces, buttressed with stone, that run for three miles along the wall of the Rift Valley in northern Tanzania. Another five hundred houses lie below, in the valley itself. There are no ruins of monuments, impressive tombs, or public buildings. The ruins are uninhabited, and none of the peoples living in the general area know for certain who built and lived in Engaruka. But the builders of Engaruka were clearly an agricultural people who farmed both the terraced escarpment and the lands of the valley. They probably grazed cattle and other domestic animals in the valley. The Masai, who today live near Engaruka, believe that it was once inhabited by the Iraqw peoples (called Mbulu by most of their Masai and Bantu neighbors), who today live some miles away, south and west of Lake Eyasi. The Iraqw, surrounded by Bantu peoples, still speak a language of the Cushite branch.

If the Iraqw originally inhabited Engaruka, as seems likely, they must have abandoned it as recently as two or three hundred years ago, in the face of armed assault from the Masai or Bantu groups who were moving into the area, and who were more warlike than the sedentary Iraqw. Engaruka itself may have been built as a last stronghold by a Cushitic population that was increasingly beleaguered by the encroachments of new peoples who used the Rift Valley as a corridor.

Reconstructing the early history of interior East Africa, it seems evident that the earliest inhabitants were the small-statured Khoisan peoples who once hunted over all the lands of eastern, central, and southern Africa. Several millennia before the Christian era, possibly as early as 15,000-10,000 B.C., the ancestors of the Cushites began entering Kenya, migrating southward down the Rift Valley. They are identified archaeologically with the Kenya Capsian, Elmenteitan, Hyrax Hill, and other stone-age cultures of this line. The few skeletons of this group show a people of tall stature, with head shapes and body configuration as much Caucasoid as Negroid. Eventually these ancient Cushites, related to the peoples who orginally inhabited Ethiopia, Somalia, and parts of the Sudan, changed their economic system from hunting and fishing to farming and herding. When this change occurred is not known for certain, but it seems to have taken place before the beginning of the Christian era.

The Cushites and Khoisan peoples, very different from each other in race and culture, inhabited East Africa for several millennia without exterminating or absorbing one another. The Cushites tilled their farms and grazed their cattle in the more fertile regions, both inland and along the coast, while the Khoisan hunters roamed the drier grasslands and forests. Prior to the early centuries of the Christian era, they seem to have had East Africa largely to themselves, with few sizable intrusions by other groups.

In the early centuries of the Christian era the human ecology of East Africa began to change rapidly. Two great waves of migrants began to move in from north and south, drastically changing the region's cultural pattern, economy, and even its landscape. (As more farmers felled trees in heavily forested areas, they created grasslands in which, even today, few trees are found.) From the south came the Bantu, both along the coast and inland up the Rift Valley and around the Great Lakes. From the north came a new group, the Sudanic peoples called Nilotes. The Nilotes were farmers and herders who migrated southward along both sides of the upper Nile toward its source in Lake Victoria. And continuing groups of Cushites arrived from time to time, from the general area of Ethiopia and Somalia.

During the first millennium of the Christian era, the Bantu were moving in substantial numbers out of their Katanga dispersal area, first to east and west, then to north and south. Some time before the end of the first millennium they reached what is known as the Interlacustrine Region, the vast expanse of land that is almost encircled by Lakes Tanganyika, Kivu, Victoria, Albert, Edward, and Kioga. There they found an environment that is perhaps the largest rich area in Africa outside the Nile valley. Well watered by rivers and lakes, with rainfalls exceeding forty inches a year, the topsoil of the area is fertile and deep. In this region the Bantu population expanded rapidly on abundant harvests of bananas, plantains, millet, sorghum, yams, and other thriving staple crops.

From the northeast, moving toward the same hospitable country, came further groups of Cushites, especially cattle herders who migrated from their homeland in what is now southern and western Somalia and southern Ethiopia. In those areas, which had been invaded long before by Semitic peoples who crossed the narrows of the Red Sea, the Somali peoples, themselves members of the widely dispersed Cushitic language group, were steadily pressing south into country inhabited both by Bantu and Galla peoples. The Galla, a Cushitic cattle-herding people, were pressing both northward into the Ethiopian highlands and southwestward into modern Kenya and eastern Uganda. Because of the great time and distance that separated them, many of these new Cushite immigrants were only distantly related to the ancient Cushitic settlers of East Africa. Whether the new Cushites penetrated the Interlacustrine Region is not known. They did, however, establish themselves in parts of Kenya and Uganda, and exercised considerable cultural and economic influence on the Nilotic peoples who were moving southward early in the second millennium.

Currently numbering about four million people, the Nilotes are not a large group, as major African peoples go. Many Nilotes absorbed Cushitic traits, including Cushitic words and a variety of cattle herding in which the milk, urine, and blood from living cattle are a major element of diet, along with the meat of slaughtered cows. These mixed

Nilotes are often called Nilo-Hamites, to distinguish them from both the purer Nilotes and the Cushites (who until recent years were referred to as Hamites).

Regrettably the history of the Nilotes (whose eastern Sudanic sub-family of languages relates them to both the Nubians and the peoples east of Lake Chad, in Bagirmi and Darfur) is very poorly known. Their homeland—east and west of the upper Nile, hundreds of miles south of modern Khartoum, in the modern Republic of Sudan—is one of the most remote in Africa, offering little access to literate peoples. Their oral histories go back only fifteen to twenty generations and cover only a few centuries at best. And the isolation of their homeland region has made it one of the least studied in Africa.

The cradleland of the Nilotic peoples is in the modern Republic of Sudan, in the general region known as the Bahr el Gazal, especially between the Nile and the modern Central African Republic. Numerous rivers originate in the higher lands around the Sudan-Central African Republic border, flowing eastward and coming together to flow into the Nile. The closer these rivers get to the Nile, the more the surrounding country becomes swampy. For thousands of square miles along both sides of the Nile, these swamps form the area known as the "sudd." Here the Nile is diverted into many small channels by the grasses and swamplands, rendering the river unnavigable except to the small canoes of peoples who know the channels from long experience.

The isolation of their central homeland apparently allowed the Nilotes to develop distinctive cultural and racial traits. But, since they are spread over a large region, both east and west of the Nile and over 1,400 miles north and south along the river, they also have developed internal heterogeneity through contact with dissimilar peoples. Nilotes were almost certainly part of the ancient Meroitic political system and of the state of Alwa which succeeded it in the south, but influences from these periods do not seem to have carried over into the Nilote way of life in their more isolated homeland.

The Nilotes are noted for their unusually tall stature and slender body build. Many Nilotic men stand well over six feet and are almost invariably of slim proportions. Generally they are dark brown in color, with typically Negroid hair and skin. Their facial features range from Negroid (large, flat noses, thick lips) to partially Caucasoid (thinner noses and lips), indicating long genetic contact with the Cushites who live to the east of the Nile in Ethiopia.

The Dinka and Nuer are the two Nilotic groups who today live nearest to the Nilote's central dispersal area. The northernmost Nilotic group is the Shilluk, who developed a highly organized kingdom late in the sixteenth century. The Luo of western Kenya and southeastern

Uganda, and the Masai (Nilo-Hamitic rather than pure Nilote) of southwestern Kenya and northern Tanzania, are the southernmost Nilotic groups.

Most Nilotes practice both agriculture and pastoralism, although the latter is generally more important because the abundant grasslands of the region are ideally suited for grazing cattle. Fishing is an important sideline in most Nilotic societies.

Nilotic culture and political organization are quite diversified. In the homeland of the Nilotes, and in many of their dispersed societies, people are politically decentralized. They live mostly in small family and clan communities, but some, such as the Shilluk, have highly organized states with divine kingships. Nilotic immigrants into the Interlacustrine Region also played a vital role in building the several powerful empires and kingdoms that dominated the history of interior East Africa.

Much of the cultural heterogeneity that characterizes Nilotic society is due to a series of migrations. During the present millennium, the Nilotes spread out of their central area, both north and south. The Nilote peoples who came into contact with Cushitic peoples (how long they have been influenced by Cushites, and vice versa, is unknown) and absorbed Cushitic influence include, in modern East Africa, the Karamojong, Turkana, Teso, Nandi, Kipsigi, Suk, and Masai, of whom the Masai, now living in Kenya and Tanzania, are the most southerly. Several groups of these peoples, in adopting Cushitic pastoral traits, have come to depend exclusively on herding for their livelihood. The Masai and Turkana, who inhabit extremely dry areas, are nomadic peoples who move their herds constantly to find new grazing lands in their countries.

As so often happens with nomadic pastoralists, the Masai are known in modern East Africa as an unusually conservative people who have fiercely resisted change. Although the governments of Kenya and Tanzania, especially the latter, officially encourage the Masai to adopt modern life styles, acquire formal education, and become full participants in the affairs of their countries, change has come slowly. To the mild chagrin of modern Tanzanian officials, for example, tourists still see an occasional Masai "morani" (a man who has passed the rites of initiation) striding down the main street of modern Dar es Salaam, long spear in hand, dressed in skins colored red with ochre, hair plaited with ochre and dung, and bedecked with the beads and bangles regarded by the Masai as fashionable.

In the arid steppes of northern Kenya, where Turkana nomads graze their herds of cattle and camels, warfare is not unknown even today. The pastoral Nilotes have often been in conflict over land with neighboring peoples, and the Turkana, like their Masai cousins several hundred miles to the south, still carry spears. Every year or so the newspapers of Nairobi carry reports of skirmishes and cattle raids in and around Turkana country, where both grass and water are precious.

The Masai and Turkana, however, do not typify either Nilotes generally or the Cushitized "Nilo-Hamites." Their pastoral nomadism is the result of adaptation, within the past two or three centuries, to the arid environments they settled as the waves of Nilotes pushed southward. Almost next door to the Masai the related, but non-Cushitized, Luo are among the most progressive people and skilled farmers in Kenya.

The numerous contacts between the Bantu and Nilotic peoples are responsible for some of the most interesting and creditable civilizational achievements of East Africa, especially in the Interlacustrine Region. In several parts of East Africa, including the area around the present Kenya-Uganda border and the eastern shores of Lake Victoria, it is a matter of controversy as to which of these migrating people settled the country first. Most scholars favor the view that the Bantu arrived first, settling east and northeast of Lake Victoria a few centuries after they settled the Interlacustrine Region to that great lake's west and north. Whatever the case, however, it is today a region in which Bantu, Nilotic, and Cushitized Nilotic speakers are all settled, and oral histories of various clans within these groups agree that there were major movements of the two Nilotic types into their present area of settlement within the past two or three centuries.

To the west and north of Lake Victoria, however, it is clear that the Bantu arrived first. Before they came, this region was inhabited by Khoisan peoples (including relatives of surviving Pygmy groups) and Cushite farmers and cattle herders, the latter probably related most closely to the Sidamo peoples of Ethiopia. The Bantu immigrants absorbed, drove out, or enslaved both the Khoisan peoples and the Cushites. Whether there was warfare between the Bantu and the Cushites is unknown; in the end, however, the Bantu became the great majority of the population, and it was their languages, their culture, and their economy that set the tone for most of the lands of the Interlacustrine Region.

The early period of contact and intermixture between the Bantu and the Cushites of the Interlacustrine Region is shadowy. From the much better-known events that took place between about 1500 and 1900, however, one can reconstruct at least the broad outlines of the process. Small Bantu family bands moved into those parts of each new locality that were best suited to the type of agriculture by which the Bantu lived: the cultivation of sorghum, millet, and the various legumes and root crops of the Sudanic, Ethiopian, and Indonesian complexes.

They found the banana to be especially useful in some parts of the fertile lake country, and many of their settlements came to depend heavily upon that plant as a staple food. The Cushites, who apparently were not densely settled in the region, increasingly came to devote their energies to the care of their cattle. A symbiotic relationship evolved by which the Bantu did the farming and the Cushites the herding.

Probably small clans of Bantu and Cushite intermingled in the evolution of this relationship, with the more numerous Bantu displaying greater energy in clearing and settling new lands. Intermarriage and acculturation must have occurred. The Cushites gradually adopted the Bantu languages and many of the Bantu customs, while at the same time retaining a sense of separate origin through their clan affiliations. And as a pastoral people who had freedom of movement and action, the Cushites eventually developed the greater prestige and power. This prestige and power, transmitted from generation to generation through the clan structures, grew greater as the former Cushites used their leisure time and their prestigious position to develop skills and graces in religious ritual and ceremonial dancing, warfare, poetry, dress, and leadership.

Over much of southern Uganda the Bantu-Cushite peoples came to be known as Hima, and as early as about 1300 several clans began to assume sufficient prominence that their names are still remembered. In the kingdom of Bunyoro, located in western Uganda, the great Hima clans that formed dynasties of rulers were the Gabu, the Ranzi, and the Chwezi. The Chwezi (it is not clear whether the Chwezi, Gabu, and Ranzi ruled various areas simultaneously, or succeeded one another) eventually established their leadership over all the other clans, and their dynasty of kings came to rule a number of small kingdoms in western and southern Uganda. Farther to the south, in what was to become the kingdom of Ankole in southwestern Uganda, another Hima group, the Hinda, established their supremacy, very much as the Chwezi were doing at the same time. Even farther south, in what are now Rwanda and Burundi, a people similar to the Hima, the cattle-herding Watutsi, established supremacy over the more numerous farmers and laid the foundations for the kingdoms of Burundi and Rwanda.

By about 1400, this process had occurred over the greater part of the Interlacustrine Region, in most of western and southern Uganda, northwestern Tanzania, Rwanda, and Burundi. Kingdoms of varying population and territory, ruled by a cattle-herding aristocracy but consisting mainly of skilled farmers, covered the region. It is thought by many authorities that the earliest Nilotes had also migrated into the area by this time, merging with the aristocracy, and thus becoming a part of the ruling cattle-herding class. No traces of Nilotic languages remain from this early period, but the great height and slender build of the Watutsi, for example, resemble the "pure" Nilotes far to the north. Whatever the case, the Bantu languages and basic culture were adopted by all the peoples of the area, whatever their origin, their class, or their clan heritage.

Of all the states established during the fourteenth century the largest and strongest was the great kingdom of Bunyoro, in the west of Uganda. By 1400 its Chwezi kings ruled a loosely knit empire or confederation of kingdoms, each ruled by other Chwezi or Hima families. At its peak of territorial expansion, the Bunyoro Empire stretched from the Ruwenzori Mountains (the fabled "Mountains of the Moon," in which some romantic European explorers of the nineteenth century eagerly sought King Solomon's mines) across Uganda to what is now the Uganda-Kenya border and from Lake Victoria north to the region of Lakes Albert and Kioga. In the fourteenth and fifteenth centuries this great kingdom was known as Kitara, and was ruled by the Gabu, Ranzi, and Chwezi dynasties. Little is known of its pattern of government, but it is abundantly clear that its Chwezi rulers claimed fealty from other Hima chiefs and kings, many of them also Chwezi.

Modern traditions revere this early period as a kind of Golden Age. The Chwezi kings developed great palaces in which areas as wide as two and a half miles were enclosed by deep trenches and earthworks, helping to demarcate and protect the king, his family and retainers, and his vast herds of cattle. At least eighteen sites of these royal dwelling centers have been discovered, the largest and most famous of which is at Bigo, today a small village lying between Lakes Victoria and Edward in southwestern Uganda. Only the worn remains of the trenches and earthen ramparts remain to show the vast extent and the complex construction of these royal centers.

In the same general area, the remains of ancient roads, some as wide as fifteen feet, have also been found. They were carefully built up of earth and protected along each side by ditches and earthen retaining walls, apparently to be used for the soldiers, the herds of cattle, and the loads of bananas and grains that moved along them.

The Hima period of Interlacustrine history lasted about two hundred years, and set an enduring foundation of culture and political organization. During this period the various ruling clans of the Hima and related peoples helped to meld together the peoples of diverse origins in each of several large areas. Out of the resulting united kingdoms some of the most highly organized states of sub-Saharan Africa would grow. It was during this age that the distinctive class structure of the region developed. This structure consisted of a ruling aristocracy of cattle owners and a commoner class of farmers, bound together by a symbiotic economic relationship, common Bantu languages, and a complex pattern of mutual obligations. In some areas, notably Rwanda and Burundi, the Watutsi aristocracy became permanently distinct, retaining its special sense of "noblesse oblige" and its racial uniqueness, despite sharing a common language and political system with the farmers over whom it ruled. In these two kingdoms the class system crystallized into a rigid caste system that has persisted into modern times and has been the cause of bitter conflict. In other areas, especially in the kingdoms of Uganda and northwestern Tanzania, the ruling class became racially indistinguishable from the commoner-farmers, and a close-knit pattern of internal unity prevailed.

In about 1500 a new wave of cattle-herding Nilotic peoples who spoke languages of the Luo group, began to move into these kingdoms: one major stream moved on the western side of the region into northwestern Uganda, another into the Mount Elgon area of eastern Uganda. Historians, both African and foreign, still disagree as to whether the Luo immigrants established themselves peacefully or seized power as they moved by force of arms. Whichever the case, they soon replaced the Chwezi rulers. A new clan of Luo origin, the Bito, brought new growth and development.

Bito kings were soon in control of Acholi, in northern Uganda, and the kingdom of Kitara in western Uganda. The latter came to be called Bunyoro, as it is today. The Bito kings, as leading members of a ruling clan that spread itself over a large territory, maintained and soon expanded the kingdoms they inherited. During the sixteenth century, Bito kings came to power not only in Acholi and Bunyoro, but in the neighboring kingdoms of Buganda, Busoga, Toro, Koki, Kizibi, and several other very small states.

The center of Bito power was Bunyoro, and there the Bito developed both a strong hold on the government of that state and an aggressive military system. Culturally they were undoubtedly crude and comparatively barbaric by the standards of the people of Bunyoro and the Hima aristocracy. To compensate for this relative cultural inferiority and to strengthen their power and prestige, the Bito adopted all the symbols of Chwezi authority: the royal great drums, covered with the skin of antelope or zebra, the ceremonial copper spears, body ornaments of monkey skin, and even the method of building royal houses of finely plaited reeds and grasses. Within a few generations, they came to relate themselves to the Chwezi and to describe the transfer of power as peaceful.

Militarily the Luo-Bito rulers of Bunyoro brought the kingdom to a new level of development, using methods that apparently originated in the days of the Chwezi. There is no evidence that the Bito introduced new weapons or military tactics; they simply made mandatory a military obligation on the part of all Banyoro (people of Bunyoro) and led their troops frequently and aggressively into battle. It was probably through the strength of Bunyoro that Bito dynasties were established in many small kingdoms on Bunyoro's borders, and it was Bunyoro strength that kept these smaller states loyal and cooperative.

Banyoro troops raided over a wide region, seizing cattle and booty, shoring up Bito rulerships in conquered states, and enforcing the payment of tribute. They are known to have marched against Rwanda, far to the south of Bunyoro itself. Rwanda traditions tell of an attempted invasion by a Bunyoro army in about 1500 to 1550. The Banyoro are described as a strange and terrible people as numerous as the grains of millet in a good harvest, carrying spears "of iron and all of one piece" and shields that were so strong that Rwanda arrows could not pierce them. Despite this legend of fierceness, the Banyoro warriors failed to conquer Rwanda, and the Rwanda kings grew stronger as they developed their defenses.

During the 16th century the small kingdom of Buganda, on the shores of Lake Victoria where the modern capital city of Kampala stands, was but one of many small states subject to Bunyoro. Buganda's former ruling dynasty (called the Chwa in Buganda tradition, and probably Chwezi) was deposed by a Luo dynasty. The new rulers of Buganda were much more substantially absorbed into the Bantu Baganda (people of Buganda) society than in most other kingdoms conquered by the Luo-Bito. By the end of the sixteenth century these rulers seem to have regarded Bunyoro as an enemy; an enemy to whom tribute had to be paid, to be sure, but from whose yoke the Buganda throne and people intended eventually to be free. About twelve generations back, during the reign of Kabaka (king) Katerega, the Baganda took advantage of a period of Bunyoro weakness that resulted from a series of defeats in Ankole, Ndorwa, and Karagwe (the latter in modern Tanzania). Baganda troops marched into several tiny kingdoms surrounding Buganda, defeated them, and established Baganda chiefs to rule over them. The annexation of these states (Butambala, Gomba, Mawokota, and Singo), during Kabaka Katerega's reign, more than doubled Buganda's size.

The Baganda added the annexed states permanently to Buganda, and established Buganda culture and identity in them. Through intermarriage, the kabaka was linked by family ties to most of his viceroys and they in turn took several local wives. By the beginning of the seventeenth century, when Buganda was expanding its territory, it had developed a strong feudal system through these intermarriages. Annexed kingdoms became counties within the unified state of Buganda;

their chieftainships were hereditary through Baganda families related to the kabaka.

During the eighteenth century Buganda continued to expand its territory, growing larger and stronger as Bunyoro grew weaker. Slowly but inexorably small states that had been tributary to Bunyoro were annexed by Buganda. The once fabled armies of Bunyoro were not strong enough to drive out the Baganda. In its aggressive imperial expansion during the sixteenth century, Bunyoro had overextended itself, and her many tributaries, ruled largely through fear of Bunyoro's military power, felt little loyalty to her. Even Bito subdynasties in these tributary states chafed under Bunyoro power, and many formed alliances with the increasingly powerful state of Buganda.

During the eighteenth century, when Buganda again nearly doubled in size, it was slowly developing both a better military system and a less feudal, more bureaucratic form of administration. Early in the century a royal bodyguard, composed of professional soldiers, was formed. Throughout the Interlacustrine Region, troops had been ordinary farmers who, however courageous and skilled in battle, were conscripted in time of war or raiding campaigns and returned to their normal occupations as soon as the brief war or campaign ended. The professional guard of the early eighteenth century, on the other hand, lived in compounds around the king's palace, were fed and clothed by him, and received handsome rewards for loyal service. With the development of this small standing army, the power of the kabaka was permanently enhanced. If there were threats of rebellion or acts of disobedience, he was able to retaliate immediately; and when he went to war to expand the kingdom, the elite corps of professionals set a standard for conscripted troops to follow.

The new system of administration that developed during the eighteenth century consisted of appointed officials, men who were both loyal to the kabaka and skilled in administration. By the end of the century, the majority of posts throughout the kingdom were filled by these appointed administrators, who could be removed by the kabaka for poor performance or disloyalty, and who had no hereditary rights to their offices. The old feudal system which had helped to assimilate new peoples into Buganda gradually declined as the new system grew. By this time, however, the central kingdom of Buganda was of large size and population and was closely knit culturally and politically. The power of the kabaka (supported by his bodyguard) was supreme.

A long-distance trade system between the coast (under the rulership of the sultan of Zanzibar, whose dynasty had been rebuilding the economy so nearly destroyed by the Portuguese) and the Interlacustrine Region had developed by then. From inland East Africa, so long isolated from the coast, there now flowed ivory and slaves, and from the coast came foreign glassware and porcelain, cloth, iron tools, and beads. Arabs and their Swahili allies played a major role in developing this trade system, but Bantu peoples who had, during the eighteenth and early nineteenth centuries, expanded into the dry central area (the Nyamwezi of Tanzania being the leaders) also acted as middlemen and porters in facilitating the movement of goods. Most of the well-organized Interlacustrine kingdoms participated in the trade by the early nineteenth century, and Buganda especially dominated commerce on the northern regions of Lake Victoria. Several important kingdoms of the Interlacustrine Region were either cut off from the coastal trade, or benefited from it only by dealing through Buganda, which controlled most of the routes of access around Lake Victoria to the coast.

The kabaka's court grew in importance because of Buganda's involvement in the trade system. New wealth flowed into his coffers. Foreigners, especially Arabs and Swahili traders, were increasingly attracted to his court, and as European curiosity about the interior of Africa and possible profits there grew, the first European explorers entered the Interlacustrine Region and were soon in Buganda. It was John Hanning Speke, the British explorer who claimed credit for establishing that Lake Victoria was the source of the Nile, who first visited the kabaka's court and published an account of it, during the reign of Kabaka Mutesa I, who ruled from 1856 to 1884.

The growth of the kabaka's power, the increasing wealth of Buganda from its own production and from trade, and the evolution of the state continued steadily during the nineteenth century, especially under Kabaka Suna, whose reign ended in 1856, and Mutesa, who succeeded him. Under these two kings the palace bodyguard was expanded into a standing army, and, during Suna's reign, the first guns (ancient muzzle loaders) were imported into the kingdom and used by a select few soldiers. Mutesa imported more guns, and formed a corps of musketeers, armed with nearly a thousand guns, who fought as a unit within his large army of spearmen. Both kabakas continued to reduce the power of hereditary chiefs and officials and expanded the number of appointed administrators.

Speke entered the Interlacustrine Region from the south, coming up from Zanzibar, in 1858-59, but got no farther on this expedition than the southern shore of Lake Victoria. In 1860 he and James Grant began another expedition, partly intended to prove Speke's theory that Lake Victoria, called Ukerewe by most Africans at the time, was the source of the Nile. In 1861, this expedition became increasingly interested in visiting Buganda, about whose power and wealth they had heard vivid reports in the south of the Interlacustrine Region. After visiting for some time with King Rumanika, ruler of the kingdom of Karagwe, Speke pushed north toward Buganda. He was escorted by an officer of the kabaka, Maula, who had been sent with a large group of soldiers and officials to bring him to the capital.

As soon as they entered Buganda, Speke was made aware of the fact that Mutesa's power extended effectively throughout the land:

> Maula led me straight to his home, a very nice place, in which he gave me a very large, clean, and comfortable hut—had no end of plantains brought for me and my men—and said, "Now you have really entered the kingdom of Uganda, for the future you must buy no more food. At every place that you stop for the day, the officer in charge will bring you plantains, otherwise your men can help themselves in the gardens, for such are the laws of the land when a king's guest travels in it. Any one found selling anything to either yourself or your men would be punished."

Speke found this largesse of little practical help; all his men were from the coast and dry regions, where millet and sorghum were the staple foods. They steadfastly refused to eat the Baganda's plantains; in the end his men had to violate Maula's instructions and purchase grain.

A few weeks after entering the kingdom Speke arrived at the capital, which stood on the site of Uganda's modern capital, Kampala:

> It was a magnificent sight. A whole hill covered with gigantic huts, such as I had never seen in Africa before. I wished to go up to the palace at once, but the officers said, "No, that would be considered indecent in Uganda; you must draw up your men, and fire your guns off, to let the king know you are here; we will then show you your residence, and tomorrow you will doubtless be sent for, as the king could not now hold a levee whilst it is raining."

As the kabaka's officers predicted, Mutesa sent for Speke the next day. The following excerpts indicate something of the style of the court, which impressed even Speke, a man usually somewhat contemptuous of Africans and their ways:

> . . . I prepared for my first presentation at court, attired in my best, though in it I cut a poor figure in comparison with the display of the dressy Waganda. They wore neat bark cloaks resembling the best yellow corduroy cloth, crimp and well set, as if stiffened with starch, and over that, as upper-cloaks, a patchwork of small antelope skins, which I observed were sewn together as well as any English glovers could have pieced them; whilst their head-dresses, generally, were abrus turbans, set off with highly polished boar-tusks, stick-charms, seeds, beads, or shells; and on their necks, arms and ankles they wore other charms of wood, or small horns stuffed with magic powder, and fastened on by strings generally covered with snake-skin.

. . . The palace or entrance quite surprised me by its extraordinary dimensions and the neatness with which it was kept. The whole brow and sides of the hill on which we stood were covered with gigantic grass huts, thatched as neatly as so many heads dressed by a London barber, and fenced all round with the tall yellow reeds of the common Uganda tiger-grass; whilst within the enclosure, the lines of huts were joined together, or partitioned off into courts, with walls of the same grass. It is here that most of Mutesa's three or four hundred women are kept, the rest being quartered chiefly with his mother, known by the title of N'yamasore, or queen-dowager.

. . . The first court passed, I was even more surprised to find the unusual ceremonies that awaited me. There courtiers of high dignity stepped forward to greet me, dressed in the most scrupulously neat fashions. Men, women, bulls, dogs, and goats, were led about by strings; cocks and hens were carried in men's arms; and little pages, with rope-turbans, rushed about, conveying messages, as if their lives depended on their swiftness, everyone holding his skin-cloak tightly round him lest his naked legs might by accident be shown.

. . . musicians were playing and singing on large nine-stringed harps, like the Nubian tambira, accompanied by harmonicons. . . .

. . . the king is said to be unapproachable, excepting when he chooses to attend court—a ceremony which rarely happens. . . .

. . . The king, a good-looking, well-figured, tall young man of twenty-five, was sitting on a red blanket spread upon a square platform of royal grass, encased in tiger-grass reeds, scrupulously well dressed in a new mbugu [cloth made of bark]. The hair of his head was cut short, excepting on the top, where it was combed up into a high ridge, running from stem to stern like a cockscomb. . . . On every finger and every toe he had alternate brass and copper rings; and above the ankles, half-way up to the calf, a stocking of very pretty beads. Everything was light, neat and elegant in its way; not a fault could be found with the taste of his "getting-up." For a handkerchief he held a well-folded piece of bark, and a piece of gold-embroidered silk, which he constantly employed to hide his large mouth when laughing, or to wipe it after a drink of plantain-wine, of which he took constant and copious draughts from neat little gourd-cups, administered by his ladies-in-waiting, who were at once his sisters and wives. . . .

. . . I now longed to open conversation, but knew not the language, and no one near me dared speak, or even lift his head from fear of being accused of eyeing the women; so the king and myself sat staring at one another for full an hour—I mute, but he pointing and remarking with those around him on the novelty of my guard and general appearance, and even requiring to see my hat lifted, the umbrellas shut and opened, and the guards face about and show off their red cloaks—for such wonders had never been seen in Uganda.

Speke spent six months at Mutesa's court, often seeing the king, and doctoring the king's mother for various ailments. All the while he sought the kabaka's permission and help to continue his journey and trace the course of the Nile. Finally Mutesa, both suspicious of Speke's motives and those of his sponsors and curious about a man of such different culture and knowledge, relented. He allowed Speke to march eastward into Busoga, which, though independent, had lost some of its territory to Buganda and on numerous occasions was entered by Baganda hunters.

By the mid-nineteenth century, Buganda had become a large and powerful state, ruled by a semidivine king whose power was almost unchallengeable. It was earning profits on the coastal trade and was beginning to learn about affairs outside the Interlacustrine Region and even outside of Africa. Yet many other states, only slightly less powerful, covered this entire inland region. Some, though militarily less powerful than Buganda and less highly developed administratively, had developed traditions of art, poetry, dance, and philosophy that rivaled or even exceeded those of Buganda. In many respects these states were undergoing processes of development that paralleled those in the forest regions of West Africa. But this development was frozen at the end of the nineteenth century by European conquest.

13 Europe and Africa: Coastal Contacts and the Slave Trade

Prior to the fifteenth century, Europe had played a minor role in African affairs. This role was limited largely to the Greek and Roman conquests and colonies in North Africa and to the growing interplay (including the Crusades) between Europe and North Africa after the twelfth century. The peoples of North Africa and the barren lands of the vast Sahara stood so formidably between Europe and sub-Saharan Africa that Europe was scarcely aware that Black Africa existed.

Then, in the fifteenth century, Portuguese ships began to explore the coasts of West and then East Africa. A long period of contact between Europe and the Black Africans on and near the coasts began. Finally, in the nineteenth century, European explorers, missionaries, and traders began to penetrate the African interior. European armies followed by the end of the century, enforcing the partitioning of Africa into colonies and spheres of influence for the aggressive manufacturing countries of western Europe.

Europe's poor knowledge of Africa before the period of exploration began is easily understood. Europe itself had not been a well-developed continent. Its peoples, despite the civilizing influences of Rome, progressed with snail-like slowness for nearly a thousand years after the decay of Roman civilization. Northern Europe was especially backward; southern Europe, bordering the Mediterranean, not only retained more of the Roman and Greek heritage, but benefited from close contact with Islamic civilization after Rome's decline. Between the fifth and fifteenth centuries, while northern Europe was in a state of near stagnation, the Mediterranean countries had at least a small share of the enlightenment that Islam brought. As conquered lands, however, they were on the periphery of Islamic civilization, especially since their peoples tended to cling to Christianity instead of accepting the new faith of their conquerors. The knowledge of Africa that Islamic writers possessed was rarely transmitted to Europeans in Spain, Portugal, or Italy.

The Islamic world, stretching from Morocco to the steppes of Asia, served as a cordon between Europe and the rest of the world for centuries after the Islamic Empire began to decay. The native Christians of Portugal and Spain expelled their Moorish conquerors by the thirteenth century, but neither they nor other European countries possessed the power to conquer the Islamic strongholds of North Africa and the East or to break through the Islamic cordon.

By the beginning of the fifteenth century, Europe was beginning to stir restlessly from the long centuries of its Medieval Age. New ideas and ambitions were spreading rapidly. One of these ideas was to find a way to bypass the Islamic world in order to gain direct access to the riches of Asia and Africa. European kings and nobles envisioned wealth of fantastic dimensions to be found in these lands from which they had been historically isolated: Cathay, China, Mali, and the Indies. During the centuries of Islamic ascendancy, many of Europe's most prized imports were from Muslim lands and from the lands beyond the Islamic world—pepper and spices, gold, ivory, gems, jewelry, metal articles, leathers, fine china and glassware, writing paper, and a host of other items associated with civilization and affluence. Europe saw in the East and Africa a possible source of the delicacies it craved—if it could find some way to flank the Islamic powers.

Added to this craving for new wealth and trade was a legend, surviving from the days of the Crusades, that there lay beyond the Islamic lands a great Christian kingdom, the land of King Prester John. Prester John's location was uncertain. Some said his kingdom lay in the interior of Africa; others said it was in India. (Ethiopia may well have been the source of the Prester John legend.) Many Europeans believed that direct contact with Prester John's kingdom might result in a powerful new Christian alliance against Islam and that this alliance might succeed where the Crusades had failed.

No European kingdom wanted to find a way around Islam to obtain the riches of the Indies and Africa and to seek an alliance with Prester John more keenly than Portugal. That small land had long been under Muslim rule and was a keen antagonist of Islam after it succeeded in expelling the Moorish conquerors and wresting its freedom.

Early in the fifteenth century, when Portugal's mariners, intellectuals, and nobles were keenly debating the possibilities of finding some direct access to the East, a wealthy and visionary member of the royal family, Prince Henry (1394-1460), provided a new style of leadership to the intellectual movement. Wealthy and ambitious (and not a mariner himself, though history has come to refer to him as "the Navigator"), Prince Henry was persuaded that properly constructed ships could sail down the West African coast and eventually make their way into the Indian Ocean, and thus to the Indies.

This was a bold idea for the times. Portuguese seamen had often sailed out into the Atlantic seeking new lands. They either returned with reports of nothing but endless ocean or never returned at all. And those who sailed down the African coast found that Cape Bojador, in Morocco, formed a point-of-no-return. South of Bojador the winds blow in a southward and westward direction most of the year. At the beginning of the fifteenth century the Portuguese, like most Europeans, were still incapable of sailing into the wind. Arabs, Indians, and Chinese had long known how to build sails that would enable a vessel to sail into the wind (or at least at angles toward the direction of the wind, so that by tacking in a zigzag pattern they could reach the same objective).

Prince Henry developed a maritime center in Portugal, where scholars and mariners studied new techniques, pored over all available charts, designed better ships, and discussed ventures of exploration. In 1434 the first of Prince Henry's exploration ships passed Cape Bojador, sailed on for a few days, then returned to Portugal. Psychologically this was a major accomplishment, although it brought no new knowledge about the coast or its peoples. But every year more ships set sail, pushing farther down the West African coast, occasionally meeting Africans and filling in navigation charts with accurate readings. By 1445-46 the Senegal River mouth was reached, and the first contact between White Europe and Black Africa was made.

Between 1469 and 1475 one of the first of the new breed of Portuguese captains, Fernão Gomes, explored as far south as the Gold Coast, a name that section of coast received because Gomes found considerable amounts of gold in the hands of the African kings with whom he made contact. In 1483 Diogo Cão made contact with the kingdom of Kongo while exploring the Congo-Angola coast. And, in 1488, Bartholomew Dias rounded the Cape of Good Hope to enter the Indian Ocean, the first European to accomplish this long-hoped-for objective. The way was at last open for Portuguese exploitation of whatever riches could be found in the East.

Up to this point, the voyages to Africa hugged the coastline. But the huge coastal bulge of West Africa made for a long voyage to the continent's southern tip. Vasco da Gama, when he made his historic voyage in 1497-1499, sailed directly southeast from the West African bulge, greatly shortening the voyage to the Cape. After reaching the Cape, he led his fleet around it into the Indian Ocean. Da Gama then sailed up the East African coast to acquire information about that region and went on to India, thus completing the grand design Prince Henry had launched more than half a century earlier. The Portuguese quickly exploited the opportunity opened up by Dias and da Gama, and within a few years the Indian Ocean was virtually a Portuguese sea.

At each place the early Portuguese captains called, they asked if the local inhabitants knew of Prester John or of a large Christian kingdom in Africa. On the East Africa coast they began to receive positive (though rather imprecise) answers, and their hopes were aroused. They never found Prester John or his kingdom, despite many decades of questioning and searching, although they did eventually establish direct contact with Ethiopia, the nearest approximation to the object of their search.

Its quest for Prester John's kingdom fruitless, Portugal also found eastern Africa, north of Mozambique, to be a less than opulent source of gold, gems, or other wealth. Portugal achieved little on the East African coast except to dampen the trade that had long supported the Swahili civilization. Its attentions, in the Indian Ocean area, were focused primarily on India and the islands and mainland of southeast Asia, with Mozambique included partly for its gold and ivory, and partly for its value as a refueling midstation and naval base between Europe and the Far East.

West Africa, however, was different. Although it never proved to be quite the source of wealth that the Portuguese had hoped to find, it was worth continuing effort. Gold was found in a number of places, and Africans were quite willing to trade it for Portuguese goods. Ivory, pepper, gums, skins, beeswax, ostrich feathers, and slaves were all available along the West African coast.

In many fundamental respects the western African coast was different from that of eastern Africa. There were fewer natural ports and much trade was conducted by ships anchored offshore or at the mouth of a river. Longboats were sent ashore, exchanging goods, then departing. There were no large towns or cities comparable to Kilwa, Mombasa, and Malindi, with their own wealth that could be had for the taking by armed assault. In West Africa the kings lived in large or small villages, and their wealth, apart from some gold and personal possessions, had to be brought from the hinterland through trade. The Portuguese were not averse to trying to seize riches in western Africa, and they showed little regard for the integrity and liberty of the African peoples. One of the very earliest chronicles of Portuguese adventure in West Africa (the *Cronica de Guine,* written in about 1453 by Gomes Eames de Azurar), aptly illustrates this Portuguese tendency:

> And when they were close to its mouth [the Senegal River] they let
> down their anchors on the seaward side, and the crew of the caravel of

Vicente Diaz launched their boat, and into it jumped as many as eight men, and among them was the Esquire of Lagos called Stevam Affonso. . . . And as soon as they reached the land, Stevam Affonso leaped out, and five others with him, and they proceeded in the manner that the other had suggested [i.e., by stealth, since the Portuguese had already learned that West Africans were not universally friendly and peaceful]. And while they were going thus concealed even until they neared the hut, they saw come out of it a Negro boy, stark naked, with a spear in his hand. Him they seized at once, and coming up close to the hut, they lighted upon a girl, his sister, who was about eight years old. . . .

Although Azurar relates that the boy was educated in Portugal as a Christian under Prince Henry's patronage, no sense of wrongdoing is expressed in describing this brutal kidnapping of children.

The Portugese soon learned that West Africans were no easy prey and that stealing unprotected children was very different from landing along the coast among communities of adult Africans. Azurar relates another incident, which took place when the ship just mentioned attempted to land near a village.

And because there were so many of those blacks on land that by no means could they disembark either by day or night, Gomez Pirez [the ship's captain] sought to show that he desired to go among them on peaceful terms, and so placed upon the shore a cake and mirror and a sheet of paper on which he drew a cross. And the natives when they came there and found these things, broke up the cake and threw it far away, and with their assegais they cast at the mirror, till they had broken it into many pieces, and the paper they tore, showing that they cared not for any of these things.

"Since it is so," said Gomes Pirez to his crossbowmen, "shoot at them with your bows that they may at least understand that we are people who can do them hurt, whenever they will not agree to a friendly understanding." But the blacks seeing the other's intentions, began to pay them back, launching at them also their arrows and assegais, some of which our men brought home to this kingdom.

But as each new Portuguese ship sailed down the African coast, it found more opportunity for trade than conflict, and the Portuguese interest in putting trade on a more permanent basis soon led to a major decision—in 1480-81, an expensive fort and trading station was built on the Gold Coast at a site which soon came to be called Elmina (el mina—the mine), because it was along the same coast where Captain Fernão Gomes, in the early 1470's, had found kings possessing gold.

King John II, who later set into motion the ambitious Portuguese missionary effort in Kongo, decided to build the fort at Elmina, despite vigorous opposition from his councillors and nobles, who doubted that the profits would justify the great expense and risks involved. An account by Ruy de Pina, who wrote a chronicle of King John II's reign, illustrates that the fort (which is still standing and is maintained by the goverment of independent Ghana as a historical monument) was a substantial undertaking:

> The King, after these arguments had been advanced, nevertheless determined that it should be built. For this purpose, he ordered that all the timber and freestones, which would be necessary for the gates, the windows, the corner-rafters of the walls, the tower, and other things, should forthwith be cut and shaped in this country, so that without any delay in the work they could be set in place immediately. Moreover, a great quantity of mixed and compounded lime was made ready, together with tiles and bricks, nails and iron tools, and provisions, and all other things pertinent to the work in great abundance. And 600 men were ordered and equipped, 100 masters of masonry and carpentry and 500 for defense and service. . . .

King John II entrusted the task of building the fort to a knight of his court, Diego da Azambuja. Azambuja is said to have been a versatile diplomat, skilled in debate and military matters and possessing practical ideas of construction and administration. It is apparent from the following account that Azambuja was an able man, who had learned (though he had no previous African experience) that Africans were not to be treated lightly on their own territory. Almost as soon as his fleet anchored, Azambuja and a large party came ashore, set up an altar to pray, and ate a meal.

> Then, after eating, he [Azambuja] ordered a richly ornamented platform to be erected; and he sat thereon, accompanied by very honorable men, and with his trumpets, tambourines, and drums [Azambuja had already been advised by Portuguese traders whom he met on the coast about some of the African customs and the symbols of royalty or powerful men] and all in an act of peace, in order to receive there, by agreement, the lord of the place, who was called Caramansa, whom the negroes called king, and to speak with him. Hither the king came, and before him a great noise of bugles, bells, and horns, which are their instruments, and he was accompanied by an endless number of negroes, some with bows and arrows, and others with assegais and shields; and the principal persons were attended by naked page-boys with seats of wood, like stools, to sit upon. The king came naked [this is probably an error; from other evidence it is known that kings of the area wore cloth robes at the time] and his arms and legs and neck were covered with chains and trinkets of gold in many shapes, and countless bells and large beads of gold were hanging from the hair of his beard and his head. The captain stepped down from his platform to receive him, amid a great sounding of his instruments; and the king gave the captain the usual sign of peace, which was to touch his fingers and then to snap the one with the other, saying in his language *"Bere, bere,"* which in ours means "Peace, peace," and

the captain returned the compliment. . . . When all were again seated the captain began his speech, with the aid of a negro, familiar with the language, who forthwith interpreted it, and the substance was: that, on account of the good report which the king, his lord, had received about them, and of the good treatment which they above all the men of that land gave to his vassals, who were accustomed to come to trade there, his highness had sent him there to treat with them and for ever to secure peace and friendship; in such a way that in that place rather than in any other of that territory there might be made, and should be, a permanent center for much, very rich merchandise, so that by their good treatment they and their descendants might always be very rich and very ennobled. . . . And forasmuch as a house was necessary, because it was reasonable that the merchandise, which they were now bringing, and would in future arrive, might always remain there continuously, fresh and secure, he asked them to give place and license and even assistance, so that it might be built at the mouth of the river, because from such a house and from the Christians, who would be stationed in it, they would always find and receive protection, profit, and favor. The king . . . there, then replied to him, saying that the people of the Christians, who up to that time had come there, were few, foul, and vile, and that the people, who had now arrived, were very different, particularly he himself, who by his clothes and appearance must be the son or the brother of the King of Portugal. At this, before they proceeded in their speech, the captain again replied to them that he was neither the son nor the brother of the king, his lord, but one of his very humble vassals, because the king was so very powerful and so great a lord that in his kingdoms, which he commanded, and which obeyed him, there were 200,000 men, greater and better and richer. They marvelled at this, and to signify their great admiration, as is their custom, they vigorously clapped their hands. . . . they gave him permission to build the house, as he desired. . . .

When the Portuguese were expelled and succeeded by the Dutch early in the seventeenth century, this treaty was put in writing; one of the treasures seized by the Asante from the Denkyira was the paper by which Elmina was leased to the Dutch.

Portugal also established trade relations with Benin in 1486. A formal Portuguese mission visited the Oba and an ambassador was sent by the Oba to Lisbon. Ruy de Pina relates it:

The king of Beny sent as ambassador to the king [of Portugal] a negro, one of his captains, from a harboring place by the sea, which is called Ugato [Gwato], because he desired to learn more about these lands, the arrival of people from them in his country being regarded as an unusual novelty. This ambassador was a man of good speech and natural wisdom. Great feasts were held in his honour, and he was shown many of the good things of these kingdoms. He returned to his land in a ship of the king's, who at his departure made him a gift of rich clothes for himself and his wife; and through him he also sent a rich present to the king of such things as he understood he would greatly prize. Moreover he sent holy and most catholic advisers with praiseworthy admonitions for the faith to administer a stern rebuke about the heresies and great idolatries and fetishes, which the negroes practice in that land. Then also there went with him new factors of the king, who were to remain in that country and to traffic for the said pepper and for other things, which pertained to the trades of the king. But owing to the fact that the land was afterwards found to be very dangerous from sickness and not so profitable as had been hoped, the trade was abandoned.

Not mentioned in this statement by de Pina is the fact that the Oba banned the slave trade in about 1500, apparently because he found it more advantageous to keep all available labor at work in Benin. Even by this early time, the slave trade was of growing interest to Portugal. The fact that no slaves could be purchased in Benin must have been a factor in the withdrawal of the trade mission.

By 1500 Portugal was solidly established along the coasts of western Africa, with formal missions in Elmina, Benin, and Kongo, and many Portuguese traders spent weeks, months, and even years in residence at other points. Portugal still had Africa almost entirely to herself, as far as the rest of Europe was concerned. Most of the European countries that were later to become great powers were far behind Portugal in maritime development. Thus England, France, Holland, Denmark, Sweden, and the cities of the Hanseatic league all contented themselves with developing trade in the North Atlantic-Baltic region or in other European countries around the Mediterranean.

Other Mediterranean countries were more nearly capable of sustaining the great voyages Portugal had pioneered. Spain, however, began its international voyages of exploration on a serious scale when it financed Columbus' little fleet in 1492. After Columbus returned, Spain concentrated its efforts on the New World, leaving Africa and the Far East to the Portuguese. Genoa and Venice, both of which had in the fourteenth and early fifteenth centuries done a small amount of exploration, had become engrossed in the lucrative Mediterranean trade, which they dominated. Both served as the main middlemen through which the Islamic world traded with Europe.

Portugal made strenuous efforts to legitimize its discoveries and trade operations in Africa and the Far East by international agreements, through which monopoly rights were claimed. Rome generally recognized Portugal's claims, making it even more difficult for other European countries to compete with Portugal in Africa. For all these reasons Africa's contact with Europe between about 1450 and 1600 was almost entirely through Portugal. Ships from other countries did call, but very

Africa in the 16th Century: Major States and Ethnic Groups

SPAIN

ITALY GREECE

TURKEY

PORTUGAL

TUNIS

ALGIERS

SYRIA

MOROCCO

TRIPOLI CYRENAICA

ARABIA

EGYPT

BERBER - ARAB GROUPS

Nile R.

SONGHAI

AÏR

BAGIRMI

WADAI DARFUR

FUNJ

YEMEN

TEKRUR

WOLOF

Senegal R.

MALI

KANEM-BORNU

ETHIOPIA

L. Tana

SERER

Niger R.

VOLTAIC STATES

L. Chad

HAUSA STATES

SHILLUK

SOMA SULTAN

MANDE and FULANI STATES

AKAN STATES

OYO

JUKUN

NILOTE

GALLA

NUPE

FON

BENIN

BANTU

INTER-LACUSTRINE STATES

Mom

L. Nyanza (Victoria)

Brava

KONGO

Congo R.

LUBA

L. Tanganyika

BANTU

Malindi Mombasa

SWAHILI STATES

ZANZIBAR

LUNDA

MAFIA

Kilwa

States in being

BEMBA

BANTU

L. Malawi (Nyasa)

States in process of development or brought together in emergency

LOZI

Zambezi R.

MWENE MUTAPA

Quilimane

CHANGA MIRE

Sofala

BANTU

KHOISAN

SOTHO

NGUNI

KHOISAN

infrequently and always at the risk of Portuguese reprisals if they were discovered.

The first recorded English voyage to Africa was that of Captain William Hawkins, in 1540. This voyage was briefly noted in Richard Hakluyt's famous collection of English explorations of the world, published in 1600: " . . . wherewith he made three long and famous voyages unto the coast of Bresil . . . in the course of which voyages he touched at the river of Sestos upon the coast of Guinea, where he traffiqued with the Negroes and tooke off of them elephants teeth and other commodities."

By the late sixteenth century, however, voyages such as those of Hawkins were becoming almost commonplace, as England, France, and Holland sent ships to Africa, the New World, and the Far East in search of trade and territories that had long been denied them by the primacy of Portugal and Spain. It was Holland, acting with great boldness and efficiency, that made the most determined assault on Portugal's claims. Dutch merchant ships, either armed or accompanied by warships, prowled the waters of the Atlantic and Indian Oceans, and soon Holland began seizing and occupying Portuguese posts. The Portuguese strongholds of Arguin Island, Gorée, and Elmina were seized and retained, while several Portuguese stations in the Kongo-Angola region were seized briefly. By the early seventeenth century the Portuguese presence in Africa was limited to a few points in Senegambia, Angola, and Mozambique, and by about 1650 rivalry among the Dutch, English, French, Danes, and Swedes was often intense.

In 1663 an English agent at Ardrah in Dahomey recorded his concern that "the Dutch told the King of Ardra that they had conquered the Portugals, the potentest nation that ever was in those countries, and turned out the Dane and Swede, and in a short time should do the same to the English, and by these discourses hindered the Company's factors from trade. . . ."

In the same year the English agent at Komenda, on the Gold Coast, reported an incident that was not unique: ". . . the Dutch [from a man-of-war based at Elmina] manned out three long boats, and continued firing at all canoes that would have traded with the English, and those canoes that were made fast to the English ship the Dutch cut from the ship's side. . . . So the English boat weighed anchor, the long boat's men giving us such base language as was not to be endured. . . ."

Neither the English nor the French intended to respect Dutch claims to the coast, any more than Portuguese claims had been respected. Both nations began to implant their own trading stations at commercially desirable locations. The French concentrated their efforts along the coast of Senegal, while the British competed with the Dutch along the Gold Coast, Dahomey, and the Nigerian coast. During the seventeenth century, if not for a much longer period, it was the Gold Coast that attracted the most intense European attention. By 1700 twenty-eight forts had been built by the Portuguese, Dutch, English, and Danes on the Gold Coast, in what is modern Ghana. In the early eighteenth century over a dozen more were constructed. These forts ranged from small stone buildings surrounded by earthen ramparts to elaborate structures of mortar with intricate passageways, water and sanitation systems, and massive defensive moats, walls, and towers. All the forts were built on lands rented from the local chief or king, under a treaty or contract that acknowledged the residual authority and sovereignty of the African ruler.

The reactions of African peoples and states to the first two and a half centuries of European trade and contact varied from area to area. As a general rule Africans welcomed the increasing trade and regarded it as in their interest. In western Africa, from Mauritania to the Congo River, the pattern was almost universally one of contact between equals. Except for islands far off the African coast—Fernando Po, Principe, São Tomé, for example—no attempt was made to establish permanent colonies of European settlers. The tiny handful of European residents clustered around the mouths and lower reaches of the Senegal and Gambia rivers, along the Gold Coast, in the forts, and in African towns along the coast of Dahomey and western Nigeria.

During the period of Portuguese trading supremacy and during the next two centuries of brisk activity by the other European nations, a considerable variety of European goods came to be in demand in Africa. Yet the African goods desired in Europe consisted of a relatively small number of items: gold dust, ivory, gum, skins, ostrich feathers, beeswax, and slaves. The longer the trade went on, the more important slaves became in it. By the beginning of the eighteenth century, European demand for African slaves far overshadowed demand for all other African goods.

John Barbot, a Frenchman residing in England, made many voyages to West Africa, and wrote one of the most widely circulated accounts of the trade there in his *A Description of the Coasts of North and South Guinea,* published in about 1682. He devoted nearly a full page to a simple listing of the numerous goods, both utilitarian and luxurious, that French traders stocked along the Senegambia coast. A few excerpts from his list serve to illustrate the range of goods being imported into Africa:

> . . . common red, blue, and scarlet cloth, silver and brass rings, false crystal . . .
> Dutch pointed knives, pewter dishes . . . French paper, steels to strike

fire . . . lines, shoes . . . brass kettles . . . Dutch cutlasses, strait and bow'd, clouts . . . white sugar, musket balls, iron nails, shot . . . looking glasses in plain and gilt frames, cloves, cinnamon, scissors, needles, coarse thread of sundry colours . . . copper bars of a pound weight . . . but above all . . . great quantities of brandy, and iron in bars. . . .

For roughly four centuries, from the first Portuguese contacts in the mid-fifteenth century until the abolition of the slave trade in the latter part of the nineteenth, all these and many other European goods flowed into the African hinterland through hundreds of trading posts that dotted the African coasts between what are now Mauritania and southern Angola. Although European merchants exerted a degree of control over the trade, the African kings along the coast or in the immediate interior played an active role in determining what goods they would buy and sell, and at what prices.

In 1758 the British Board of Trade expressed the reality of this situation in a frank statement to William Pitt, the prime minister:

> The British interest, both in Possession and Commerce, depends chiefly, if not entirely, on the good Will and Friendship of the Natives, who do not allow us even these Possessions, limited as they are to the bare spots on which our Forts and Factories are situated, without the payment of an annual Quitrent . . . The Natives have ever expressed great jealousy at every attempt made by Europeans to discover the Nature and Produce of their Country and particularly their Gold.

Europeans had been restricted almost entirely to the coasts by African policies, by the physical difficulties of traveling into the interior, by the diseases that took so heavy a toll of European lives, and by the fact that they hesitated to jeopardize profits by deviating from the traditional pattern of coastal trading.

The Portuguese, during the fifteenth and early sixteenth centuries, had sent several parties into the interior. In 1494 and 1534 Portuguese missions traveled up the Senegal River and then overland to Mali. On several occasions in the early sixteenth century, under the sponorship of King John II, Portuguese missions visited Tekrur and Timbuktu. As late as 1623 a Portuguese expedition opened a gold mine fifteen miles inland from the coast on the Ankobra River (which flows into the ocean some sixty miles west of Elmina). This mine proved to be a rich one, but in 1636 it was destroyed by an earthquake. (The local people, noting that the mine had been sunk in a hill long regarded as sacred, and assuming that the earthquake was a sign of divine wrath, rounded up the few Portuguese survivors and buried them in the hill as a sacrifice.)

The records of these few Portuguese ventures into the interior were filed away in tightly guarded Portuguese archives so that other Europeans would remain as ignorant as possible of Africa. The great distances that had to be covered to reach the bustling trade cities in the interior, the lack of navigable waterways, uncertainty about cooperation from the numerous African states that had to be traversed, and a high toll in sickness and death discouraged even the Portuguese, and gradually their initial ventures came to a halt.

The physical deterrent to European penetration of the African interior was formidable. The coast of western Africa contains few natural harbors. Most of the rivers are not navigable for more than a few miles inland from the coast. Then there were the great rain forests of West Africa, which Europeans believed were virtually impenetrable. (The rain forests are not nearly so mysterious and difficult to traverse as early Europeans, often on the basis of deliberate African exaggeration, came to believe; but a myth grew up about them, which lies at the base of the modern misconception that Africa is teeming with jungles.)

African disease, especially malaria, also discouraged European expeditions into the interior. The death rate of European sailors engaged in the West African trade was high. An old chanty sung by English sailors warned:

> Beware and take care
> Of the Bight of Benin,
> For one that comes out
> There are forty goes in.

The entire West African region, from the coast all the way to the Sudan, was populated with thriving agricultural societies that had begun to develop centrally organized states under the rule of kings. These emerging states participated in the great trading system that linked almost all of West Africa. The arrival of European ships, filled with attractive goods and men eager to exchange them for African goods, gave the West African forest states a new, and much larger, outlet for their goods. These states were not eager for Europeans to bypass them to reach directly into the far interior. As the trade grew larger and became better organized, jealousy among these states grew, as did their unwillingness to allow Europeans direct contact with the richer states of the interior.

This situation characterized the entire African-European commercial system and the economics of West Africa. In the fifteenth century, when the first Portuguese ships began calling, the center of economic activity in western Africa lay along the Sudan, in favorable areas at the headwaters of the Senegal, the Gambia, and the Niger, at convenient termini of the trans-Saharan trade routes, and at natural crossroad sites (such as the Hausa states, Bobo-Dioulasso, and Kong) where goods from the forest regions converged for transshipment to the Sudanic markets. Most of the states that lay in or near the forest regions were on the far periphery of this commercial network although they were part of it. They included Wolof, Serer, Mende, Temne, Bambara, the Voltaic states, the Akan states of Denkyira, Akyem, Akwapim, Asante, the states of the Ga, Ewe, and Fon, the Yoruba states, and the decentralized societies of what is now eastern Nigeria and western Cameroun.

Most of these states were small and poorer than the more favorably situated states of the Sudan, which were at the center of the commercial network. (Benin was an exception; it had grown rich and powerful very early, despite being on the far edge of the Sudanic trading system.) European trade created a situation hitherto unknown in West Africa: goods could flow relatively short distances from the southern parts of the Sudan and from the forest region to markets on or near the coast. For the first time the states of the coast and of the forests were at the center of an important commercial system. The Atlantic trade encouraged a shift in the flow of goods. Gradually the flow of goods north to the Sudan diminished and that south to the Atlantic increased. This shift took place over the centuries and never completely destroyed the inland commercial centers. In the mid-sixteenth century, more than a hundred years after the Atlantic trade began, both Songhai and Kanem-Bornu were at the zenith of their careers, and Mali, though slowly declining in power and wealth, was by no means dead. The Hausa states, close to and an intimate part of the Sudanic system, thrived and grew during the period when the Atlantic trade system was developing, partly because they were in a unique position to participate actively in that system as well as in the Sudanic-trans-Saharan system.

The Sudanic trade system drew goods from wide areas into several major entrepôt regions—one around Tekrur, another around the headwaters of the Senegal and Niger rivers in the western Sudan, another in the Timbuktu-Jenne-Gao area where the Niger makes its great bend to the north, another around Hausa country, and another still farther east around Lake Chad in the Kanem-Bornu area. Similarly, the Atlantic trade system centered around several major entrepôt areas, in which transportation networks from the interior converged. One such region was around the mouth of the Senegal River. Into this area flowed goods from Mauritania, the lands along the Senegal River, the Futa Toro plateau, Tekrur, and much of the region covered by ancient Ghana. A few hundred miles to the south was another such region, the area between the mouth of the Gambia and the islands that dot the coast of what is now Guinea (Bissau). Goods from Futa Jallon, the lands along the Gambia River, and the lands of the Bambara and other

Mande peoples flowed into this region. For the next thousand miles of coast no trade centers of such importance developed during the centuries when the Atlantic trade was forming.

Along what was called the Gold Coast, or modern Ghana, one of Africa's most important trading regions developed. This area, though possessing few good natural harbors, proved to be an excellent trading region since its highly organized states (the Fante states on the coast and the states of Denkyira, Asante, and of the other Akan peoples inland) effectively channeled goods from a large and rich hinterland. Into the many trading stations that soon developed flowed goods from the Voltaic lands, from what is now eastern Ivory Coast, all of modern Ghana, and western Togo. The coast country along the Gold Coast is relatively dry and free of forests. Thus it is more attractive and healthy for Europeans, adding another point in favor of trading there. The Dahomey coast was the next important trade entrepôt region, channeling goods from most of Togo, Dahomey, the eastern part of Upper Volta, the western part of Nigeria, and northwest Nigeria down the Sudanic belt to Ardrah, Ouidah, and other trade towns. Around Badagry and Lagos another important trade area developed, drawing goods from what is now western Nigeria and the western parts of northern Nigeria.

Next came the Niger delta (later to be called the Oil Rivers, for the large quantity of palm oil which was brought there). The delta region served eastern Benin, Iboland, and the rich country that lies up the Niger and Benue rivers. (Europeans were ignorant of the fact that the Oil Rivers were the outlets to the sea of the great Niger.) East of the Niger delta lay the last of the great trading areas of West Africa, encompassing the mouth of the Calabar River and the neighboring coast of western Cameroun together with the offshore island of Fernando Po. Most of the remaining coast for another six or seven hundred miles was an area of only intermittent trade, comparable to the coast between Sierra Leone and the Gold Coast in importance. But a rich trade region began with Loango, in modern Congo (Brazzaville), running south to modern Luanda, the capital of Angola. Between the mouth of the Congo and Luanda lay Kongo, and on both sides of Kongo were other flourishing states that had goods to trade, and were well organized to ensure orderly trading conditions. This area became the most important single source of slaves for the Portuguese trade, and it was the only area to which the Portuguese were able effectively to claim a right.

South of Luanda there were no other important trade areas except where the modern Angolan towns of Lobito and Benguela are located. Beyond these towns, the coast grows increasingly desolate as it merges into the great coastal Namib Desert, one of the most barren areas on earth. No trading areas could develop along this inhospitable coast, nor

Late seventeenth-century British fortress on the
Gold Coast. (Nineteenth-century drawing.)

even along the coasts of South Africa, because the interior was sparsely
populated and poor. The next major trading area, after the Benguela
region, was all the way around the southern tip of the continent in
Mozambique.

These areas of trade concentration between the Senegal River
mouth and Angola channeled trade goods from an area where some two
thirds of the people of Black Africa lived. Through these regions, a
large variety of European goods flowed into Africa in exchange for a
smaller variety of African goods. African rulers accumulated wealth by
taxing the goods that flowed into and out of their kingdoms. The
many luxury items from Europe enhanced the prestige of the chief,
his court, and his vassals, and provided him with disposable wealth
with which he could reward loyal service, maintain fighting forces, and
support the state's administrative structure. As time went on, guns,
powder, and shot gave rulers a significant new measure of power, as they
equipped troops with these modern tools of war. In areas where European goods were purchased in greatest quantity, such as the Fante
states along the Gold Coast, indigenous enterprise was occasionally
dampened. Iron working, for example, became less important when
European knives, swords, axes, adzes, and hoes could be imported at
less cost than those produced in Africa. Cheap European cloth easily

competed with the relatively expensive cloth woven by Africans. Thus, there was popular demand for useful items as well as for luxury goods. Over a long period of time, African rulers and their subjects became dependent upon the imports to which they had become accustomed.

Of the African goods that Europeans sought none were more highly prized than slaves. The longer the Atlantic trade developed, the more important became the buying and selling of slaves. The slave trade, in one sense, was simply a major component of the total African-European trade relationship, yet it was something unique, the likes of which have never occurred in any other part of the world.

Europeans did not start the slave trade. African societies had practiced a form of slavery for centuries before contact with Europe. Africans had sold slaves to each other, and for export to North Africa and Asia across the Sahara and through Ethiopia and the Azanian ports. But the sheer volume of the slave traffic across the Atlantic and the brutality with which African slaves were treated renders the European slave trade fundamentally different from anything that took place within Africa itself.

African slaves were captured, both by African kings and by North African and Egyptian slavers, and sold in Egypt, Asia, and southern Europe as early as the first millennium before Christ. Aesop, whose fables are familiar throughout Western civilization, was himself an African, the son of Negro slaves owned by wealthy Greeks. Aesop probably was born in about 620 B.C. In these early times there was no organized African slave trade. But individuals, taken in battles between the Egyptains, the Libyans, the Phoenicians, and others against Negro and Berber Africans, were frequently sold.

During the first millennium of the Christian era, a small but steady trade in Negro slaves took place across the Sahara and through the Red Sea-Indian Ocean trading system. Slaves crossed the Sahara with caravans moving between Ghana and Tekrur and Morocco, and between ancient Kanem and Libya. By the ninth century the slave trade with East Africa was sizable enough to have produced a large Negro population in Iraq and Persia, who rebelled in the Zanj Rebellion of 869-883 and set up an autonomous but short-lived state around Basra, in Iraq.

In these early times, slaves were usually taken in battles or raids conducted for other purposes. In the trade between Kanem and North Africa and between East Africa and Arabia, slaves were important enough to rank with ivory, gold, and skins. Yet there is no evidence of any organized effort to procure slaves especially for trade. They seem to have been a by-product of the expansion of various African states, such as Kanem, Axum, and Meroe, whose leaders captured slaves in order to increase their own supply of farm workers, soldiers, and artisans. They were manpower, and their destiny was in the hands of a king or chief. Slaves were not considered primarily as a commodity, nor were most slaves sold; but chiefs and kings could and did sell slaves if the products they received in exchange seemed of greater value than the labor the slaves were expected to render. If a king was a powerful ruler whose territory was adjacent to a well-populated but poorly organized area, his troops could produce a large enough supply of slaves to satisfy domestic demand and still leave a modicum for exchange abroad.

Where there were no well-organized states, foreigners frequently resorted to slave raids. This was especially true along the East African coast, where Arabs settled in sufficient numbers that they could send military parties a few miles into the interior and capture slaves. Berbers in some parts of the western Sahara also engaged in slave raiding. (And sometimes the tables were turned, with Berbers ending up as slaves to Negro kings.)

It is unlikely that any figures can be compiled on the volume of the pre-European African slave trade. Its volume was substantial, at least at some times and in some areas, as attested by the existence of as many as 100,000 African slaves in Iraq and Persia. A large but unknown number of African slaves from Kush and areas to its south was captured by Egypt over the millennia of its history. These slaves ultimately merged with the population along the Nile valley. Yet in most areas that were in contact with early Africa and in a position to buy slaves—Greece, Rome, ancient Persia, India, China—the number of African slaves cannot have been very large before the Arab-Islamic period. In those lands African slaves, though known, were but a small proportion of slaves from other areas in Asia and Europe.

The growth of the Arab Empire stimulated an increase in the African slave trade, chiefly into the Arab homeland and adjacent regions of Iraq, Persia, and the Near East. In these areas, great agriculture and engineering enterprises were undertaken, and there were shortages of labor. African slaves were imported into the burgeoning Arab-controlled cities of North Africa during this period, between about 700 and 1400, as a source of labor. In all parts of the Arab Empire, African soldiers, purchased as slaves but assigned to military service, formed important units in the Arab armies. If they accepted Islam—and most did—they could rise to positions of power and prestige through military service and personal assistance to sultans and amirs and could win their freedom.

No reliable estimates are available on the size of this expanded flow of African slaves. The flow of slaves, however, was not large enough to result in sizable African or mixed populations in any but a few local areas, such as the Iraq-Persia area. Many Negroid physical traits are today found in North Africa, but to what extent this admixture was produced by mixtures between the descendants of slaves and the Berbers or by intermarriages between contiguous Negro and Berber peoples is difficult to ascertain. Certainly both these processes were long at work to produce the racial blends so common today in parts of North Africa.

Within Africa itself slavery took two forms, neither of which was comparable to the stark chattel slavery of the Atlantic slave trade. Most African "slaves" were more properly serfs or vassals. They were conquered peoples who lived within a kingdom or empire and who were regarded as different from and on a slightly lower level than the people of the conquering group. These serfs were required to perform labor in the fields as well as in various crafts. Serfs were generally not sold and were protected by custom from capricious treatment by the ruler. This form of "slavery" was prevalent in many of the Sudanic and forest states. The other form of slavery was similar to that practiced by Muslims. Under this second system, captives taken in war were brought from their native land to that of their captors and kept as slaves in the service of the king or his vassals. These slaves, though their descendants gradually melded into the capturing society, were frequently used as soldiers, palace guards, personal servants, and artisans for the king. They often rose to positions of great prominence and power.

Willem Bosman, a Dutch slave factor (trade representative) on the Gold Coast, writing about African societies and customs in 1704, noted that slaves usually led the caravans that brought slaves for sale to the European slave traders from inland states.

> Those who come from the inward part of the country to traffick with us are chiefly slaves: one of which, on whom the master reposes the greatest trust, is appointed the chief of the caravan. But when he comes to us he is not treated as a slave, but as a very great merchant whom we take all possible care to oblige. . . . Indeed, I have observed that some of these slaves have more authority than their masters; for having long exercised command over their master's dependents, by their own trading they are become possessors of some slaves themselves, and in process of time are grown so powerful, that their patrons are obliged to see with their eyes only. . . .

R. S. Rattray, one of the first observers to write a thorough study of the Asante of the Gold Coast, noted that a slave in that society "might marry; own property; himself own a slave; swear an oath; be a competent witness; and ultimately become heir to his master. . . . Such briefly were the rights of an Ashanti slave. They seemed in many cases practically the ordinary privileges of an Ashanti free man. . . . An Ashanti slave, in nine cases out of ten, possibly became an adopted member of the family, and in time his descendants so merged and inter-married with the owner's kinsmen that only a few would know their origin. . . ."

The slaves and serfs of an African king were important components of his wealth and power; he therefore had a vested interest in their welfare and good performance. As good farmers they increased the production of food with which the ruler fed his large retinue and family. Food was also used as a reward for good service by the king's followers. As craftsmen, slaves turned out the furniture, personal orna-ments, tools, and even weapons that were essential to the king's prestige. As soldiers, they defended their lord in a tradition unfettered by family connections with conspirators or aspirants for power. A wise ruler re-warded loyal service by his slaves, and a wise slave performed well. Both masters and slaves often deviated from this ideal relationship, and Africa knew its acts of capricious cruelty by slave owners, as well as rebellion and disloyalty by slaves. Yet these were deviations from the rule and were less common than the prescribed relationship that bound mas-ter and slave in mutual need.

The taking of African slaves by Europeans began almost as soon as European ships began visiting the coasts of West Africa. In 1441, in one of the early voyages, a young Portuguese captain, Antam Gonçalvez, de-cided to return home with a captured "Moor" or two with which to surprise Prince Henry, in whose service he was engaged. Gonçalvez, with another Portuguese captain, Nuño Tristão, returned to Portugal with twelve captives, intended as slaves for Prince Henry. In Portugal these captives aroused great interest, especially when one explained that he was of royal birth and could be ransomed for a larger number of slaves. He was returned to his home in exchange for ten Negro slaves.

There were markets for slaves in a number of cities of Europe at the time. Both Portugal and Spain still depended upon some slave labor for domestic service in the households of nobles and wealthy merchants, and for work in the fields, on ships, and in military service. And in several European trading cities, especially Venice and Genoa, captives were regularly traded to the Muslims of North Africa and the eastern Mediterranean world, where slaves still played an even more important economic role. The church in Rome was, at the time, becoming highly skeptical of the moral justification of slavery and prohibited the sale of Christians. But the Church could not effectively prohibit slavery, and even Christians continued to be sold by the energetic and amoral merchants of Venice and Genoa, despite Rome's denunciations.

Thus the early Portuguese mariners, who sailed to Africa for pur-poses other than finding slaves, quickly recognized that the ease with which they could capture or buy slaves in West Africa meant an extra dividend from their expeditions. Prince Henry, who had expended large sums for maritime study, ship building, and expeditions, soon began to appear in a better light to his critics: "... when they saw the first Moorish captives brought home," wrote the Portuguese chronicler, G. E. de Azurar, "and the second cargo that followed these, they became already somewhat doubtful about the opinion they had at first expressed; and altogether renounced it when they saw the third consignment that Nuño Tristão brought home, captured in so short a time, and with so little trouble. . . ."

The slave cargoes brought back by Gonçalvez and Nuño Tristão raised the priority of slaving in the African adventure almost at once. In 1444 an expedition of six ships was dispatched to the Moroccan coast. It returned with 235 men, women, and children, all captured by armed slaving parties. Within ten years, a regular slave trade had been organized and had shifted from direct capture to purchase from local Berber chiefs, who in turn purchased slaves from African rulers south of the Sahara, chiefly in what is now Mauritania. Alvise da Ca Da Mosto, a Venetian who sailed with the Portuguese to the Gambia River in 1456, left a record of how the slave trade was developing: "These [Berbers] have many Berber horses, which they trade and take to the land of the Blacks, exchanging them with the rulers for slaves. Ten or fifteen slaves as usually given . . . for one of these horses. . . ."

Arguin Island, just off the coast of Morocco, was the earliest base used by the Portuguese for this new trade in slaves. Da Mosto noted that a thousand slaves a year were shipped to Portugal from Arguin—only fifteen years after the first slaves were taken by Gonçalvez. By about 1506 Duarte Padheco Pereira, writing of the slave trade along the entire West African coast, estimated that "when the trade of the country was well ordered, it yielded 3,500 slaves and more, many tusks of ivory, gold, fine cotton and much other merchandise."

In the first few decades of the slave trade, slaves were taken to Portugal from West Africa, Kongo, and Angola. These slaves were sold in the markets of Portugal and Spain, with most purchased by Spaniards to serve as laborers on the large estates of that country. Yet the demand for slaves in Spain and Portugal was limited. A new market, however, developed quickly, in the islands Spain and Portugal were colonizing and developing off the West African coast—Madeira, the Canaries, the Cape Verdes, São Tomé, and Principe. In the fertile fields of these islands, colonists planted vineyards, sugarcane, vegetables, and fruits, all of which required inexpensive labor. During the early sixteenth century, these islands became an even larger market for slaves than the Mediterranean area, and so the slave trade continued to grow.

But it was the energetic Spanish enterprises in the New World, following the voyages of Columbus, that opened up, very slowly at first, a slave market with a seemingly infinite demand. By 1500 Spanish ships were regularly exploring the islands of the West Indies and the mainlands bordering the Caribbean. These lands had been granted to the Spanish crown as a monopoly for exploitation, and were so beckoning in their promise of gold, silver, and precious stones that they absorbed the attention of Spain during the sixteenth century. Mines of gold and silver, requiring large supplies of labor, were found. At first Spaniards and slaves from Spain (Moors, Africans, and some Spanish indentured servants) were brought to the New World to perform the arduous work in the mines. Then an attempt was made to require the indigenous Indian inhabitants to work the mines and the plantations that were being established. These Caribs, however, not only resisted efforts to make them work but died in large numbers from European diseases to which they had no immunity and from the sheer pressure of work under cruel Spanish overseers. In 1547, protests by a shocked Spanish priest, Bishop Bartolomé de las Casas, who witnessed the cruelties suffered by Indian laborers, persuaded King Charles of Spain to forbid further use of forced Indian labor.

Since both the church and the crown were reluctant to permit widespread use of Christian European labor in the harsh conditions of the New World mines, it was decided to import more African slaves. Las Casas himself had suggested this as the best available alternative. The Spanish authorities in the New World were not particularly pleased with this decision. African labor was already in use and had proven less than ideal, due largely to the intractable attitudes of Africans to enslavement and forced labor. Planters and administrators complained that the African slaves who had been brought to the New World from Spain often escaped and had on several occasions fomented rebellions among the Indians. In the end they accepted the necessity of using more African slave labor, however, and the flow of slaves directly from West Africa to the New World began.

Although African slaves ultimately proved to be the most effective solution to the problem of abundant labor in the New World's mines and plantations, they continued to show their desire for freedom and their antipathy to enslavement. There were slave rebellions in Hispaniola in 1522, in Puerto Rico in 1527, in Santa Marta in 1529, and in Panama in 1531. By this time it had been found necessary to organize a special police force trained to subdue slave rebellions and to pursue runaways. Africans were at a distinct disadvantage in their rebellions. They were often separated from their families, their friends, and even their fellow tribesmen: they were in unfamiliar surroundings and often did not known the language and customs of the indigenous people.

In many cases they had been taken into slavery as children and knew little of any life except that of slavery. In the New World their Africa-bred capacity for hard, sustained labor under tropical conditions enabled some not only to survive (at least in a larger proportion than the Indians who had been enslaved) but to produce under difficult and harsh conditions.

Over several generations, the African slave population in the New World adapted itself, however unwillingly, to the new life from which escape was so difficult. The number of slaves, constantly replenished by larger and larger new shipments, slowly grew. In 1550 about 12,500 African slaves had been landed in Spanish America. By 1600 this number had swelled to 75,000, and another 50,000 had been shipped to Portuguese Brazil. During the sixteenth century the volume and organization of the slave trade steadily grew, and Portuguese forts and trading posts were established from Morocco to Angola. Direct capture of slaves had virtually ceased. Slaves were supplied through a regular trade system in which Portuguese slave merchants bartered for batches of slaves with Berber and African rulers and with merchants all along the Atlantic Ocean coasts of Africa.

During the sixteenth century, when the annual rate of the African slave flow increased by an average of 1.5 percent a year, the Portuguese had the trade largely to themselves. The Spanish and Portuguese colonists of the New World were by far the largest buyers of slaves, as the demand for slaves in Europe and the Atlantic islands slowly declined. Between 1450 and 1600, about 55 percent of the slaves shipped from Africa were sold in the New World, which by the end of the period was almost the sole market for slaves. The mines, though still producing substantial quantities of gold and silver, were slowly giving way to great plantations, especially for the burgeoning production of sugarcane and processed sugar.

In 1515, only twenty-three years after Columbus first discovered the New World, the first shipment of slave-grown sugar left the Spanish West Indies, and throughout the century sugar production steadily increased in volume and importance. Sugar, by 1600, was the chief item on one leg of the "triangular trade" system in which manufactured articles flowed from Europe to Africa; slaves flowed from West Africa to the New World; and sugar, gold, silver, indigo, tobacco, and other products flowed from the New World to Europe. The greatest profits in this triangular trade accrued in Lisbon and Spain, with the next largest profits being made in the New World. The smallest share of profit was made in Africa. This pattern persisted for many years in the trade systems of other New World colonizers: British, Dutch, French, Danish, etc. Over the centuries other valuable New World products—

rum, cotton, skins, foodstuffs, and timber—joined sugar and metals as major components of the trade with Europe. But slaves remained the chief item in the Africa-America trade well into the nineteenth century.

The English and the French entered the slave trade on a very small scale in the mid-sixteenth century, as interlopers in a system that the Portuguese claimed as a legitimate monopoly. English and French ships slipped through the widely spread Portuguese naval net, sometimes trading with African chiefs for slaves, occasionally landing armed parties to capture a few slaves directly, and sometimes seizing Portuguese slave ships and making away with their human cargo. In the New World, the English and French captains could be sure of finding a ready and lucrative market for their human booty. Their audacious forays into the slave trade served as one of the many irritants that prompted the Spanish throne (which ruled Portugal at the time) to send its famous Armada against England in 1588.

The Dutch joined the English-French effort to break the Spanish-Portuguese monopoly in Africa and the New World, early in the seventeenth century, and were more systematic and more successful. By the middle of the seventeenth century Africa was largely open to European trade, and the growing interest of the English, Dutch, and French in their own colonial ventures in the New World stimulated them all to trade in African slaves.

During the sixteenth century the European powers other than Spain and Portugal had played only a minor role in the exploration and colonization of the New World. In the early seventeenth century, however, they began to move into the West Indies and North America. By the end of the century England, France, and Holland were firmly established on the North American continent. These three nations, along with Denmark, had also established flourishing colonies in the Caribbean. In former years, traders from these nations had intruded into the African slave trade in order to profit from selling slaves to the Spanish and Portuguese colonies. Now colonies of their own countrymen were eager for slaves. By the end of the seventeenth century, Portuguese and Spanish merchantmen were carrying many fewer slaves than those of the slave traders from northern Europe.

English and French planters in the West Indies began to plant sugar and tobacco in the mid-seventeenth century. Like the Portuguese and Spaniards, they needed slave labor to clear and till the fields. As sugar production mounted, the need for slaves climbed with it.

Between 1600 and 1650, a period when the need for slaves was still confined largely to the Spanish and Portuguese colonies, the annual importation of slaves averaged around 7,300 a year. After 1650 the annual

Slaves being marched to the coast. (Sketch in Livingstone's *Last
Journals*, 1874, illustrating the cruelty of the slave traders.)

rate began to increase steadily, with the growth of other European
colonies. For the quarter century 1651-1675 the annual rate doubled to
14,700. Between 1676 and 1700 it averaged 24,100. By 1720 it was over
45,000, and it continued to mount until, in the period 1761-1780, it
averaged around 65,500 slaves a year. By this time cotton, in the West
Indies and the English colonies of southern North America, had not
only joined sugar and tobacco as big business, but had begun to surpass
them.

The steadily growing volume of the slave trade tells only one part of
the iniquitous story. Much sadder is the human aspect, from initial
capture, to forced marches to the slave markets on the coast, to con-
finement while awaiting sale and shipment, to the tortures of the trans-
Atlantic "middle passage," to sale in the New World, to a life of toil and
suffering. Each part of the enslavement experience brought new fears
and new torments to the bewildered individuals who were torn from
home and family, often as children. Paradoxically the initial capture,
frightening and harsh though it was, was by no means the worst of the
experience. Capture in warfare and raids had long been known in
African societies, but for most people it was usually followed by a period
of serfdom which was not drastically worse than the life before. The
autobiography of Olaudah Equiano, an Ibo who was captured at the
age of ten and sold into slavery, offers a vivid picture of individual

suffering under slavery. Equiano, unlike most slaves, acquired an education and eventually earned enough money to purchase his freedom from a comparatively benevolent master.

Equiano was born in about 1745, nearly three centuries after the slave trade had first begun. At the time, some 55,000-60,000 slaves a year were being landed in the New World. As an Ibo, Equiano lived in a society which, though well developed culturally, had no central political organization. The Ibo people, who were highly prized for their intelligence and ability to perform a variety of tasks well, suffered disproportionately from the slave raids. When Equiano was captured, slaving in Iboland had become so prevalent that children were posted each day as lookouts in trees. They sounded the alarm when kidnappers (who usually operated in small groups, rather than in large armed parties) appeared. On several occasions Equiano himself spotted kidnappers, but when he was about ten his luck forsook him:

> One day, when all our people were gone out to their works as usual and only I and my dear sister were left to mind the house, two men and a woman got over our walls, and in a moment seized us both, and without giving us time to cry out or make resistance they stopped our mouths and ran off with us into the nearest wood. Here they tied our hands and continued to carry us as far as they could till night came on, when we reached a small house where the robbers halted for refreshment and spent the night. We were then unbound but were unable to take any food, and being quite overpowered by fatigue and grief, our only relief was some sleep, which allayed our misfortune for a short time.

Two days later Equiano and his sister, still apparently in Ibo country, were separated and each sold to other slave agents, a process that recurred several times before he reached the coast:

> The next day proved a day of greater sorrow than I had yet experienced, for my sister and I were then separated while we lay clasped in each other's arms. It was in vain that we besought them not to part us; she was torn from me and immediately carried away, while I was left in a state of distraction not to be described. I cried and grieved continually, and for several days I did not eat anything but what they forced into my mouth.

After about six months, during which Equiano experienced both kindness and cruelty from the many people through whose hands he passed, he arrived at the sea and was placed on board one of the numerous slave ships that lay at anchor all along the Biafran coast. Here his sufferings began to increase, accentuated by his first sight of white men (whom he, like many Africans, suspected of being cannibals):

The first object which saluted my eyes when I arrived on the coast was the sea, and a slave ship which was then riding at anchor and waiting for its cargo. These filled me with astonishment, which was soon converted into terror when I was carried on board. I was immediately handled and tossed up to see if I were sound by some of the crew, and I was now persuaded that I had gotten into a world of bad spirits and that they were going to kill me. . . . Indeed such were the horrors of my views and fears at that moment that, if ten thousand worlds had been my own, I would freely have parted with them all to have exchanged my condition with that of the meanest slave in my own country. When I looked round the ship too and saw a large furnace or copper boiling and a multitude of black people of every description chained together, every one of their countenances expressing dejection and sorrow, I no longer doubted my fate; and quite overpowered with horror and anguish, I fell motionless on the deck and fainted. . . .

. . . I was not long suffered to indulge my grief; I was soon put down under the decks, and there received such a salutation in my nostrils as I had never experienced in my life: so that with the loathesomeness of the stench and crying together, I became so sick and low that I was not able to eat, nor had I the least desire to taste anything. I now wished for the last friend, death, to relieve me; but soon, to my grief, two of the white men offered me eatables, and on my refusing to eat, one of them held me fast by the hands and laid me across I think the windlass, and tied my feet while the other flogged me severely. I had never experienced anything of this kind before. . . .

Equiano was later reassured when some of the adult Africans told him that they were to be taken to another place to work and would not be eaten. His fear of the strange white men, however, was soon renewed:

I then was a little revived, and thought if it were no worse than working, my situation was not so desperate: but still I feared I should be put to death, the white people looked and acted, as I thought, in so savage a manner; for I had never seen among my people such instances of brutal cruelty, and this not only shewn toward us blacks but also to some of the whites themselves. One white man in particular I saw, when we were permitted to be on deck, flogged so unmercifully with a large rope near the foremast that he died as a consequence of it; and they tossed him over the side as they would have done a brute. This made me fear these people the more, and I expected nothing less than to be treated in the same manner.

After a few weeks on the slave hulk an ocean-going slave ship arrived, and Equiano and his companions began the torment of the notorious six- to ten-week "middle passage" to the New World:

At last, when the ship we were in had got in all her cargo, they made ready with many fearful noises, and we were all put under deck so that

Olaudah Equiano.

we could not see how they managed the vessel. . . . The stench of the hold while we were on the coast was so intolerably loathesome that it was dangerous to remain there for any length of time, and some of us had been permitted to stay on the deck for the fresh air; but now that the whole ship's cargo were confined together it became absolutely pestilential. The closeness of the place and the heat of the climate, added to the number in the ship, which was so crowded that each had scarcely room to turn himself, almost suffocated us. This produced copious perspirations, so that the air soon became unfit for respiration from a variety of loathesome smells, and brought on a sickness among the slaves, of which many died, thus falling victims to the improvident avarice, as I may call it, of their purchasers. This wretched situation was again aggravated by the galling of the chains, now become insupportable, and the filth of the necessary tubs [for use as toilets], into which the children often fell and were almost suffocated. The shrieks of the women and the groans of the dying rendered the whole a scene of horror almost inconceivable.

Another part of Equiano's testimony tells of being sold in a slave market in Barbados, in the British West Indies:

We were not many days in the merchant's custody before we were sold after the usual manner, which is this: On a signal given (as the beat of a drum) the buyers rush at once into the yard where the slaves are confined, and make choice of that parcel they like best. The noise and clamour with which this is attended and the eagerness visible in the countenances of the buyers serve not a little to increase the apprehensions of the terrified Africans, who may well be supposed to consider them as the ministers of that destruction to which they think themselves devoted. In that manner, without scruple, are relations and friends separated, most of them never to see each other again. I remember in the vessel in which I was brought over, in the men's apartment there were several brothers who, in the sale, were sold in different lots; and it was very moving on this occasion to see and hear their cries at parting. . . .

Willem Bosman, the Dutch slave trader who wrote one of the few intelligent accounts of African life along the Gold Coast during the late seventeenth and early eighteenth century, described the assembling and buying of slaves at a slave factory on the Dahomey coast. His account gives even more vivid detail than that of Equiano:

> When these slaves come to Fida [Ouidah] they are put in prison all together, . . . they are thoroughly examined, even to the smallest member, and that naked too both men and women, without the least distinction or modesty. Those which are approved as good are set on one side; and the lame or faulty are set by as Invalides. . . . These are such as are above five and 30 years old, or are maimed in the arms, legs, hands, or feet, have lost a tooth, are gray haired, or have films over their eyes; as well those which are affected with any venereal distemper, or with several other diseases.
>
> The Invalides and the maimed are thrown out . . . the remainder are numbered. . . . In the meanwhile a burning iron, with the arms or names of the companies, lyes in the fire, with which ours are marked on the breast.
>
> I doubt not but that this trade seems very barbarous to you, but since it is followed by meer necessity it must go on; but we take all possible care that they are not burned too hard, especially the women, who are more tender than the men.
>
> . . . we send them on board our ships at the very first opportunity; before which their masters strip them of all they have on their backs; so that they come aboard stark-naked as well women as men: in which condition they are obliged to continue, if the master of the ship is not so charitable (which he commonly is) as to bestow something on them to cover their nakedness.

Another European, a British physician named Alexander Falconbridge, who served for several voyages as ship's surgeon on slavers, was so disturbed by the experience that he became a prominent abolitionist and in 1788 wrote of the Atlantic middle passage:

> . . . having occasioned the port-holes to be shut, and the grating to be covered, fluxes and fevers among the negroes ensued. . . . I frequently

went down among them, till at length their apartments became so extremely hot as to be only sufferable for a very short time. . . . The deck, that is the floor of their rooms, was so covered with the blood and mucous which had proceeded from them in consequence of the flux, that it resembled a slaughter house. It is not in the power of human imagination to picture to itself a situation more dreadful or disgusting. Numbers of slaves having fainted, they were carried up on deck, where several of them died and the rest were, with great difficulty, restored. It had nearly proved fatal for me also.

Falconbridge noted that a common measure to maintain a semblance of health during the voyage was to bring the slaves on deck for forced exercise, usually dancing:

. . . if they go about it reluctantly, or do not move with agility, they are flogged; a person standing by them all the time with a cat-o-nine tails in his hand for that purpose. Their music, upon these occasions, consists of a drum. . . . The poor wretches are frequently compelled to sing also; but when they do so, their songs are generally, as may naturally be expected, melancholy lamentations of their exile from their native land.

These scenes, as described by Equiano, Bosman, and Falconbridge, were repeated thousands of times, over a period of four hundred years. The modern mind boggles at the barbaric conditions that attended the whole process of the slave trade and the sheer magnitude and time span of this unholy traffic in human lives.

During most of the time the slave trade flourished, people in Europe were aware of it, but only vaguely so. In many ports of origin in Africa and in government offices and commercial agencies in Europe records were kept of the number of slaves bought, the number of ships licensed, the number of slaves sold in the New World, and so on. Yet the variety of origins, systems of transport and sale, and countries of destination was so great that no comprehensive quantitative study of the slave trade has ever been performed. No one can answer, with close accuracy, for example, which regions of Africa supplied the largest numbers of slaves, much less which tribes were the worst sufferers from the slave trade.

It is generally clear, however, that the densely populated inland areas of western and central Africa, from modern Guinea (Bissau) and Senegal down to Angola, produced more slaves than the far interior of the Sudan, interior East Africa, and the East African coast. Angola, which was exploited by the Portuguese throughout the centuries of the slave trade, was also exploited by the British, Dutch, and French between the late sixteenth and late eighteenth centuries. It not only produced consistently large numbers of slaves, but suffered extensive depopulation and political and social disorganization in the process. Large numbers of slaves came from West Africa; the area between Senegal and southern Angola provided roughly 80-85 percent of all the slaves exported to the New World. Scarcely a tribal name from this region is absent from any account of the ethnic origins of slaves: especially hard hit at one period or another were the Wolof, Malinke, Mende, various Akan peoples, Ewe, Fon, Yoruba, and Ibo.

Although the flow of slaves from various areas fluctuated considerably over the years, names of great slave-trading towns and localities stand out—Gorée in Senegal, Guinea (Bissau), James Island (at the mouth of the Gambia), several Gold Coast towns (Assini, Elmina, Seccondi, Dixcove, Anamabu, Accra), several Dahomey towns (Popo, Ardrah, Ouidah), and a host of towns and posts along what is now the Nigerian coast (Badagry, Lagos, Gwato, and Warri near Benin, Brass, Bonny, Calabar, and several small trade villages near the mouth of the Cross River). Along the coasts of what are now Cameroun and Gabon there were few major slave entrepôts until the development of early Gabon, but slave ships frequently called all along this area of coast. Between the mouth of the Congo and along the coast of Angola down to the Benguela region there were a number of trading settlements. The export of slaves was maintained more consistently here than in almost any other part of Africa.

Routes along which slaves flowed from the interior to the trading stations along the coast are difficult to delineate with any real precision. In general, there were no well laid out roads along which slaves were marched, and for the most part the flow of slaves was not sufficiently regular and sustained from any one region to result in long-used slave trails. But there were exceptions. The Senegal and Gambia rivers, which stretch into the far interior, long served as routes for transporting slaves, together with other African products, to the major trading towns at their mouths. Asante slaving parties marched slaves from the far north, as well as east and west, through central Asante to the ports they controlled on the Gold Coast, especially Elmina and Accra. Slaves taken in the territory that now comprises eastern Ghana, Togo, Dahomey, and western Nigeria converged on the narrow Dahomey coast for sale at Ardrah, Ouidah, and Popo.

Slaves from Nupe, Borgu, Hausaland, the Nigerian plateau, and Yorubaland were moved on a number of converging roads to Abomey and Lagos, although some from the far north were transported down the Benue and Niger rivers for sale at numerous small trading stations along the creeks and rivers of the Niger delta. The mouths of the Calabar and the Cross rivers served as focal points for slaves taken in northeastern Nigeria and western Cameroun. In northern Angola there were no clearly marked roads or river systems along which slaves were moved from the interior to the coast, but slaves were taken to the port areas where Luanda and Benguela now stand.

The bulk of the slave trade, especially after the sixteenth century, was handled through highly organized systems, involving European trading firms and African kings. Each major European country that engaged in the trade had companies licensed by the crown (such as England's Royal African Company). These firms were granted a monopoly on the trade in slaves as well as other goods for particular areas of Africa. (Competition from the companies of other European powers, as well as from numerous privately owned ships, effectively prevented any company from exercising a monopoly for long, however.) On the African side, the trade was controlled largely by kings, in those areas where there were organized states, or by merchants, in areas where there were no strong states. Along the delta of the Niger, an area where centralized states had never developed, individual merchants formed trading companies, usually based on family and clan ties. These merchants, in essence, were kings of small territories. They maintained small armed forces, fleets of war canoes, and a complex system of agents.

The manner of the trade is well described in an account by Thomas Phillips, who traveled to Ouidah on a slave ship, the *Hannibal*, in 1693-94:

> This morning I went ashore at Whidaw, accompany'd by my doctor and purser, Mr. Clay, the present Capt. of the *East-India Merchant,* his doctor and purser, and about a dozen of our seamen for our guard, arm'd, in order here to reside till we could purchase 1,300 negro slaves, which was the number we both wanted, to compleat 700 for the *Hannibal,* and 650 for the *East-India Merchant,* according to our agreement in our charter-parties with the royal African company; in procuring which quantity of slaves we spent about nine weeks.
>
> As soon as the king understood of our landing, he sent two of his cappasheirs, or noblemen, to compliment us at our factory . . . to invite us there that night, saying he waited for us, and that all former captains used to attend him the first night: whereupon being unwilling to infringe the custom, or give his majesty any offense, we took our hammocks, and Mr. Peirson, myself, Cap't. Clay, our surgeons, pursers, and about 12 men, arm'd for our guard, were carried to the king's town, which contains about 50 houses. . . .
>
> According to promise we attended his majesty with samples of our goods, and made our agreement about the prices, tho' not without much difficulty; he and his cappasheirs exacted very high, but at length we concluded as per the latter end; then we had warehouses, a kitchen, and lodgings assign'd us, but none of our rooms had doors till we made them, and put on locks and keys; next day we paid our customs to the king and

cappasheirs, as will appear hereafter; then the bell was order'd to go about to give notice to all people to bring their slaves to the trunk to sell us. . . .

When we were at the trunk, the king's slaves, if he had any, were the first offr'd to sale, which the cappasheirs would be very urgent with us to buy, and would in a manner force us to it ere they would show us any other, saying they were the Reys Cosa [the term indicates the ancient Portuguese influence], and we must not refuse them, tho' as I observed they were generally the worst slaves in the trunk, and we paid more for them than any others, which we could not remedy, it being one of his majesty's prerogatives: then the cappasheirs each brought out his slaves according to his degree and quality, the greatest first, etc. and our surgeon examined them well in all kinds, to see that they were sound of wind and limb, making them jump, stretch out their arms swiftly, looking in their mouths to judge their age; for the cappasheirs are so cunning, that they shave them all close before we see them, so that let them be never so old we can see no grey hairs in their heads or beards; and then having liquor'd them well and sleek with palm oil, 'tis no easy matter to know an old one from a middle-age one, but by the teeths decay; but our greatest care is to buy none that are pox'd, lest they should infect the rest aboard. . . .

During the centuries of slave trading along the western African coast, until near the end of the eighteenth century, eastern Africa had been neglected except for a comparative trickle of slaves from Mozambique. North of Mozambique virtually no slaves were taken during this period (although there was an insignificant flow from the coastal trading cities to Arabia). During the second half of the eighteenth century, however, two events helped shift the slave trade toward eastern Africa. First, a number of European countries were beginning to question the moral and economic justifications for slavery, and the market in North America, the British Caribbean, and the Caribbean islands of France, Holland, and Denmark was declining. Some African kings were themselves beginning to question the validity of the trade. Second, the French were colonizing and planting sugarcane on the fertile Indian Ocean islands of Mauritius and Réunion; the Arabs were developing a new prosperity on Zanzibar and Pemba; and the Sakalava rulers of Madagascar were beginning to buy slaves as farmers and herders. French interests opened a new flow of slaves from Mozambique and the areas to the north, especially Tanzania; and Arab and Swahili organizers began to work with emerging African states in the interior (the Yao in southern Tanzania and Malawi and the Nyamwezi in central and western Tanzania) to develop a major network of roads leading down to the coast, especially to major slave markets in Kilwa and Zanzibar.

When the first flow of slaves from Mozambique to Mauritius and

Réunion began as an organized traffic, in 1735, it involved only three to four hundred slaves a year. It grew slowly and, as the sugar plantations began to expand to meet new demands in Europe and Asia, it swelled to more than 4,000 a year in the 1790's. In 1776, a French slaver named Jean-Vincent Morice signed a treaty with the sultan of Kilwa to purchase slaves there and at Zanzibar. These slaves were destined for the burgeoning labor demands of Mauritius, Réunion, and Madagascar, and a new supply of slaves to these places began at a rate of about 1,000 per year. By 1811, somewhere between 6,000 and 10,000 slaves each year passed through the booming slave market of Zanzibar, which was becoming the economic and political center for the entire Kenya-Tanzania coast. In 1818 cloves (which required considerable labor for clearing, planting, pruning, harvesting, etc.) were introduced into Pemba and Zanzibar, and a new, large market for slave labor opened there, under the ownership of both new Arab immigrants and ancient Swahili landowners. By 1839, the Zanzibar slave market was handling between 40,000 and 45,000 slaves a year, and customs records from Kilwa show that 97,203 slaves passed through that city's market between 1862 and 1867, for an average of more than 19,000 per year (although some of these were sent on to the market in Zanzibar for resale).

The destinations of slaves in both the Indian Ocean islands and the New World are better documented than their origins. The following table [1] summarizes the important figures for the Atlantic slave trade for its entire duration, from 1451 to 1870:

Area of Importation	Number of Slaves (1451-1870)
Brazil	3,646,800
British Caribbean	1,665,000
French Caribbean	1,571,900
Spanish America (Caribbean, Mexico, Central and South America)	1,552,000
Dutch Caribbean	500,000
British North America (U.S. and Canada)	427,300
Danish Caribbean	28,000
Old World (Europe, Atlantic islands)	175,000
Total number of slaves	9,566,000

These figures are surprising to most Americans, since it has long been assumed that the U.S. was one of the most important buyers of slaves, and the figures do not correlate well with modern populations of African-descended peoples in the Western Hemisphere. The reason for

[1] From *The Atlantic Slave Trade: A Census*, by Philip Curtin, Madison, University of Wisconsin Press, 1969.

this is found in the great differences in slave mortality rates in the New World, although why these differences were so great is not so well understood; in the United States slaves early achieved a low death rate and a high birth rate, and by the middle of the eighteenth century the number of slaves was increasing rapidly, independently of new imports. The Caribbean Islands, on the other hand, long showed higher death than birth rates. New imports of slaves were necessary right up to the nineteenth century so that the slave population could remain sufficient for the labor demands of the islands. Brazil, which bought more than one third of all the slaves shipped to the New World, was another area that long had high death rates and low birth rates, plus a constantly enlarging demand for slave labor as the enormous sugar and coffee plantations expanded.

Spain, whose American colonies were the chief market for slaves in the sixteenth and seventeenth centuries, imported comparatively few slaves considering the long period covered and the enormous area of the Spanish colonies. Cuba, which began to develop rapidly in the early nineteenth century, accounted for 702,000 slaves, nearly half of all slaves imported into Spanish America. The large number of fertile small islands in the Caribbean that were colonized by the British, Dutch, and French purchased well over three and a half million slaves, which, in view of the small land area of the islands, represents a massive use of slaves.

The Atlantic slave trade grew at a steadily increasing annual rate until about 1760, when it leveled off at its highest peak (varying from 50,000 to 65,000 slaves a year) for about fifty years. After 1810 it began to decline slowly until 1840, when it began to drop sharply. The Atlantic slave trade finally ended, except for a minor amount of smuggling, in about 1870. The causes for the leveling off at a high rate in the latter half of the eighteenth century are various: an equilibrium, requiring continuous imports but no increase in rates, was achieved in some of the Caribbean islands; in others, small natural population increases began to lower the number of slaves needed; and in still others (such as Cuba), new and increased demands helped balance the smaller numbers required in some of the British and Dutch islands.

The decline in the slave trade after 1800 was due primarily to a drop in demand in North America and the Caribbean islands of Britain, France, and Holland. By this time all these areas had a nearly stable or growing slave population, and needed fewer and fewer new slaves to meet labor needs. In the U.S. and the British islands, the efforts of the abolitionists resulted in the slave trade's being declared illegal after 1808, further reducing the slave trade to the New World.

Efforts to abolish the slave trade were widespread but took many years to become effective. By the mid-eighteenth century, as the slave trade was leveling off at its highest volume, a growing band of Christian clergymen, liberal politicians, ex-slaves (such as Equiano, whose *Travels,* quoted in this chapter, were used extensively as anti-slave trade propaganda), and intellectuals in Denmark, France, Britain, and the United States were agitating to have the trade abolished. Their work began to bear fruit very early in the nineteenth century. Denmark forbade any of its ships and merchants to deal in slaves, and its colonies to buy slaves, in 1805. The United States and Britain followed suit in 1808, although both countries had made it difficult for their nationals to transport slaves several years earlier. The United States was slower to enforce its ban on slave trading and importing because it was occupied with its internal affairs and the War of 1812, but Britain increasingly began to enforce its bans on its own nationals and to pressure other nations to follow suit.

By about 1825, there was little importation of slaves into the American areas controlled by Britain, France, Denmark, Holland, and the United States. But Portugal, Spain, and Brazil—an independent nation after 1822—continued to buy, transport, and sell slaves. Portuguese and Brazilian ships were the chief carriers of slaves by this time, and Portugal and Brazil had agreements with Britain that their trade south of the equator would be unmolested. (British warships, later joined by French and American vessels, were by this time patrolling the West African coast in an effort to stamp out the slave trade there.) North of the equator the slave trade was prohibited, although for many years Brazilian and Portuguese slavers continued to trade actively there, avoiding the thinly spread antislave patrols.

As a result of these developments during the first three decades of the nineteenth century, the slave trade along the West African coast declined fairly rapidly. In the great markets along the Nigerian coast, however, and in Dahomey, African kings were still eager for the trade (Brazilian tobacco was greatly in demand there) and the antislave patrols were hard pressed to cover the numerous trading points along the coast well enough to suppress the Brazilian and Portuguese traders. Conditions inside Nigeria were, at the same time, producing larger numbers of slaves than ever before: the Fulani jihad produced large numbers of refugees on the Nigerian plateau and in Yorubaland who were easy prey, and the political upheavals in Yorubaland added still others. Thus numerous trading towns along the Bights of Benin and Biafra, from modern Dahomey to the Cameroun, continued to engage in the trade until the 1850-60 period, when Britain finally mounted a major antislave offensive, occupying Lagos and using it as a naval base for antislave patrols.

The antislave efforts pushed the center of gravity of the slave trade farther south. The area between modern Cabinda and Luanda became the area of heaviest export. Increasing numbers of slaves from Mozambique and East Africa were diverted to the Atlantic trade, to satisfy the voracious demand in Brazil, Cuba, and Puerto Rico. Finally, however, both countries became increasingly diligent in preventing their nationals from buying, transporting, or importing slaves. By 1870 the Atlantic trade was dead.

In East Africa the trade still flourished, despite constant efforts by the British to persuade the sultan of Zanzibar to end it. But in 1873 the sultan signed an agreement with Britain prohibiting the trade, and it soon ended in eastern Africa, except for a minor smuggling effort that lingered on for a few more years.

In the four and a half centuries of the slave trade nearly ten million slaves were sold in the Atlantic trade, and perhaps another two million in the Indian Ocean trade. But the toll in African lives was far greater than even these staggering numbers indicate. The death rate across the Atlantic, under the inhuman conditions on the slave ships, averaged roughly 15 percent throughout the period of the trade. This means that some one and a half million Africans died in passage between Africa and the New World. No figures are available for the number who died on the African coasts while awaiting shipment, on the marches from where they were captured down to the coastal slave entrepôts, or in the battles and raids in which slaves were taken. (Accounts during the mid-nineteenth century by British observers in East Africa, including the famous Dr. David Livingstone, indicate that the death rate in capture and on the march to the coast was very high.) It is estimated that at least one African died before being sold at the coast for every one who was sold. Thus, some 25 million to 26 million Africans were killed or removed from Africa between 1451 and 1870, as a result of the slave trade on both sides of the continent.

What effect did this monstrous traffic in humanity have on Africa?

To a large extent there is no answer to this fundamental question. Too much time has elapsed, too little information is available, and too few studies have been carried out. Efforts to answer the question have usually concentrated on three areas: the effects of slavery on the population and demography of Africa, on African political and economic life, and on attitudes and morals in Africa or in the African-European relationship.

As to the first, too little is known of the demography of Africa during and before the slave trade to arrive at very meaningful conclusions. Only two areas, Angola and the Mozambique-Tanzania-Malawi region, show definite evidence of depopulation as a result of the slave trade.

West Africa, the area that produced the largest number of slaves between about 1700 and 1850 (the peak period for the trade), is today
one of the most densely populated regions on the continent. It is possible
that the slave trade served (as wars and plagues have often done in
other parts of the world) to prevent the population from increasing so
rapidly that it might have become too large for the land to support. In
other words, the slave trade may have served to control the rate of
population increase. Whatever the case, the only sure conclusion is that
West Africa is not, despite centuries of the slave trade and its ravages,
depopulated or even underpopulated.

To the extent that the slave trade, during its peak periods in various
areas, may have served to underpopulate Africa (setting aside Angola and
part of eastern Africa), the population apparently increased rapidly
enough afterward to compensate, at least in part. In general, therefore,
one may reasonably conclude that the slave trade did not serve to
produce drastic, long-term reductions in the African population,
except in two areas where it resulted in a significant population decrease
that had not until recently been reversed.

Clearly the effects of the slave trade, as well as trade for other
African products, on political and economic conditions in Africa were
more extensive than the demographic effects. Yet this also is an area that
has been inadequately studied. Many Europeans have maintained that
most of the prominent states of western Africa (Wolof, Asante, Dahomey, Oyo, Yoruba, Benin, Kongo, et al.) were at best rudimentary
before the slave trade but grew to power and prominence as they engaged in it. Historical analysis, however, has shown clearly that the
process of state formation and growth in Africa began long before contact of any kind with Europe and would certainly have continued had
there been neither European contact nor the slave trade.

Yet the trade with Europe in general, and the slave trade in particular, did have some importance for African political development. Only
one state, Dahomey, derived its wealth and power so largely from the
slave trade that it seems unlikely that it would have achieved its power
and prestige without it. The neighboring states of Asante and Benin,
which profited from it, would just as certainly *have* achieved their
greatness had there been no slave trade. Benin, in fact, was at the
height of its development before the slave trade began and refused to
participate in it until the late seventeenth century. The serious
debilitation of other great states, such as Kongo and Mwene Mutapa,
seems to have been partly due to their participation in the slave trade.

When future research reveals the precise effects of the slave trade
on each African society, including those that had no centralized political structure, it will undoubtedly show that poorly organized peoples

suffered more from it than those with strong central governments. The Ibo, as Equiano eloquently exemplifies, were easy prey for a long time, despite the fact that they were a highly developed people socially and culturally. They had no central political organization that would have allowed them to band together in mutual defense against the raiders and kidnappers. The neighboring Edo peoples of Benin were less likely to be enslaved because they had a powerful king and state structure. (As the case of Kongo illustrates, however, a strong central government did not always guarantee that a people would not suffer from the slave trade.)

The slave trade enhanced the development of those states that benefited from it largely by increasing the wealth available to the king of the state. By protecting and taxing the goods flowing through his kingdom, a king accumulated surplus wealth that allowed him to exhibit greater prestige, reward loyal supporters, support an army, and maintain the bureaucratic superstructure necessary to administer a large state or empire. Prior to European contact, it was the rulers of the Sudan who profited most from contol of trade systems. With the establishment of direct trading contact between Europe and the African peoples of the coasts and forest regions, the peoples of the forest were in position to control the trade system that developed. Gradually the wealth and power of forest region kings increased, while that of Sudanic region kings decreased, and the growth in the European trade plus the decline in the trans-Saharan trade was clearly important in this shift.

While slaves were not the only commodity African rulers near the coasts had to trade, they constituted an increasingly major addition to the available exports—gold, silver, ivory, spices, skins, gums, grains, wax, and other goods. In return for these goods, the rulers and their peoples received a large enough variety of European goods to support an economic base of great importance. The more goods, including slaves, that were produced in or channeled through his kingdom, the more imported goods a king and his people were able to acquire. With these imported goods a ruler could equip at least some of his soldiers with European weaponry. This gave him an enormous advantage over neighboring peoples who fought with traditional African weapons. And the spread of attractive foreign goods served as a powerful inducement to the ruler's followers and vassals to support him in wars of conquest, which usually increased the supply of African goods, including slaves.

It would be surprising if African rulers had ignored the fact that the slaves they could capture in war would add to their wealth and power. Dahomey, for example, must have waged wars in which the taking of captives for sale was an important objective, even though other objectives may have existed. Dahomey's power and prestige depended upon profits from the slave trade to a greater extent than that of almost any other West African state.

Looking backward from the mid-twentieth century, one cannot but feel that the most enduring, and the most pernicious, effect of the slave trade lay in the attitudes that Europeans developed about Africa and Africans, and the sense of deep, historic injury that modern Africans and "Africans of the diaspora" (as many Black Americans regard themselves) feel when they view the centuries of the trade and its aftermath.

European attitudes about Africans developed into a complex set of derogatory myths. Africa was depicted as a Dark Continent of jungles and dank, mysterious swamps, and Africans were thought of as savages with no history and no "culture." European ignorance of the African interior contributed to the myth of African inferiority, but the slave trade played the more active role in creating myths. Most Europeans were exposed to African slaves (when they had contact with Africans at all) rather than to Africans who were free men. And the whole situation of the uprooted, enslaved African made him appear in an unfavorable light.

But it was not always so. In the first century or two of European-African contact, the relationship between African and European was between equals. Even though Europeans' education and technology gave them an edge, they recognized the basic intelligence, skills, and wisdom of the Africans whom they visited. Even the haughty, acquisitive Portuguese reflected little, in their writings, of any view of Africans as innately inferior. Portuguese factors often took Africans as wives, and the Portuguese adapted themselves to dealing with African rulers and institutions. The sparse literature written by other Europeans (English, French, and Dutch) during the same period also reflects little of the basic racist views that were to become so widespread during the seventeenth century and later.

By the end of the seventeenth century more books about Africa began to appear. More often than not they were written by Europeans who had spent time in Africa, usually in the slave trade. One of the most widely read books, John Barbot's *Description of the Coasts of North and South Guinea,* illustrates the growing tendency to characterize Africans in an unfavorable light. In one section Barbot painted the people of the Gold Coast as "men of sense and wit enough, of a sharp, ready apprehension and skill in business," and the people of Senegambia as "genteel and courteous in their way, but leud and lazy to excess; . . . generally extremely sensual, knavish, revengeful, impudent, liars, impertinent, gluttonous, extravagant in their expressions and so intemperate that they drink brandy as though it were water."

In another section Barbot claimed that the more or less benign quality of the slave trade represented a means of delivering the average African from a miserable life in Africa:

> The king and chief Blacks of Acra [Accra, now capital of modern Ghana] were, in my time, very rich in slaves and gold, through the vast trade the natives drove with the Europeans on the coast, and the neighboring nations up the country. . . .
>
> There slaves are severely and barbarously treated by their masters, who subsist them poorly, and beat them inhumanely, as may be seen by the scabs and wounds on the bodies of many of them when sold to us. They scarce allow them the least rag to cover their nakedness, which they also take off from them when sold to Europeans; and they always go bare-headed. The wives and children of slaves, are also slaves to the master under whom they are married; and when dead, they never bury them, but cast out the bodies into some by place, to be devoured by birds, or beasts of prey.
>
> This barbarous usage of those unfortunate wretches, makes it appear, that the fate of such as are bought, and transported from the coast to America, or other parts of the world, by Europeans, is less deplorable than that of those who end their days in their native country; for aboard ships all possible care is taken to preserve and subsist them for the interest of the owners, and when sold to America, the same motive ought to prevail with their masters to use them well, that they may live the longer, and do them more service. Not to mention the inestimable advantage they may reap, of becoming Christians, and saving their souls, if they make a true use of their condition. . . .

Between 1700 and 1750, at a time when the slave trade was booming, the number of books about Africa increased; twenty English and seven French volumes are known to have been published during this period. Yet these works did little to enhance any true knowledge of Africa. It was during this period that the celebrated British intellectual Lord Chesterfield could state: "The Africans are the most ignorant and unpolished people in the world, little better than the lions, tigers, leopards, and other wild beasts, which that country produces in great numbers." And in 1782, in the second edition of his *New Universal Geographical Grammar,* the geographer Thomas Salmon devoted two of his book's 770 pages to Africa. He began with a frank admission of ignorance: "This immense territory is very little known; there is no traveler that has penetrated into the interior parts, so that we are ignorant not only of the bounds, but even of the names of several inland countries."

The fundamental philosophical dilemma that the slave trade created within a Europe that regarded itself as Christian and enlightened could only be relieved by evolving a view of Africans as something less than human. By the beginning of the nineteenth century this view had taken such deep root in the European mind that it defied challenge.

The slave trade eventually became both distasteful and unprofitable to Europe, especially to the growing industrial powers of northern Europe, and it was abolished. Yet the racist legacy of the slave trade could not be legislated out of existence. Perhaps, if a century of egalitarian and amicable relations between Africans and Europeans had followed the end of the slave trade and the abolition of slavery, racism might have begun to wither away under the weight of its own illogic and the growth of European knowledge of Africa's cultural values and achievements. This was not to be the case, however: at the very time that the abolitionist movement was growing strong enough to achieve its goals, a new European economic force, concomitant with the industrial revolution, began to see in Africa the possibility of further profit. This new force stimulated exploration of the interior, then seizure of the continent. The men who justified the second drive to derive profit from Africa recognized the unassailable logic of the abolitionists. Yet they soon created a new philosophical justification for exploitation. They proposed to open up Africa so that its peoples could be exposed to the enlightenment of Christianity and Western values, and could be taught skills and thus work to improve their material conditions. According to this rationalization it was presumed that Africans should be imbued with European democratic ideals so that they could eventually free themselves from the shackles of their own tyrannical political systems and leaders.

The implicit foundation of this entire argument, which appealed even to many abolitionists and freed Africans, was that Africans were inferior to Europeans. The one major difference from the older views of the slavery era was that Africans were potentially educable. But, during the nineteenth and early twentieth century, the underlying racist view of African inferiority received major reinforcement from the new view. Thus the great evil legacy of the slave trade was nourished and kept alive, albeit in slightly different guise, for another century and a half after the abolition of slavery itself.

14 Exploration, Exploitation, and Conquest

As the nineteenth century began, European manufacturers, newly created by the industrial revolution, needed mounting supplies of raw materials: cotton, wool, lumber, skins, coal, ores, and vegetable oils. Their expanding factories also needed mass markets for the cloth, woolens, tools, soaps, dishes, glassware, pots, pans, guns, and hundreds of other items that poured out in ever increasing quantities.

There was no sharp break in Europe or in Africa between the end of the first period of European-African trade contact and the beginning of the second. For decades after abolition, there was much sentiment in Europe (and in Africa) that the slave trade should be revived, and smugglers from England, France, the United States, and other countries continued to engage in it until the risks far outweighed the profits. And long before Europe began to raise serious questions about the interior of Africa and the possible profits to be found in trade there, prophetic voices were heard. Malachi Postlethwayt, one of the most prominent writers on economics in eighteenth century England, and no enemy of the slave trade, paid tribute to the fundamental economic importance of Africa in one of his numerous pamphlets:

> Are we not indebted to those valuable People, the Africans, for our Sugars, Tobaccoes, Rice, Rum, and all other Plantation Produce? And the greater the Number of Negroes imported into our Colonies, from Africa, will not the Exportation of British Manufactures among the Africans be in Proportion; they being paid for in such Commodities only? . . . May we not say therefore . . . that the general Navigation of Great Britain

owes all its Encrease and Splendor to the Commerce of its American and African Colonies?

In the next year, 1745, Postlethwayt followed up this recognition with an argument that was prophetic, though a century later it would become commonplace:

> If the trade to the Spanish Indies and the Brazils is so inviting, it is equally certain that the Inland Trade, duely extended upon the Continent of Africa . . . may be rendered little inferior to either, if not equal to the united Advantages of them both. The Continent of Africa is of great extent, the Country extremely populous, and this Commerce, by Reasons of its Discouragements hitherto, but yet in its Infancy.

A few years later, in 1758, he carried this argument a step further:

> If we could so exert our commercial policy among these people, as to bring a few hundred thousand of them to cloath with our commodities, and to erect buildings to deck with our furniture, and to live something on the European way, would not such traffic prove far more lucrative than the slave-trade only?

Finally, in 1759, Postlethwayt reached the conclusion that was to become European policy at the end of the nineteenth century and early in the twentieth:

> Were this country planted by the Europeans in colonies and settled habitations, towns and cities built, and people brought out to inhabit as in the American plantations, something like what the Portuguese have already done in Africa, the whole commerce of this part of the world might, in all probability, be considerably more extended among those people than it ever has been.

But Europe was not ready for Postlethwayt's urgings. Ignorance and myth dominated European thinking about Africa (except for the Portuguese, who were by this time a weak and impotent power, unable to exploit the vast African territories they claimed, except for a few settlements in coastal Angola and around the Zambezi and a few coastal islands in Mozambique). Few Europeans were prepared to devote time, money, and manpower to test Postlethwayt's thesis.

Over the fifty years that followed, however, events in England were to make Postlethwayt's arguments more attractive. England was in the forefront of the industrial revolution, and was the first country to sense a massive need for new sources of raw materials and new markets for its flood of products. The English abolitionist movement, more powerful than similar movements in other countries, tended to go beyond advocating the end of slavery. Some abolitionists felt they had a responsibility to make amends, largely by introducing Christianity and Western civilization into Africa. It was thought that such a course would bring Africa's peoples into intercourse with the rest of the world on a more egalitarian basis. In addition, England's intellectual community was growing more curious about the flora, fauna, geography, and customs of the entire world. In short, England, in the late eighteenth century, was peculiarly ripe for a new age of adventure and exploration.

In 1756, the great Seven Years' War broke out and Britain fought a far-flung naval and colonial war with France in the Atlantic and Indian oceans, in North America and the Caribbean, in India, and on the African coasts. With Prussia, Britain also faced an alliance of France, Austria, Russia, and the Germanic states on the European continent. When the war ended in 1763, Britain emerged with a national feeling of destiny and energy that many historians have compared with that of the Elizabethan era. In 1768, Captain James Cook embarked on a series of voyages that were to expand British, and European, knowledge of the Pacific Ocean. This voyage helped to whet British appetite for further explorations in unknown parts of the world.

James Bruce, the famous British explorer, came to manhood during this period of British curiosity about the world. Born in 1730, the eldest son of a Scottish gentleman, Bruce received a good education, but became disenchanted with the rigors of schooling while studying law at Edinburgh University. He left school and devoted himself to country life for several years, becoming especially skilled at riding, hunting, and shooting. Marrying the daughter of a London wine merchant, Bruce then entered the business world; but he left business after the death of his wife and began to devote himself to study of languages and drawing. By this time, Bruce was thinking seriously of becoming a full-time traveler with an interest in science. In 1759, after traveling for a few years around Europe, Bruce reentered business as a partner in an ironworks. He made a considerable success of the venture, and within two years had a substantial independent income. At age thirty Bruce was financially well off, possessed of a wide knowledge of languages and foreign customs, and still obsessed with the desire to travel and learn. (Years later, in the dedication of his great book *Travels to Discover the Source of the Nile,* Bruce characterized the climate of the times which had so captured his imagination: "It was a golden age, which united humanity and science, exempted men of liberal minds and education, employed in the noblest of all occupations, that of exploring the distant parts of the globe, from being any longer degraded, and rated as little better than the Buccaneer or pirate, because they had, till then, in manners been nearly similar.")

Bruce's friend Lord Halifax, a secretary of state at the time, suggested that Bruce go to North Africa as British consul in Algiers. Lord

Halifax promised Bruce that he could appoint a vice-consul, then take leave to explore the ancient ruins of North Africa. Halifax even suggested that Bruce might become interested in solving one of the most famous of all European riddles, locating the source of the Nile.

Bruce was appointed consul at Algiers in 1762. He was able to do a certain amount of traveling, but never with the freedom that Halifax had promised. Bruce's strong views and independent personality earned him many enemies among British interests in Algeria, and his appointment was terminated in 1765. Then, at age thirty-five, he began the explorations that were to mark him as one of the greatest explorers in British history and as the first modern European to penetrate the African interior. Bruce's wealth was sufficient to finance his journeys. He was physically robust, standing six and a half feet tall, with red hair and a lordly bearing, and his varied experiences had provided him with an unusually wide range of skills: riding, shooting, fencing, drawing, medicine, science, languages, geology, and cartography. His interest in Islam and his residence in North Africa had given him an intensive knowledge of Islamic customs and language; he wore Arab dress and posed as a Muslim scholar, without which he might never have made it through the numerous hostile Muslim societies that encircled Ethiopia.

After wandering through a number of countries around the eastern Mediterranean between 1765 and 1768, Bruce arrived in Egypt and began to plan a visit to Ethiopia. He established contacts with many powerful peoples, including the Patriarch of Alexandria (who was spiritually the acknowledged head of the Ethiopian Church) and Ali, the Mamluk bey of Cairo, who provided him with letters of introduction to various Muslim monarchs and officials. Posing as an Arab mystic scholar and armed with these powerful letters, Bruce set forth in 1769 from Cairo down the Red Sea to Jidda, then across the sea to Massawa, the chief port on the African side of the sea. With numerous halts and sometimes hazardous encounters (despite his letters of protection), he arrived in Gondar, Ethiopia's capital, in February 1770. There Bruce presented his credentials from the Patriarch of Alexandria and shed his Arab guise. Bruce remained in Ethiopia for nearly three years, under the protection of Tecla Haimanot, the young king, and Ras Michael, the "duke" of Tigre province and the most powerful man in Ethiopia.

In 1773 Bruce returned to Great Britain after an absence of nearly ten years. In London, his accounts were eagerly received, but his tendency to be outspoken and overbearing had grown, and soon he had more critics than supporters. Gradually his attractiveness to the London social-intellectual elite began to wane. Finally, Bruce retired to Scotland, remarried, and for ten years was little heard from. Then his second wife died, and he began to write his great work, which was published in 1790. His *Travels* were soon, as Lord Sheffield wrote to his friend Edward Gibbon, ". . . to be found on every table."

Bruce solved few geographical problems for Europe: his contention that he had discovered the source of the Nile was incorrect (he visited the source of the Blue Nile, but he gathered no information on the more important White Nile). Besides, Portuguese Jesuits had visited the same spots 150 years earlier. But Bruce did bring to the attention of literate Europe, with sensitive understanding, the drama of life in a remote Christian kingdom virtually unknown to the most learned Europeans. He made many authentic drawings of plants, birds, and animals, kept comprehensive notes of language and culture, and recorded exact cartographic details. And his accounts of court life, intrigues, military campaigns, relations between church and state, and the culture of medieval Ethiopia gave Europe a sense of Africa that no previous writer had ever achieved.

Bruce's personal appearances in London, in 1773-74, came at a time when Britain was stirring with interest in exploration. His book, however, stimulated more interest and had a more decisive impact. During the seventeenth years between Bruce's return and the publishing of his book other events had turned Europe's attention increasingly toward Africa. During the 1780's Olaudah Equiano's autobiography had appeared and in the same decade, two other books by freed African slaves, Ottobah Cugoano, a Fante, and Ignatius Sancho, born on a slave ship and brought to England when he was two, were published. These three books, written in respectable English by Africans who obviously had keen minds, were instant publishing successes. Equiano's book went through eight editions in five years, and its subscription list was headed by a royal duke. Sancho's book (which contained two plays, several poems, a work on the theory of music, and letters between himself and such friends as the brilliant actor David Garrick) was said to have had the longest subscription list of any publication since the first issue of the *Spectator* fifty years earlier.

Joseph Jekyll, a member of parliament and prominent social figure in London, collected Sancho's works and published them, with an anonymous introduction, shortly after Sancho died in 1780. The growing enlightenment about Africans (which unfortunately was never great enough to wipe away the discreditable myths) was well stated in Jekyll's introduction:

> He who could penetrate the interior of Africa, might not improbably discover negro arts and polity, which could bear little analogy to the ignorance and grossness of slaves in the sugar-islands, expatriated in infancy, and brutalized under the whip and the task-master. And he who surveys

the extent of intellect to which Ignatius Sancho has attained by self-education, will perhaps conclude that the perfection of the reasoning faculties does not depend on a peculiar conformation of the skull or the colour of a common integument.

These three books by Africans, virtually forgotten until recent years, played an important role in stimulating growing British curiosity about Africa. They also paved the way for the impact of Bruce's book, which followed them into print by only a few years.

In 1788, the African Association, which was to stimulate and sponsor much of the energetic British exploration of Africa that Bruce had pioneered, was formally chartered. Although Bruce himself played no direct role in its formation, his accounts influenced many of the men who flocked to the Association to offer their service in the exploration of the African interior.

The African Association—or, more formally, the Association for Promoting the Discovery of the Interior Parts of Africa—was active from 1788 to 1815, and its greatest achievements came in its first fourteen years. Formed by twelve wealthy men, eight of whom were members of parliament and all of whom had liberal yet practical minds, the Association launched a series of explorations into western Africa that gave Europe its first real knowledge of that hitherto mysterious region. During its first decade, the Association launched or attempted to launch nine significant journeys of discovery, several of them abortive and most ultimately fatal to the explorers who led them. But these explorations added significantly to Europe's knowledge of Africa's interior, especially of the Saharan and Sudan regions, and they helped to stimulate wider interest in Africa among British intellectuals and political leaders, and among the wealthy manufacturing and commercial circles.

The visit by Mungo Park to the Niger, and his subsequent book, *Travels in the Interior Districts of Africa*, represent the Association's crowning achievement. Ironically, the dramatic feature of Park's success was his discovery that the great Niger River flowed eastward—a fact known to millions of Sudanic Africans, and presumably to numerous Arab and Berber traders who had visited the Niger region for over a millennium. But prior to Park's journey, Europe knew only that the great river flowed somewhere in Africa's interior.

The chief value of Park's journey, however, was his book, which was comparable to Bruce's in some respects. It was unusually well written, detailed in many sections, authentic and objective, and replete with information about a vast area that had hitherto been the subject of wild and ignorant speculation in Europe.

From today's perspective, Park's contribution lies in his references

Africa about 1800: Major Power Centers

to a group of powerful kingdoms clustered around the headwaters of the Senegal, the Gambia, and the Niger: Bondou, Bambuk, Galam, Kasson, Kaarta, and Bambara (Segu). These were the states, inhabited mainly by Mande-speaking peoples, that had inherited the mantle of Ghana and Mali, after the decline of these great empires. Kaarta and Segu, both kingdoms of Bambara peoples, were perhaps the strongest. They were often at war with each other as well as with other neighbors, and each struggled to gain control of territory and trade routes upon which empires in the Sudan had traditionally been built. Just as Bruce visited Ethiopia at a period of internal disunity, Park visited the Sudan at a time of struggle between states. His accounts of the perils he encountered, especially when attempting to move from one state to another, vividly portray the breakdown of the long-distance security system that the Sudanic empires had achieved. His contacts with kind and understanding people, both noble and commoner, highlight the hospitable and generous characteristics of the African peoples of the Sudan. As Park himself noted, after witnessing the reunion of one of his companions, an African blacksmith, with his blind, aged mother, "From this interview I was fully convinced that whatever difference there is between the Negro and the European in the conformation of the nose and the colour of the skin, there is none in the genuine sympathies and characteristics of our common nature."

Sensitively bearing out Park's recognition of the commonality between Africans and Europeans was his moving account of the kind treatment he received, at the lowest ebb of his fortunes, from an aged Fulani woman. For several months he had been detained in the Berber state of Ludamar, north of the kingdom of Bambara. Robbed of his goods, virtually starved, and kept under threat of torture and death, Park finally escaped and made his way southward toward Bambara. A few days before he reached the borders of Bambara, he met his benefactress in a small Fulani village:

> About sunset, however, . . . a woman, returning from the labours of the field, stopped to observe me, and perceiving that I was weary and dejected, inquired into my situation, which I briefly explained to her; whereupon, with looks of great compassion, she took up my bridle and saddle, and told me to follow her. Having conducted me into her hut, she lighted up a lamp, spread a mat on the floor, and told me I might remain there for the night. Finding that I was very hungry, she said that she would procure me something to eat. She accordingly went out, and returned in a short time with a very fine fish; which, having caused to be half broiled upon some embers, she gave me for supper. The rites of hospitality being thus performed towards a stranger in distress, my worthy benefactress (pointing to the mat, and telling me I might sleep there

without apprehension) called to the female part of her family, who had stood gazing on me all the while in fixed astonishment, to resume their task of spinning cotton; in which they continued to employ themselves a great part of the night. They lightened their labour by songs, one of which was composed extempore; for I was myself the subject of it. It was sung by one of the young women, the rest joining in . . . chorus. The air was sweet and plaintive, and the words, literally translated, were these.—"The winds roared, and the rains fell.—the poor white man, faint and weary, came and sat under our tree.—He has no mother to bring him milk; no wife to grind his corn. Chorus: Let us pity the white man; no mother has he, etc., etc." Trifling as this recital may appear to the reader, to a person in my situation the circumstance was affecting in the highest degree. I was oppressed by such unexpected kindness; and sleep fled from my eyes. In the morning I presented my compassionate landlady with two of the four brass buttons which remained on my waistcoat; the only recompense I could make her.

Just as these—and many other—passages in Park's book ought to have given Europe a truer view of the African character, his descriptions of African towns, commerce, and politics ought to have counteracted the growing European belief that the interior of Africa was a vast, undifferentiated land of savages. Typical of his accounts is his sketch of Segu, capital of the main Bambara state:

> Sego, the capital of Bambarra, at which I had now arrived, consists, properly speaking, of four distinct towns; two on the northern bank of the Niger, called Sego Korro and Sego Boo; and two on the southern bank, called Sego Soo Korro and Sego See Korro. They are all surrounded by high mud-walls; the houses are built of clay, of a square form, with flat roofs; some of them have two stories, and many of them are whitewashed. Besides these buildings, Moorish mosques are seen in every quarter; and the streets, though narrow, are broad enough for every useful purpose, in a country where wheel carriages are entirely unknown. From the best enquiries I could make, I have reason to believe that Sego contains altogether about 30,000 inhabitants. . . . The view of this extensive city; the numerous canoes upon the river; the crowded population, and the cultivated state of the surrounding country, formed altogether a prospect of civilization and magnificence, which I little expected to find in the bosom of Africa.

Yet Mungo Park's accounts, even when supplemented by those of fellow explorers sent to the African interior by the African Association, and later by the British government and various private and governmental agencies in France, Holland, Germany, Sweden, and Denmark failed to shake the deeply imbedded European myth of African inferiority and savagery. The simple fact that many of the explorers died, from diseases, accidents, or murder by brigands, seemed to carry more weight in supporting the myth of Africa's inhospitality than the more sanguine statements in the written accounts of many explorers. Park himself was killed on a second journey, in 1805, when he and his party were set upon by warriors. As the expedition's boat passed over rapids at a narrow point in the Niger River, Park and one of his companions, according to an African member of the expedition who escaped and later told his story to the British on the coast, jumped into the river and drowned.

Just as Park's accounts, widely circulated in England and very influential (his book is still in print), were counterbalanced by his tragic death at African hands, so the disappearance of Frederick Hornemann, a young German explorer sent to Africa by the African Association seemed to argue more forcefully against Africa than Hornemann's own letters argued for it. In a letter he sent back to the Association from the Fezzan (in southern Libya), capital of Marzuk, he noted that "we have a very unjust idea of these people, not only with respect to their culture and natural ability, but also of their strength and the extent of their possessions."

The difficulties that beset Park, Hornemann, and other explorers, often at the hands of hostile Africans, together with reports of possible riches in trade and agricultural production, sharply changed British interest in Africa. Within ten or fifteen years, the earlier emphasis on exploration for the sake of science and on contact with the interior for the possible benefit of Africa, was changing to a harder, more avaricious interest in penetrating the interior and exploiting its commercial possibilities. No less a person than Sir Joseph Banks, whose name came to symbolize the exploration of Africa, was a spokesman for the new point of view. In 1799, following Mungo Park's return, Banks declared: "We have already, by Mr. Park's means opened a Gate into the Interior of Africa into which it is easy for every nation to enter and to extend its Commerce and Discovery from the West to the Eastern side of that immense continent."

Sir Joseph suggested that the few hundred miles between the upper Gambia and the Niger was the logical route by which to divert the trans-Saharan trade down to the Atlantic (and into the ships of eager British merchants). He also claimed that five hundred well-chosen troops, two hundred of them armed with field guns, could overcome "the whole Forces which Africa could bring against them." The members of the Association thereupon resolved formally that Britain should strive to "take possession of the banks of the Joliba [Niger]."

Banks at once informed the president of the British Board of Trade of the resolution, suggesting that it be brought to the attention of the Cabinet. First, Banks proposed, the British government should "secure to the British throne, either by conquest or by Treaty the whole of the Coast of Africa from Arguin to Sierra Leone; or at least to procure the cession of the River Senegal [France's traditional sphere of influence and trade] as that River will always afford an easy passage to any rival nation who means to molest the Countries on the banks of the Joliba [the Niger]." If this were accomplished, Banks suggested, there would be "little doubt that in a very few years a trading Company might be established under immediate control of the Government, who would take upon themselves the whole expense of the measure, would govern the Negroes far more mildly and make them far more happy than they are now under the tyranny of their arbitrary princes, would become popular at home by converting them to the Christian Religion by inculcating in their rough minds the mild morality which is engrafted on the tenets of our faith and by effecting the greatest practicable diminution of the Slavery of Mankind, upon the principles of natural justice and commercial benefit."

During this period, when the roots of modern imperialism in Africa were forming, Britain and France were engaged in a series of wars. France, under Napoleon Bonaparte, had lost much of its naval strength of earlier years. Although still interested in Africa, France's attentions were focused on continental struggles, internal affairs, and the Mediterranean. (It was at this time that Napoleon invaded Egypt and ruled it for three years, presaging later European moves to acquire and rule African territory.) French explorers were few and concentrated on northern Africa and the Senegal River area. Even this interest, however, suffered during the Anglo-French wars, when Britain blockaded French posts along the Senegambia coast and even seized the important French bases at Gorée (near modern Dakar) and St. Louis in Senegal, holding the latter until 1817 before returning it to France.

The difficulties that impeded French exploration and development in Africa did not cause France to lose sight of Africa completely. In 1802, Napoleon issued instructions to the governor at St. Louis, F. Blanchot, which, though they could not be fulfilled, indicated the sweeping ambitions of Bonaparte's policies:

"Up to now Senegal has been regarded only as a factory limited to exploiting certain branches of trade native to the country. Citizen Blanchot will lift his thoughts above such narrow bounds. The power of the metropolis of France grows daily under the hands that govern it; it is necessary for the colonies to feel the same dynamic. It is not enough for Senegal to exist as a mere stake for the republic in the rich territories of Africa; it must serve as a growing point, making use of every possible form of contact. . . ." The governor was also ordered to build "every sort of practicable relationship between the Senegal and the interior of Africa."

Almost as soon as these instructions were issued, France became reengaged in European tensions: Napoleon assumed the title of emperor in 1804, and in 1808 a major continental war began, with England and France again on opposite sides. The grand design of linking Senegal with the interior languished, until the appointment of Louis Faidherbe as governor in 1854.

One great French explorer of Black Africa did emerge, however, in the 1820's: René Caillié. Born in 1799, Caillié was inspired during his youth by the accounts of the great English explorers, especially Bruce and Park. By 1820 he had already traveled twice to Senegal; in 1824 he began to study Arabic and Islam, very much as Bruce had done fifty years earlier, and in 1827 he set out from the British colony of Sierra Leone, disguised as an Egyptian, to reach Timbuktu, an objective he accomplished after a journey of a year (including five months of illness). Caillié was the first modern European to visit Timbuktu, long the most famous city of interior Africa. He received high honors and a large cash prize from the Geographical Society of Paris for his feat. After reaching Timbuktu, Caillié traveled across the Sahara, following the ancient caravan route that connected ancient Ghana and Mali with Morocco. He finished his journey in Fez.

Caillié made his exploration at a time when a new wave of British exploration was beginning. Britain's position as the world's greatest naval power gave her the means to keep up the pace of exploration in order to exploit possible riches before France or other powers could do so. The Sierra Leone Company, founded to establish a home for freed slaves on the West African coast, received fairly consistent British encouragement on any ideas it originated leading to expansion into the interior. Sierra Leone served as a staging point for several expeditions (including Caillié's) and as a center of information about conditions in the interior.

In 1808, the British government undertook formal responsibility for Sierra Leone, which became a crown colony. This committed the British to an African role that was quite different from subsidizing the great trading companies or encouraging societies such as the African Association.

The African Association itself began to wane at about this time, partly because some of its most active members were growing old and few new members joined to replace them. Much attention was being paid to the movement to abolish and suppress the slave trade, and some wealthy liberals who might have supported the Association were now drawn more into the antislavery movement. But the British government itself had begun to appreciate the potential values of exploration, and it began financing small expeditions to take up where the Association had left off. Dr. Walter Oudney, in 1820, was dispatched to North Africa to investigate routes across the Sahara. In 1822 Dr. Oudney (who had by this time been joined by Captain Hugh Clapperton, a Scottish naval officer, and by Major Dixon Denham) departed from Tripoli and crossed the Sahara to Lake Chad. Oudney, Clapperton, and Denham were the first Europeans known to have seen Lake Chad.

Oudney died soon after leaving Lake Chad, but Clapperton continued on to become the first European to visit Kano and Sokoto. In Sokoto he was received by Sultan Bello, the great son of Usman dan Fodio. When Bello refused to allow him to travel south to the Niger, Clapperton returned to Lake Chad, rejoined Denham, and together they returned across the Sahara to Tripoli.

As soon as Clapperton reached England he was asked to undertake another expedition, this time to explore a route from the sea northward to Hausaland from the Lagos-Badagry area and to negotiate a formal diplomatic relationship with Sultan Bello. Accompanied by Richard Landers (who acted as Clapperton's servant, later becoming an even more celebrated explorer than Clapperton) and three other English companions, Clapperton left Badagry early in 1825. Within a few days, two of the Englishmen died, a third split off to follow an independent route through Dahomey, and Clapperton and Landers continued on to Kano. There Clapperton left Landers while he proceeded to Sokoto in search of Sultan Bello, whom he soon learned was away from the capital on a military campaign. Clapperton eventually found Bello, who was so preoccupied with the war that he was uninterested in a treaty with England. To a powerful ruler of Bello's stripe, England seemed a far-away and shadowy place. Clapperton died on this expedition, but Landers finished the trip and wrote a highly acclaimed account of their adventures in Hausaland.

Landers, despite his humble status, then persuaded the British government to finance a new expedition on which he proposed to verify the theory that the Niger flowed into the sea in the region of the Bight of Biafra. In 1830, Landers left England for Badagry. He made his way to Hausaland with his younger brother, John. After traveling down the Niger in canoes, the Landers brothers eventually reached the trading town of Brass, at the Niger delta.

Richard Landers' successful expeditions marked the end of the first phase of western African exploration by Europeans. Between 1832 and 1860, both the British government and several private companies (a number of which in 1879 united to form what was later renamed the

Royal Niger Company) sent several expeditions up the Niger. These expeditions established consulates and trade stations, experimented with steamer navigation, and gradually laid the foundation for British hegemony over the whole lower Niger from Hausaland to the sea. (At this period, Hausaland was the richest country in Sudanic Africa, overshadowing the formerly great cities of Timbuktu, Jenne, and Gao.)

With Britain energetically exploring and beginning to exploit the lower Niger, France began to seek a similar role up the Senegal toward the upper Niger. Eventually, France controlled the upper and middle Niger and Britain controlled the lower Niger, including Hausaland. By this same time, around 1850-60, Britain had begun to formalize and deepen its control of the territory around the mouth of the Gambia River, Sierra Leone, the Gold Coast, and the Lagos region. Dahomey, still active in the slave trade with Brazil, refused to accept any power as supreme along its coast, so that Britain, France, Germany, Brazil, Portugal, and several other countries continued to trade there (though most traded for copra and coconuts, rather than slaves). But western Africa, from the Sahara and the Sudan down to the sea, was known at least roughly to Europe, and European trading stations were proliferating along the three great rivers—the Senegal, Gambia, and Niger—as well as along the coast.

In the interior of West Africa, during this part of the nineteenth century, there was considerable political activity among the Sudanic societies of the region. The principle force in this political activity was a widespread tendency toward religious and political reform among the Muslim communities. These reform movements resulted in attempts to create a number of new empires based on strict Islamic law and principles of administration. The great jihad led by Usman dan Fodio in Nigeria was the most successful and permanent of these movements, but similar efforts were undertaken in the central and western Sudan as well.

At the beginning of the nineteenth century, the western and central Sudan was broken up into a number of states, most small, but some fairly large. These states were ruled by kings of various Mande, Atlantic, and Voltaic ethnic groups. Perhaps the most powerful was the Bambara state ruled from Segu, which Mungo Park had visited. Islam was widely spread, although still more concentrated in the towns than in the countryside. Still, many states with a number of Muslim inhabitants were ruled by non-Muslim kings. To the more devout Muslims, the subordination of Islam in many states to native African religions was a source of dissatisfaction. In the Islamic world at large, once the center of world power and civilization, Islam seemed to be suffering repeated setbacks at the hands of Christian or pagan forces.

Throughout the Islamic world there were tendencies toward reform movements designed to aid the devout in carrying out the fundamental charge of the Koran: to spread the faith, by force of arms where necessary, into the lands of nonbelievers. Muslim brotherhoods were attracting increased support. One such spiritual brotherhood, the Qadiriyya, which dated back to the twelfth century, when it was founded by Abd al-Qadir, a saint of Baghdad, had attracted many devout Fulani, including the great Usman dan Fodio.

The Qadiriyya brotherhood was widespread in the central and western Sudan, but it was not alone. Many devout men were attracted to a new movement, the Tijaniyya, founded by Ahmad al-Tijani in Arabia late in the eighteenth century. More mystic and exclusive than other Muslim brotherhoods, the Tijaniyya preached the need to establish Islamic control of political units wherever possible. It held that the adherents of the Tijaniyya were superior in faith to all other brotherhoods, although it collaborated with others when its interests were furthered by cooperation.

The jihads of the Sudan were powerfully affected by the success of dan Fodio's movement in Hausaland. One of his followers, Seku Ahmadu, a Fulani from the state of Masina in the western Sudan, raised an army and proclaimed a jihad to free Masina from the rule of Muslims who collaborated with pagans. Dan Fodio sent Ahmadu a flag that sanctified the jihad, and, in 1818, Ahmadu's forces began their war of holy conquest. Between that time and 1844, when Ahmadu died, he established a small Islamic empire that stretched from Jenne to Timbuktu.

Seku Ahmadu's small empire, of which Masina was only a small part, was soon absorbed into a larger empire. This larger empire resulted from a new jihad launched by Al-Hajj Umar, a Tukulor from Futa Toro who had joined the Tijaniyya brotherhood while on a pilgrimage to Mecca. For several years after returning to Africa Umar resided in Hausaland, where he fought alongside Sultan Bello in several campaigns. He married one of Bello's daughters and accumulated a large number of slaves. Though a Tijaniyya, Umar respected the Qadiriyya leadership and the precepts of the dan Fodio movement, but when he returned to his own country, in 1839, he was deeply hostile to the collaboration he found between Seku Ahmadu's descendants and various powerful non-Muslim kings in the central and western Sudan. Resolving to renew the jihad, he settled in Futa Jallon, where he began training a growing cadre of disciples in his faith, and purchasing firearms along the Atlantic coast in return for slaves and other products.

In 1848 Umar and his disciples undertook a *hijra*, or holy emigration, from Futa Jallon to Dinguiray, a small kingdom near Futa Toro. There he continued to build up strength until he felt conditions were ripe for his jihad. In 1862, after forty days of meditation, Umar received the call and launched the offensive, first against Futa Toro, his own land. He was repulsed, although many of his Tukulor kinsmen flocked to his support, swelling his army as he retreated. Umar's strength grew, and he went on to capture a number of towns and small kingdoms in the western Sudan, finally capturing Segu and Masina. By this time, however, a new element had entered Sudanic affairs: the French forces of Governor Faidherbe. Umar's troops fought several battles against the French, whose firearms (including some small field guns) were superior. A stalemate resulted and Umar's advance down the Senegal and into Futa Toro became impossible. Faidherbe's advance farther up the Senegal into Umar's loosely knit empire was also checked.

Umar's armies, during more than twenty years of campaigning, captured many of the great cities of the western and central Sudan: Masina, Jenne, Timbuktu, Kaarta, Segu. For a brief period, Umar thus ruled an empire that began to approximate Mali and Songhai in extent, though it never reached the size of these earlier empires. But French pressures on the west, continuing opposition from both Muslim and non-Muslim chiefs and warlords within his own conquest area, and the lack of peaceful access to great markets all helped to render his empire unstable and short-lived. By 1878, the French again began to advance into his territory, and the rising power of Malinke kingdoms threatened from the south. Soon Umar's empire crumbled, and with it went the reformist zeal of the Islamic jihadists in the western and central Sudan.

One other great African imperial effort was made in the western Sudan before the area was finally conquered by the French. But this final effort, the campaign of Samori Touré, a Soninke trader and professional soldier, who built a substantial empire in the country around the headwaters of the Niger and the adjacent forest regions of Guinea and Sierra Leone, was not primarily religious in inspiration. Between 1860 and 1870, Samori seized control of the small kingdom of Kumadugu, and established his capital at Bissandugu, its chief town. (Samori was a Muslim, and in 1874 he took the title of Al-mami, or political-religious leader. But Islam seems not to have played a major role in the development of his ideas or methods.)

Operating from Bissandugu, Samori systematically captured control of surrounding chiefdoms. He organized a system of administration in which twenty or so villages were grouped into a district. (Eventually there were 162 districts.) Districts were grouped into ten provinces, each of which was under the control of a governor who was a relative or close supporter of Samori. At both district and provincial levels, Samori provided armed support for the chiefs. He made sure, however, that the burden of taxation was sufficiently light that people would not be alienated.

Samori maintained a personal guard of five hundred well-trained troops, armed with repeating rifles (purchased from the British in Sierra Leone) and wearing uniforms consisting of cap, tunic, and yellow trousers. But each of the ten provinces had a professional cadre, together with a national system of required military service, in which each village was required to supply one soldier for every ten men in the village. These reserves devoted at least half the year to farming, except in time of national emergency. Each year, even in times of peace, the reserves went forth to extend the territory of the empire by conquest.

Recognizing that his troops were no match for French soldiers who were armed with cannon and machine guns, Samori relied heavily on his own version of guerrilla warfare, avoiding stands in fortified positions. His army was divided into three groups. One group, armed with rapid-fire rifles, was charged with defense and fighting the French. A second group, armed with older guns, was responsible for internal security, guarding the civilian population, and for evacuation when necessary. The third unit, armed like the second, was used for extending territory in wars of conquest. Since most of the territory seized was to the east, and the French were on the west, Samori's main government and army continually shifted to the east when pressed too hard by the French. The French, after meeting resistance from Samori's elusive and fast-moving first corps, would enter his territory only to find it evacuated.

Samori had a good sense of diplomacy, and occasionally communicated with the British in Sierra Leone and the French along the Senegal, discussing the possibilities of peace with the French or alliance with the British. Gradually, however, he lost more territory to the French (although he gained additional lands at the expense of Umar's empire), and his efforts at diplomacy merely staved off his ultimate defeat. Ironically, a diplomatic effort led to Samori's downfall. In 1898, while negotiating with the French, he was captured by a party of French riflemen whom his guards had mistaken for negotiators. Samori was then exiled to an island off the coast of Gabon, where he died in 1900.

During the nineteenth century European involvement along the West African coast, beginning with the French colony at the mouth of the Senegal and the British proclamation of colonial status for Sierra Leone, grew steadily. Liberia, founded with American support in 1822 as a home for freed slaves, never became, as did Sierra Leone for Britain, a political colony of the United States. Yet it maintained close links with American philanthropic circles and with Black Americans, and developed a cultural and political system that borrowed from the American model.

In the Gold Coast, much of the nineteenth century was dominated by the constant efforts of the Asante to maintain their far-flung empire. In the interior, there were frequent small wars as the Asante subdued rebellions by vassal states, but the trade in slaves, gold, ivory, spices, and soon, cocoa, continued to bolster the prosperity of most inland peoples. Along the coast itself, British commercial suzerainty, marked by deepening involvement in Fante and Ga politics, resulted, in 1874, in the proclamation of the Gold Coast Colony.

Dahomey, to the east of the Gold Coast, struggled, as did Asante, to maintain its territorial integrity during the nineteenth century. But the end of the slave trade, bitterly opposed by the king of Dahomey, seriously weakened the Fon empire, which, more than most others in Africa, depended upon the slave trade for its guns, ammunition, and luxury goods. Basically a poor country, Dahomey was left with only ʾa small supply of copra from its coconut palms once the slave trade ended. By the end of the third quarter of the century, shortly before the European scramble for African territory began, Dahomey was in its weakest condition.

Farther east, along the Yoruba coast, Lagos and Badagry had emerged by the mid-nineteenth century as the remaining important entrepôts for the slave trade. The dying of the Oyo Empire and the great Yoruba civil wars produced a fresh supply of slaves. At the same time, however, the production of alternative trade goods was made difficult. In 1861 Great Britain annexed Lagos, partly to stamp out the slave trade and partly to use the city as a base for helping to bring peace to Yorubaland so that a new pattern of trade could be opened there.

The Niger delta region, long a major center of slave export, was one of the first areas to develop a viable alternative to the slave trade. There the trade chieftains of the Ijaw and Efik peoples, who inhabited the dense mangrove and oil palm lands around the delta and lived under decentralized political structures until the slave trade permitted individuals to gather wealth and create small states, developed the oil palm trade. These same enterprising chiefs had created a trade network up the Niger and in Iboland to serve the slave trade. Early in the nineteenth century, sensing the need for a good alternative to the slave trade, the chiefs began to use the same network to encourage the production of oil palm nuts for shipment by canoe down to Brass, Bonny, and other ports. European manufacturers prized these nuts as a major source of oil for soaps, lotions, and industrial uses. By the time the slave trade began to decline, the oil trade was already an important source of revenue.

After the Landers brothers had traced the Niger's course to the sea, the enterprise of the delta trade chiefs came into direct conflict with the explorations of the British. Steam vessels were seen by the British as a means to get directly at palm nuts and other products. The delta trade chiefs saw the steamboats as a direct threat to their position as middlemen in the palm nut trade. Between 1840 and 1860, armed canoemen attacked British boats frequently, and African producers who traded directly with the British were subject to reprisals. By the 1860's, however, British and French trading posts were established all along the Niger, and British gunboats patrolled the river as far north as the Niger-Benue confluence. From that time on, the economic position of the Ijaw and Efik trading states declined.

This was a period when the British and French were at peace and cooperated, although uneasily, in African commerce. Britain was better established along the Niger, from Hausaland to the sea, but it hesitated, for international reasons, to prohibit the French or other nationals from trading there. Even in the mid-twentieth century, French commercial companies operated in British areas and the British (to a lesser extent) operated in French areas.

Thus, by the middle of the nineteenth century, British and French influence was becoming entrenched along the Atlantic coast of western Africa, and was pressing into the interior, especially up the Senegal and Niger rivers. South of the Niger, however, there was little change in the classic pattern of the previous three centuries: trading posts and small forts, owned by European governments or chartered companies, continued to trade along the coast, while the interior remained largely unexplored. Along the coasts of Cameroun, Gabon, and Zaire, British and French traders controlled most of the commerce. As the slave trade declined, ivory became a major export from this region, brought from the far interior by middlemen of the Fang nation between Cameroun and Gabon, and the Teke along the Congo coast.

In Gabon, France had established a beachhead in 1849, similar to that of the British in Sierra Leone. The town of Libreville in Gabon, like its counterpart, Freetown in Sierra Leone, became headquarters for freed African slaves and their French supporters. Late in the nineteenth century, Portuguese efforts in Angola were still confined largely to the coasts, especially at Luanda and Benguela, although many racially mixed Portuguese-African traders, known as "pombeiros," were established at interior African towns, and facilitated the flow of goods to and from the coast.

Along the Indian Ocean coast, European interests were minor. The Portuguese still confined themselves to the coast and the lower Zambezi in Mozambique, while the British directed their attention to the affairs of the sultan of Zanzibar, who ruled the coasts of East Africa from the Rovuma River in southern Tanzania northward to Somalia. By

Tippu Tib
(Muhammed bin Hamad).

the mid-nineteenth century, the sultan had extended his commercial influence into the interior, but he had little direct political authority more than a few miles inland. His Arab and Swahili trading agents had established themselves around the shores of Lake Tanganyika, in the interior of Tanganyika, along the tributaries of the upper Congo, and in parts of the Interlacustrine Region. In these areas, they stimulated a thriving trade in slaves and ivory.

One of the most notable of the Arab-Swahili traders was Muhammed bin Hamad, known to Europeans as Tippu Tib. Born of a Swahili father and an Arab mother (an immigrant from Oman), Tippu Tib established a complex network of settlements and trading stations in central Africa, often in alliance with great African trading nations such as the Nyamwezi, and by 1870 had become the most powerful man in the region; it was said that he commanded a force of fifty thousand guns at the peak of his power. Tippu Tib became virtually an emperor of an inland empire, though he described himself as only a trader and claimed consistently to be loyally subordinate to the sultan of Zanzibar. In the 1880's, in fact, when he foresaw the coming European onslaught on the interior,. he attempted to gain European recognition of his area of influence as part of the sultan's empire, though without success.

Although the Zanzibar-based traders exercised their greatest influence in what is now Tanzania and eastern Zaire, they spread during the nineteenth century to Bunyoro, Buganda, Karagwe, and various parts of Kenya and Mozambique, where they established permanent liaison with African traders. The prosperous states of this area had been isolated from the coastal trade. But within decades after Arab and Swahili traders from the coast effected their liaison, the great states of the Interlacustrine Region began to participate actively in the Indian Ocean trade system, and their long isolation began to disappear.

During the first two thirds of the nineteenth century, when these developments were taking place in western and eastern Africa, with African leaders very much in control, a quite different process was at work in South Africa. There, Britain was intensifying and expanding its physical presence in what had long been a Dutch area of influence. In South Africa, European influence was already setting the tone for developments, and Africans were increasingly swept along by forces too powerful for them to control.

The early Dutch settlement at Cape Town had grown slowly between its founding in 1652 and the late eighteenth century: few new settlers came from Holland, the land was so vast that natural population increase among the Boers exerted little pressure except within a few hundred miles of Cape Town, and Holland itself undertook no campaigns to open up the interior. It was not until 1770 that the first contacts began between Boer settlers and Black African inhabitants. When the Boer settlers reached the area of the Fish River, they found the Xhosa, a large and comparatively powerful Bantu-speaking population.

A modern South African myth holds that there were no Africans below the Fish River when this territory was first claimed by Dutch settlers, and that the Xhosa, whom they found east of the Fish, had only just arrived. This myth conveniently ignores the thousands of Bushmen and Hottentots who were living west of the Fish when the Dutch arrived. Years of conflict between the Dutch and the Hottentots resulted in the extinction of the Hottentots. Bantu-speaking Africans, furthermore, had settled the country east of the Fish as early as the fourteenth century, but had not moved west of the river because that country was already settled by the pastoral Hottentots.

Great Britain, by the late eighteenth century, had come to recognize the importance of Cape Town to its naval interests in the Indian Ocean. England seized Cape Town and the government of the province from its

Dutch administrators in 1795, during the first Napoleonic War. Holland, by this time, had fallen under French protection, and was a part of the French alliance. One of Britain's first acts, during the war, was to seize Dutch colonies in various parts of the world, partly to expand British trade, and partly to deny the French navy the ability to use colonial ports. Although the Cape was returned to the Dutch as a result of the Treaty of Amiens in 1803, the British seized it again in 1806 when the war was resumed. This time they kept it permanently.

British administration of the Cape reflected some of the growing British liberalism on the slavery question. After 1806 Britain began introducing reforms which, by the 1830's, became intolerable to many of the Boer settlers, threatening their way of life and its attendant use of African slave and serf labor. In what was known as the Great Trek, family after family sold or abandoned their lands near the Cape and joined great caravans (very similar to those used by American pioneers to cross the great plains) that moved hundreds of miles north and east, beyond British rule. The abolition of slavery and the enactment of laws designed to protect the depressed African population of the Cape offended some of the deepest beliefs of the Boers, as a letter written by Anna Steenkamp, sister of one of the Trek's leaders, illustrates:

". . . It is not so much their freedom [the slaves] that drove us to such lengths as their being placed on equal footing with Christians, contrary to the laws of God and the natural distinction of races and religion, so that it was intolerable for any decent Christian to bow beneath such a yoke; wherefore we rather withdrew in order thus to preserve our doctrines in purity."

British liberalism was, however, only one facet of the new style of administration. Britain recognized, far more clearly than earlier Dutch officials or even many of the Boers, that the Cape was more than a pleasant land and a strategic base. Britain saw it as a potential colony with the same promise as their earlier New World possessions and their Pacific holdings in Australia and New Zealand. Developing a modern economy in the Cape, attracting British settlers and merchants to the country, and implanting Western civilization among the indigenous peoples were goals of the British plan, which led to major change in South Africa from the early nineteenth century on. The tendency of independent-minded Boers to move into the interior in no way conflicted with the British design. Lands vacated by the Boers could be settled by British immigrants, and the Boer push into the hinterland opened that area for later use by Britain.

The history of South Africa after the early nineteenth century is one of incessant conflict between Boer and Bantu, and between Boer and Briton. The trekking Boers, with their conviction of being a unique,

A British news artist's version of the warfare between the Nguni
Zulu and Xhosa soldiers of South Africa and British troops.

superior people, separate from all others in their way of life, constantly
fought with the Xhosa, Sotho, Zulu, Tswana, and other African peoples
whose grazing and farming lands were necessary to satisfy the Boer
drive for expansion. The northward push of the Boers was a major
factor in the rise of the Mfecane, or time of troubles, referred to in
Chapter 11. This turmoil prompted the rise of the Zulu military system
and the migrations of many Africans throughout southern and central
Africa in the first half of the nineteenth century. Until the 1860's,
African military resistance against the guns of the determined Boer
pioneers was stubborn but generally unsuccessful. But after the discovery of diamonds at Kimberley, when African workers could purchase guns and ammunition from European traders (indeed, some
African workers were paid in guns in lieu of cash), African troops
began to win battles against forces of Europeans. On numerous occasions
in the 1870's and 1880's it proved necessary for the Cape government to
send small armies to battle against Xhosa, Basuto, Zulu, Tswana,
and Pedi troops; the British government even briefly annexed the Boer
republic of Transvaal in 1877, under the pretext of protecting its
European population from the successful campaigns of the Bapedi people under Chief Sekukuni.

The Bapedi were the eastern branch of the Sotho peoples, other branches of whom lived in Basutoland (modern Lesotho) and Bechuanaland (modern Botswana). They lived in the Transvaal region and suffered greatly from Boer encroachments onto their traditional grazing and farming lands. The Bapedi had taken a considerable beating from the migrating Nguni peoples during the Mfecane, and afterward had developed a more capable military organization to protect their lands and herds. They were ultimately defeated in their war against the Boers and the British, but they put up a stout and courageous defense before succumbing to better trained and equipped European forces.

The northward movements of the Boers produced surprisingly little knowledge of interior South Africa for the British or other Europeans. The Boers were not a highly literate people, and those of their community who were literate were not interested in writing accounts for European reading. Boer explorations were for Boer settlement, and Boer settlers were primarily interested in being left alone to work out their own destiny in Africa. It was missionaries from Britain and France, especially Britain, who relayed back to an interested Europe vital information on the geography, the peoples, and the economic conditions in southern and central Africa.

Missionaries of the Paris Missionary Society worked in Basutoland, under the enthusiastic sponsorship of King Moshesh, while the London Missionary Society worked farther to the west, in what is now Botswana. Robert Moffat, a leading missionary of the London group, helped to inform British liberal and Christian circles about the constant aggressions of the Boer settlers against African farmers and pastoralists. His campaign to attract protection for these Africans added substantially to the growing British sense of proprietorship for southern Africa and also helped to attract numerous recruits into the missionary field. One of these inspired recruits was David Livingstone, who was persuaded by Moffat to devote himself and his medical talents to the missionary effort. Livingstone went on to become possibly the most famous European explorer of Africa.

Toward the conclusion of his study of medicine at Glasgow, Livingstone met Moffat, who encouraged him not to go to an old station, but to advance to unoccupied ground. From then on, Livingstone's ambition to go to Africa, to seek the villages where no missionary had ever been before, burned fiercely. He left England for Cape Town in December 1840, qualified as a doctor and ordained as a minister by the London Missionary Society. He was then twenty-seven years of age. For more than thirty years, until his death in 1873, he traveled almost continually in Africa. He had a lively interest in the people he found, in contrast to some of the explorers of western and eastern Africa, whose main interests were adventure and the discovery of geographic facts and oddities.

Livingstone's several major journeys of exploration, between 1841 and 1873, took him through thousands of miles of southern and central African territory, in the lands now covered by Angola, Botswana, Zaire, Malawi, Mozambique, Rhodesia, South Africa, Tanzania, and Zambia. It was a time of great population movements, conflict between the African peoples and white settler and commercial interests, the introduction of modern warfare, and the savage depredations of the slave trade. Livingstone contacted, and often spent time with, the peoples of most of the great Bantu states: Botswana, Makololo, Matabele, Lozi, Mashona, Mwene Mutapa, Mwata Yamvo, Mwata Kazembe, and Bemba. He traversed central Africa from Luanda in Angola to Quilimane in Mozambique, explored the Zambezi from the Indian Ocean to its origins, "discovered" Victoria Falls and Lake Nyasa, and roamed inquisitively up and down the great continental watershed that separates the Congo from the Zambezi.

Livingstone wrote very well, and his books were widely read in Europe and America. Over a period of years his accounts allowed the cartographers to fill in, with considerable accuracy, great voids in the maps of southern Africa. From the European point of view, his great fame was justified by the amount of information that resulted from his explorations.

Yet Livingstone's unique quality was his interest in African peoples and an objectivity in describing them that was rarely achieved by other European explorers of the nineteenth century. His religious background and his missionary calling provided him with strong moral and ethical standards that evoked many personal judgments about what he found in Africa. Yet, unlike most missionaries of the day, he often saw beyond his own values and reported African customs and beliefs with occasional humility and frequent objectivity. This ability to see Africans as human beings of the same essential worth as other human beings resulted in friendships between Livingstone and many Africans, including several famous chiefs.

Livingstone spent considerable time with two chiefs, Sechele of the Bakwena and Sebituane of the Makololo. His descriptions and evaluations of the two men differed radically from those brought back from the interior by big-game hunters, traders, and Boer travelers. Chief Sechele ruled the populous Bakwena clan of Tswana peoples who today comprise much of the population of Botswana. In 1885, they were forced to accept a British protectorate in order to prevent further encroachment into their territory by the Boer Republics. Sechele's people were a peaceful group, devoted to growing grain and herding cattle over the dry grasslands of their country. Chief Sebituane's Makololo people were related to the Tswana, both being Sotho speaking, but they had embarked on a long migration northward as a result of Zulu raids and pressures. Fighting other groups every few years, the Makololo, under Sebituane's capable leadership, eventually reached what is now southern Zambia, where they conquered the highly organized Lozi kingdom. Both men were painted as ignorant savages by their European detractors (both had had conflicts with the Boers); Livingstone's descriptions tend to emphasize their high intelligence, their political shrewdness, their leadership qualities, and their wit. Sebituane, Livingstone noted, "was decidedly the best specimen of a native chief I ever met"; "always led his men into battle himself"; and possessed qualities of "tenacity in defeat," "mercifulness," and "affability even to humble strangers."

Livingstone's ability to understand Africans and their beliefs is aptly illustrated by his passage on rainmaking among Sechele's Bakwena people:

> As the Bakwains believed that there must be some connection between the presence of "God's Word" in their town and these successive and distressing droughts [there had been no rain since Livingstone's arrival], they looked with no good will at the church bell, but still they invariably treated us with kindness and respect. I am not aware of ever having had an enemy in the tribe. The only avowed cause of dislike was expressed by a very influential and sensible man, the uncle of Sechele. "We like you as well as if you had been born among us; you are the only white man we can become familiar with; but we wish you to give up that everlasting preaching and praying; we can not become familiar with that at all. You see we never get rain, while those tribes who never pray as we do obtain abundance." This was a fact; and we often saw it raining on the hills, ten miles off, while it would not look at us "even with one eye." If the Prince of the power of the air had no hand in scorching us up, I fear I often gave him the credit for doing so.
>
> As for the rain-makers, they carried the sympathies of the people along with them, and not without reason . . . and in order to understand their force we must place ourselves in their position, and believe, as they do, that all medicines act by a mysterious charm.

Two burning interests drove David Livingstone throughout his nearly thirty-five years of explorations: an insatiable urge to explore new country and experience new things and a deep hatred of slavery and the attendant degradation of the African people. Consistent with the European liberal spirit, Livingstone felt that African enslavement and exploitation could best be ended by opening up access routes to the Africans of the interior, converting them to Christianity and Western tastes, and substituting a peaceful trade in goods for the traffic in slaves. His attitudes toward Africans, paternalistic and condescending by today's standards, were at the time in the forefront of European liberal thought.

Livingstone's last great expedition took him to the Great Lakes, where he sought to explore the watershed system and the origin of the Congo River. In 1865, he wrote Sir Roderick Murchison, president of the Royal Geographical Society, to accept the mission of exploration. "What my inclination leads me to prefer is to have intercourse with the people, and do what I can to enlighten them on the slave-trade, and give them some idea of our religion . . . I shall enjoy myself, and feel that I am doing my duty," he stated. Livingstone left Zanzibar in March 1866, for the mouth of the Rovuma River. He planned to follow that river inland to Lake Tanganyika and the area he was to explore. After his departure, Europe heard nothing further from Livingstone: the letters he sent back periodically never arrived. By this time his fame was widespread, and his "disappearance" became a matter of public interest and concern.

In 1869, the *New York Herald* dispatched Henry Morton Stanley, one of its most venturesome reporters, to find Livingstone. Stanley arrived in Zanzibar in January 1871, organized a large expedition, and, on November 10, met Dr. Livingstone at Ujiji, uttering the now famous "Dr. Livingstone, I presume?" After spending four months with Stanley, Livingstone continued his explorations, and died on May 1, 1873, while still in Africa.

During his journey to find Livingstone, Stanley had developed a passion for African exploration. Over a period of years, he explored the Great Lakes area, found the source of the Congo River, followed the river from the lakes to the Atlantic, and mapped the area of the Congo basin. But Stanley was interested in much more than exploring. He quickly became obsessed with visions of European exploitation of the great heart of Africa, the Congo basin. Stanley's explorations and his vision played a vital role in the European conquest of Africa in the last years of the nineteenth century.

Livingstone's explorations also played a strategic role in the later exploitation of much of southern and central Africa. Seen from the perspective of history, his reports of the vast regions that lay between the European settled areas of South Africa and southern Tanzania served to complete European knowledge of the geography of all of eastern Africa, when added to the information being produced by another, unrelated series of British explorations in Tanzania, the Great Lakes of East Africa, and the upper Nile valley.

In the 1850's four British explorers, all adventurers with considerable experience in big-game hunting, military matters, and traveling in unexplored areas, began a series of expeditions that filled in the last major pieces of the puzzle of African geography.

Sir Richard Francis Burton, with extensive military and hunting experience in India, undertook the first European expedition from the Somali coast inland to Harar and Galla country, in 1854-55. Seriously wounded and faced with numerous dangers, Burton successfully completed this mission, which was largely self-financed, and returned to England with much information about Somalia and southern Ethiopia. Later, with support from both the Royal Geographical Society and the British government, he explored Tippu Tib's country, in company with John Hanning Speke, and was the first European (only a few years before Livingstone) to visit Lake Tanganyika.

John Hanning Speke, also a soldier with Indian experience, accompanied Burton on a portion of his Somali expedition as his second-in-command. On the expedition, Speke went off on a side trip to find Lake Victoria. He was the first European known to have seen it, and returned to claim that this great lake, Africa's largest, was the source of the Nile. (Burton and Speke became bitter enemies on these expeditions, each writing accounts that portrayed the other in poor light.) In a second expedition in 1861-63, Speke, this time accompanied by James Grant, a much more congenial companion than Burton, visited Buganda and found the source of the Nile at the north end of Lake Victoria.

The independently wealthy Sir Samuel White Baker, who had a varied experience in Europe (he was educated in Germany) and Ceylon, was one of the great big-game hunters of his day. In 1862, he left Khartoum on a privately financed expedition on which he hoped to explore the Nile and to meet Speke and Grant as they traveled north down the river. Traveling with three ships and a hundred men, he experienced considerable difficulty with navigation problems and his unruly crew. He visited the kingdom of Bunyoro in 1864 (where the king, Kamrasi, extorted much of his scant remaining supplies, as he had done to Speke and Grant a few months earlier), discovered Lake Albert, and finally met Speke near the town of Gondokoro, on the Nile. Baker and his wife then returned to Egypt. Baker was knighted and was widely acclaimed for his explorations of the Nile. In 1869-73 he and his wife returned to southern Sudan and Uganda, this time with an appointment from the khedive of Egypt as governor-general of the Nile basin. His mission was to help stamp out the brutal slave trade in that region, and to attempt to extend the Egyptian frontiers into Uganda.

Although these British explorations were the primary sources of European information on the vast region between Lake Tanganyika and

Egypt, German missionaries added much knowledge of the same region, as well as of the interior of what are now Tanzania and Kenya. John Ludwig Krapf and John Rebmann, for example, both employed by the Church Missionary Society, were the first Europeans to visit Mount Kilimanjaro, Africa's highest mountain, and to make contact with the progressive Chagga people who lived on its slopes.

After these historic journeys, the interior of eastern Africa lay open to increasing European penetration, and year after year the number of missionaries, explorers, hunters, and traders increased. By the 1860's and 1870's, most of the African continent was known to Europe. The earlier coastal installations were being used, in Senegal, Gambia, Sierra Leone, the Gold Coast, Nigeria, Angola, South Africa, Mozambique, and parts of North Africa, as springboards for the extension of European influence and control into the interior.

European activity in North Africa, which was much closer to Europe both physically and historically, also helped set the precedent for later conquest. Like South Africa, it unwillingly became a major part of Africa to experience early European colonialism. During the first half of the nineteenth century, when European efforts in western and eastern Africa were still largely confined to coastal trade and exploration of the interior, Europe was already developing an increasingly possessive attitude about North Africa's wealth, mostly because of Napoleon's earlier conquest of Egypt.

The European role in North Africa stemmed in part from the long conflict between Christian Europe and the Islamic powers of North Africa and the Middle East. By the late eighteenth century, this conflict had carried over into numerous tensions between Europe and the Turkey-based Ottoman Empire. The Ottomans had long held part of Europe within their empire, particularly Greece and Albania. Europeans were quite interested in pushing Ottoman influence back into Asia. Europe had also come to regard the Mediterranean as a European sea, and North Africa, which (except for Morocco) was still claimed by the Ottoman Empire, was seen by Europe as an area of legitimate concern. The fact that North Africa still controlled some profitable trade with the Sudan, that its fertile coastal plains were the source of significant exports of grain, olives, dates, and wines for European markets, and that its harbors could be used either as bases for European ships or as lairs for pirates, all enhanced Europe's interest.

Unlike most of Africa, North Africa had long been inhabited by urbane and wealthy peoples who were in close and direct contact with Europe. North African ships sailed the Mediterranean and called at European ports, and every North African city had consuls and trade representatives from several European countries. North Africa played a role in Mediterranean affairs and was a part of its broader political system, even if on a minor key since the decline of the Muslim Empire.

At the beginning of the nineteenth century, Egypt was wracked by internal disunity, corruption, and lethargy. It was nominally ruled by the Ottoman sultan. In 1798 Napoleon invaded Egypt, partially in response to the British seizure of South Africa, and quickly defeated the Egyptian army. Although his French forces were expelled three years later, with British assistance, Egypt became the first African power in modern times to suffer major European invasion and conquest.

After the expulsion of the French, a period of near-chaos wracked Egypt. In the midst of this episode, filled with uprisings, intrigue, and disputes between various factions, a bey of Albanian origin, Muhammad Ali, rose to power, and in 1805 was made pasha, or governor, of Egypt. For six more years, Muhammad Ali fought to consolidate his power. By 1811, he had succeeded in killing or exiling all the Mamluks, including the Albanians who had helped him to seize power. He ruled Egypt as the representative of the Ottoman sultan, paying the latter a token tribute each year, but in actual fact he was independent and, in many respects, stronger than the Turkish overlord. In 1839, Ali's modernized Egyptian army inflicted a major defeat on the sultan's Turkish army. Ali might have become head of the entire Ottoman Empire had the European powers not intervened.

Muhammad Ali was a complex blend of the ancient autocratic ruler and the modern dictator; he brooked no challenge to his personal power, yet he introduced many reforms that led to modernization in Egypt. He built a major canal connecting the port of Alexandria with the Nile and introduced cotton into large-scale production in the Nile delta. Ali also broke the power of the Turks and established a new class of officials who were decidely Egyptian in outlook. And he vigorously sought European capital, technology, and scientific knowledge to aid in Egyptian development. He conquered most of the modern Republic of Sudan as a part of a major campaign to expand Egyptian territory.

Muhammad Ali's first aggressive international move was the major reorganization of the Egyptian army. All Turkish and Albanian officers were removed; a new cadre of Egyptian and Black African officers was installed; and European trainers were employed to train the new army, which was outfitted with European arms. By 1820, Ali was ready to send the army into the Sudan, and as his forces moved up the Nile, they proved worthy of his ambitions. The cities of Dongola and Sennar were captured, and a new capital was built at Khartoum, from which an Egyptian governor could rule the entire territory. Year after year, the army campaigned farther to the south, but the powerful Shilluk, despite their lack of modern weapons, slowed the Egyptian advance until 1841, when it finally broke through Shilluk country. The Shilluk, Dinka, Nuer, and other Nilotic peoples, however, were never fully conquered. They maintained an attitude of hostility and rebelliousness that made the Egyptian occupation tenuous. Although Egypt later sent Sir Samuel Baker through the lands of the Nilotes in an effort to extend Cairo's control into Uganda, he was unsuccessful. The modern Sudan-Uganda border became the effective limit of Egyptian influence.

Ali's imperial efforts were not confined to Africa alone. He occupied the Sinai Desert, Palestine, Syria, and adjacent lands, and held them for years until forced by the threats of Britain and other European powers to pull back toward the Suez region. He developed a major naval facility, and at the request of the sultan sent a combined naval-military force to Greece, which at that time was struggling to regain its independence from Ottoman power. Ali's force, led by his son Ibrahim, defeated the Greek navy, and was well on the way to a complete conquest of the Greek army when European intervention forced Ali to recall his troops.

Ali's methods were harsh and ruthless, and he was a master of intrigue—a necessary quality in the Egypt of the Mamluks. Under his rule, Egypt's peasants, the fellahin, suffered greatly from heavy taxes and forced labor and military requirements. And the country's finances were seriously strained by Ali's extravagant efforts at modernization and development. Yet he left Egypt a great legacy, and introduced changes in administration, the military, and economy that set Egypt on the road toward equal participation in modern power politics.

Ali died in 1841. His first two successors proved incapable of furthering Egypt's expansionist thrust. But his grandson Ismail, who assumed the title khedive, renewed Ali's program in the early 1860's. Ismail completed the Suez Canal (which had been begun in 1859) and attempted a drive down the Red Sea to the Indian Ocean and the Somalia-Kenya coast. His forces were defeated by the Ethiopians when they attempted to bring that land under Egyptian control. Pressure from the sultan of Zanzibar, with British backing, prevented conquest of the Indian Ocean coasts. Ismail pressed a massive modernization effort that resulted in a more effective army, school system, and civil service. This effort, however, required such extensive borrowing that Egypt was near bankruptcy when Ismail was deposed by the Ottoman sultan in 1879. In 1881, a group of army officers led a successful military coup against the government that succeeded Ismail; but by this time European interests, based on their heavy claims against Egypt's finances, led to a joint British-French decision to intervene. Because of domestic problems French forces failed to participate, and in 1882 British forces alone began a long-term occupation and rule. This unilateral British conquest of Egypt was to be the first important event sparking the European "scramble" for Africa from 1884 onward.

The increasing involvement of Europe in North African affairs, of which Napoleon's invasion of Egypt in 1798 was a harbinger, took its earliest permanent form in Algeria, which was invaded by France in 1830 and eventually annexed as a colony. During the Napoleonic wars in 1792-1815, Algeria aided France by fulfilling much of its wartime need for grain. After the French defeat, a huge debt to Algeria had been accumulated, and the new French government that replaced Bonaparte was unwilling to pay it. After years of acrimonious tension between the two countries, France invaded Algeria, and by 1832 had defeated the official armies of the bey and had occupied all the coastal cities and plains. The fiercely independent Berber hill people, however, were not so easy to subdue, nor were the Arab herders who had long been established in the steppe regions near the Sahara. The Turkish rulers of Algeria had largely ignored the Berbers and Arabs of the interior, and at first the French seemed inclined to follow suit. The Arab-Berber peoples, however, were devout Muslims, and they began to react against the French occupation with an antipathy born of religious fanaticism. For the first time in centuries Arabs and Berbers began to come together into a confederation, in order to oppose French rule.

The leader chosen to head this new state was Abd al-Qadir. Still in his mid-twenties, he had already built a reputation for piety, wisdom, and leadership. A group of Arab tribes in western Algeria, his own home area, asked him to become amir and to lead a jihad against the French, in 1832. Abd al-Qadir immediately set out to unite the hundreds of small Arab and Berber communities of interior Algeria. He established a system of finance and a central treasury, an army, a comprehensive system of administration, and a system of schools and courts that rigorously followed Koranic precept. By 1840, Abd al-Qadir had his state firmly organized, under a fervent Islamic ethic. Qadir's energetic state-building process, however, was neither purely political nor religious in objective: in the process he had assembled an army of 10,000 men, well trained and equipped with guns. He had also built a chain of strategic fortresses along the foothills that led down to the French-occupied plains.

The French initially recognized Abd al-Qadir as the ruler of an autonomous interior state, and attempted to concentrate their attention on settling Europeans in the cities and fertile plains. Conflicts began very quickly, however, and after 1840, they grew into full-scale war. By 1846, the French, who had come to regard Algeria as a prize worthy of considerable sacrifice, had built up a massive army, consisting of 108,000 troops. In 1847 French forces surrounded Qadir's troops and Qadir himself was captured. He was sent into exile, but resistance from his people continued intermittently until 1879. By that time France ruled Algeria, but Qadir's name stood as a symbol of national pride to the conquered Algerian people.

French settlers, as well as settlers from Spain, Italy, and other Mediterranean countries, were attracted into coastal Algeria, where the French army helped them to settle on the more fertile lands by forcefully removing the Algerian farmers and resettling them farther in the interior. By 1840, there were 100,000 European settlers in Algeria, and by 1880, the number had grown to 350,000. European enterprises— businesses, artisan shops, light manufacturing—and commercial farms developed rapidly. Algeria soon began to produce major supplies of grapes, olives, grains, and fruits for the French and Spanish markets. One large area of Africa had become, by the middle of the nineteenth century, the first large European colonial conquest.

In 1835 Ottoman rule was reestablished in Tripoli following a period of internal unrest. The Turkish sultan's forces, however, were unable to establish their rule over the Fezzan, the large oasis and highland area in southern Libya, and this region continued as an autonomous territory. Tripoli had long been an important trading entrepôt, into which flowed most of the trans-Saharan slaves, gold, and ivory from the Hausa states, Kanem-Bornu, and the eastern Sudanic states of Wadai and Bagirmi. During the 1830's and 1840's, however, this trade was disrupted by internal struggles in Bornu and by feuds among the leading families of the Fezzan; throughout this period it was possible for only one large caravan a year, under heavy guard, to get through to Tripoli.

In 1843, and in following years, another of the great Islamic religious movements that played such a vital role in northern and western African affairs brought peace to the central and eastern Sahara, and trade to Tripoli resumed and even expanded. This movement, the Sanusiyya brotherhood, was founded by a scholar and religious reformer named Muhammad al-Sanusi. Born in Algeria in 1787, al-Sanusi traveled widely in North Africa and Arabia. In Mecca, in 1837, he formed a religious order. His objective was to induce Muslims to return to the life and government of early Islam. Arabian opposition forced al-Sanusi to return to Africa, and he retreated into the remote oasis of Jaghbub in the desert south of Cyrenaica, the eastern province of Libya. There he organized a monastery, attracted many followers, and developed Jaghbub into a major intellectual and religious center. The men who were initially attracted to the order were Bedouin Arabs living in the eastern Sahara, but as the movement gained in prestige Berbers and Black Africans also joined.

Within a few years devout disciples of the Sanusiyya brotherhood were living throughout Cyrenaica and had begun to spread westward along the Saharan trade routes, into the Fezzan, Wadai, and Tibesti (another great plateau region in the central Sahara, in what are now northern Chad and southern Libya). Sanusiyyan lodges were far more than religious retreats: they served as centers of education, commerce, banking, law, social activity, and even politics. Many of the Sanusiyya were wealthy merchants and caravanseers, and their membership in the brotherhood brought them into a strong bond of mutual cooperation and assistance. The Sanusiyya movement never resulted in the creation of a political empire comparable to that of Usman dan Fodio in Nigeria, but Sanusiyya controlled Cyrenaica and had great influence on the politics and commerce of the central and eastern Sahara. Tripoli itself, though not a Sanusiyyan center, benefited considerably from the peace the movement brought to the Sahara.

Libya was remote from the centers of European activity in North Africa in the nineteenth century, and only Italy regarded it as an area of special interest. Because of Libya's internal unity and prosperity, and Italy's internal weakness, however, Libya remained largely free of Italian or other European influence until the twentieth century. (Libya was not one united nation during the nineteenth century: its two large provinces, Tripoli, and Cyrenaica, were separately governed by Ottoman representatives, with the Sanusiyya sharing power in Cyrenaica. Libya did not become one state until the twentieth cenutry.)

Tunisia, in general the most progressive and westernized country in nineteenth century North Africa, was too closely tied to European affairs to escape the darkening cloud of European intervention. Under the enlightened leadership of largely autonomous beys, who paid tribute to the Ottoman sultan, Tunisia early abolished slavery and the slave trade, and was one of the first African states to adopt a constitutional government, in 1857-61. Alarmed by the French aggressions in neighboring Algeria, Tunis sought and obtained close British ties in 1837. Despite warm British-Tunisian relations, however, French proximity next door in Algeria caused French influence to grow while British influence declined. French trading firms were solidly established in Tunis, and France increasingly came to regard Tunisia as its special sphere of interest. In 1881, France, after several years of commercial and diplomatic struggle with Italy—itself by now deeply interested in North Africa—invaded Tunisia and forced the bey to sign a treaty giving France control of finances and foreign affairs. Although the bey's government continued to manage internal affairs, Tunisia became another victim of the European seizure of Africa.

Of all the North African countries, Morocco had remained most isolated from both Ottoman and European affairs. Foreign entanglements were shunned, and foreign visitors were not as welcome as in other North African countries: the sultan's government, sovereign and free of the Ottoman claims that played a role in the affairs of other North African states, feared that foreigners might become involved in the country's internal affairs as they had in neighboring Algeria and Tunisia. And Morocco's people, conservatively Muslim, were suspicious of infidels. The country was governed by a sultan, but district governors, Islamic *ulama* (spiritual leaders), and Berber chieftains all held considerable power, serving both to force the sultan to rule by diplomacy and to evoke frequent internal rivalries. On the surface Morocco was united, and its large population and independent government made it appear far less vulnerable to European intervention than its neighbors.

In the 1840's, however, the sultan, who followed both African and international events closely, aided Abd al-Qadir's struggle by providing supplies and sanctuary. The French decided to retaliate. A French army entered Morocco from Algeria in 1844, and inflicted a serious defeat on the sultan's army. Almost immediately European governments and commercial agents became bolder. More consuls and traders entered the country, steamships began making regular calls, and Moroccan nobles and traders connived with their foreign counterparts to escape the sultan's taxes and authority. An intelligent and able sultan, Sidi Muhammad, ruled from 1859 to 1873, and made some progress with a modernization program, despite subversive opposition from many of the European traders and financial interests and conservative, xenophobic elements in his own state. Spain invaded Morocco at the beginning of Muhammad's reign, and again the Moroccan army was defeated by a modern European force. According to the terms of the peace treaty, Morocco had to recognize Spain's right to rule the coastal cities of Ceuta and Melilla, and had to pay Spain a large indemnity in order to secure the withdrawal of Spanish troops.

Throughout the 1860's and 1870's, the influence of European trade and financial interests increased, and the sultan's difficulties in maintaining the internal integrity of his state grew. In 1873 a new sultan, Mawlai al-Hasan, succeeded Sidi Muhammad, and carried forward the modernization of the army, the improvement of ports, the building of roads, and a number of administrative reforms, including reestablishment of central authority over most of the local governors. Al-Hasan ruled until 1894, and the country knew a greater sense of internal stability than it had for several decades. Although there were no further invasions or military actions, European involvement continued to grow, as ever larger numbers of trading firms set up agencies and the various European powers agreed among themselves as to what privileges they would have in Morocco. On the whole, however, Morocco maintained its sovereignty and internal structure intact well into the twentieth century.

By 1884, as the formal European "scramble" was launched, much of North Africa had already succumbed to the growing expansionism of imperialist Europe: Algeria in 1830, Tunisia in 1881, Egypt in 1882, leaving only Morocco and Libya for later attention. With the firm British presence in South Africa, large chunks of northern and southern Africa had been brought under Europe's domination.

During this period, only three European powers, Britain, France, and Portugal, had maintained a serious presence on African soil. Other countries—Italy, Spain, the United States, the German states, Belgium, and Holland—had engaged in the African trade, had sent missionaries, or had occasionally exhibited some interest in Africa, but had shown no tendency to become officially and permanently involved. But the European world of the late nineteenth century was a tense one, marked by wars, commercial and diplomatic struggles, and constantly shifting alliances and quarrels. Although the European scramble for Africa had earlier beginnings, it acquired its greedy character largely from the complex events occurring in Europe itself.

The British invasion of Egypt in 1882 served as an important generating factor. The unilateral British invasion of Egypt produced a bitter French reaction and the French became suspicious of British intentions in the rest of Africa, where both powers had for several decades cooperated and competed commercially. Suddenly France, whose national pride had been sorely wounded by German defeat and the loss of Alsace-Lorraine in the Franco-Prussian war of 1870, began to fear that Britain had broader designs in Africa south of the Sahara. (For some years before 1882, Britain and France had shared a concern in Egypt. They were the chief lending nations during the heavy borrowing that financed Khedive Ismail's modernization program.)

Germany's brilliant chancellor, Otto Bismarck, saw in this new French suspiciousness of British intentions an opportunity to strengthen his own position in the German elections of 1884, and to divert French attention from Alsace-Lorraine and other Franco-German tensions. He began to raise questions himself about British intentions in Africa, and specifically attacked the British support of Portuguese claims to the lands at the mouth of the Congo, which many Frenchmen believed threatened the security of the French position in Gabon.

To understand this critical development, it is necessary to return to Henry Morton Stanley, and to examine the liaison that Stanley had formed with Leopold II, King of the Belgians. A few years after his expedition to find Livingstone, Stanley undertook a second expedition to explore the Great Lakes and the Congo River. During this expedition he traversed the continent from Zanzibar to the mouth of the Congo. Stanley saw in the Congo basin a vast source of riches, and in the Congo River a made-to-order system of transportation with which to exploit these riches. As soon as he reached the Atlantic in 1877, after his three-year journey in central Africa, he set forth to Europe with the intention of interesting the British government in the vast opportunities he saw in the Congo.

In a letter to the *London Daily Telegraph*, Stanley wrote:

> I feel convinced that the question of this mighty water-way will become a political one in time. . . . If it were not that I fear to damp any interest you may have in Africa, or in this magnificent stream, by the length of my letters, I could show you very strong reasons why it would be a politic deed to settle this momentous question immediately. I could prove to you that the Power possessing the Congo, despite the cataracts, would absorb in itself the trade of the whole enormous basin behind. The river is and will be the grand highway of commerce to West Central Africa.

Britain, for many reasons, was at the time uninterested in taking on the burden of responsibility that administering and developing the Congo basin would require. Although British traders on the coast were engaged in the Congo trade, the government felt that the British commercial interest was secure without formal governmental involvement in central Africa.

But Leopold of the Belgians, unlike the British government, regarded the Congo as a dazzling opportunity. In 1876, even before Stanley had completed his journey, Leopold had formed the International African Association, supposedly to combat the slave trade and to protect and extend the work of Christian missionaries in eastern and central Africa. More probably the association was to give Leopold, a very ambitious sovereign of a small state, an acceptable cover under which to establish his own claims in Africa. As soon as Stanley reached Europe in 1877, Leopold's agents began to woo him to join the king's service, and finally Stanley agreed; formally employed by the International African Association, he worked directly under Leopold's control and in very close communication with the king.

Stanley's mission was to negotiate agreements with the chiefs and kings of the Congo, allowing him to establish a system of trade and river transportation in the entire Congo basin. His methods were ruthless and forceful; he used deception and trickery on numerous occasions to persuade chiefs to sign agreements and to provide labor and trade goods. He used force or intimidation when necessary. But with these methods he succeeded, between 1879 and 1884, in laying the foundations for one of the most profitable colonial enterprises ever to appear in Africa.

Some Frenchmen, if not the French government, were concerned about the Leopold-Stanley venture, and in 1880 Pierre S. de Brazza, a French naval officer sponsored by the French Committee of the International African Association but unofficially acting for the French government, launched a French expedition from Gabon into the interior. De Brazza headed for the Stanley Pool on the Congo River to obtain agreements with African chiefs that would legitimize French claims to the territory north of the river. With no clear French government authority, since he was supposedly acting for the International African Association, he signed a treaty with King Makoko of the Bateke people, who controlled most of the territory north of the river. Although the treaty was at first disavowed by France, it soon was formally ratified and proclaimed as the legal basis of French claims to a Congo empire, stretching from Gabon to the Congo River.

By this time Portugal had become aroused, fearing that these developments would nullify her four-centuries-old claims to the lower Congo—claims that had been neither exercised nor challenged. Portugal secured Britain's promise of support for the claim of Portuguese legal control over the Congo. This promise, however, was soon challenged by British trading firms on the lower Congo, who regarded Portuguese sovereignty as a threat to their interests. By the end of 1883 a crisis of great complexity, involving Britain, France, Portugal, King Leopold, and Germany, surrounded the question of the Congo.

In 1884, Leopold announced the formation of the Congo Free State, under the sponsorship of his International African Association. He declared that the whole Congo basin and lower river should be open to free trading by all countries and legitimate firms. Within months Germany and the United States formally recognized the Congo Free State, and France followed suit. At the same time, Germany proposed the historic Berlin Conference (which was convened in December 1884) to resolve the complicated Congo question and to air disputes over colonial expansion. While all the interested European nations, as well as the United States, were agreeing to attend the Berlin Conference, Germany announced to a surprised world that she had become a colonial power in Africa by declaring German protectorates over Kamerun (Cameroun), South West Africa, East Africa, and Togo.

The German action was a surprise, largely because Germany had played a comparatively minor role in most of Africa. Even in the four territories it annexed, its claims were not based on any substantial German presence or investment. German missionaries had set up numerous stations in these as well as other African countries, and German industrial and commercial firms had begun to develop African trade relations. But in each of the areas that Germany claimed, Britain, France, and other European nations had played an equally important role, usually for a much longer time. The German action stemmed primarily from a growing feeling in Germany that colonies were necessary to international prestige. The four areas chosen by Germany had been explored, to a certain extent, by Germans and were areas in which none of the rival powers maintained major trading missions, consulates, or other internationally honored interests. (German East Africa, now Tanzania, was an exception; there Britain had a more recognized interest because of its long role in Zanzibar affairs: Germany rather adroitly annexed only the mainland, Tanganyika, where both the sultan's authority and the British stake were more tenuous than on Zanzibar and the Kenya coast.) Clearly Bismarck was gambling with Germany's audacious move, and events showed that his gamble was successful—at least for another three decades, until World War I broke out.

The fourteen powers that attended the Berlin Conference had to accept, as a *fait accompli,* Leopold's Congo Free State and the new German acquisitions, as well as the established claims of Britain, France, and Portugal over various parts of the African continent. A number of lofty resolutions were passed, dealing with the need to stamp out any remaining vestiges of the slave trade and to protect the freedom of trade on the Congo and the Niger, and it was generally agreed that further acquisitions of African territory would not be recognized unless the acquiring country mounted an effective occupation and administration. The latter point was designed to prevent the claiming of African territory by mere proclamation. Instead it served to stimulate Africa's partition by encouraging military occupation and the imposition of formal control over recalcitrant African rulers.

The almost philanthropic tone in which the agreements of the conference were couched was aptly (and quite innocently) stated in 1888 by Emile Banning, chief archivist of the Belgian government and a close supporter of King Leopold:

> The Berlin Conference fulfilled a double task: it endorsed the creation, in the very heart of Equatorial Africa, of a great interior state, commercially open to all nations, but politically shielded from their competition. It also set up the bases for economic legislation which was immediately applicable to the central zone of the continent but which virtually demanded more extensive application. These regulations, inspired by the most liberal ideas and discarding all whims of selfish exploitation, will protect both the natives and the Europeans in their relations with the colonizing powers. The conference also upheld the principles—justly dear to our age—of religious and civil liberty, of loyal and peaceful competition, and it broke with the antiquated traditions of the former colonial system.

It has often been said that the race to conquer Africa began when the Berlin Conference ended, and indeed the two decades between 1885 and 1905 witnessed the rapid conquest of those parts of Africa that had not yet been placed under European control. But the events of 1885-1905 were not without precedent. The Berlin Conference, important though it was, was only a signpost, marking the rapid acceleration of a race that had already begun.

By the time the conference ended, North Africa was largely under European colonial control. Egypt was occupied by Britain, Algeria was formally a part of France, and Tunisia was under French protection. Only Morocco and Libya remained under African control.

In West Africa, France had continued the expansion of its control up the Senegal River. By 1879, a Franco-Senegalese army was marching up the headwaters of the Niger River, into the empire of Ahmadu Sefu, the son of al-Hajj Umar. After several years of clashes, Ahmadu's resistance collapsed, and Bamako was captured in 1883. The French advance up the Niger continued, both before and after the Berlin Conference, although it was seriously slowed between the late 1880's and 1898 by the army of Samori. In 1894, however, Timbuktu was taken. And in 1896 the town of Say in modern Niger was taken, bringing the French to Hausaland, which by then had come under British control.

Britain, in turn, had established a formal protectorate over the Gold Coast, and had tense relations with Asante, whose territory the British were to invade in 1896. The small island colony of Lagos had become a center of British strength. Following the Berlin Conference, Britain expanded rapidly from Lagos into Yorubaland and the interior. British firms were established throughout northern Nigeria and began to maintain armed forces with which to control local rulers. France had earlier attempted to challenge British supremacy on the lower Niger, but eventually abandoned the effort when it was seen how effectively the British were in charge.

Basic factors in Europe itself influenced the patterns of colonial expansion prior to the Berlin Conference and the speeding up of the process after the conference. Before the 1880's, Britain had been the undisputed industrial leader of the world. This superiority encouraged the British government to prefer a free-trade, laissez-faire policy toward Africa, and to regard formal colonial responsibility as costly and troublesome. As long as British traders had relatively free access to African goods and markets, British industrial superiority guaranteed British profits against all competitors. In those areas, such as the Gold Coast and the lower Niger, where Britain had some internationally recognized influence, she kept tariffs low and permitted traders from other nations to operate more or less freely. British openness in these areas allowed

Britain to argue against monopoly and in favor of free trade in other vast areas, such as Cameroun and the Congo.

France, largely because her less efficient and less productive industries were no match for British competition, tended to seek monopoly positions in African markets. As soon as French commercial and naval power in a particular area was strong enough, France took measures to prevent or impede trade by British or other European traders. Thus in the lower Senegal, along the coast of French Guinea and the Ivory Coast, and in Gabon, France maintained a vigilant watch against foreign competitors, discouraging them by high tariffs, poor cooperation, and even refusal of trading rights. Despite the high cost of conquest and colonial administration, therefore, France had, long before the Berlin Conference, begun to expand its areas of legal control, especially up the Senegal and along the upper Niger. This French colonial tendency became even stronger after the British invasion of Egypt.

Germany, which had played no colonial role and little commercial role in Africa during the nineteenth century, had developed into an industrial power rivaling the British. The union of German states into a federation in 1870-71, and the crushing defeat of France in the Franco-Prussian war, gave Germany a new sense of national pride. This pride made the acquisition of colonial territory, which Germany had never before possessed, a matter of great public interest. And the great German merchant and industrial houses desired guaranteed access to markets and raw materials.

Portugal, by now a small, enfeebled, and poor country, played a defensive role in the European scramble for Africa. Through diplomacy, Portugal sought to preserve the vast holdings she had claimed for more than four centuries. At the conference tables Portugal came out surprisingly well in view of her weak power position: she kept the very large areas of Angola and Mozambique, the small mainland and island country of Guinea (Bissau) in West Africa, and the island of São Tomé. To Angola was added the small enclave of Cabinda, which remained in Portuguese hands even after Leopold won an access route to the sea for the Congo Free State between Cabinda and Angola.

Spain, whose sole interest in Africa was in the northwest portion of the continent, played a minor role in the scramble. But eventually Spain won recognition of her rights to Spanish Sahara, long claimed by Morocco, and to the ports of Ceuta and Melilla on the Moroccan coast.

Italy's interests, also minor, concentrated on Libya and the Horn of Africa, including Ethiopia, Eritrea, and Somalia. Neither Ethiopia nor Libya was "given" to Italy, but Italy later attempted to participate in the African conquest in these countries.

Of the three most powerful states with African objectives—Britain,

France, and Germany—Britain was less territory-conscious than France and Germany, and her belief in free trade led her to underestimate the eagerness of other powers to protect their trade by seizing colonial territory. Thus the swiftness with which Germany moved into Africa in 1884 took Britain by surprise. Similarly, Leopold's speed in consolidating his position in the Congo Free State and the rapidity of France's thrusts into the West African interior caught Britain almost unaware. By the beginning of 1885, she found her traditional trade supremacy in Africa restricted by the actions of these powers. Much of North and West Africa was emerging as a French sphere of influence. German claims to Cameroun and South West Africa abruptly ended the free exercise of British interests in those regions. Leopold held the upper hand in the rich Congo trade, and a large part of East Africa had slipped from the control of the sultan of Zanzibar and his British mentors. Even in South Africa the fiercely independent Boer republics in Transvaal and the Orange Free State were a cause for constant British concern and a potential obstacle to free British exploitation of southern Africa.

In 1885 Lord Salisbury became British prime minister and launched a campaign to regain British primacy in Africa. Salisbury's term of office ended in 1892, but by that time he had made up for Britain's lost time in the African colonial conquest. The priorities of Salisbury's African policy were to continue the British occupation of Egypt, to consolidate and expand British rule in South Africa, and to establish British suzerainty in all territory between the Cape and Cairo. To ease French bitterness over Egypt, Salisbury played down British concerns over the mounting French drive in West Africa, and contented himself in that region with solidifying existing British interests in the Gambia, Sierra Leone, the Gold Coast, and Nigeria.

Recognizing Bismarck for the master strategist and diplomat that he was, Salisbury moved quickly to settle the many difficult questions raised by the German annexations in 1884. In 1886 Salisbury and Bismarck worked out an agreement recognizing both British and German legitimacy in East Africa. In 1890 Britain ceded the North Sea island of Heligoland to Germany, in return for German recognition of British rights in Zanzibar, Kenya, Uganda, Northern Rhodesia, Bechuanaland (bordering on German South West Africa) and eastern Nigeria (bordering on German Kamerun). In 1890 Britain proclaimed a protectorate over Zanzibar and the neighboring island of Pemba, which was promptly recognized by Germany in accordance with the agreements between Bismarck and Salisbury. The sultan of Zanzibar, who a few decades before had been a powerful monarch, had no alternative but to submit to the British action.

The Bismarck-Salisbury agreement eased tensions between Britain and Germany, and Salisbury turned his attention to Britain's other great rival in Africa, France. Two areas were the source of considerable tension between France and Britain—Madagascar and eastern Nigeria. In Madagascar, where Britain had established a major trade presence and where numerous British missionaries were serving, France was pursuing an increasingly aggressive role. In 1883, the French navy captured Tamatave, one of Madagascar's chief ports. In 1885 the French forced the king of the Hova state of Merina, Madagascar's most powerful monarch, to sign a treaty placing the island's foreign relations in France's hands. In the rich trade areas of eastern Nigeria, which include part of the Niger delta and the area at the mouth of the Calabar River, French merchants disputed British claims to control commerce. Britain needed clear recognition of her supremacy over eastern Nigeria in order to safeguard its growing stake in the lower Niger, Hausaland, and Yorubaland.

In 1890 Salisbury negotiated a treaty with France recognizing Madagascar as a French protectorate, in return for French concurrence in Britain's claim over eastern Nigeria. With another tension eased, Salisbury was able to give full attention to the third of his major objectives: British control of southern Africa.

During Britain's negotiations for other parts of Africa, Salisbury's attention had never swayed from his vital interest in southern Africa. In 1886 gold was discovered on the Witwatersrand of the Transvaal Republic, attracting a rush of British prospectors and miners. With the insistent collaboration of South Africa's Cecil Rhodes, who had become wealthy from the Kimberley diamond industry and was ambitious for British expansion to the north, Salisbury concerned himself with two problems: tensions with the Boer republics of the Orange Free State and Transvaal, and agreements with Portugal defining the lines between British and Portuguese holdings.

On both questions Salisbury had to reckon with Cecil Rhodes, by then prime minister of the Cape Colony and one of the wealthiest men in the world. Rhodes, born in 1853, had come to live with his settler brother in Natal in 1870 because of his failing health. Within two years he had not only regained robust health, but had, with his brother, joined the ranks of diamond diggers in Kimberley, in the far west of the Cape Province.

In 1881, when all South Africa was tense due to conflicts between British and Boer settlers, Rhodes entered politics as a member of the Cape assembly. He soon developed a political philosophy that played a major role in building the Union of South Africa: as a staunch, almost fanatical believer in the greatness of the British Empire (he felt Britain ought to rule the entire world), he helped rally British support. As a believer that South Africa should play its proper role in the empire as a self-governing state where all white settlers could share equally in its fortunes, he appealed to many of the Boer settlers in the Cape and Natal. He soon developed great appeal, receiving both British and Boer votes.

Rhodes regarded British expansion in Africa as his own particular obligation. In 1884, concerned over Boer encroachments into Bechuanaland, Rhodes was appointed resident deputy commissioner in that country. There he influenced Britain to halt Boer expansion. The western borders of the Transvaal Republic were defined under British pressure, and British troops were sent to Bechuanaland to ensure that the Boer commandos, who had terrorized the African population along the border, stay within the Transvaal.

By this time Germany had annexed South West Africa, on Bechuanaland's west, and Rhodes became afraid that Germany and the Transvaal might forge an alliance that would connect them north of Bechuanaland, cutting off any possibility of further British expansion. He sent personal emissaries to Lobengula, king of the Matabele on the Rhodesian plateau (as the country was later called in honor of Rhodes), to develop trade relations. In 1889 he completed arrangements for the creation of the British South Africa Company, whose charter allowed it to trade in, exploit, and help to govern the territory between Portuguese Angola and Mozambique north of Bechuanaland. This area ultimately came to be known as Northern Rhodesia (Zambia), Southern Rhodesia, and Nyasaland (Malawi). British acceptance of the German annexation of Tanganyika thwarted Rhodes's dream of seeing all of Africa from the Cape to Cairo under British rule. But his initiative in the Rhodesias and Nyasaland, combined with British moves to establish control over Kenya and Uganda, brought a great part of eastern Africa under British rule.

Rhodes became prime minister of Cape Colony in 1890, and made a great impact on its policy toward Africans (he helped to restrict the possibility of Africans' voting or becoming involved in white affairs), its educational system, and its economic development. Rhodes's downfall came in 1896, as the result of an abortive raid in which an armed force of British South Africa Company troops under L. Starr Jameson, administrator of the company in Rhodesia, was discovered marching into the Transvaal to help British miners and settlers rebel against the Boer government. Although Rhodes was later cleared of complicity in Jameson's entry into the Transvaal, opinion toward him was so hostile that he was forced to resign.

Rhodes spent the last few years of his life (he died in 1902) in Rhodesia, helping to develop that vast dominion. He established the railway from South Africa up to Bulawayo, developed the country's mines, and attracted British settlers to the country. In 1899, when war finally broke out between Great Britain and the two Boer republics, he returned to South Africa, and helped to defend the mining city of Kimberley when it was besieged and nearly starved by Boer forces. He died just before the peace treaty was signed, and thus failed to witness the British victory that made possible the realization of one of his great ambitions: the federation of the Cape, Natal, the Orange Free State, and the Transvaal into a united South Africa.

Lord Salisbury (for whom Rhodesia's capital was named) went on to secure British access to the north through Bechuanaland, acquire the Rhodesias and Nyasaland, and negotiate the respective boundaries between the Portuguese and British African possessions.

France, meanwhile, was busily engaged in northern and western Africa, bringing under her control the vast territories that had fallen under her sphere of influence by 1886. By 1896, the French advance from the headwaters of the Senegal to the upper Niger had brought the French to Hausaland, where French expansion was checked by the British Royal Niger Company which was moving upstream. The Royal Niger Company, under the direction of George Goldie, had established treaty relations with the Sultan of Sokoto, thus gaining legal access to much of the Fulani empire of northern Nigeria. The emirates of Nupe and Ilorin had resisted Goldie's efforts to establish commercial control, but the army of the Royal Niger Company had defeated them. When French forces began to operate on the Hausa borders, they frequently clashed with the Royal Niger Company army, and in 1900 the British government took over direct control of the treaty territories in northern Nigeria.

In 1893 France had declared French Guinea and the Ivory Coast as colonies, and in that same year had invaded Dahomey, deposing that country's King Behanzin. After 1896, having gained command of the entire Niger country down to Hausaland, France began to extend its control from the Niger down to the coasts of Guinea, Ivory Coast, and Dahomey. By 1900 that process was complete. The Mossi states and the various Mande kingdoms had all been defeated by French armies, usually after dogged resistance.

At about the same time France moved to link its territory in North Africa with its newly subdued lands in Sudanic West Africa and with Gabon. Expeditions were dispatched from Algeria southward across the Sahara, eastward from the Niger, and northward from Gabon. These forays were to converge in the area of Lake Chad, after forcing all peoples in their paths to submit to French rule. By 1900, units of these three military groups had met at Lake Chad. But again they found that the British had moved equally fast. By 1900, British missions had occupied Kano, the richest of the Hausa states, and had claimed much of Bornu west of Lake Chad. (Thus the ancient empire of Kanem-Bornu fell victim to the accidents of boundary-setting that characterized the partition of Africa: Kanem and part of Bornu fell to the French, while another part of Bornu became British.)

This same French thrust led to occupation of most of the important Saharan oases by 1900, although resistance by Berber bands continued in some areas until the 1930's. From Lake Chad, French forces moved east, conquering Wadai and Bagirmi, after a fierce war with the Bagirmi army under Rabih, an Arab who had set up an expanding trade empire.

The final drama of the colonial partition of Africa came in the last five years of the nineteenth century, in the Sudan and Ethiopia. The Sudan was ruled by Sayyid Muhammad Ahmad, who had proclaimed himself the Mahdi (he whom God guides aright) in 1881. Ahmad, after a long and increasingly successful rebellion against the Egyptian rulers of the Sudan and their British supporters, captured Khartoum in 1884. The Mahdi's rebellion was the last great jihad of Muslim reform in modern African history: the Mahdi was a devout religious reformer, who set out not only to free his native Sudan, but to reestablish the rule of the Koran as widely as possible.

When Muhammad Ahmad proclaimed himself the Mahdi in 1881, political and religious leaders in Khartoum refused to accept his claim. An armed force sent to seize him was defeated, greatly boosting the Mahdi's prestige. Victory followed victory, and soon he was master of most of the western parts of the Sudan. The governor of Khartoum appealed to Cairo for help. Cairo was unable to send help at that time, and the Mahdi's forces continuing to grow. Soon his followers had taken much of the eastern Sudan, and Khartoum and the Nile valley were caught between the two Mahdist strongholds.

By this time Britain, intimately involved in Egyptian affairs, had become concerned, and at the request of the khedive sent an army from the Red Sea. In 1883 this force was met by Mahdist troops and annihilated almost to the last man. Then the khedive sent Charles George ("Chinese") Gordon, one of the most experienced and colorful British officers of the day, to take command of Khartoum. There Gordon, who was aware that the Mahdi was attracting great popular support because of the corruption and cruelty of the Egyptian administration in Khartoum, declared the Sudan separate from Egypt and recognized the Mahdi as ruler of Kordofan. By this time, however, a massive wave of religious zeal had made the Mahdi too strong for appeasement. In March 1884, Khartoum was besieged and surrounded by thousands of Mahdist troops. In January 1885, when the city was virtually starved, the Mahdist army stormed it, killing Gordon and the remaining administrators. With the fall of Khartoum, the Mahdi ruled the Sudan.

Egypt and Britain were not willing to accept the loss of the Sudan, and in 1886 Lord Kitchener, in command of a large Anglo-Egyptian army, began moving up the Nile. In 1898 Kitchener's army met the Mahdist army under the Khalifa (the Mahdi's successor; the Mahdi himself died six months after the fall of Khartoum), and in the Battle of Omdurman, which claimed 20,000 Sudanese lives, the Anglo-Egyptian force crushed the Sudanese army and ended the short-lived Mahdist reign.

During the 1880's and 1890's Italy, which had played little role in the partition and conquest of Africa, began to build an Italian colonial empire. First Italy seized a portion of the Eritrean coast that had been claimed by Ethiopia. Italy then negotiated a peace treaty with Ethiopia which, by Italian interpretation, allowed Italy to control Ethiopia's foreign relations. In 1896 Italy seized the eastern coast of Somalia (Britain claimed the northern coast, on the Red Sea), and decided to bring most of the Horn of Africa under Italian rule. She overlooked, however, the foresight and determination of Menelik II, emperor of Ethiopia.

Menelik was outraged when he discovered that Italy represented itself before the world as responsible for Ethiopia's foreign affairs. A strong, intelligent man, deeply imbued with a sense of Ethiopia's ancient history but thoroughly conscious of the complexities of the modern world, Menelik had vigorously strengthened Ethiopia in anticipation of an eventual test of Italy's claims. Menelik was a master diplomat, who was keenly aware that a divided Ethiopia would be easy prey for Italy or other European powers; when he succeeded to the throne in 1889, at the age of 45, Ethiopia was in a state of acute disunity. The rulers of each of the ancient provinces (Tigre, Gojjam, Wello, Harar, Kaffa, Wellegga, etc.) maintained as much independence as possible and resisted the authority of the emperor if he showed signs of weakness.

Menelik used constant diplomacy to win the support of the various powerful provincial rulers. At the same time, he signaled to the great powers of Europe his intention to rule an independent Ethiopian Empire. He had signed the disputed Italian treaty in the same year that he succeeded to the throne, and as soon as he realized how Italy was interpreting the document, he renounced it, repaying to Italy a large loan that had been made to Ethiopia as a part of the treaty. In 1891 he sent a letter to the heads of state of Britain, France, Germany, Italy, and Russia, in which he set forth the boundaries of the Ethiopian Empire and stated his position bluntly:

> While tracing today the actual boundaries of my Empire, I shall endeavour, if God gives me life and strength, to reestablish the ancient frontiers [tributaries] of Ethiopia up to Khartoum, and as far as Lake Nyanza, with all the Gallas.

> Ethiopia has been for 14 centuries a Christian island in a sea of pagans. If powers at a distance come forward to partition Africa between them, I do not intend to be an indifferent spectator!

Menelik also bought firearms and ammunition as rapidly as possible, and equipped his various armies with them. His resolute position on Ethiopian unity and his resistance to Italian aggression struck a highly sympathetic chord in the hearts of the Ethiopian people, who, as later events proved, were more loyal to Menelik than to his subordinates in the provinces. Italy was steadily building up its armed forces in Eritrea, and frequently engaged in minor military incursions into Ethiopian territory. This further aroused the growing nationalism of the Ethiopian masses.

In 1895 Italy sent its troops into Tigre province, seizing the towns of Addigrat and Adowa. Menelik, who had continued to seek an end to Italian aggression by diplomatic means while increasing his military capability, assembled his armies from the major provinces, and began to march toward the Italians in Tigre. (Many stories have been told of Menelik's strategy: he prepared inaccurate maps that were allowed to fall into the hands of the Italians, and had his agents, posing as guides, volunteer erroneous information.) In March 1896, the two armies met at Adowa, and the Italians were crushed in the largest military action between Africans and Europeans that had ever taken place. Only a tattered remnant of the Italian army managed to escape, and the defeat was so decisive that Italy abandoned its Ethiopian ventures until the 1930's, when Mussolini vowed to avenge the still-remembered humiliation.

Menelik went on to reconstitute the ancient Ethiopian Empire. He sent his armies into Somali-occupied lands in the Ogaden and the modern Kenya-Ethiopia border area; he strengthened his control over the provinces of Ethiopia, modernized the system of administration, founded the modern system of education, and attracted large numbers of European advisers, traders, investors, and technicians. He was the creator of the modern Ethiopian state, as well as the African ruler who proved that Europe was not invincible. He was paralyzed by a stroke in 1908, and died in 1913, a hero both to Ethiopia and the conquered peoples of Africa.

With the exception of Ethiopia (and tiny Liberia, whose independence was protected by its vague ties with the United States), the partitioning of Africa was nearly complete by 1900, awaiting only the French occupation of Morocco in 1912 and the Italian seizure of Libya in 1911-12. When these two ancient lands fell to Europe, all Africa was in European hands.

15 The Imposition of Colonial Rule

Emile Banning, the official Belgian archivist, summarized, in glowing tones, the new concept of colonialism in Africa:

> National interests are reconciled with universal interests in a synthesis of which the final result will be to give the world another continent; to production, the resources of a wealth and variety scarcely glimpsed; to militant humanity, a new family whose native faculties have already caused considerable surprises and which will reserve, after a century of culture, a goodly number more for future generations.[1]

There was little correspondence between the high tones of these comments and the grim reality of the colonial conquest of Africa. Although the partitioning of Africa was accomplished peacefully enough, the imposition of colonial conquest on the peoples of Africa was far from peaceful. European technology and armaments made the end result certain, but many lives were given in the struggle that began soon after the Berlin Conference.

By 1900, the scramble for African territory was almost over. Of the major African states and areas, only Libya, Morocco, Liberia, and Ethiopia remained under African rule. (In 1879 France had tried to establish a protectorate over Liberia, and did seize some Liberian territory, but the United States, in one of its few acts of responsibility toward Liberia, persuaded France to abandon its effort.) Libya was to fall to Italy in 1911-12. Morocco succumbed to France and Spain in 1912, with France taking the major part of the kingdom as a protectorate and

[1] *La partage politique de l'Afrique d'après des transactions internationales les plus recentes, 1885 à 1888*, Brussels, 1888; translation by Irene and Raymond Betts.

Spain claiming the barren coastlands and adjacent interior that came to be called Spanish Sahara. With these actions the formal partitioning of Africa came to an end.

The thirty years between 1880 and 1910 were years of misery for Africa, as the several European powers quickly and ruthlessly moved to expand and "pacify" the territories they were claiming so that other European nations could be denied access to them. To a large extent this period was one of conquest, resistance, retaliation, rebellion, and repression. Few African rulers welcomed European claims of protection and supersovereignty. Many of those who signed treaties did so (as in Bechuanaland and Basutoland) because accepting European protection was the lesser of two evils. Africans, of course, often learned that they had agreed to something that meant one thing to them and something different to the Europeans (Menelik's treaty with Italy provides the most famous case of such a treaty).

There is a myth that Africans accepted colonial rule passively, even eagerly, and were happy in their faith that European civilization would relieve them from misery. Nothing could be farther from the truth. Not only African rulers, but thousands of ordinary people, bitterly opposed the establishment of colonial rule and its subsequent administration.

There is no way to estimate the number of African lives exacted by the wars, reprisals, massacres, and executions that accompanied European conquest. What figures are available, however, bear grim testimony to the African spirit of resistance. Some 20,000 Sudanese lives were lost in the bloody battle of Omdurman alone, when Kitchener and his Anglo-Egyptian army defeated the troops of Mahdist Sudan.

Two other series of wars, both resulting from German "pacification" efforts, show the dimension of African resistance as well as the brutal determination of Europe to implant its rule on Africa. In South West Africa (which is today called Namibia by the United Nations and the African liberation movement that is trying to free it from alien rule), the Herero-German war of 1904-06 is believed to have resulted in the death of approximately two thirds of the entire Herero population. The Herero, a Bantu people, live in central and western South West Africa, earning a living by growing grain and herding cattle. Traditionally, they have been seminomadic, living in small family settlements that are moved from time to time to take advantage of the best grazing and tilling conditions in their dry homeland. Before the German conquest, the Herero lived in a decentralized society, and ruled through clans headed by presiding chiefs and councils of elders.

German policy called for the Herero to concentrate their population in certain localities, to grow cash crops, and to work for the German colonists who soon began to arrive. The Herero resisted, and the ensuing skirmishes resulted in the death of several German settlers. Germany then assembled a small but well trained and armed force that was determined to exact reprisals. In the war that followed, the Herero, armed with spears and bows, were killed in large numbers. Many communities were destroyed by the ruthless German punitive force, and starvation killed thousands. By 1906, when effective Herero resistance had ceased, between 60,000 and 75,000 Herero had been killed, leaving a population of only 25,000 or 30,000.

In Tanganyika the toll in lives was even higher. There the Germans met resistance almost from the moment they set up a government, a few years after 1884. The coastal Swahili began a war of resistance in 1888, when the first German garrisons were set up in the coastal cities. They forced the Germans to evacuate Kilwa, Lindi, and Mikindani, and attacked the main German fort at Dar es Salaam. At first the German forces were heavily on the defensive and were unable to make headway against the Swahili troops. In 1889, however, the German navy, aided by ships from Britain, Italy, and Portugal, blockaded the coast, shutting off supplies of arms and ammunitions. By 1890, the Germans had finally defeated the Swahili and restored an uneasy peace to the coast.

Swahili resistance on the coast was only the forerunner of the African reaction to German conquest. In 1891-94 the Hehe and Gogo peoples of central Tanganyika fought fiercely against the German troops that came to set up garrisons in the interior. Well-equipped German soldiers and a brutal German policy of reducing villages to ashes and destroying crops and food supplies subdued the two peoples. The Chagga peoples who live around the slopes of Mount Kilimanjaro in northern Tanganyika, and the Yao and Ngoni peoples of southern Tanganyika also resisted valiantly. But, between 1892 and 1895, they too were defeated by superior German arms and organization.

The attitude of Tanganyika's African peoples was abundantly clear: they opposed German rule and colonization, and were prepared to defend their freedom and their lands. In 1890, Chief Macemba, head of the Yao peoples in southern Tanganyika, stated the position in a letter, written in Swahili, to Herman von Wissman, leader of the German campaign in the south:

> I have listened to your words but can find no reason why I should obey you—I would rather die first. I have no relations with you and can not bring it to my mind that you have given me so much as a pesa [fraction of a rupee] or the quarter of a pesa or a needle or a thread. I look for some reason why I should obey you and find not the smallest. If it should be friendship that you desire, then I am ready for it, today and always; but to be your subject, that I can not be—If it should be

war you desire, then I am ready, but never to be your subject. . . . I do not fall at your feet, for you are God's creature just as I am. . . . I am sultan here in my land. You are sultan there in yours. Yet listen, I do not say to you that you should obey me; for I know that you are a free man . . . As for me, I will not come to you, and if you are strong enough, then come and fetch me.[1]

Although the wars of resistance took thousands of lives, they were modest compared to the great "Maji-Maji rebellion" in Tanganyika, which came some twenty years after Germany first claimed the country. In 1904, the African population of central Tanganyika had been "pacified." Yet it grew increasingly resentful of the German style of rule. German administrators, backed by garrisons of professional officers and African mercenaries, had levied heavy taxes on all adult males and had used harsh methods to force African labor to work on numerous construction projects. One especially odious and clumsy effort was a German experiment of introducing cotton as a cash crop, and attempting to force African subsistence farmers to grow it for market.

In 1905, when resentment was widespread, a semireligious movement began, led by African priests who preached that men who took certain potions and oaths would be rendered immune to German bullets, which would turn to water ("maji" in Swahili) when fired. Like wildfire this movement spread among the discontented peoples and soon sparked African attacks on German administrative posts, settlers, and missionary stations. Over a wide area of central Tanganyika, Africans suddenly rose up in anger, determined to rid their lands of the hated German oppressors. At first the German armed forces were overwhelmed. African freedom fighters, terming themselves "askari ya mungu" (soldiers of God), cut telegraph lines, burned posts, destroyed roads and bridges, and besieged a number of German settlements. In the end, however, the Germans were too strong. They again resorted to a massive scorched-earth policy and pursued African troops relentlessly. Soon starvation was rampant, and group by group the Africans laid down their arms and surrendered. By 1908, when the rebellion finally ended, the death toll had reached between 75,000 and 125,000 (the German official report, probably conservative, listed 75,000) men, women, and children. Thousands had been killed in battle or were executed by German troops, and tens of thousands died from starvation. By this time the exhausted and beaten peoples of Tanganyika recognized the impossibility of further armed resistance, and the German conquest was complete.

German rule was also contested in Togo, Cameroun, and Ruanda-Urundi (modern Rwanda and Burundi). The latter country was an-

1 *The African Past*, by Basil Davidson, Boston, Little, Brown and Company, 1964, pp. 357-58.

nexed by Germany after its seizure of Tanganyika. In none of these countries, however, was the death toll as high as in Tanganyika and South West Africa. Yet in each case, German troops had to battle and defeat African troops in a series of wars before German rule was finally established.

The French had to fight battle after battle in the years of their expansion up the Senegal, in their invasions of Guinea and Dahomey, and in their occupation of the great plains of the Sudan. The French military role in the enormous lands that their empire included continued well into the twentieth century. And many of the freedom-minded Berber and Arab tribes of the Sahara continued to resist French rule until the 1940's.

The British were able to occupy some of their territories, such as the Fante states along the Gold Coast, with relative ease. But a series of wars was necessary to crush Asante power and resistance, and several thousand Asante lives were lost in the process. Small-scale military actions were necessary in many parts of Nigeria before British rule was secure. Had the British not used the policy of "indirect rule" in Hausaland, ruling through the established political structures of the Fulani emirs, there might have been a major war in that region. As it was, military action was necessary in several of the Hausa states.

In South Africa, British rule required frequent military action over a long period. But British rule came almost as a relief to many of the African peoples who were subjected to Boer conquest and exploitation. David Livingstone in his book *Missionary Travels and Researches in Africa,* published in 1858, described the Boer forays against the peaceful Bechuana (Tswana) people:

> But how is it that the natives, being so vastly superior in numbers to the Boers, do not rise and annihilate them? The people among whom they live are Bechuanas, not Kaffirs [here he means the warlike Zulus] though no one would ever learn the distinction from a Boer; and history does not contain one single instance in which the Bechuanas, even those of them who possess firearms, have attacked either the Boers or the English. . . . They have defended themselves when attacked, . . . but have never engaged in offensive war with Europeans. . . .
> The plan pursued [in raids] is the following: one or two friendly tribes are forced to accompany a party of mounted Boers, and these expeditions can be got up only in the winter, when horses may be used without danger of being lost by disease. When they reach the tribe to be attacked, the friendly natives are ranged in front, to form, as they say, "a shield"; the Boers then coolly fire over their heads till the . . . people [attacked] flee and leave cattle, wives, and children to the captors. This was done in nine cases during my residence in the interior, and on no occasion was a drop of Boers' blood shed. . . .

Yet these brutal little raids were minor when compared with the hundred years of war with the Xhosa, the great battles with the Zulu, the wars with the Basuto and their northern kinsmen, the Pedi, and the extinction of the thousands of Hottentots. Europe's South African conquest began in 1652, and has gone on for more than three centuries. Africans still rebel against European rule in South Africa, and the threat of incursions by guerrilla forces based in neighboring countries hangs over the heads of the white-ruled government.

Ironically, British expansion in South Africa led to a particularly violent war of resistance by the Boers. In 1899, the Boer republics of Transvaal and the Orange Free State resorted to open military defiance of the growing British presence. During three years of pitched battles by armies and numerous guerrilla activities, the British lost 5,774 men and the Boers lost some 4,000, making this one of the bloodier wars of resistance to the colonial conquest of Africa.

North of South Africa, Britain was able to begin its rule more or less peacefully. But within a few years, resistance began to form in Nyasaland (Malawi), Rhodesia, and Northern Rhodesia (Zambia). The widescale uprising by the Shona and Matabele peoples of Rhodesia was the largest violent confrontation, comparing with the Maji-Maji War in the number of Africans involved. Yet, its ultimate death toll, in excess of 10,000, was modest compared to the Tanganyika uprising.

The British South Africa Company had induced several thousand British settlers, both from South Africa and from Britain, to come to farm the fertile lands of the Rhodesian plateau. The company also attracted many employees for mining, trading, and administration. Both the Shona, the land's ancient inhabitants, and the Matabele, the conquerors of the western part of the plateau only a few decades before, lost large tracts of land, found their movements and freedoms severely constricted and the demands made upon them for labor and taxes onerous. In 1896, the two peoples, acting in a coordinated effort that was remarkable considering the traditional hostility between them, attacked British farms, mission stations, and settlements. They also sent large armed parties to attack the larger towns. Their onslaught was so vigorous that the British were almost overwhelmed, retreating into the sanctuary of several of the larger towns. The well-equipped troops of the British South Africa Company, even when augmented by the settlers, had to appeal for help from both the British government and Cecil Rhodes. This help came almost immediately, in the form of new troops and supplies, and soon the Africans were driven from areas around the towns and near the major roads. Less than a year after the war started, most African belligerents were conducting guerrilla campaigns from remote areas. Within a few more months the beleaguered Matabele were ready to discuss peace terms, and Rhodes himself came to arrange a treaty. The Shona continued to fight for nearly a year longer, until most of their leaders had been captured and executed.

African resistance in Rhodesia involved so much of the population that it was more of a popular revolution than a series of skirmishes. Old men, women, and even children joined in some of the attacks against the hated white oppressors, despite the hail of machine gun bullets that killed them by the hundreds. The causes of this fervent popular uprising are various but had much to do with the proud history of the people. This was, after all, the land of Changamire and Great Zimbabwe, where the Shona had for a thousand years tilled their fields while their rulers created a great culture and imperial state. The state, and its noble Rozwi rulers, had been smashed decades before, when the Zulu forces of Zwangendaba destroyed Zimbabwe and the Rozwi houses and shrines. Though there was no longer a centralized political system, and the Rozwi held power only in a few areas, their prestige was still alive in the memory of many ordinary Shona. The leaders who helped organize the uprising against the British included many Rozwi. Their stature encouraged the people to believe that they might humble the arrogant whites and, at the same time, restore an ancient glory.

The Matabele in the west were themselves intruders, disliked by the Shona whose lands they had occupied. But they had come to develop their own roots in the country and to absorb some of its culture. They also had as much reason as the Shona to detest the British settlers. The two groups planned jointly and coordinated their attacks and campaigns. When the leaders of the Matabele accepted peace in 1897, one group of warriors joined the Shona and continued the fight.

British expansion into Kenya and Uganda and Britain's assumption of responsibility for Zanzibar were comparatively peaceful, evoking only minor opposition in Kenya and Uganda. The greatest African resistance in these areas arose many years later, in the 1950's, when the Kikuyu people of Kenya produced the Mau Mau rebellion.

The greatest toll in African lives during the European conquest was not in any of these specific battles, wars, uprisings, and rebellions: it was in the extensive, sustained, and brutal reduction of the Congo Free State by Leopold II, between 1884 and about 1908. This was a campaign carried on almost as a deliberate policy of genocide. Deep in the interior of the Congo River basin, Belgian operations were virtually hidden from the outside world. After about 1900, however, the bloody results came increasingly to the attention of the outside world through reports from traders and missionaries, and, in 1908, the government of Belgium was forced to assume responsibility for the Congo. Several years later, an official commission of the Belgian government estimated that during the

Congo conquest between 1889 and 1908 roughly half the African population had been killed, either by force of arms or through starvation and malnutrition.

Part of the reason for this shocking process was the unique status of the Congo Free State. King Leopold had vast ambitions. He made investments in various European industrial and financial ventures and followed closely the activities of various governments in acquiring foreign trade rights and colonial territories. Africa, especially, fired his imagination, and he believed, like Stanley, that in its interior were vast potential riches awaiting energetic exploitation. His involvement with the International African Association, as a wealthy private individual rather than as king, enabled him to keep abreast of explorations for new sources of trade and mineral wealth, and he saw in Stanley's explorations and speculations a unique opportunity in the heart of Africa, in an area where no European power had staked a claim.

When Leopold employed Stanley to explore the water system of the Congo and to seek treaties granting trading rights with African chiefs, he envisioned the creation of a giant colony in the interior that would be largely under his personal control. The first step was taken in 1879, when the Belgian Committee of the International Association changed its name to the International Association of the Congo, which was controlled by Leopold and several Belgians in his service. In 1884, Leopold sought formal international recognition of the International Association of the Congo as an independent nation. The United States was the first major power to give this recognition. In 1885, after the Berlin Conference, the name of the state was changed to "État Indépendant du Congo," which came to be called the Congo Free State. In the same year, Leopold persuaded the Belgian parliament to authorize him to become the sovereign of the Congo state. A formal resolution authorized the king ". . . to be the chief of the state founded in Africa by the International Association of the Congo," and made it clear that "the union between Belgium and the new state of the Congo shall be exclusively personal."

Thus Leopold became as near the owner of the Congo as one man could. He was not required to answer to anyone in his administration of the territory, and he was convinced that as the Congo developed he would become wealthy beyond belief. Leopold was aware that he had to act as rapidly as possible to press this development, partly to recover some of the money he was already spending from his personal fortune and partly to make sure that no other European power could grab parts of the territory. (In Katanga, Leopold soon faced the equally ambitious and energetic Cecil Rhodes as both sought possession of the lands that soon came to be known as the Copper Belt. Part of the rich area became part of Leopold's Congo; the other portion became part of Northern Rhodesia.) This meant building roads and railroads, subduing resistance, establishing administrative centers, building river steamers, port facilities, and other necessary infrastructure, and at the same time devising ways by which the government could reap a sure profit on the goods produced and sold. Within the first few years of the development of the Congo, Leopold spent 20 million of his own francs, in addition to other moneys raised in loans and funds that various companies expended to develop plantations, mines, warehouses, and transport facilities.

The development of the vast lands of the Congo into a modern area of production would have been a formidable task even for the government of a large and wealthy European country. For a private enterprise, which the Congo Free State essentially was, it was staggering. Leopold's ambitions were equal to the task, however, and he determined to open the Congo and make it profitable as quickly as possible. Indeed, his resources were not sufficient to allow the process to drag on for long. Several measures, taken early in the process of setting up the Congo government, were designed to maximize profits and facilitate the speed of development: all lands not under cultivation were declared government property (a drastic blow to Africans, who used the shifting-plot method of farming, which required that plots remain idle for several years); forced labor was declared an obligation of all Congolese; taxes, in cash or in products, were levied; and a large and well-equipped police force was organized. The police force resembled a mercenary army, with European officers and African troops employed on contract.

Leopold's actions were met with widespread opposition and resentment, but the police, under administrators who were obligated to facilitate development and maximize profits, met resistance with immediate retaliation. Recalcitrant chiefs were punished and fined. Hostages were taken to ensure compliance. Women and young girls were raped. As time went on, whole villages were pillaged and burned, chiefs and rebels executed, tax laggards publicly punished (often by cutting off hands or ears), and a reign of terror became almost the order of the day.

Ivory and wild rubber were among the first products to be brought under government control, and soon both could be sold only to the government or to government-licensed firms. This set off a tendency toward monopoly, which violated the Berlin agreements and further constricted the Africans, who now were even more at the mercy of government administrators and the mercenary police. To all this was added a system of concessions for European companies organized for Congo ventures (and usually owned in part by Leopold's Congo government). These companies were granted vast tracts of territory to develop, almost as small states, into rubber plantations, cotton plantations, mining areas, or simply areas in which to harvest the wild rubber. In this way, the great Union Minière du Haut Katanga was formed as one of many firms that exploited the copper resources of the rich Katanga copper-belt.

Reports of this harsh administration and exploitation began coming out of the Congo before 1900. By about that time, committees were organized in the United States and Great Britain to protest these practices. In 1903, the British House of Commons formally requested the British government to consult with the Berlin powers "by virtue of which the Congo Free State exists, in order that measures may be adopted to abate the evils prevalent in that state." Belgian public opinion was also aroused, and, in 1904, Leopold appointed a commission of enquiry (composed of several Belgian and Swiss jurists) to investigate the validity of the criticisms. After several months the commission, although it paid guarded tribute to the many beneficial aspects of the Congo development program, reported that many of the suspected evils were true. The panel recommended a number of measures to alleviate some of the crueler and more debasing aspects of the Congo administration. A measure of European attitudes toward Africans at the time was the commission's explicit recognition that the development of the Congo's riches required such techniques as forced labor and the issuing of concessions to private companies. It addressed itself to ways of alleviation of vicious excesses rather than to any questioning of the fundamental ethical problem of forcing Africans to work for European profit. Among the committee's recommendations were more liberal interpretation of the land laws (which prevented African farmers from growing the food to sustain themselves and their families), better supervision to ensure that Africans were not forced to work away from their farms for more than forty hours per month, withdrawal of the rights of concession companies to employ compulsory measures, and better regulation of the army and police.

In 1906, Leopold signed a decree that was said to ameliorate conditions along the lines of the commission's recommendations, but there was widespread criticism of its limited approach. Reports of the suffering of African communities, the use of harsh punishments and tortures, and of starvation and malnutrition again began to flow out of the Congo. Public ire in Belgium and other countries mounted. The British government, both the Senate and President (Theodore Roosevelt) of the United States, Belgian legislators, and many French citizens and groups began to issue firm statements demanding fundamental change in the Congo. Finally, in 1908, the Belgian parliament approved an act that, in effect, confiscated the Congo Free State from Leopold (with generous compensation), and created a new administration under the authority of the Belgian government. Thus ended twenty-four years of Leopold's rule of an independent, private fiefdom, at a cost of untold

African suffering and the death of as many as a million and a half Africans.

The full story of the inhuman repressions that characterized the exploitation of the Congo people during the Free State period will never be known; Leopold destroyed many of the documents that might have told it, with the comment "They can have my Congo, but they've no right to know what I've done there." Leopold himself emerged with a considerable profit. He had used Congo revenues to build royal palaces and gardens in Belgium, and the compensation granted him by the Belgian government included absolving him of all debts ensured by his Congo government. In addition he received a large cash settlement. For years afterward some 20 percent of the Congo's revenues went into reducing the debts incurred under Leopold.

These several examples, notably Tanganyika, South West Africa, South Africa, Rhodesia, and the Congo, illustrate the extensive African reaction to European partition, conquest, and administration. Few African chiefs, even those in remote and poor areas, were under major illusions about the European motive in setting up protectorates and legal systems in their territory. Many resisted at once, and wars, in which a determined, superbly equipped Europe had the clear advantage, resulted. Others resisted within a few years after the beginning of European administration, when it became clear that the European presence implied a fundamental change in the life, culture, and welfare of whole populations. Thus uprisings that amounted to civil war took place in the Maji-Maji rebellion of Tanganyika and the Shona-Matabele uprisings in Rhodesia. Similar rebellions and acts of resistance broke out in most parts of Africa repeatedly between the 1880's and about 1910, when European forces finally established an uneasy peace.

The European attitude during this bloody period hardened into a view of Africans that was, if anything, even more deprecatory than during the height of the slave trade. Africans were increasingly thought of as inhuman savages, ignorant, lazy, devoid of the finer emotions, and without history or culture. One of the most vivid expressions of this view was an official German order of 1911, addressed to German officers serving in Tanganyika. The order instructed officers on the characteristics of the African and how to handle him:

> The negro does not love us but only fears our power. Any sign of weakness which he thinks he sees in us will be a temptation to him to take up arms and to drive us from his country. Cruel by nature, the negro does not understand devotion, gratitude or loyalty in our sense.
>
> He will, therefore, support those whom he fears or who offer him the greatest material advantage.

This material instinct is influenced by superstition and . . . racial hatred. . . .

There are certainly no tribes whatever on whose loyalty we can with certainty depend.

The myth of African inferiority was essential to protect European sensitivity from the stark contradiction between the finer European ethical views and the base exploitation of Africa that underlay the colonial system. Some colonial pioneers were overtly crass and motivated purely by profit and adventure; the administrators, police, and company officials of Leopold's Congo were liberally spiced with such men. Others were convinced that they were, in the long run, developing Africa for the benefit of its people. The former colonial personnel assuaged their consciences by convincing themselves that Africans were scarcely human. The latter, much less given to cruel punishments and overt injustice, justified their paternalistic actions with the belief that Africans were childlike and irresponsible and had to be firmly handled for their own well-being.

With their minds well encased in a sheath of stereotypes, the European nations partitioned Africa, crushed resistance and rebellion, and set up a thin but viable network of administration. By the eve of the great World War, when the comparative amicability that had prevailed among the contending European nations was at last disrupted, Africa was not only partitioned and largely pacified, but boundaries had been demarcated, networks of administration set up, and a skeletal system of transportation developed to facilitate both administration and economic exploitation.

Once resistance was subdued and an administrative system introduced, the next order of business was to open the interior to commerce and production as rapidly as possible. At the turn of the century, European governments in their own home lands were concerned primarily with internal stability, providing a means of political expression, conducting international relations, and facilitating commerce and economic pursuits: today's vast array of social and educational services were then considered the responsibility of private and religious agencies rather than government. This situation prevailed equally in the new colonial administrations. The governments of colonies saw as their tasks the quelling of resistance and violations of the law, the administration of justice, the facilitation of transportation and communications, and the encouragement of economic enterprise. While bringing Western religion, education, and culture to the Africans was regarded as an ultimate object of the colonial mission, it was generally felt that this was better done by missionaries and private agencies.

Generally, the economic potentialities of most of the new colonial territories were either unknown or known very poorly. The centers of European influence that had long existed along the coasts of West Africa had witnessed development of new products, following the end of the slave trade: Senegal was producing groundnuts (peanuts); the Gold Coast was producing palm oil, cocoa, timber, gold, and wild rubber; Dahomey was growing a limited quantity of copra and coconuts; Lagos and Yorubaland produced cocoa, palm oil, and rubber; and eastern Nigeria was producing palm oil. In these regions, the African populations had made a satisfactory shift from the earlier slave economy to the production of cash crops for sale to Europe, and by about 1900 were exporting these goods. The colonial governments had this as a precedent, as they pressed into the interior of each colony, seeking to encourage African farmers to produce for sale whatever crops would grow in their areas.

The chief crops thus encouraged were cocoa, palm oil, and palm kernels. Coffee was encouraged in the forest areas. Groundnuts and cotton were encouraged in the savanna region. France's success with groundnuts in the grassy plains of Senegal set the pattern for most of the vast territory of French West Africa, all of which lay in the Sudan country except for the coastal lands of Guinea and Ivory Coast. Shortly after 1900, France consolidated the huge areas it had conquered in West Africa into one coordinated unit, French West Africa, administered under the supervision of a governor-general in Dakar, the capital of Senegal. Under Dakar were seven territorial units other than Senegal: Mauritania; Soudan, or modern Mali; Guinea; Niger; Ivory Coast; Upper Volta; and Dahomey.

In all seven of these territories the pattern was roughly the same. French military forces were quickly followed by civilian administrators, who worked energetically to persuade African farmers to grow cash crops. Much of the money needed to establish the administrations of each of the territories came from the revenues of Senegal. That country had long been self-supporting, and the French government expected its example to be followed in the new territories. Since the governor-general in Dakar was responsible for developing the other territories, he had to employ funds available to him from within Senegal and from Dahomey, at first the only other territory that produced a surplus of wealth. (The funds came largely from customs duties on imports and exports.)

France soon found that the upper Senegal and the upper Niger were unreliable means of transportation, especially for heavier boats capable of carrying large cargoes. Railways had already proved effective stimulants of revenues. In the 1880's a line laid from Dakar to St.

Louis on the lower Senegal River had resulted in increases in ground-nut production all along the line and up the Senegal. Between about 1890 and 1910, other lines were built or begun. These connected the Niger with the Senegal River, Guinea's port of Conakry with upper Niger country, and the Niger with Abidjan in the Ivory Coast and Cotonou in Dahomey. The loans that financed most of this railway construction were made possible because of revenues from commerce in Senegal and Dahomey.

In both the French and British colonies of West Africa the colonial governments assumed responsibility for economic development. Although companies that wished to trade or invest were encouraged, the earlier use of powerful trading firms as rulers and exploiters of territory was discontinued. Most lands remained in African hands and patterns of land ownership and use were not seriously affected by colonial rule.

In the four British colonies in West Africa, Gambia, Sierra Leone, the Gold Coast, and Nigeria, the same general economic process took place, although the four were separately administered, each with its own government. (Nigeria was administered as three colonies until shortly before World War I—Lagos and Yorubaland, the Oil Rivers, and Northern Nigeria.) In each colony the earlier coastal economies produced revenues that supported the administration and development of the colony, including building railroads into the interior. In the French territories cash crops alone were the stimulus for railroad construction. In the British colonies there were minerals also. Gold mines in the Gold Coast stimulated the building of the first railroad to the interior, thus opening an important lumber industry. The Gold Coast was the wealthiest colony in all West Africa. By 1914 it was producing more than $10 million in cocoa annually, and more than $8 million worth of gold, as well as more than $1 million worth of timber.

In 1906 Britain amalgamated the Lagos Protectorate and the Protectorate of Southern Nigeria. Its revenues came largely from customs duties levied on the export of cocoa from Yorubaland and palm products from the eastern region. Northern Nigeria was much poorer. It had to be supported by grants from the British government, and was forced to use the governmental structure of the Fulani emirates for most of its administration. Some years later tin mines and groundnuts became important sources of revenue in the north, but it consistently lagged behind the south in most aspects of development.

Most of central Africa, including the German colonies of Kamerun (Cameroun), Togo, and South West Africa, the French colonies of Equatorial Africa, Leopold's Congo Free State, and the British colonies of the Rhodesias and Nyasaland, had no precolonial economic systems upon which to build programs of exploitation and development. To open the interiors, the French adopted the same system of concession companies used so profitably (and so painfully) in the Congo. Mineral and agricultural rights were granted to any company that agreed to build the roads, railroads, or navigation routes that would stimulate production in a given territory. The French colonial administration, however, supervised concession companies more carefully than did Leopold's Congo government. Alienation of Africans from the land and the enforcement of labor were lessened, though not eliminated.

The concession system, however much it may have lessened African entrepreneurship, enabled the colonial government to open a vast territory in a comparatively short time, without large grants from the metropolitan country's budget. In central Africa, the colonial governments seized on the concession system as the least expensive and most expeditious method of creating an economy that would produce revenues.

The Germans adopted a different approach, especially in Tanganyika and South West Africa. They encouraged German settlers to come to the colonies to set up farms, using the abundant and cheap African labor to produce cash crops on a large scale. Portugal, motivated by the European scramble to exploit the interior of Angola and Mozambique, resorted to the same device. By 1914, there were thousands of settlers in Angola, Mozambique, South West Africa, and Tanganyika.

Although Great Britain had no official policy of encouraging settlement in its African territories, British farmers were attracted in increasing numbers to the highlands of Southern Rhodesia and Kenya. Other Britons came to the copper mines in Northern Rhodesia. By 1914 there were more than 10,000 British settlers in Southern Rhodesia, and at least 3,000 each in Kenya and Northern Rhodesia. Much smaller numbers came to Nyasaland and Uganda, both of which had relatively dense African populations on the better lands. In Uganda, the Baganda people, in return for their assistance to Britain in conquering the rest of Uganda, were given large land holdings and soon developed a major and highly profitable cotton production. Uganda quickly became self-sufficient.

The policies by which European governments developed a basic cash economy in their African colonies thus differed according to local conditions, historical developments, and the attitudes of the metropolitan power. In every case, however, the object was to install a colonial government that was adequate to keep the peace, to facilitate production of crops or minerals that could support the colonial government, and to create a basic pattern of roads, railways, and harbors.

By 1914, the colonial territories were producing substantial supplies of cotton, sugarcane, wild rubber (although the demand was declining, with the growth of plantation rubber in Indonesia and South America), groundnuts, cocoa, coffee, tea, sisal, and bananas, in addition to the palm oil, copra, and ivory that had traditionally been produced. Gold and diamonds were being produced in Sierra Leone, the Gold Coast, Congo, Angola, Rhodesia, and South Africa. Copper was being produced in Congo and Northern Rhodesia; and tin in Nigeria. Prospectors were lured to the unexplored lands of the vast African interior in search of gold, diamonds, tin, semiprecious stones, iron, copper, and coal. With each new find revenues increased, and new prosperity was brought to areas near the mines and along the railways that carried their products to the sea.

Exports from the more developed and better endowed territories rose sharply between 1900 and 1914 as the African interior was opened up and new mines and new farm lands began producing. Exports from the Gold Coast increased five-fold during this period, while those of Sierra Leone quadrupled and those of Nigeria increased three and a half times. The growth of the more isolated and less richly endowed territories was disappointingly slow, however. Nyasaland, Togo, Dahomey, Niger, Upper Volta, and Ruanda-Urundi experienced little new growth in production, for example, and Northern Rhodesia (where the highly profitable copper mines were yet to open) seemed stagnant. South Africa was flourishing, especially with the expanding production of gold and diamonds, as was Southern Rhodesia, where gold was being mined in substantial quantity.

Just as the major patterns of economic development varied from territory to territory, so the kinds of administrative systems differed widely. Yet several broad patterns emerged as characteristic. Each colonial power began with its own preferences and philosophy, adapting these to the requirements of governing each territory. The French, influenced by their own history during the eighteenth and nineteenth centuries, had developed a strong sense of mission regarding their own culture, and in their colonial territories were prone to feel that it was important to acculturate the subject peoples and bring them into the great French cultural sphere. In their earlier experience with Black Africa, the French had applied this philosophy in Senegal, where numerous Black and mixed inhabitants in and around the coastal towns became as fiercely French as the Parisians, voting in French elections and playing an enthusiastic role in French politics and national affairs.

The British were much less prone to feel that British culture needed to be spread among the world's people. In most of Africa, the British were interested in stimulating trade and ensuring order. They believed in expending only that amount of money, energy, and manpower necessary to achieve this interest. Thus Britain, more often than France, was willing to work through African rulers and to allow African peoples to go about their own affairs, so long as economic development and peace were achieved. Between the two major colonial powers these broad colonial policies produced fundamental differences in African colonial territories. While a Frenchman regarded it as natural that a properly Gallicized African, speaking good French and acquainted with the refinements of French civilization, should be accepted as French and vote, the Briton could never forget that a basic difference existed between himself and all other peoples. This basic difference in philosophy influenced the development of education especially. Schools in French colonial Africa invariably were conducted in French and had the inculcation of French culture as a deep objective; in British territories, on the other hand, missionaries often learned the local language and conducted classes in it. They were more concerned with imparting literacy and the tenets of Christianity than with creating Black Britons.

In the Congo the Belgians followed a policy that was fundamentally akin to that introduced by Leopold. Economic development was the sacred objective, and everything was subordinated to it. African culture was not thought to have any particular relevance, nor was the spread of Belgian culture seen as important. Whatever was needed to induce the African to work, to desire goods, and to produce goods or services was relevant. Education, which began to spread through missionary efforts even during the days of the Congo Free State, consisted exclusively of primary schooling, with an emphasis on literacy, artithmetic, and the glorification of work.

German rule was similar to that of the Belgians. It emphasized the economic transformation of the peoples of the colonies into producers and consumers. German administrators tended to set up rigorous and comprehensive models (what to farm and how, how to behave, what work habits to follow, etc.) that Africans were expected to follow.

The Portuguese had the least coherent colonial philosophy. They tended to leave their African territories to themselves until stimulated by the scramble of other European powers. After Portugal developed its colonial empire, its approach was somewhat contradictory. Emphasizing the values of the ancient Portuguese civilization, the Portuguese professed to govern their colonies in such a way as to transform the African peoples into Black Portuguese, with all the rights and privileges of any Portuguese. There were few legal distinctions between the handful of "assimilados" in the main towns and the native Portuguese. But overall, Portuguese policy was quite different: its nationals used forced labor and other techniques to require Africans to produce goods and services, but provided little in return.

Despite these differences, the colonial patterns of all the powers were similar in broad outline and in fundamental objectives. The purposes of colonial rule were to maintain peace and order, to open up the African continent to trade, to find new sources of raw materials, and to organize African manpower to these ends. In general colonial administration and African development were expected to be financed by African financial resources rather than by subsidies from the metropolitan country. Since many African societies possessed no sources of money except those developed from European trade, a circular system of financing often developed in colonial territories: taxes, usually a per capita or "head" tax or a "hut" tax on each household, were levied, then Africans had to grow new products with which to earn the tax money or else had to sell their labor to the European administrations or commercial enterprises.

Road building quickly became an African responsibility. The colonial administration would plan the roads and provide engineering expertise, but each local chief was required to provide manpower for building the road through his area, and for maintaining it afterward.

Since the taxes paid by African populations were rarely sufficient to pay the total cost of colonial administration, much less the cost of developing railroads, ports, and economic enterprise, two other devices were utilized: duties on imports and exports and forced labor. Customs duties to generate revenue for governments had long been used by African rulers. They were neither unique nor unfamiliar in the African colonial experience; they did, however, tend to force the price of imported goods to high levels, making them difficult for the African to afford.

Head taxes and forced labor quickly became a special, critical matter in most colonies. A French researcher, writing about French West Africa, noted bitterly that "the idea of colonization becomes increasingly more repugnant to me. To collect taxes, that is the chief preoccupation. Pacification, medical aid, have only one aim: to tame the peoples so that they will be docile and pay their taxes. . . ."[1] Taxes were vital because the cost of maintaining colonial administrators and military forces was high, and the cost had to be met almost entirely from within the territory. Both taxes and forced labor had an additional importance, however: they were essential to the overall colonial strategy of opening up the continent and developing profitable new products for the great commercial and industrial firms of the metropolitan countries.

As a 1922 circular on Congo government policy put it, "It is a mistake to believe . . . that once taxes are paid and other legal obligations met, the native may remain inactive. Under no circumstances may

[1] Michel Leiris, quoted in *Africa Dances: A Book About West African Negroes*, by Geoffrey Gorer, Alfred A. Knopf, Inc., New York, 1935.

magistrates or officials express this opinion. In every case, I should consider this to be a lack of discipline violating the recommendations of the government and our most positive duties toward our black subjects."

The policies of the colonial powers proved effective in forcing Africans out of their traditional economic systems into cash systems dictated largely by European needs for products, markets, and profits. For centuries before the colonial era the three great trading systems of Africa—the trans-Saharan, the coastal Atlantic, and the Arab-Swahili Indian Ocean trade—had helped to create economic patterns linking Africans with the outside world, but only a relatively few states and urban or royal classes were affected. In the colonial period, foreign-linked economic activity and influences were extended to the masses in interior Africa. Between about 1880 and 1950, millions of ordinary African men, pushed by the burden of colonial taxes or forced labor and pulled by the lure of wages with which to buy new goods and education, abandoned their traditional economic pursuits partially or wholly.

Western views of Africa during the colonial period rarely recognized the massive extent of change in the lives and values of ordinary Africans. Americans and Europeans imagined an Africa in which a tiny percentage of peoples living around the urban centers began to adopt new ways and new attitudes, while the vast majority of African peoples lived in an unchanging cultural system. Yet in the 1920's the Catholic Apostolic Prefect of Ubangi district in the northern Congo, stating a complaint that was no way unique to his area, noted that "the territory of Ubangi is emptied of every able bodied man. The majority of the young men, the hope of the future, are taken from their district of origin and transplanted in the country from which they will return, if they ever do, corrupted and contaminated by every kind of subversive idea which they will spread upon returning here." [1]

To achieve their objectives colonial governments had two alternative methods of administration available: direct rule, whereby European or professional African administrators governed the people; and indirect rule, under which the European administrators governed primarily through the existing African political structure. In general, the British tended to favor indirect rule, citing as the ideal model the precedent set in northern Nigeria, where a handful of British residents and police officers ruled almost from behind the scenes through the governments of the Fulani emirs. The French, using their experience in Senegal as a precedent, tended to favor direct rule by French or Gallicized Senegalese administrators, although in many areas they installed new chiefs or kings after defeating those who opposed their conquest.

[1] Quoted in *The Native Problem in Africa*, Vol. II, by Raymond Leslie Buell, The Macmillan Company, Inc., New York, 1928.

The Belgians, Germans, and Portuguese applied direct rule almost exclusively: the need to develop their relatively poor colonies quickly, along lines chosen by the metropolitan power and its officials in Africa, made the use of traditional rulers impractical.

Whether the pattern of rule was direct or indirect depended partly on the strength and power of existing political structures. The great rain forests of central Africa, ruled by Belgium and France, were economically poor areas where great states had never developed. In this region indirect rule was impossible, simply because there were few African rulers powerful enough to command more than a few thousand people. Indirect rule was also rarely used in those areas where white settlers were present, since there was too much likelihood of conflict between the interests of the settlers and those of the Africans. European sensitivity necessitated governments of Europeans to safeguard the interests of the white settlers.

Direct rule was practical in many areas where strong African governments existed and were willing to collaborate (either without military pressure or after being defeated) with the European colonial authority. The French found it impolitic to destroy the complex administrative structure of the sultan of Morocco, and worked out a blend of direct and indirect rule in that country, just as they had done in Tunisia. In most of the Sudan, where they were opposed by the traditional rulers and had to defeat them in battle, the French divested them of power and substituted direct rule, backed up by seasoned military forces of French officers and Senegalese troops. Britain, on the other hand, used the Fulani emirs of northern Nigeria for administration even after defeating them in battle (although a new, more cooperative, emir was usually chosen after conquest) and relied heavily upon Baganda officials in governing Uganda.

Despite the variations between direct and indirect rule, the overall effect of colonialism was to weaken traditional African political structures and to substitute a new form of government based on Western principles of organization and administration. In the colonial territories where direct rule was applied most stringently, the authority of kings, chiefs, and councils was rather quickly replaced by the authority of district administrators, usually from the European metropole. But even in those areas where indirect rule was policy, with a district administrator working through and buttressing the authority of the local chief, the position of the chief was gradually undermined. All too often he was used to implement the more unpleasant rules and requirements and had little power to challenge the orders of European administrators. The people increasingly realized that the real power lay with the European administrator rather than with the chief. Frequently the authority of the chief in matters of religion and custom continued, while his political and judicial authority declined.

A former French colonial administrator, reviewing the results of French attempts at indirect rule, concluded as follows:

> In fact, we are confronted with opposing and mutually contradictory necessities: on the one hand we are well aware that it is essential to preserve the native character of the canton chief and to make use of the traditional feudal spirit which still survives in him; on the other hand the very fact of colonization forces us to shape him to our administrative outlook. Our major fault is lack of method in our dealings with him. We demand from him too many trivial tasks and we set too much store by the way in which he performs them . . . we make his authority a travesty by using him as an intermediary in small affairs—provisioning a camp, receiving a vaccinator, collecting witnesses for a petty court case, providing a supply of chickens. We think that because he is a native, we are carrying out a native policy with his assistance, while in fact by putting menial tasks on him we treat him as sub-European.[1]

In the most striking applications of indirect rule such as in British northern Nigeria, colonial administrators were more successful in preserving the authority of African rulers; the Fulani emirs emerged still strong and respected when colonial rule ended. Still, they found themselves ruling under a traditional political philosophy within a larger national state based on a radically different political philosophy. Their people, deeply influenced by the economic, educational, and cultural influences of Europe during the colonial period, were divided uneasily between respect for their surviving authority and for that of the more powerful nation state.

Thus the net effect of colonial rule was to introduce changes in the political structures and values of Africa that could only mean the deterioration of traditional patterns of rule. In a Tanzania, where direct rule was vigorously implemented by the Germans and to a lesser extent by their British successors and where precolonial systems of government were often less deeply entrenched than in some of the great African state systems, the national government after independence had little problem with the vestiges of traditional political authority. In a northern Nigeria, the political position of the emirs at the time of independence was formidable, and the national government faced the difficult task of either accommodating to them or challenging their traditional authority.

Another far-reaching effect of colonial rule was the spread of Western education, first to small numbers of young people near the coasts,

---

1 *Freedom and Authority in French West Africa,* by Robert Delavignette, London, 1940.

then to more and more children in the interior. Education in Western schools influenced change in all areas of life by providing bright young Africans with a command of the ideas and means of expression that underlay Europe's political and economic strength.

Colonial administrations rarely established schools in the first few decades of the colonial era. This task was left to the missionary. Only in French areas, where the official policy was to acculturate and assimilate the African into French culture and society, was there an official acceptance of governmental responsibility for education early in the colonial period, and even in these areas, funds were not sufficient for the colonial government to establish more than a handful of schools.

Before World War I, schools had been established only in the areas where Europeans had long been involved in Africa: Senegal, Sierra Leone, the Gold Coast, coastal Nigeria, Gabon, a few settlements in the Congo, South Africa, and North Africa. By World War I missionaries were beginning to spread rapidly into the interior, sometimes preceding conquest and pacification, sometimes following it. But the colonial powers were still concerned almost exclusively with extending political control, putting down rebellions and uprisings, building transport systems, and encouraging the rapid development of cash crops or mineral products. One interesting exception was the Congo, where the single-minded devotion of the colonial government to propelling the Congo's people into a new economic pattern of production and consumption led to official encouragement of Catholic missions, operating under governmental license. Even under Leopold's harsh regime, primary schools had expanded rapidly, and by 1908 there were 100,000 pupils in school.

Throughout colonial Africa the masses of Africans soon came to see formal education as a means of acquiring the envied knowledge and power of the European conquerors. It took no brilliant insight for Africans to realize that the European administrators, missionaries, and commercial agents had superior power, wealth, and know-how, and that African skills and power were inferior by comparison. The African ascribed the European superiority to his education. The appeal of education was strengthened by the African realization that educated men earned more money and achieved higher position in the European-dominated world.

After World War I, a period of world prosperity brought higher prices for African products, and colonial policies were generally reviewed and reexamined. This review of policy brought with it a recognition that education was important for the future well-being of the colonies and that colonial governments would have to take more direct responsibility for it. Thus in 1923, the British Secretary of State for the Colonies appointed a prestigious Advisory Committee on Education in

British Tropical Africa. In 1925, the committee set forth a clear statement of the changing view of colonial responsibility:

> As a result on the one hand of the economic development of the British African Dependencies, which has placed larger revenues at the disposal of the Administrations, and on the other hand of the fuller recognition of the principle that the Controlling Power is responsible as trustee for the moral advancement of the native population, the Governments of these territories are taking an increasing interest and participation in native education, which up to recent years has been largely left to the Mission Societies. . . .
>
> Government welcomes and will encourage all voluntary educational effort which conforms to the general policy. But it reserves to itself the general direction of educational policy and the supervision of all Educational Institutions, by inspection and other means. . . .
>
> Education should be adapted to the mentality, aptitudes, occupations and traditions of the various peoples, conserving as far as possible all sound and healthy elements in the fabric of their social life; adapting them where necessary to changed circumstances and progressive ideas, as an agent of natural growth and evolution. Its aim should be to render the individual more efficient in his or her condition of life, whatever it may be, and to promote the advancement of the community as a whole through the improvement of health, the training of the people in the management of their own affairs, and the inculcation of true ideals of citizenship and service. *It must include the raising up of capable, trustworthy, public-spirited leaders of the people, belonging to their own race.* . . . [Italics added.]

As the italicized statement suggests, by the 1920's colonial governments were not only beginning to accept basic responsibility for education, but had realized that education was a critical influence on the development of a new African leadership that might ultimately supplant both the chiefs and the colonial authorities.

In the four areas in which colonial rule introduced the most fundamental changes in Africa—transport and infrastructure, economy, political structure, and education—developments tended to fall into several phases, each heavily influenced by events in Europe and by world affairs.

The first phase lasted roughly from about 1885 to 1914, and was characterized by energetic efforts to conquer and pacify, open the interior, develop a system of efficient administration, stimulate new crop and mineral production, and lay the foundations for changes in African ways and values. World War I diverted the attention of the colonial powers from these efforts, but Africa was inevitably pulled into the war effort. African troops were heavily involved on both sides of this conflict between colonial powers. African troops and laborers were re-

cruited into the European armies, and many saw service outside Africa.
African oils, groundnuts, copra, and grains were valuable to Europe
during the war. Although production was stepped up wherever possible,
planned, systematic development activity was largely suspended.

The conflict between Germany and the Allies involved considerable
military action in Africa, as British, French, Belgian, and South African
forces invaded the German colonies and eventually defeated their defenders. South Africa took the lead in invading South West Africa (although many Boers were sympathetic to the German cause) and
acquired the right to govern that territory after the war's end. When the
League of Nations was formed, South Africa accepted official mandate
responsibility for South West Africa under the League. Belgian troops
from the Congo defeated the Germans in Ruanda-Urundi, coordinating
their campaign with that of the British, who directed their main thrust
against German troops in Tanganyika. Both Belgium and Britain accepted League of Nations mandate responsibility for these territories
later; the British acquisition of Tanganyika brought into reality Cecil
Rhodes's old dream of a British dominion stretching from Cape to
Cairo. France and Britain collaborated to attack German forces in Togo
and Cameroun. After the war, both territories were divided into zones,
one under British administration, the other under French rule. Britain
administered her Togo zone together with the Gold Coast, and her
Cameroun zone with Nigeria. France administered her portions of both
Togo and Cameroun as parts of French West Africa.

The acceptance of League mandate responsibility by the several
colonial powers marked a new development in colonial affairs. By the
terms agreed upon in the founding of the League, a nation with mandate responsibility accepted administration of a colonial territory as "a
sacred trust of Civilization" until the people of the territory were "able
to stand on their own feet in the strenuous conditions of the modern
world." Although it took several more years, and pressure from anticolonial forces in both Africa and the outside world, most colonial powers
eventually began to move in the direction suggested by the League
mandate agreement.

The second phase lasted from the end of World War I until the
beginning of World War II. In the early 1920's, as world prosperity began to revive, more revenues became available to the colonial governments, and comprehensive, systematic development of the colonies became a matter of long-term policy. But the Great Depression in the
United States beginning in 1929 touched off a world depression, so that
by the 1930's African products brought low prices and African colonial
governments had to suspend many of the development plans that had
been conceived in the 1920's. By 1940, when prosperity was beginning

to return to Africa, World War II erupted and Africa was again caught up in the European struggle.

Africa's second involvement in a European war was felt more heavily than before. Tens of thousands of African troops and laborers were recruited into European armies, European troops poured into bases in the African territories, and European governments courted the new elite in Africa in an effort to retain its loyalty in the struggle with the Axis. Although formal development activities were suspended, the impact of the war on Africa was substantial. African troops outside Africa learned that there were European peasants and lower classes, not just the lordly colonial administrators, commercial agents, and educators seen in Africa. African products brought high prices in European markets, and European troops stationed in Africa brought new ways and attitudes into the African-European social relationship.

A third, and final, phase of the colonial era began a few years after World War II, as Europe began to recover from the effects of the war, and as world currents of self-determination, anticolonialism, and egalitarianism began to exert their influence. These currents, combined with developments inside Africa, were to bring to a hasty conclusion the half-century of European colonial rule in Africa, and to allow Africans to regain the control over their own destinies that they had lost so utterly in the 1885-1910 period of conquest.

The era of colonial rule set into motion in Africa such a complex and fundamental set of changes that today the term "revolution" is used to describe these still active forces. The colonial era represented an explosive, externally imposed acceleration of a process of change that had gone on throughout African history. Goods and ideas had trickled into Africa for millennia—across the Sahara, down from Egypt, across the Indian Ocean, and, since the fifteenth century, across the Atlantic—and goods and ideas had filtered out of Africa by the same routes. African societies influenced change in each other. But the pace was gradual, almost stately, and African societies were able to absorb incoming influences gracefully.

The colonial era, though it lasted only a matter of decades, shattered the tranquillity of Africa's long process of change and evolution. For most of the colonial period, the shock of European conquest and control prevented African leadership from exercising more than feeble and sporadic influence over the accelerating changes. Traditional rulers were removed or placed under the firm hand of colonial administrators. Until the very end of the colonial period, African participation in the governing process was precluded. African men were forced, directly or indirectly, to spend time growing new crops on their own lands or to sell their labor on the European controlled plantations, mines, and transport routes. A new type of education began to spread, changing irrevocably the tastes, ideas, and values of the growing number of young Africans who could gain access to it.

Viewed from outside, either through the eyes of colonial administrators who had a professional contempt for the abilities and opinions of their African subjects or through European stereotypes that grossly distorted the reality of African cultures and human resources, Africa seemed to be asleep before and during the colonial period. Viewed from a different perspective, either through the eyes of Africans or in the light of African history, the colonial period was a painful and humiliating episode, during which traditional values and structures were shattered by the invasion of European economic and political interests. Numbed and anesthetized rather than asleep, Africans soon began to seek control over their own destinies.

16 The African Reaction: Nationalism and Freedom

During the initial decades of the colonial period, the African was clamped tightly into a position of impotence. The European colonial administrators and their commercial compatriots were supremely confident that the power and technology of Western civilization justified their unfettered manipulation of Africa. The rapidity with which they had suppressed African resistance greatly strengthened their sense of confidence.

Having foreclosed the possibility of organized resistance by Africans, colonial administrators maintained a vigilant firmness to ensure that the traditional sources of African initiative, the chiefs, became collaborators. In some territories chiefs were swept aside under the policy of direct rule, becoming little more than arbiters of custom and religion. In many areas where indirect rule was applied, chiefs were protected so long as they carried out colonial policies, but were removed and replaced if they became obstructionist. In either case, the net effect was to weaken traditional African institutions of leadership, during the period of the greatest change African peoples and their societies had ever experienced.

During this period of fundamental change, the long-term goals of colonialism, stated so eloquently during the 1880's, received scant attention. Europe's attention, when it focused on Africa at all, concentrated on maintaining the political status quo and continuing the development of the colonies into economically self-sufficient units that were profitable to trading firms, mining companies, and plantation owners from the metropolitan country. Yet the terms of the League of Nations mandate reflected a gradually growing realization that sooner or later Africans would have to prosper and play a role in managing their affairs. Philosophically most colonial administrators and political leaders in Europe had no problem in accepting this long-term objective; practically, however, they doubted the ability of Africans to manage their own affairs. They tended to concentrate on building up revenues and products, and to postpone any actions needed to turn back to African control what Europe was building.

Senegal was an exception to this rule. There, French missionaries, both Protestant and Catholic, had begun providing education in non-Islamic areas early in the nineteenth century, just as British missionaries were doing in Sierra Leone, the Gold Coast, and South Africa. But in 1903, the governor-general of French West Africa, Ernest Roume, set forth an outline of an educational system for all the territory, marking the first time that the head of any colonial government in Black Africa had expressed official concern for African education. Roume stressed that most education was to be vocational and agricultural. Literacy in French and elementary computational skills were also considered fundamental. For the few students selected for secondary and higher education, Roume specified an education identical to that in France. In the same year, the government established the William Ponty School in Dakar, a center of higher education for teachers, pharmacists, and lawyers from all of French West Africa. Roume's early concern for African education was limited: most education was still being provided by Christian missionaries, who were not allowed to operate in the Islamic areas that comprised so much of the French area, and the government had limited funds either to build schools or to aid mission schools. Yet, more than twenty years before Britain addressed herself to the same problem and before France concerned herself officially with education in French Equatorial Africa, a start had been made.

To the average colonial administrator between about 1890 and 1920, Africa appeared both inferior and conservative. The colonial administrator tended to form a view of African behavior in which he saw certain traits as characteristic: unwillingness to take initiatives, passivity, clumsiness, surliness on occasion, childlike bewilderment, evasiveness, lack of motivation, and lack of purpose.

The average colonial administrator, of course, was seeing what his prejudices led him to expect. Any individuals exposed to new cultures and forced to perform in them, with few of their own institutions available to provide guidance and security, appear awkward and naive. Yet such people are constantly changing and absorbing the values and ways of the new culture. Africans, forced to perform in a context defined by Europeans, appeared to be backward, especially to those who expected it. In the minds and hearts of millions of Africans, however, vast and fundamental changes were underway.

The most visible index of these fundamental changes was the steady growth of a new kind of urbanized society, based on Western values, Western tastes, and Western techniques. Some parts of Africa had long had urban populations, but the new urban centers created under the colonial influence had a permanency and a breadth of impact totally unlike these older ones. Thousands of Africans clustered around St. Louis, Dakar, Freetown, Conakry, Accra, Cape Coast, Cotonou, Lagos, Ibadan, Onitsha, and dozens of other towns and cities. They came to enter the cash economy and to seek and receive Christianity and Western education; they also had a strong desire for the houses, foods, clothes, books, bicycles, tools, and luxury goods that came into these cities from Europe.

Each of these cities soon developed an elite group that had mastered European knowledge and skills and could compete and excel in the new context. As Africans in the interior completed the mission education that was spreading rapidly into the hinterland, they migrated to these towns and cities, seeking more education, good jobs, and a less traditional way of life. Yet the cities also attracted uneducated men and women, especially men. Cash and Western goods inspired men with a taste for adventure, with wanderlust, or with ambition to become wealthy and powerful to travel to the cities in search of jobs.

The people of the growing cities tended to migrate there permanently. They abandoned a way of life in the rural areas where traditional society still held sway. Yet they tended to maintain personal contact with their home villages and to retain the ties of kinship and some of the traditional values. They were both products of change and agents of it, helping to keep open lines of communication between the rapidly changing culture of the cities and a less rapidly changing culture at home.

During the nineteenth century this urban class played a strategic role in some of the growing changes in Africa. Educated Senegalese were widely employed to help administer new territories seized by France, and Senegalese troops made up the backbone of the French armies and occupation forces. Educated men from Sierra Leone were active in Lagos and other parts of Nigeria, setting up businesses or working as clerks, teachers, and administrative assistants. Educated men from the Gold Coast and from Nigeria played an active part in spreading Christianity and education among the people. Before the colonial period of the late nineteenth and twentieth centuries, educated and urbanized Africans were important and respected. They represented to the liberal European the natural heirs of the new Africa. With the full imposition of colonial rule, however, attitudes toward the new kind of African changed.

Broken lines indicate borders appearing after
1945 or in existence as administrative units.

Africa: 1945

When the colonial period began in the late nineteenth century, the number of Western-educated Africans was not large, and there were certainly more Africans educated in Islamic culture and literacy. But these Africans were generally opposed to the European presence and were regarded by Europeans as unreliable. Africans who had acquired Western education clustered around the mouth of the Senegal River, the coastal area of Senegal, the coasts of Sierra Leone and Liberia, the coastal fringe of the Gold Coast, a few areas of southern Nigeria, and urban South Africa. Many were ex-slaves, or the children of slaves, who had been freed during the abolition campaign of the mid-nineteenth century and had resettled in West Africa. There seemed to be a vast gulf between these educated Africans and the traditional masses, a gulf Europeans assumed to be as wide as that existing between themselves and the African masses.

Some of the earliest of these Christian, educated Africans identified strongly with European values, tending even to reflect the European view of Africans as barbarians and heathens. Because of this, Europeans accepted the handful of acculturated Africans more as equals, and there was at least an area of common purpose, especially in trying to convert Africans to Christianity. Yet the African Christians rarely rejected their African identity completely, and often labored faithfully to establish schools, raise the living standards of their non-Christian compatriots, and combat the evils of the slave trade.

One of the very earliest and most notable of this group of African pioneers was Philip Quaque of the Gold Coast, a Fante who, as a boy of thirteen, was sent to England for education by the Society for the Propagation of the Gospel in Foreign Parts. Quaque returned to the Gold Coast in 1766, at the age of twenty-five, as a fully ordained priest of the Church of England. He was appointed missionary for the society and chaplain of the fort at Cape Coast, which served as the Gold Coast headquarters of the British Company of Merchants Trading to Africa; he lived with European colleagues in the castle, held church services for them, and even was sent on occasional assignments as acting head of subsidiary trading posts.

Quaque's education in England made him a "marginal" man: he was intermediate between two very different cultures, not fully a part of either. His Christian, British views led him to condemn much of African culture and religion, often with more vehemence and patronization than most European missionaries. In a description of the funeral of Cabosheer Cudjo, the powerful commercial leader who had first nominated him for study in England, Quaque exhibited his embarrassment and contempt for African customs:

> . . . the funeral ceremony . . . was pompously exhibited . . . after the blacks' usual customs or manner of burying their deceased . . . this

Edward Wilmot Blyden.

mighty exhibition could not well be acted without songs of shouting, drinking and that to a very great excess, with dancing and all kinds of juvenile festivity, which scenes appeared to me more like their harvest feasts than that of mourning or sorrow.

Yet despite his alienation from his African cultural heritage, Philip Quaque was devoted to the education of his people. His most enduring accomplishment was the establishment of a small school at the fort, which was the direct forerunner of a much larger Government School established in Cape Coast in the nineteenth century, and indirectly it served as the precedent for the Gold Coast system of education in the late nineteenth and twentieth centuries.

A hundred years after Quaque's time there were many distinguished Africans, as well educated and as able as he, who refused to share his rejection of African culture and values. Philosophically, Quaque cannot be held up as a pioneer of modern African nationalist thinking; his thinking was too much that of the eighteenth-century European. But his efforts to educate Africans give him a special, revered place in the pantheon of modern Africans who helped to prepare Africa to throw off European rule.

Of the nineteenth-century Africans who worked to create a philosophy that would unite Africans into a constructive pattern of resistance to their second-class status in the world, the most renowned and prophetic was Edward Wilmot Blyden. Blyden was born in 1832 in the

Virgin Islands, then under Danish rule, of free parents. When he was ten his family moved to Venezuela for two years. There, Blyden learned Spanish and realized that he had a taste and aptitude for languages. When he was eighteen he went to the United States, with the help of American missionaries working in the Virgin Islands. Unable to find an institution that would accept him for theological study because of his race and fearful of his personal safety, Blyden moved to Liberia seven months later.

By this time Blyden, though possessed of less than a proper high school education, had already exhibited some of the qualities that would enable him to become perhaps the most famous Negro of the nineteenth century: penetrating intelligence, intellectual curiosity, strong convictions, and an urge to act on his ideas. He had also developed a strong consciousness of race and a deep feeling that the Black race must find its own salvation through pride in its race and history.

In Liberia, Blyden found the formal education he had unsuccessfully sought in the United States by enrolling as a part-time student at Alexander High School. He finished that course and became a teacher in the school, an ordained Presbyterian minister, and eventually principal of the school. Blyden remained in Liberia for most of the next twenty-five years, studying, writing, and becoming increasingly involved in Liberian politics and public affairs. He served in several cabinet posts, headed a number of important diplomatic missions and commissions, and became a professor of classics and then president of Liberia College. He ultimately was on the losing side of a major Liberian domestic dispute between a political faction in which mulattoes held the power and another that stressed purity of race; Blyden believed that Negroes should retain as much racial purity as possible, and he was antagonistic to mulattoes because of the feeling of superiority he had found them to possess in America, Liberia, and Sierra Leone. After this dispute, Blyden moved to Sierra Leone, in 1885; for much of the remainder of his life (he died in 1912, at the age of eighty) he alternated residence between Liberia and Sierra Leone, while traveling extensively to Britain, the United States, Egypt, and many other countries on government missions, study tours, and speaking engagements.

During the earlier years of his career, Blyden felt that Negroes from all over the world should return to Africa and work with the indigenous people to regenerate the continent. At first he had a poor opinion of native Africans, believing them to be barbaric and uncultured; but as he began to learn more about African culture, his view changed to one of considerable respect. His appeals to Negroes to return to Africa were well stated in an appeal to the United States government to finance a major migration of freed slaves to Africa:

> In visions of the future, I behold those beautiful hills, the bands of the charming streams, the verdant plains and flowery fields, the salubrious highlands in primeval innocence and glory, and those fertile districts watered everwhere . . . I see them all taken possession of by the returning exiles from the West, trained for the work of rebuilding waste places under severe discipline and hard bondage. I see, too, their brethren hastening to welcome them from the slopes of the Niger, and from its lovely valleys—from a sequestered nook, and from palmy plain—Moham-medans and pagans, chiefs and people, all coming to catch the inspiration the exiles have brought—to share in the borrowed jewels they have imported, and to march hand in hand with their returned brethren towards the sunrise for the regeneration of a continent. . . .

Soon after becoming active in Liberian affairs, however, Blyden's disparaging conception of native African cultures began to change (unlike those of many Liberians); in 1853, following his participation in a Liberian military expedition against a hostile Vai leader, King Boombo, Blyden wrote in an article for the *New York Colonization Journal* that Boombo's town was "remarkably fortified," giving evidence of "the inventive genius of the natives" and proof of "the unfairness of those who represent the native African as naturally indolent, and living in a state of ease and supineness." The more Blyden learned about the indigenous Africans of the interior, many of whom lived in Islamic societies, the more impressed be became. In 1866, he spent three months in Egypt, Lebanon, and Syria to perfect his knowledge of the Arabic language and to visit, in Egypt, the ruins of ancient African civilization. There he found evidence that Blacks had been an important part of ancient Egypt, and presented, in an article in the *Methodist Literary Quarterly*, the first serious attempt by a modern Black to reconstruct part of this early history. His emotional exhilaration at his discoveries of a glorious achievement by the Black race was sensitively expressed in the article:

> This, thought I, was the work of my African progenitors. . . . Feelings came over me far different from those I have ever felt when looking at the mighty works of European genius. I felt that I had a peculiar heritage in the Great Pyramids built . . . by the enterprising sons of Ham, from which I descended. The blood seemed to flow faster through my veins. I seemed to hear the echoes of those illustrious Africans. I seemed to feel the impulse from those stirring characters who sent civilization to Greece . . . I felt lifted out of the commonplace grandeur of modern times; and, could my voice have reached every African in the world, I would have earnestly addressed him . . . "Retake your Fame."

By this time Blyden was forming a comprehensive theory of race, paying ever more attention to African cultures and accomplishments. By the beginning of the twentieth century, he had developed a strong conviction about the "African Personality" (nearly half a century before this concept became a major political and intellectual theme of emergent Africa); he made the first serious attempt to define the common characteristics and fundamental qualities that made African culture unique. In 1908 he wrote a comprehensive thesis on the subject, in which he tried to prove the existence of "an African Social and Economic System most carefully and elaborately organized, venerable, impregnable, indispensable."

Blyden contrasted the Negro character with the European: the latter, he argued, was harsh, individualistic, competitive, and combative; highly materialistic, worshiping science and industry even more than God. The Negro character, by contrast, contained "the softer aspects of human nature," with such qualities as cheerfulness, sympathy, and willingness to serve. The special contribution of the African to world civilization would be in the spiritual realm, he said. Anticipating the social philosophy that underlies much of modern African nationalism, Blyden used terms such as socialistic, cooperative, and equitable to describe the African social system.

Edward Wilmot Blyden was one of the truly great Black thinkers and spokesmen. He quarreled with some of the most powerful Black leaders of his day, and he showed a lack of tact and diplomacy that prevented him from assuming the full mantle of leadership in Liberia or any other country. Yet his eloquent writing, his vast knowledge, his systematic effort to build racial pride among the world's Africans, and his impressive intellect won him an audience that was worldwide. (Although he remained Christian, he became convinced that Islam had more to offer Africa than Christianity. For this reason he was widely read in the Islamic world and his name was as well known in Constantinople, Cairo, and Damascus as it was in London or New York.) He also developed a comprehensive set of relationships throughout most of the Black world, especially West Africa, and in Great Britain and the United States. He was thus able to influence and assist many fellow Black thinkers.

Perhaps more than any other man, Blyden was the voice, albeit a few decades before times were propitious, of the dynamic philosophy that later galvanized millions of Africans and gave expression to their ardent movements to win freedom from colonial rule. Born while the slave trade still thrived in several parts of the world and when white views of Africa were hardening into systematic racism, Blyden stood out as both a living refutation and a formidable opponent of racist theories.

He was unable to crush the strong racism that had gripped the white mind where Africans were concerned, but he laid out for Africans (both in Africa and in the diaspora) an intellectually brilliant, emotionally compelling rationale for African regeneration and self-confidence. He played a major role in the creation of an ideology of racial pride and African progress that helped guide the several later generations of literate, educated Africans who laid the foundations for African freedom after World War II.

As Blyden counseled the members of the Freetown Unity Club in 1891, so his life's message was to all Africans:

> Your first duty is to be *yourselves*. . . . You need to be told constantly that you are Africans, not Europeans—black men not white men—that you are created with the physical qualities which distinguish you for the glory of the Creator, and for the happiness and perfection of humanity; and that in your endeavors to make yourselves something else, you are not only spoiling your nature and turning aside from your destiny, but you are robbing humanity of the part you ought to contribute to its complete development and welfare, and you become as salt which has lost its savour—good for nothing—but to be cast out and trodden down by others.

A contemporary of Blyden's, for whom he expressed great admiration, was Samuel Ajayi Crowther, the first African bishop of the Anglican Church in Nigeria. Crowther was a distinguished example of the growing efforts of Westernized nineteenth-century Africans to create the institutions necessary for the development of Africa in the twentieth century. Born in about 1809, Crowther was captured and sold into slavery as a boy of eleven. While on a ship bound for America, he was rescued by a British antislavery warship. Taken to Sierra Leone (where many liberated slaves were repatriated), he received his basic education in a missionary school, then returned to his home country, Yoruba, as a missionary. In 1842, the Church Missionary Society awarded him a scholarship to study theology at the society's college in London; in that year, having passed the course outstandingly, he was ordained and sent back to Nigeria. There he spent the rest of his life (he died of a stroke in 1891) building a major network of missions, schools, and native church activities. He translated the Bible and prayerbooks into Yoruba, and worked to spread literacy in Yorubaland. In 1864 he was consecrated first Bishop of the Niger Territories, thus becoming titular head of the Anglican Church in his homeland.

Bishop Crowther was not the intellectual and renowned spokesman that Blyden was, but he was an eminently successful educator and organizer. He trained dozens of able African ministers and missionaries who spread both Christianity and Western schools over a large area of southern Nigeria. Under Bishop Crowther and his protégés, Abeokuta became one of the most important church centers in West Africa. Crowther and his Nigerian missionaries lived and worked with their people, building an indigenous religious and educational system that touched the lives of thousands of Yoruba. Under their tutelage, this new system was firmly implanted in southern Nigeria, so that it became part of the new culture that was emerging in that populous region.

The winds of change that were helping to create a new kind of Africa along the coastal regions of West Africa were not only intellectual and religious; a new system of commerce was spreading under African entrepreneurship, and a class of African businessmen whose wealth came solely from trade began to grow. Merchants from Sierra Leone and Liberia set up trading posts and distribution systems in many parts of West Africa.

Thus the long European contacts along the West African coast had begun to produce real effects by the time Africa was partitioned and the colonial era began in earnest. Schools had been established, many towns and cities had an educated populace, an intellectual tradition was being founded, Christianity was sinking roots, and a new kind of African business class had emerged, acting often as intermediaries between the African producers inland and the European trading companies in the port cities. These developments were only weakly related to the political and cultural life of the vast majority of Africans farther inland, but such men as Blyden and Crowther clearly recognized, and acted upon, the necessity for unified development among both the Westernized and the traditional Africans. Europe, so long as its main concern was with the coast and adjacent areas, encouraged, and cooperated with, the emerging new Africans.

Under colonial rule, however, Europe's attitude changed rapidly; the resistance of Africans in the interior showed that Europe's rule had to be imposed and maintained by force of arms. The appeals of a Blyden, tolerated and even welcomed in the 1870's and 1880's, became potentially subversive by the beginning of the twentieth century. Blyden, after all, had begun to form a concept of Black Power, which appealed to many Africans, as the following excerpt from his inaugural address, upon assuming the presidency of Liberia College in 1881, reflects:

> The African must advance by methods of his own. He must possess a power distinct from that of the European.
> We must show that we are able to go it alone, to carve our own way. We must not be satisfied that, in this nation European influence shapes our polity, makes our laws, rules in our tribunals, and impregnates our

social atmosphere. We must not suppose that the Anglo-Saxon methods are final. . . . We must study our brethren in the interior who know more than we do the laws of the growth for the race.

Colonial authority welcomed no expression by Africans that might dispute the civilizing rationale of colonialism. In the more enlightened colonies, African representation on legislative and advisory councils was shifted away from the urban elite toward the traditional chiefs, who, in the fiction of the period, were thought to be the only legitimate spokesmen for Africa—despite the fact that they owed their own continued position largely to the colonial authority. The urban elite, when they were given official forums at all, were appointed to councils such as the legislative council of Lagos, that had limited powers only for local and municipal affairs.

The development of African expression under the tight lid of colonialism took many forms. In the French West African territories it most often focused on the struggle for full rights as Frenchmen and on participation in French affairs. In British West Africa it flowed into the educational field, into the churches, into appeals to liberal British elements for support, and into personal development in business or the professions. In the Belgian and Portuguese areas, where suppression of political activity and anticolonial tendencies was especially harsh, nativist religious movements became, during the twentieth century, an important means of expressing resentment toward European domination. (In South Africa, where suppression was equally tight, it has been estimated that about 1,500 separatist churches, based originally on Christianity, appeared during the late nineteenth and twentieth centuries.)

A typical, and important, separatist religious movement grew under the direction of Simon Kimbangu, a carpenter and evangelist in the Thysville district of the lower Congo. In 1921, Kimbangu began to proclaim that he had been empowered by God to establish a revitalized religious movement in Africa. He preached that his powers included the ability to heal sickness. Quickly followers began to join his movement, flocking to hear him preach, appealing to him to heal their afflictions. Kimbangu, a member of the Bakongo nation, preached no political message, yet his reputed powers and divine mission touched the deep resentments of the Kongo people at the disintegration of their once great kingdom and the harsh exploitation by the Belgian colonial government. The colonial power sensed the explosive potential of the movement and soon jailed Kimbangu; he remained in jail or in detention until his death in 1951. His incarceration, however, made him a martyr, and his movement began to spread even more rapidly, retaining a continuing vitality despite Kimbangu's removal and careful Belgian supervision of the movement's activities. It has remained active until today, claiming the devotion of thousands of adherents who worship Simon Kimbangu as a prophet of the same stature as Christ.

Generally the British colonial administrations permitted more overt African intellectual and political expression and organization that did the other colonial powers. In both the Gold Coast and Nigeria the constantly growing community of educated and affluent Africans, though denied the freedom of expression and action that they desired, continued to read and to be inspired by the works of Blyden and other Black intellectuals in Africa and abroad. Schools, established both by these Africans and by the rapidly growing missionary network, continued to turn out ever larger numbers of Africans with a basic literacy and a thirst for greater knowledge and personal development. These young Africans were readily absorbed into the growing colonial administrative and commercial system, as clerks, bookkeepers, translaters, guards, soldiers, messengers, and aides. The more fortunate were offered positions as teachers and ministers in the missionary effort, and a few went to England, and later to America, for higher and professional education.

Yet even in the more liberal atmosphere of British colonialism, the expanding class of educated, urbanized Africans suffered setbacks and handicaps, when compared to the precolonial period. The small but vital entrepreneurial group found it increasingly difficult to compete with the great commercial companies from Europe. Periods of low prices could virtually wipe out the African small businessman yet leave the large European firm, with its massive capital reserves, unscathed. By the 1920's the African commercial group played a proportionately lesser role in West African commerce than before the imposition of colonial rule.

The beginning of the colonial era helped to stimulate a large increase in the number of young European missionaries attracted to Africa, particularly between 1890 and 1914. Although the longer-term impact of their numbers was to spread Western culture, Christianity, and education more widely, they served coincidentally to weaken the leadership efforts that Africans had made during the nineteenth century. In Nigeria, for example, British missionaries wrested control of the Niger Mission from Bishop Crowther and his colleagues between about 1874 and 1890, on the basis of complaints by jealous white missionaries and antagonistic white traders that his administration was inefficient and many of his African-managed stations were lax in moral and theological standards. History has vindicated Bishop Crowther: studies have concluded that his management and administration were quite capable compared to European missionaries. But Crowther was a victim of the times: a pattern of humanitarian partnership between white and Black that, earlier in the nineteenth century, had helped to found Sierra Leone and Liberia, educate and ordain dozens of African ministers, and provide European funds and guidance for an African-led improvement program was rapidly giving way to a white paternalism more compatible with colonial conquest.

The setbacks to African development were not limited to restrictions on the role of the educated and urban Africans. Even in the political realm, the nineteenth century had produced ideas that, had they been followed, might have made for a dramatically different history of Africa in the twentieth. The British, at least, had earlier thought seriously of transferring to African management the administrative responsibilities they had assumed along the coast in Sierra Leone, the Gold Coast, and Nigeria. In 1865, a British Select Parliamentary Committee on West Africa had recommended that British policy be directed toward "encouraging in the natives the exercise of those qualities which may render it possible for us more and more to transfer to them the administration of all the Government. . . ." Toward this end legislative councils had been set up in the British territories of West Africa to advise the government. Many of the new African elite were thus provided with a formal, if limited, means of political expression.

These limited, but progressive, vehicles through which Westernized Africans might express their views and gain experience were frozen during the first several decades of the colonial era. The authority of the legislative councils was severely limited, and educated Africans whose opinions were considered too progressive were dropped from them. They were replaced either by chiefs or by town Africans who supported the general position of the colonial government.

The attention of colonial governments turned toward the traditional rulers, and away from the educated Africans of the towns, who had been regarded only a few decades before as the logical cadre for leading Africa into a new phase of development as a Christian, Westernized continent. Yet the power and the leadership of the traditional rulers had been severely weakened by the imposition of colonial rule.

It was perhaps inevitable that the colonial conquest produce this situation. European political rule, virtually unknown in most of Africa until the end of the nineteenth century, had to be imposed by force, and African resistance, actual or potential, had to be contained by stern measures. Older ideas of Black educators and missionaries creating, with the egalitarian support of their white friends and mentors, a new African society that could manage its own affairs and deal with Europe on equal terms were contradictory to the facts and the philosophy of colonial rule. The colonial powers thus quickly wove a

Dr. W. E. B. DuBois.

net of containment over the colonial territories. This served to prevent independent-minded and creative Africans from undertaking anything that might threaten the security of colonial rule.

Colonial rule so effectively discouraged the development of a powerful voice for freedom in Africa that the main activity in the growth of the African freedom movement took place outside Africa during the first several decades of the twentieth century. Much of its leadership came from Black Americans and West Indians working alone and with young Africans who came abroad to seek higher education.

Outside Africa, the philosophical ideas that had possessed Blyden and his disciples were continuing to develop. Two events are of special significance: the growth and decline of the Black Zionist movement, and the rise of the Pan-African movement.

The Black Zionist movement, though it had long historical antecedents, was largely the creation of Marcus Garvey, a forceful and charismatic Jamaican who used New York as a base of operations. Garvey traveled widely in Central and South America, and lived and worked in London for several years, where he collaborated with an Egyptian nationalist, the editor of the anti-imperialist *African Times and Orient Review*. A man of both conceit and vision, Garvey came to believe that Negroes all over the world could never prosper under white domination, and must ultimately return to Africa to build a new state and civilization. He launched his Universal Negro Improvement and African Communities League in New York in 1920, with adherents coming from many countries to attend the inaugural convention. Although the movement collapsed in 1925, and Garvey, deported from the United States, died forgotten in London in 1940, the meteoric rise of his movement and its associated organizations aroused the passions of millions of Negroes in America and the West Indies, and helped to stimulate thinking even in Africa itself. Partly because of Garvey's appeals, both Africans and their descendants overseas came closer to universal acceptance of the view that Black freedom could come only when Africa itself was free.

Strongly opposed to the Garvey aim of returning Negroes to Africa was the brilliant American sociologist and civil rights leader, Dr. W. E. B. DuBois, who helped to build Pan-Africanism into a powerful force. DuBois opposed the Garveyite notion of physically repatriating Negroes to Africa; he argued that this was impractical and that Negro rights must be won wherever there were Negro populations. But he recognized the necessity for Africa to be free, and held that Africans all over the world must unite in order to achieve justice and freedom for the race. DuBois helped to found the National Association for the Advancement of Colored People in the United States, then took major responsibility for promoting the aims of Pan-Africanism in the interest of achieving freedom in Africa.

The concept of Pan-Africanism, which meant basically the forging of unity among the peoples of Africa in order to free the continent from imperial rule, originated with Henry Sylvester-Williams, a lawyer from Trinidad who had studied and practiced in England, where he came to know visiting chiefs and students from Africa. He had organized a small Pan-African conference in London in 1900, attended mainly by a few West Indian, North American, and British Negroes. Although this conference, protesting colonialism and calling for aid from liberals and abolitionists on behalf of African peoples, drew some attention, Mr. Sylvester-Williams died a few years later and the idea remained dormant until after World War I.

DuBois set out for Paris immediately after the war to petition the victorious Allies for a charter of human rights for Africa, partly as a reward for the support rendered by Africans during the war. According to DuBois' own admission, he had little political support, and the idea might have died had it not been for the vigorous intervention of Blaise Diagne, a distinguished Senegalese whom France had appointed as the French African delegate to the peace conference. Diagne, a close friend of Clemenceau's, had played a vital role in recruiting African troops; by 1918 Black Africa had contributed 680,000 soldiers and 238,000 laborers to France. (Diagne later went on to prominence in French politics, as a deputy in the French assembly and as Under Secretary of State for Colonial Affairs in 1931.) Suspecting that the United States government, which had domestic reasons for not wanting Dr. DuBois to have a Paris platform, might join with colonial interests in persuading France to forbid a Pan-African meeting, Diagne secured permission from Clemenceau and joined DuBois in calling the congress. Fifty-seven delegates from various African colonies, the West Indies, and the United States met in Paris in 1919, and attracted at least some of the desired attention from the powers around the Versailles peace table.

The New York *Evening Globe* noted that the first Pan-African Congress was "the first assembly of its kind in history, and has for its object the drafting of an appeal to the Peace Conference to give the Negro races of Africa a chance to develop unhindered by other races. Seated at long green tables in the council room today were Negroes in the trim uniform of American army officers, other American coloured men in frock coats or business suits, polished French Negroes who hold public offices, Senegalese who sit in the French Chamber of Deputies. . . ." Although few realized it at the time, this meeting formally launched the philosophy and pattern of political cooperation that, thirty years later, was to become the victorious battle cry of the suppressed but evolving elite of the new Africa.

DuBois, in company with similarly minded Africans, Americans, and West Indians, kept the concept of Pan-Africanism alive. Other congresses were convened in London in 1921, London and Lisbon in 1923, New York in 1927, and Manchester in 1945. With each succeeding meeting the interest of young Africans increased; in 1920 the first African nationalist political organization to emerge during the colonial era, the West African National Congress under the leadership of Gold Coast barrister Joseph Casely-Hayford, endorsed the program of the Pan-African Congress and pledged full support for it.

Each of the Pan-African congresses adopted platforms calling for the introduction of a code of just law into colonial territories; the holding of African land in trust for Africans and the prevention of alienation of the land to settlers; regulation of the activities of capitalist developers of Africa; the final abolition of slavery, forced labor, and corporal punishment; greater access to education by Africans; and progressive African participation in government. Although the recommendations of the congresses carried little weight with the colonial powers and produced little visible amelioration of the exploitation and suppression under which Africa existed, the ideas of Pan-Africanism inspired many educated Africans.

In 1935, the development of Pan-Africanism, race consciousness, and African freedom movements was accelerated by the brutal Italian invasion and conquest of Ethiopia. Ethiopia had a peculiar emotional significance both for Italians and for the world's Africans and African descendants. For many Italians it was a symbol of national humiliation:

Adowa represented a burning memory for the millions of Italians who smarted under poverty, ignorance, and a feeling of inferiority. For the world's Africans, it was the great occasion of Black victory over white, the one successful defense by Black men of their freedom and territorial integrity against the hordes of militarily and technologically superior Europeans. Italy had never forgotten, nor had it ever completely dropped the idea of avenging its defeat and acquiring Ethiopia as a colonial empire.

Italy's invasion of Ethiopia had been planned long before 1935 (Mussolini is believed to have accepted the concept and begun to plan for it as early as 1925), and ominous signs of it had begun to appear several years before it began, even while Mussolini was speaking of eternal peace and friendship between the two countries. Surveys of Eritrean defense needs, secret missions into Ethiopia to compile maps, publicity about border skirmishes between Ethiopian and Italian forces, and frequent Italian efforts to sow dissension within Ethiopia had all been undertaken. Ethiopia's emperor Ras Tafari, Haile Selassie I, had been convinced of the plans for invasion several years before 1935, but had hoped for, and striven tirelessly to build, League of Nations guarantees against it.

As events showed, Haile Selassie's hopes for international support were futile; every European country was contemptuous of the Italian designs on Ethiopia (even Hitler's Germany denounced it, and Germans demonstrated against it), but not one was willing to act in Ethiopia's behalf. Popular support for the Ethiopian cause, even before the invasion, was widespread and enthusiastic: citizen and youth groups in Scandinavia, Germany, France, Belgium, England, Turkey, Hungary, and other European countries, and similar groups in the United States and many South American countries, were organized to show solidarity with Ethiopia. An American Committee for Ethiopia and the International African Friends of Ethiopia attracted support from hundreds of thousands of Black Americans and Africans. Prominent among the members of the latter group were Jomo Kenyatta, Kenya's first president but then only a teacher; George Padmore, one of the leading proponents of Pan-Africanism; and J. B. Danquah, later called the "doyen of Gold Coast politics."

African devotion to Ethiopia as a symbol was powerful. Marcus Garvey had constantly praised Ethiopia as the leading symbol of Black civilization and pride, and many of his followers called themselves Rastafarians, after the name of the emperor. Black Americans had emigrated to Ethiopia, and both they and Africans looked to it as the last bastion of African freedom from white rule. In every African town and city discussion groups were formed in 1934 and afterward to follow the progress of the Italian threat, and later the war. When Italy's powerful army finally moved, the invasion was watched by the most unified and sympathetic Black world community that had yet been achieved.

Italy, conscious of its defeat at Adowa, made sure in 1935 that there could be no doubt of the outcome. In its two territories adjacent to Ethiopia, Eritrea and Italian Somaliland (in both territories there was a history of conflict with Christian Ethiopia), it built modern military bases and assembled an army that eventually numbered more than 500,000 men. The war could hardly have been made more unequal. The hundreds of thousands of Italian troops and reserves were augmented by nearly as many thoroughly trained and armed Eritreans and Somalis, under Italian officers. They were equipped with some five-hundred airplanes, thousands of cannon, tens of thousands of machine guns, thousands of armored cars and supply vehicles, a vast store of food, medical supplies, ammunition, and gasoline, and large naval units to keep the supplies flowing and to bring reinforcements if needed. In addition, the Italian army was secretly stocked with large quantities of poison gas, chiefly mustard gas, which was used massively when fighting began, despite a world convention prohibiting its use.

Against the Italians Ethiopia was able to field fewer than 350,000 men, three fourths of whom had never received military training and only a few thousand of whom were uniformed. The Ethiopian troops had 400,000 rifles, most old and in poor repair; about two hundred obsolete cannon; about fifty assorted antiaircraft guns; and perhaps a hundred armored and unarmored cars, most old and poorly serviced.

The Ethiopian strategy provided for deliberate retreat near the Eritrean border, where the invasion began, to draw the Italians deep into Ethiopian territory and difficult terrain. For two months, the vast Italian force moved slowly into Ethiopia, meeting almost no resistance, and the Italian people were wild with joy at their army's advance. Then, just before Christmas 1935, the ill-fated but defiant Ethiopians counterattacked. They began to drive the Italians back in a furious onslaught involving hand-to-hand combat, at which the Ethiopians almost invariably proved superior. Italy was plunged into a national panic, and the specter of Adowa suddenly appeared.

But the Italians soon rallied and began to push back an Ethiopian army that had already been crushed by days of aerial bombardment, by constant pounding of artillery, and by thousands of deaths from mustard gas. The Italian advance toward Addis Ababa continued, marked by sporadic battles that came more like massacres as Italian bombs, tanks, gas, flamethrowers, and artillery destroyed unit after unit. And still the Ethiopians continued to fight.

The war ended in May 1936, after seven months of resistance and tens of thousands of Ethiopian casualties. Haile Selassie went into exile to maintain a campaign of resistance, and inside the country Italian mopping-up operations continued for another year. Guerrilla actions, led by men who were not professional soldiers but were genuine folk patriots, continued to harass the Italian occupiers. The Italians were defeated and expelled in 1941 when, as a result of Britain's entry into World War II, a force of British and Ethiopian troops, accompanied by Haile Selassie, invaded the country from the Sudan. The Ethiopians, many of whom had fought as guerrillas, had been secretly trained. In their second conflict with the Italians they were also properly equipped and supplied. Although the invasion force consisted initially of one hundred British soldiers and 2,000 Ethiopians, thousands of Ethiopian guerrillas joined them, and thousands of Ethiopian troops in the Italian army defected. In six months the main Italian army surrendered (Britain was able to blockade the country completely, preventing any supplies from reaching the Italians), and Haile Selassie triumphantly reentered his capital.

Ironically, the brutal Italian conquest and initial occupation had been followed by a major Italian effort to develop Ethiopia economically and educationally as thousands of Italian farmers and businessmen flooded the country. Haile Selassie, who showed an admirable spirit of forgiveness after Italy was expelled, many times paid tribute to the efforts of ordinary Italians to aid Ethiopia and to establish fraternal relations with the Ethiopian people. His own campaign to unify and modernize his country thus received a boost from the Italian occupation, however cruel and merciless it may have been.

The effect of the Italian conquest on the development of the African freedom ideology was substantial. There had been little world protest of the colonial conquest of Africa in the 1880's and 1890's, and communication among the world's Blacks was sufficiently poor that the conquest did not arouse any unified, popular revulsion. The Italian action was a different matter. All over Africa, Europe, and the Americas millions of Black people, many of whom were well educated and able to communicate their thoughts effectively, watched the Italian invasion and the world's inaction with horror and indignation. White disregard of Africa's people and its dignity were illustrated wantonly and callously as the gallant Ethiopians died to defend their country. Salt, in effect, was rubbed into a festering wound. After World War II Africans began to clamor for freedom in a way, and to an extent, that had never before been seen; the Ethiopian conquest had given the call for freedom urgency and had spread its appeal.

The deep feelings that the Italian invasion aroused in the Black world were overshadowed by world preoccupation with World War II. Yet individual Africans continued to seek personal advancement, to think of the fundamental facts of Africa's bondage, and to seek kindred spirits, new ideas, and forums through which their yearnings might be expressed. Immediately after the war, in 1945, the Pan-African movement felt that the time was ripe for a larger, more urgent congress. To this end the Fifth Pan-African Congress was convened.

The Fifth Pan-African Congress—like the first—was designed to take advantage of the end of a world war in which Africans had made a significant contribution to Allied victory. Millions of Africans had been involved in the war effort, as front-line troops, laborers, producers of strategic war materials, and loyal spokesmen against fascism and tyranny. Sustained high prices for African goods had brought a new measure of prosperity to individual Africans and to African colonial governments. The thousands of educated Africans long denied a voice in their own affairs justifiably felt that the success of democracy over tyranny should have meaning in Africa.

This congress brought the veterans of previous congresses together with many of a new breed of African, young men who had left Africa between the two world wars to gain higher education and who had formed strong ideas and aspirations in America and Europe. The latter group included Kwame Nkrumah and Jomo Kenyatta, both destined to become the first African heads of state of their respective countries, Ghana and Kenya.

The end of World War II brought about forces and trends that made achievement of the aims of Pan-Africanism and the long-postponed African renaissance practicable to a greater degree than ever before. The balance of power in the world had shifted from the colonial powers, themselves almost prostrated from the war, to the United States and the Soviet Union, neither a colonial power and each committed, in its own way, to anticolonialism. Even the United States, close friend to the leading colonial powers, found it impossible to speak in their defense against the mounting cries for freedom in Asia and Africa.

Anticolonial attitudes in Europe itself had been strengthened during and after the war. The strongest argument that could be mustered in favor of continued colonial rule—that the colonial power should continue to govern until it had developed the African peoples and their economies to the point of self-sufficiency—was one that financially depleted governments in Britain and France found less than compelling. Nevertheless, this was the justification most often advanced, and both Britain and France began to make funds available for the systematic development of African education, health services, transport, agriculture, industry, and governmental infrastructure on a scale never before attempted.

Africans themselves saw the rapid erosion of European superiority during the war. Hundreds of thousands of American and European troops were stationed in Africa, behaving in ways very unlike the colonial administrators, missionaries, and commercial agents who were the only Europeans most Africans had known. And the hundreds of thousands of Africans serving abroad saw ordinary Europeans, dated European girls, and realized that Europeans were little different from Africans. Belgium and France were both defeated nations, while Britain for a time seemed on the verge of defeat; the fortunes of war helped Africans realize that there was nothing eternally impregnable about their colonial masters; the defeat of Italy and the reestablishment of Ethiopian sovereignty added to African determination.

World War II destroyed the vitality of colonialism irreparably, much more effectively than even aspiring Africans realized at the time. At the same time, the leaders of the anticolonial movements, even though they expected decades of further struggle before final victory, began to organize more energetically and hopefully than ever before. Ghana, the first African country south of the Sahara to gain freedom, provides a clear case in point. To understand the events that helped bring independence to Ghana, it is necessary to begin a few years before the Fifth Pan-African Congress.

In the 1930's there was a trickle of young West Africans to Europe and the United States, seeking the first-class higher education that was unavailable in Africa. One man, Nnamdi Azikiwe of Nigeria, went to the United States, worked his way through college, spent time in other West African countries, wrote numerous pamphlets and books, and returned to Lagos in 1937. (Almost at once he founded a powerful newspaper, the *West African Pilot,* and in 1943 he helped to form an outspokenly nationalist political party in Nigeria, the National Council of Nigeria and the Cameroons.) Azikiwe's achievements, especially in America, inspired hundreds of young West Africans. Among them was a young Gold Coaster, Kwame Nkrumah, who followed Azikiwe to Lincoln University in 1935. After completing his education in America, Nkrumah went on to London to study British law and to establish closer contact with the large colony of Pan-Africanist intellectuals and West African students who operated from London. He assisted in preparations for the Fifth Pan-African Congress, and was, with George Padmore, its joint political secretary.

At the Fifth Pan-African Congress Nkrumah was rapporteur of two important sessions when West African colonies were discussed. The resolutions presented to the Congress by Nkrumah, on the basis of discussions during these sessions, reflected the views that he later put into practice in Gold Coast politics. Among the numerous resolutions several are especially significant:

> . . . That since the advent of British, French, Belgian, and other European nations in West Africa, there has been regression instead of progress as a result of systematic exploitation by these alien imperialist powers. The claims of "partnership," "trusteeship," "guardianship," and the "mandate system" do not serve the political wishes of the people of West Africa.

> . . . That the democratic nature of the indigenous institutions of the peoples of West Africa have been crushed by obnoxious and oppressive laws and regulations, and replaced by autocratic systems of government which are inimical to the wishes of the peoples of West Africa.

> . . . That there has been a systematic exploitation of the economic resources of the West African territories by imperialist powers to the detriment of the inhabitants.

> . . . That the industrialization of West Africa by the indigenes has been discouraged and obstructed by the imperialist rulers, with the result that the standard of living has fallen below subsistence level.

> . . . That the workers and farmers of West Africa have not been allowed independent trade unions and cooperative movements without official interference.

> . . . That the British Government in West Africa is virtually controlled by a merchants' united front, whose main objective is the exploitation of the people, thus rendering the indigenous population economically helpless.

The congress at large unanimously adopted these and other West African resolutions, as well as many resolutions dealing with North Africa, southern Africa, East Africa, and the plight of Negroes in America, Europe, and the West Indies. It stated the spirit of the aroused delegates in unequivocal terms:

> We are determined to be free. We want education. We want the right to earn a decent living; the right to express our thoughts and emotions, to adopt and create forms of beauty. We demand for Black Africa autonomy and independence, so far and no further than it is possible in this One World for groups and peoples to rule themselves subject to inevitable world unity and federation.

> We are not ashamed to have been an age-long patient people. We continue willingly to sacrifice and strive. But we are unwilling to starve any longer while doing the world's drudgery, in order to support by our poverty and ignorance a false aristocracy and a discarded imperialism. . . .

> Therefore we shall complain, appeal, and arraign. We will make the

world listen to the facts of our condition. We will fight in every way we can for freedom, democracy, and social betterment.

The voice of the New Africa had been heard, and movements to translate these words into action spread throughout Africa.

After his work with the Pan-African Congress, Nkrumah helped to organize a West African National Secretariat in London, for the purpose of implementing the congress's resolutions. Then, in 1947, he was called back to the Gold Coast to become general secretary of a new political group, the United Gold Coast Convention, formed by the leading educated Africans of his homeland. Nkrumah soon found himself in basic disagreement with the political philosophy and tactics of the UGCC leadership. The chief point of disagreement was the extent to which the party should appeal to the nonurban, noneducated masses of the Gold Coast, an objective Nkrumah regarded as essential. To Nkrumah, African power ultimately lay with the masses, both in the cities and in the rural areas. Many of the older intellectuals of the UGCC believed the uneducated rural peoples were unready for direct political involvement and should be represented by the urban elite in alliance with the chiefs.

In 1949 Nkrumah resigned his position, and formed the Convention People's Party, with strong support from labor unions, women's groups, farmers' organizations, youth, and many of the younger intellectuals of the urban areas. Asserting that his demand was for "Self-Government Now," while that of the UGCC was for "Self-Government in the shortest possible time," Nkrumah noted in his letter of resignation that "I am fully aware of the dangers [from the colonial government's predicted suppression] to which I am thus exposed, but firm in the conviction that my country's cause comes first. I take the step and chance the consequences. I am prepared if need be to shed my blood and die if need be, that Ghana [the revered name Nkrumah had chosen for the Gold Coast upon independence] might have self-government now."

The ringing appeal of Nkrumah's nationalism, and his bold assertion that Africans must be free to rule themselves immediately, swept across the Gold Coast with hurricane force. Thousands of that territory's people, from the "tribal" bush as well as from the towns and cities, flocked to join the new Convention People's Party. A few months later, when Sir Charles Arden-Clarke, the new governor, arrived at Accra to assume his office, Nkrumah greeted him with a public letter of welcome printed in the *Evening News*. The letter stated the new African attitude politely but uncompromisingly:

> Your Excellency, much lies ahead of you. Your stay with us will be good or bad as you wish it. Those who think that they can still govern

us from Downing Street against our will are tragically mistaken, and it is up to you to inform and advise them as "that man on the spot," that Britain can only henceforth rely on the friendship and cooperation of the Gold Coast, our beloved Ghana, by first granting her her freedom now.

Your Excellency, Welcome to Ghana.

To much of the world, Africa was still the "slumbering giant," but to Nkrumah, and to the tens of thousands of Africans who shared the new philosophy, Africa was fully awake and ready to fend for itself again.

Nkrumah himself has stated that "the political and social revolution in Ghana may be said to have started at midnight on 8 January, 1950, when Positive Action began." Positive Action emerged when, in late 1949, the British government Coussey Commission issued a report on unrest in the Gold Coast, and recommended a new constitution providing for a substantial measure of internal self-government by a partially elected Assembly. To Nkrumah and his colleagues in the CPP, this was both too little and too late. Not only had he been excluded from membership on the commission, while several of his former associates of the UGCC served on it, but the tenor of the recommendations, to Nkrumah, smacked of compromise and privilege for the elite and the chiefs. To engender an atmosphere of direct struggle by the people, the CPP launched Positive Action, a program of strikes and boycotts.

Because of his Positive Action campaign, Nkrumah and several colleagues were imprisoned on charges of incitement, libel, and sedition, while Sir Charles Arden-Clarke's government proceeded with plans to implement the new constitution. Despite Nkrumah's imprisonment, the CPP decided to campaign energetically, nominating Nkrumah and a party slate for elected offices. In February 1951 elections were held, resulting in victory for the CPP. The popular support of the party so impressed the colonial government that Nkrumah was released from prison to take his seat in the Assembly, and he in turn agreed to work within the new constitution to gain his objectives. After several new elections (in each of which the CPP power grew), and several changes in the constitution, Ghana became independent in March 1957. It was the first colonial territory south of the Sahara to regain its freedom.

As an ardent participant in the international Pan-Africanist movement, Nkrumah regarded Ghana's freedom as but one step in a historic revolutionary process. Even in his speeches at Ghana's independence celebrations Nkrumah took note of his view that all Africans, in Africa and abroad, shared common roots and a common destiny. "There exists a firm bond of sympathy between us and the Negro peoples of the Americas . . ." he declared.

"It is our earnest hope that the Ghana which is now being reborn will be, like the Ghana of old, a center to which all the peoples of Africa may come and where all the cultures of Africa may meet."

"The success or failure of our efforts to make Ghana into a happy and prosperous state will extend far beyond the frontiers of Ghana itself. A failure on our part would have tragic consequences for other African territories striving towards independence. We must not fail. We shall not fail."

The pattern of events in Ghana was being repeated, usually only a year or two behind, in almost all the British territories. Ghana was unique only in that vigorous and insistent leadership among the new educated elite proved ready to harness the restless energies of the people a few years earlier than in other territories.

The process of nationalist organization and the acceleration of compromises by the colonial power did not always proceed as smoothly as they had in Ghana, however. And there were other forms of protest against colonial rule. The emergence of the Mau Mau movement in Kenya in 1951, described by the British at the time as a primitive, tribalist movement with no political significance, was actually a violent civil protest, amounting almost to a civil war, against some of the conditions for which the colonial period was responsible. Mau Mau was largely confined to the numerous Kikuyu people, a Bantu-speaking farming group whose home had long been on the cool and fertile highlands of central Kenya. Britain encouraged the settlement of white farmers in Kikuyu country in the late nineteenth century, and by about 1950 there were as many as 50,000 white immigrants there. Inevitable population expansion among the Kikuyu produced a hunger for more land, a hunger that was frustrated by the large landholdings of whites. The Kikuyu had not traditionally been organized into a central state, but their natural cultural unity had been given special expression by several outstanding Kikuyu educators and nationalists, Jomo Kenyatta being the most prominent. In the 1930's Kenyatta and a close associate, Mbiyu Koinange, had worked with Kikuyu clan leaders and wealthier farmers to create a Kenya Independent Schools Association to provide education for a larger number of young people than the colonial government was willing or able to provide.

With the natural Kikuyu tendency toward progressiveness being expressed and given institutional form by such distinguished men, the land hunger that reached acute form during World War II took on a more organized and political tone. Its approach, however, was militant and violent; the first signs of its existence were the murders of several British farmers with large holdings, the mutilation of their livestock, and the murder of several Kikuyu leaders suspected of collaborating with the government and the white settlers. The reaction of the Kenya government was vigorous, but, as later analysis showed, somewhat ill-advised. Kenyatta and a number of other educated and politically active Kikuyu leaders were arrested and accused of conceiving and leading the insurrection. Thus, the leaders who might have channeled the movement into a less violent political protest were detained and isolated. The government met force with force, executing captives, using torture to force some suspects to talk, pressuring many Kikuyu into collaboration, and resettling large numbers of Kikuyu into fortified villages. The violence spread rapidly as the secret movement of guerrillas, hidden in the dense forests of the Aberdare Mountains and Mount Kenya, turned increasingly against Kikuyu landholders, officials, and workers suspected of collaboration.

After nearly four years of intensive military action, at a cost of some $60 million and the lives of some hundred Britons and several thousand Kikuyu, the rebellion was finally subdued and its leaders confined or executed. Jomo Kenyatta's years of detention had made him a martyr to both the Kikuyu people and the nationalist-minded Africans of Kenya's other tribes. When he was finally released in 1961, there was national jubilation. To most African nationalists, many of whom undoubtedly were repelled by the savage methods of the Mau Mau (as well as the equally savage methods of the police fighting Mau Mau), the movement had become a war of freedom, and its dead leaders national heroes.

The focus of attention on the Mau Mau war inevitably retarded the orderly development of the Kenya nationalist movement along the lines of Ghana, Nigeria, and most other countries under British rule. Yet even with attention diverted, and Kenyatta in detention and other leaders in exile, younger Kikuyu nationalists and nationalists from tribes not implicated in the Mau Mau movement continued to organize. After Kenyatta's release, the stage was set for a rapid transition from colonial status to independence.

In the French territories forces very similar to those in the British territories were at work before, during, and after World War II. Yet these forces appeared deceptively different at the time due to a resurgence of French efforts to build a worldwide French community of which the French African territories would be members. Under this policy many outstanding leaders of the African elite spent much of their time in France, often engaged in French politics or labor affairs, and devoted major efforts to winning a greater African voice in French circles. Rigorous colonial discouragement of independence politics seemed to hold open the possibility that the African territories would develop within the French community.

Yet nationalist attitudes were gaining wider currency than was ap-

Addis Ababa, the capital of Ethiopia.

parent. Senegal's Leopold Senghor, a brilliant teacher and poet who had spent much of his life teaching and writing in France, became the leading spokesman for the philosophy of "Negritude," which stressed "the affirmation of the values of African culture." After World War II he returned to Senegal to strengthen his political base. He still maintained his roots in France, but was deeply motivated by the desire to build a distinctively African political force within the French Union. In 1946, leaders from most of the French territories assembled at Bamako, Mali, and founded the Rassemblement Democratique Africaine with heavy support from the Communist Party of France. Senghor, fearful of Communist domination of the movement, refused to attend the assembly and began to form an alliance against the powerful RDA and its president, Felix Houphouet-Boigny of the Ivory Coast. (Although Senghor was initially correct in his judgment that the RDA would be Communist-dominated, in the longer run he was wrong; during the 1950's, the RDA became the major voice of African nationalism in the French territories, eventually breaking completely with the French Communists.)

In the ten years after World War II political consciousness in the French territories of West Africa expanded rapidly, under the leadership of Senghor, Houphouet-Boigny, and a number of other skilled leaders of the new African elite. African demands within the French Union could not be ignored, and in 1956 the Loi Cadre (Outline Law) was proclaimed, giving a measure of internal autonomy to each of the twelve territories of French West and Equatorial Africa, and leaving to France control of foreign policy, defense, and strategic economic development. The accelerating progress toward self-government and full independence in the Gold Coast and Nigeria was undoubtedly an important factor in this development, helping to kindle French African aspirations for control over their destiny, and demonstrating to France that it could no longer ignore the fundamental processes of change occurring throughout Africa.

In 1958, when Charles de Gaulle returned to power in France and created the Fifth Republic, France offered the colonial territories full independence, with no further French aid, or self-government within a new French Community, with the promise of even greater French assistance. Only Guinea, under the leadership of Sekou Touré, chose complete independence, and de Gaulle dramatically canceled all French support of that country. Yet, the surge for full freedom continued to mount in the eleven territories that had elected to remain in the French Community, and, in late 1959 and 1960, all the others negotiated agreements that gave them full sovereignty without the drastic reprisals Guinea had endured. French economic and technical assistance continued after independence, and French influence remained important.

North Africa, which had been regarded by imperialist Europe as very different from sub-Saharan Africa, gained freedom from colonial rule even earlier after World War II. Egypt, which had regained internal self-government in 1922, became fully independent as soon as British wartime occupation ended in 1944, although a British force remained along the Suez Canal until 1956. The Sudan became independent in 1956, when the British relinquished their control over that nation; Egypt, which had jointly ruled the Sudan with Britain since 1936, had canceled its claims in 1951. Libya, which had been ruled by Italy, was reunited by King Idris in 1951, and became independent a few months later. Morocco and Tunisia broke into major rebellion early in the 1950's, and finally won their independence from France in 1956. Algeria, with more than one million European settlers, faced a very different problem: France stubbornly claimed that Algeria was an integral part of France. Violence began in 1945, and broke into full-scale war in 1954. After eight years of brutal fighting, Algeria won complete freedom in 1962.

The great sweep of African nationalism and the surge toward freedom from alien rule came first, and met least resistance, in North and West Africa, but it was the product of a reaction to outside domination that covered the entire continent and touched all its peoples. Even the Congo (now Zaire), where Belgium ruled with an iron hand and tolerated no African political expression that might threaten Belgian rule, began to give way to change. In the 1950's the colonial government speeded up the formation of local government bodies on which Africans sat, especially municipal councils, and the first African political figures began to come to the notice of the outside world and of the Congolese people. By this time the country had been transformed by the firm policy of fundamental development of the economy and people according to a strictly controlled plan.

At the beginning of the 1950's, there were no university graduates, but hundreds of thousands of Congolese had attended the extensive school system, which provided primary schooling and specialized training in agriculture, mechanics, secretarial and commercial subjects, theology, medical assistance, nursing, and other practical fields. Many Congolese had gone into business and had created profitable small companies. In these respects, the Congo had become one of the most extensively developed countries in Africa, and its economy was powerful and bright with potential new wealth from agriculture and mining. The people and the country were making solid, controlled progress. Yet the traditional rulers had been removed or rendered impotent, and the educated class had been prevented from rising to the academic levels being achieved by Africans elsewhere or from acquiring the type of liberal education that Belgium believed produced anticolonial ideas.

The desire of the Congolese for freedom was as great as that of other Africans, and there was a cadre of nationalist leadership that was ready to arise, given the opportunity. These leaders were found in the ranks of the army, in the mission schools, in the business world, and in the ranks of petty administrators such as postal clerks, and they began to appear once controls were loosened. (Patrice Lumumba, who emerged in 1959-60 as the most nationally appealing leader, had been a postal clerk.) By the late 1950's, numerous political parties, with limited platforms and localized followings, had mushroomed all over the country, and their leaders were beginning to meet to discuss the possibilities of united national action. As of about 1958-59, they called for a phased transfer of power from Belgian to African leadership (a cautious objective by West African standards, but radical compared to the Congo of five years before).

Belgian officials recognized that things were moving much more rapidly than they had envisaged, and in 1959, in a move that surprised the emerging Congolese leadership as well as the rest of the world, it announced that it would confer full independence in 1960. This Belgian move has been widely regarded as an act of pique, somewhat in the same vein as de Gaulle's sudden withdrawal from Guinea in 1958. Underlying Belgium's move, however, was a more sober recognition that Belgium was too small, too weak, too concerned with internal economic and political problems to face a mounting, and possibly violent, African campaign for independence. Apparently some Belgian officials felt that the Congo would fall into disarray once the unifying force of Belgian rule was removed, and they imagined that both Congolese and world opinion would favor Belgium's return. In the first part they were correct; the lack of previous national political growth, the inexperience and localized power bases of the leaders, and the simple lack of educated Congolese to man the state's vast administrative structure helped to produce civil war and disunity. So far, however, the country has survived two civil wars, and shows signs of growing stability and prosperity.

It was in the white-ruled countries of South Africa and Rhodesia and the Portuguese colonies of Guinea (in West Africa), Mozambique, and Angola that the movement for African freedom met formidable obstacles. By 1968 every African country had achieved African rule except six: Angola, Guinea, Mozambique, Namibia (South West Africa), Rhodesia, and the Republic of South Africa.

In South Africa, and to a lesser extent Rhodesia, Christianity, Western education, and the cash economy had spread as they had in other parts of Africa. Thus the conditions for creating a new expression for African freedom existed, except for the presence of a large body of white settlers who had built a prosperous way of life based on the subjugation of Africans and their use as laborers. Although African nationalist organizations were formed and attracted considerable popular support, their appeals were not for full freedom but for a greater voice for Africans in the affairs of the country. White power was too great, and too permanent, to permit development of a force that called for African rule. After World War II, South Africa's whites, prompted by the rapid development of the African freedom movement to the north, moved to limit African expression even further: in 1948 the Boers, who today call themselves Afrikaaners, won political control of the country and introduced the program of "apartheid," or separate development, which is intended to make white rule permanently secure, at least in large parts of the country.

Theoretically, apartheid intends ultimately to divide South Africa into a number of areas: one large area, stretching in a belt from Cape Town along the Indian Ocean and through the center of the country to the central Transvaal, for whites, and a number of small areas for African tribes. The term "Bantustan" is frequently used to describe these African areas, where different tribes are supposed to develop their own national cultures in a unique form and ultimately become independent. The Bantustan areas, however, are already overcrowded and consist of the poorest soils in the country. Over half the African population of South Africa lives outside them in the white-designated region. Slow progress has been made in implementing the separate development concept since it was introduced in 1948, and the white economy is now more dependent on African labor than ever before.

At the same time, South Africa has introduced a complicated set of laws and regulations designed to control both the physical movements and the political activities of Africans and any white supporters they have had. A police state of incredible internal control has developed. African political expression and activity are forbidden and are rigorously punished when they appear. The Africans are disenfranchised and powerless in their own land, and white power seems presently impregnable. The result is a proliferation of other forms of expression of African desires for dignity, progress, and freedom: large numbers of separatist churches, strong efforts at personal advancement within the system, and extremely covert political activity in association with the two principal African nationalist movements, the African National Congress and the Pan Africanist Congress. Both parties have abandoned the older platforms of participation in national affairs and now call for total African freedom on a "one man one vote" basis; since Africans outnumber whites four to one, this would mean African control of the country. Both parties, banned inside the country, have sought support from the Organization for African Unity and friendly African governments, and both have trained a number of freedom fighters and political action specialists. So far a tight lid of secrecy cloaks their activities inside South Africa. No outside observer believes the present situation can go unchanged, but clearly the movement for African freedom has been at least temporarily halted in South Africa.

A comparable situation exists in Namibia, the name often used outside South Africa for South West Africa. Namibia is tightly controlled by the whites of the Republic of South Africa, in the name of its League of Nations mandate, despite decisions by both the United Nations and the World Court that South Africa no longer has a legal right to Namibia. In that country South Africa has begun to implement a policy of apartheid, and some 80,000 white settlers of German and South African origin occupy its small fertile regions, while the Africans are relegated to the driest, least fertile lands. The legal position of the United Nations, which claims responsibility for the country, sets Namibia apart from South Africa. Yet so far South Africa has refused to accept the UN position, and the UN has been unwilling to use force to break South Africa's hold on the territory.

The case of Rhodesia is different still. There, where some 250,000 white settlers rule four million Africans, the development of African nationalism followed the typical pattern, despite the fact that Britain granted self-government (but not independence) to the white-dominated government in 1923. As long as Britain was the ultimate authority, African nationalism developed and expanded, and there seemed to be some distant prospect of the country's achieving independence with an African majority in the government. In 1965, however, the white government declared its full independence from Britain, and moved toward an internal system that will secure white control permanently. Britain denounced the move, and the United Nations joined Britain in a program of economic sanctions that was purported to undermine the country's economy in order to force its government to renounce independence and seek terms with Britain. In early 1972, with indecisive results from the sanctions program, Britain and Rhodesia began to seek a peaceful termination to the stalemate.

Africans in Rhodesia, although slightly less restricted than those in South Africa, have been prevented from forming nationalist organizations, and most nationalist leaders are under detention. Those not incarcerated have fled the country, and maintain active offices of the rival Zimbabwe African National Union and Zimbabwe African People's Union in neighboring countries. Both parties have declared a campaign to free the country by force, both have trained freedom fighters, and both maintain a military effort inside the country that consists primarily of armed raiders crossing from Zambia, engaging in skirmishes, then retiring to the bush or into Zambia. Since both the nationalist parties and the Rhodesian government refuse to divulge details of the extent of the military conflict, it is not known whether there is a serious civil war in progress.

Portugal proved to be the most intransigent of all the colonial powers in Africa; it has long termed its colonies "overseas provinces" of Portugal, denying that they are colonies at all, and maintains that their peoples have the same rights as do mainland Portuguese. Large numbers of Portuguese settlers have immigrated to Angola (some 300,000) and Mozambique (some 175,000) since the late nineteenth century. Presumably they are developing the same feeling of permanence that white settlers in Rhodesia and South Africa have. Portugal itself has a nondemocratic form of government, so its white settlers have no significant political power either in Africa or in Portugal; certainly the African peoples of the Portuguese territories, who are among the economically and educationally least developed people in Africa, have no political rights. Since political expression is prohibited in the African territories, African nationalism has developed, since about 1960, into open fighting.

Guerrilla wars have begun in Angola, Mozambique, and Guinea. In Guinea, a small, tropical territory located between Senegal and the former French colony of Guinea, there are few Portuguese settlers, and the strong African resistance movement has liberated more than half the country. In both Angola and Mozambique, where Portugal maintains large armies (over 60,000 soldiers in Angola and 50,000 in Mozambique), small-scale fighting has gone on since the early 1960's. Small areas of Angola are believed to be essentially under African control, while at least two of Mozambique's nine provinces are held by the Mozambique Liberation Front (FRELIMO), which was founded, and led until his assassination in 1969, by Dr. Eduardo Mondlane, an American-educated anthropologist who was previously a professor at Syracuse University and a member of the United Nations Secretariat.

With these southern African exceptions, Africa has successfully ended the colonial era that began in the nineteenth century. Yet complete freedom from Europe has been elusive. Every African country is structured along the lines that developed before and during the colonial period, with a Western bureaucracy, Western ideas of national economic development, a Western-oriented economy, and financial needs that have meant a certain degree of continued dependence on Europe (and America, China, and other powers outside Africa). Teachers, advisers, technicians, and specialists in large numbers have been essential to the basic administration of the new nations, especially to assist in carrying out the aggressive programs of economic and social development to which every African government is committed.

In each of the new nations virtually all the significant mining operations, manufacturing and industrial establishments, and the larger trading institutions were owned and controlled by Europeans at the time of independence. Some nations had substantial African activity in the commercial and agricultural production fields, but even in these nations the powerful European commercial and industrial firms had depressed African economic initiative. Banking was controlled almost exclusively by European financial interests; even surplus and reserve funds possessed by some of the new nations at the time of independence were held in Europe in the form of currency and investment credits.

African nationalist leaders often use the term "neocolonialism" to describe the fundamental dependence upon European economic and financial institutions that existed at the time of political independence and that has proved far more durable than the political ties of colonialism. Even the economic systems upon which many of the new nations depended were European constructs. Each of the crops in these economies, cocoa in Ghana, for example, is subject to considerable fluctuation in world markets, and these markets either consist of European countries or are centered in Europe.

The leaders of Africa's new nations have found that political independence is only a prelude to independence in economy and other areas of national life. They face a long and difficult struggle to diversify their products and trading partners and to wrest policy control of economic institutions from European managers, directors, and investors. At the same time they must attract new sources of investment and assistance to expand their economies. Some nations are more fortunate than others in this struggle: they possess greater natural resources and richer agricultural lands, or they began to develop a healthier economic system much earlier than many African territories. Ghana, for example, began to produce cocoa in large quantities before the twentieth century, at a time when it was already exporting gold. Its exports in lumber, diamonds, and manganese were all built up before independence. Since independence vast deposits of bauxite have been tapped, and a major scheme has evolved to use the electicity potential of the Volta River to produce power for mining and refining the bauxite. Senegal, on the other hand, although it was an urbane and well-developed area after some two centuries of close contact with France, was utterly dependent upon peanuts at the time of its independence, and has discovered no important new sources of wealth since.

Despite such problems, many of the newly free African nations have surged ahead dramatically; in many the economic achievements (in developing new crops, finding new mineral sources, and creating some manufacturing and processing industries) in the first ten years of independence were as great as those of the previous thirty or forty years under colonial rule. To African leaders. economic development is a matter of national life or death; to colonial governments, it was much more a matter of turning a profit, keeping the peace, and keeping the colonial territory self-financing. On the whole, Africa remains the poorest and least-developed continent on earth, yet there has been a burst of developmental energy that political freedom and responsibility unleashed, and considerable progress has resulted.

Alongside the economic problems that had to be faced after political independence was the problem of developing united, smoothly functioning nations. Most African nations owe their present boundaries and senses of identity more to the European partitioning process than to prior African realities. African states and empires either ceased to exist before the colonial era began or were systematically destroyed by it. The territories that once lay within a Ghana, a Mali, or a Songhai were split among several colonial administrative units—Mauritania, Senegal,

The unshaded areas are either colonial
dependencies or white ruled.

Africa: 1972

Guinea, Mali, and Niger—during the French conquest of the nineteenth century. Even the African states and empires that were developing during the nineteenth century were broken up, so that parts of the territories once unified by Umar, Ahmadu Seku, and Samori are now parts of Senegal, Guinea, and Mali.

Where former African polities were not divided into new territorial units they were absorbed into even larger colonial areas in which they were prevented from playing a role of leadership. The burgeoning empire of Asante, for example, was absorbed into the Gold Coast, along with the Fante states. Even though the Gold Coast approximated Asante in territory, Asante hegemony was deliberately crushed: Dagomba, Gonja, Mamprussi and other tributary states were freed of Asante rule and placed under the rule of the new colonial administration. Both the British and the weaker states within the Gold Coast were fearful of Asante power and expansionism, and thus took special pains to make sure that Asante peoples had no opportunity to establish themselves in positions of leadership in Gold Coast affairs. Similar situations obtained in Dahomey and the Congo. In the Congo much of the territory of the Luba and Lunda was absorbed into Leopold's area, and the power of their kings and chiefs was broken so that they could not threaten the rule of the European administration. The once great state of Kongo was split among the French territory of Congo, the Belgian territory of Congo, and Portuguese Angola.

Thus the colonial era effectively crushed whatever possiblity there may have been for African political systems to play a unifying role in the new nations. These new nations in most cases consisted of several ethnic groups, shorn of traditional leadership and brought together as Africans in common opposition to colonial rule. Most of the new nations thus consisted of populations belonging to dozens or even hundreds of ethnic groups, each with its own tradition, its own sense of history, its own language, and its own identity.

This problem is not, one must add, either as serious or as fraught with deep tensions as the outside world has perceived. Most African ethnic groups were never oganized into the type of fiercely self-serving "tribe" that the colonialists described. African states and empires, although based on ethnic groups, have customarily included peoples of other ethnic origin without severe antagonisms, and the migratory history of Africans has resulted in an intricate mosaic of ethnic distribution.

The colonial era fabricated a picture wholly unlike the reality of Africa (and anthropologists during the nineteenth and twentieth century, traditionally concentrating their studies on individual tribes, have unintentionally contributed to it). According to the colonial view, Africans lived in tribes that inhabited a common territory, spoke a common language, owed common allegiance to a chief of council, shared a common history and religion, and were fundamentally xenophobic and hostile to members of adjacent tribes. This unreal impression neglects the trading systems that spanned dozens of ethnic groups, the numerous states and empires that included people of many ethnic groups, the tendencies of Africans to travel and migrate into new lands, and the sociological basis of most African societies, which were organized primarily on units of family and clan.

Modern African leaders face a problem of "tribalism" in their nation-building efforts, but it is a problem of competition by both individuals and groups for scarce political positions, goods jobs, school places, development funds, and roads. In this situation, most politicians find it easier to build a basis of political strength among peoples of their own ethnic origin (although there are many exceptions), and to reward support with patronage and "pork-barreling," in a tradition familiar to the student of American politics. Modern political activity in the new African nations actually creates "tribal" feelings as a by-product of the political process, but these feelings are not deep or immutable.

In this connection, it is interesting that there have been few boundary disputes between the newly independent nations, despite the fact that boundaries were typically drawn by agreement between the partitioning powers on bases that had little to do with ethnic distribution. There are few countries in modern Africa that do not include some people who have ethnic kin in adjacent territories. Where disputes do exist, they usually have origins that predate the colonial era.

The fundamental problem facing each of the new nations of Africa is one to which neocolonialism and ethnic heterogeneity contribute: the transformation of an entire people, with all their cultural and institutional heritages, into a modern, affluent, progressive, technologically proficient society. This is what Africa and its peoples seek. The humblest African shares two deep yearnings with the most exalted: he is dissatisfied with personal and national poverty, and he refuses to accept the underprivileged, exploited, despised status that has been Africa's for the past four centuries.

There is indeed a revolution underway in Africa. After independence was won, Africa's people began to judge their own leaders by increasingly pragmatic criteria, the chief one being how effectively they advanced the material and national progress. Leaders who have lagged, who have proved indecisive, or who have been corrupt have found it difficult to stay in power long. The African revolution proposes to surmount enormous obstacles in the briefest possible time, and the people easily lose patience with a leadership that seems to be failing. The old political institutions, much of the former culture, and many old values have become matters of history for the modern African. He is willing to consider any reasonable replacement for them, so long as it advances the revolution to which he is committed. He is thus quite willing to see his culture evolve. He is conscious that it is evolving. And he is not demoralized by change.

Underneath the rapid changes that are sweeping Africa, the ancient values continue to influence African beliefs and behavior. Underlying the widespread acceptance of Islam and Christianity, to which nearly half the African people subscribe, are the old concepts of reverence for the ancestors and propitiation of their spirits as intermediaries between the living and God. African family structures, though eroded by the powerful influences of education, modernization, and urbanization, remain surprisingly resilient and durable. The basic gracefulness of the African approach to daily life, characterized by a blend of seriousness and relaxed good humor, still obtains almost everywhere on the continent. No one can predict Africa's future, but continuing vast change is inevitable as the African thrust for modernity blends with many special values and qualities to produce a new pattern of society and culture.

Bibliography

For the reader who wishes to pursue African history further, there are numerous sound books. The suggested readings in this list are only a tiny sample of the available sources. They have been drawn from among the scores of books which contributed to this *History,* because of their readability, their general soundness, and their treatment of topics that the present *History* is able to treat only briefly. Most have good bibliographies, to help those readers who may wish to learn even more in specific areas.

GENERAL HISTORIES OF AFRICA

Hallett, R., *Africa to 1875,* Ann Arbor, The University of Michigan Press, 1970.
   A good general treatment of African history, especially of the European influence, by a scholar with long experience in the study of African history.
The Horizon History of Africa, New York, American Heritage Publishing Co., Inc., 1971.
   Contributors include some of the best scholars in the field. Profusely and richly illustrated. An excellent anthological supplement accompanies each chapter.
July, R., *A History of the African People,* New York, Charles Scribner's Sons, 1970.
   Generally sound and comprehensive. Its best sections are those on the European influence. Written by a good scholar primarily as a textbook, it is nevertheless of general interest.
Oliver, R., and John Fage, *A Short History of Africa,* 1962. (Reprinted by Penguin Books, Baltimore, 1963.)
   An inexpensive paperback edition of a work by two experienced scholars which was for many years the standard general history of Africa. Still

worth reading. Stresses influence of Arab contact in northern and western Africa.

ANTHOLOGIES OF ORIGINAL DOCUMENTS

The following anthologies contain excellent excerpts and documents on various phases of African history, written by Arabs, Europeans, and Africans. In several cases they have been the source of numerous quotations in this *History*, and grateful acknowledgment is made to their authors and publishers.

Blake, J. W., *European Beginnings in West Africa,* 1942. (Reprinted by Greenwood Press, Westport, Conn.)
    Detailed coverage of the first two centuries of European contact; useful for reference.

Cartey, W., and M. Kilson, *The Africa Reader,* Vols. I and II, New York, Random House, 1970.
    Volume I deals with colonial Africa, Volume II with the independence movement and modern Africa. Excellent selections in both volumes.

Davidson, B., *The African Past,* Boston, Little, Brown, and Company, 1964.
    Excerpts covering ancient Egypt to the present. The best single anthology available for the general reader. Quoted frequently in this *History*.

Donnan, E., *Documents Illustrative of the Slave Trade to America,* 4 vols., 1930. (Reprinted in 1965 by Farrar, Strauss, and Giroux, New York).
    The most comprehensive collection of readings describing the conduct of the slave trade. Useful for reference.

Freeman-Greenville, G. S. P., *The East African Coast,* London, Oxford University Press, 1962.
    Limited to the East African coast, covers from ancient to recent times. Quoted frequently in this *History*.

Hodgkin, T., *Nigerian Perspectives,* London, Oxford University Press, 1960.
    Many excellent selections on Hausaland, Kanem-Bornu, and other parts of Nigeria, covering a thousand-year period. Frequently quoted in this *History*.

HUMAN ORIGINS AND PREHISTORY

Clark, J. D., *The Prehistory of Africa,* New York, Frederick A. Praeger, Inc., 1970.
    A comprehensive, well-written review of human evolution and tool technology in Africa; incorporates all relevant discoveries up to 1970, synthesized by an ancient scholar.

NORTHEASTERN AFRICA

Aldred, C., *The Egyptians,* New York, Frederick A. Praeger, Inc., 1961.
    A good standard treatment of ancient Egypt.

El Mahdi, M., *A Short History of the Sudan,* London, Oxford University Press, 1965.

Very short indeed, but written by a sound Sudanese scholar. Covers the Sudan from ancient Kush and Meroe to recent times. Readable, and a useful introduction. Available in paperback.

Jones, A. H. M., and E. Monroe, *A History of Ethiopia*, London, Oxford University Press, 1965.

Somewhat dated; first published in 1935. Some of its conclusions have been disputed by recent scholarship, yet it is still the best general (and brief) history of Ethiopia.

Levine, D., *Wax and Gold*, Chicago, University of Chicago Press, 1965.

Combines historical, political, and anthropological perspectives, providing useful insights on the development of modern Ethiopia from earlier times.

Montet, P., *Eternal Egypt*, New York, New American Library, 1964.

A popular and generally sound work on ancient Egypt, translated from the French.

Pankhurst, R., *The Ethiopian Royal Chronicles*, Addis Ababa, Oxford University Press, 1967.

Translation of Ethiopian documents, especially the *Kebra Nagast*. Frequently quoted in this *History*.

Shinnie, P., *Meroe*, New York, Frederick A. Praeger, Inc., 1967.

A comprehensive history of ancient Meroe by an archeologist and historian who worked for many years excavating the ruins. Good photographic illustrations.

NORTH AFRICA

Barbour, N., *A Survey of North West Africa*, London, Oxford University Press, 1959.

Not primarily concerned with ancient times, it still provides a useful historical summary for Algeria, Tunisia, and Morocco, as well as more contemporary description.

Bovill, T., *The Golden Trade of the Moors*, 2nd ed., London, Oxford University Press, 1968.

A kind of classic. A beautifully written study of the western Sahara, with much information on the Maghrib and the Sudanic states. Written some years ago, it has been revised and updated recently by Robin Hallett. Highly recommended.

Lewis, B., *The Arabs in History*, London, Hutchinson and Co., 1966.

A brief but authoritative and readable introduction to the history of Islam, including its influence on northern Africa.

WEST AFRICA

Ajayi, F. Ade, and I. Espie (Eds.), *A Thousand Years of West African History*, Ibadan, Ibadan University Press, 1965.

A very useful collection of short chapters by numerous authorities, including a number of African scholars.

Burton, R., *A Mission to Gelele, King of Dahome,* 1864. (Reprinted in 1966 by Frederick A. Praeger, Inc., New York.)
> A useful, colorful account of the court and people of Dahomey in the mid-nineteenth century. Quoted in this *History.*

Davidson, B., *A History of West Africa to the Nineteenth Century,* Garden City, Doubleday & Co., 1966.
> An inexpensive paperback, the most popular and readable introduction to West African history up to about 1800.

Fage, J., *A History of West Africa,* London, Cambridge University Press, 1969.
> Brief but comprehensive. A useful book.

Ibn Battutah, Muhammad, *Travels in Asia and Africa, 1324-1354,* translated and selected by H. A. R. Gibb, New York, McBride, 1929.
> An abridgement of the famous Berber explorer's original Arabic volumes. Excellent descriptions of Mali and North Africa.

Niane, D. T., *Sundiata: An Epic of Old Mali,* London, Longmans, Green & Company, 1965. (Translated from the French by C. D. Pickett).
> The best available written account of the oral history of the founding of Mali.

CENTRAL AFRICA

Collins, R., *Problems in African History,* Englewood Cliffs, Prentice-Hall, Inc., 1968.
> Basically an anthology by scholars, contains an excellent section of articles by various authorities on Bantu origins and migrations.

Vansina, J., *Kingdoms of the Savanna,* Madison, University of Wisconsin Press, 1968.
> A little difficult to read, but still the best available treatment in English of the great Bantu states of Kongo, Luba, Lunda, etc.

SOUTHERN AFRICA

Davidson, B., *The Lost Cities of Africa,* Boston, Little, Brown and Company, 1959.
> Somewhat romanticized treatment of the great cities, states, and monuments now being excavated in various parts of sub-Saharan Africa. Good sections on Zimbabwe, the Swahili cities, and the Interlacustrine kingdoms.

Fagan, B., *Southern Africa During the Iron Age,* London, Thames and Hudson, 1965.
> Archeological in approach, this is the best available summary of research on earlier southern Africa. Well written and illustrated.

EAST AFRICA

Davidson, B., *East and Central Africa to the Late Nineteenth Century,* Nairobi, Longmans, Green & Co., 1967.
> Intended primarily as a textbook for East African high schools, it is well written and interesting. A good introduction.

Oliver, R., and G. Mathews, *A History of East Africa*, London, Oxford University Press, 1963.
    Only Volume I of several projected volumes has been published, but it provides a comprehensive and authoritative survey of East African history up to the nineteenth century.

EUROPEAN CONTACT AND THE SLAVE TRADE

Betts, R., *The "Scramble" for Africa*, Boston, D. C. Heath and Company, 1966.
    A brief paperback collection of analyses by participants and modern scholars of the Berlin Conference and related events. Very useful.
Curtin, P., *Africa Remembered*, Madison, University of Wisconsin Press, 1967.
    A collection of writings by Africans, selected and annotated by a number of modern scholars, on the slave trade.
Curtin, P., *The Atlantic Slave Trade: A Census*, Madison, University of Wisconsin Press, 1969.
    Mainly statistical, but the most authoritative quantitative study of the slave trade yet done. Useful reference.
Hallett, R., *The Penetration of Africa*, New York, Frederick A. Praeger, Inc., 1965. An excellent summary and analysis of the state of Europe's knowledge of the African interior, reasons for exploration, and the launching of explorations, during the eighteenth and early nineteenth centuries. Several quotations used in this *History*. Highly recommended.
Iliffe, J., *Tanganyika Under German Rule*, Cambridge, Cambridge University Press, 1969.
    A useful summary and analysis of German rule, and African reactions.
Oliver, R., *Africa Since 1800*, Cambridge, Cambridge University Press, 1967.
    A brief but valuable summary of developments in Africa after 1800.
Perham, M., and J. Simmons, (Eds.), *African Discovery*, London, Faber and Faber, 1958.
    An anthology from the journals of several of the more notable European explorers of Africa; interested readers can use the bibliography for further exploration into the published journals themselves.
Pope-Hennesy, Jr., *Sins of the Fathers*, New York, Alfred A. Knopf, 1968.
    A well-written, carefully researched story of the slave trade. Informative and interesting, and very useful.

NATIONALISM AND INDEPENDENCE

Hodgkin, T., *Nationalism in Colonial Africa*, New York, New York University Press, 1957.
    A well-written and penetrating analysis of the emergencies of African nationalism.
Lynch, H., *Edward Wilmot Blyden: Pan-Negro Patriot*, London, Oxford University Press, 1967.
    An excellent biography of Blyden, well written and researched. Quotes

Blyden frequently. Several Blyden quotations in this *History* are taken from Professor Lynch's useful book.

Padmore, G., *Pan Africanism or Communism,* London, Dennis Dobson, 1956. An authoritative account of the growth of the Pan-Africanist movement by one its main participants. Excellent analysis of the ideology of Pan-Africanism, and argument that it is incompatible with Communism.

Wallerstein, I., *The Politics of Independence,* New York, Random House, 1961. Available in paperback, a well-written and insightful review of the drive for freedom and self-determination in modern Africa.

Index